CLASSICS IN THEORY

General Editors

BROOKE A. HOLMES MIRIAM LEONARD TIM WHITMARSH

CLASSICS IN THEORY

Classics in Theory explores the new directions for classical scholarship opened up by critical theory. Inherently interdisciplinary, the series creates a forum for the exchange of ideas between classics, anthropology, modern literature, philosophy, psychoanalysis, politics, and other related fields. Invigorating and agenda-setting volumes analyse the cross-fertilizations between theory and classical scholarship and set out a vision for future work on the productive intersections between the ancient world and contemporary thought.

Praise for *Rethinking Metonymy*

'This important book sheds light on four quite different fields: Greek poetic usage in its greatest age, and German, in its; translation studies; and, above all, poetic theory. The most important outcome is a new and greatly enhanced understanding of metonymy. Crucially, Matzner's theory of metonymy insists on the primacy of literary usage, and he conducts his theorizing, as all such theorizing should be conducted, as a negotiation between existing theory and significant literary instances. In the process, the limitations of existing theory—still stuck in the world of Greco-Roman rhetoric, with or without some pointers (but little more) from Roman Jakobson and some distractions from cognitive linguistics—are patiently, lucidly, and sensitively exposed. This is a work of great acumen and striking originality.'

Professor Michael Silk, King's College London

'Matzner's study makes a unique contribution to ancient literary criticism and rhetorical theory, and to theories of metaphor and figurative language more generally. A great strength of his approach lies in his deft orchestration of a Formalist focus on usage and aesthetic aspects of metonymy that produces a far-ranging and focused analysis. As the trope is central to ancient imagery, and yet has been poorly understood since Aristotle, we should be all the more grateful to Matzner for his lucid approach to key problems in defining its parameters and illuminating its intricacies.'

Professor Nancy Worman, Barnard College and Columbia University

Rethinking Metonymy

Literary Theory and Poetic Practice from Pindar to Jakobson

Sebastian Matzner

OXFORD UNIVERSITY PRESS

Great Clarendon Street, Oxford, OX2 6DP,
United Kingdom

Oxford University Press is a department of the University of Oxford.
It furthers the University's objective of excellence in research, scholarship,
and education by publishing worldwide. Oxford is a registered trade mark of
Oxford University Press in the UK and in certain other countries

First published 2016
First published in paperback 2019

Published in the United States of America by Oxford University Press
198 Madison Avenue, New York, NY 10016, United States of America

British Library Cataloguing in Publication Data
Data available

Library of Congress Cataloging in Publication Data
Data available

ISBN 978–0–19–872427–8 (Hbk.)
ISBN 978–0–19–872428–5 (Pbk.)

ACKNOWLEDGEMENTS

Books certainly make fine travel companions. This one, in its protracted *statu nascendi*, has accompanied me on an academic journey that took me from Germany to London, then on a tour around England, and, finally, back to London—a journey over the course of which I have accumulated a great debt of gratitude that I could not hope to repay, but that I nonetheless wish to acknowledge in these first pages.

My academic studies would not have been possible without the continuous support I have received from both German and British institutions dedicated to the promotion of research in the humanities. I am grateful to the Studienstiftung des deutschen Volkes (German National Academic Foundation) for awarding me a scholarship as an undergraduate student in Germany as well as a Hölderlin Scholarship, which enabled me to come to King's College London as a Master's student, where my interest in the theory of poetic language was first sparked in a seminar on theories of metaphor. I am indebted to the Arts and Humanities Research Council for allowing me to pursue this interest with the award of a doctoral research grant. A Leverhulme Early Career Fellowship at the University of Oxford and a Junior Research Fellowship at Corpus Christi College, Oxford gave me much appreciated time to further refine the arguments I present here, while a swarm of wonderful colleagues at the University of Exeter sustained me with their encouragement, camaraderie, and sense of humour on the crucial final metres on the road to publication.

As this book began its life as a PhD thesis, special thanks are due to Michael Silk, who supervised my doctoral research. It has been a privilege, and indeed a great pleasure, to rethink metonymy together with him. His subtle guidance, active interest in my research, and unfailingly challenging yet always constructive criticism have exceeded by far what I could have asked for from a supervisor. While I have benefited immensely from his engagement with my work, our discussions and explorations have also given me the lasting impression of an ideal of scholarship in which originality of thought and scholarly rigour are never pursued at the expense of one another, but always give rise to each other.

I have had the pleasure of presenting various versions of different parts of this book at research seminars at the universities of St Andrews, London, Chicago, Oxford, and Cambridge, and my thanks must also go to the audiences for providing much useful feedback and criticism (as well as to the seminar convenors for their kind invitations).

I am very grateful to the editors of Classics in Theory, Brooke Holmes, Miriam Leonard, and Tim Whitmarsh, for enthusiastically welcoming my book into the ranks of this exciting new series, and to Charlotte Loveridge and her team at Oxford University Press for all their support (and patience) during the writing and publication of this book. The two readers for the press and my PhD examiners, Chris Carey and Charlie Louth, also deserve many thanks and much credit for their helpful suggestions, which substantially improved the final product.

While my work on metonymy quickly became a metonym for my own life, my friends always made sure that the two never became synonymous—and for this I am deeply grateful to them.

What I owe to my family and especially to my parents, Angelika and Gerhard Matzner, goes beyond anything that could be expressed in writing. Their love, support, and example are the *conditio sine qua non* not just for this book but for so much more. I hope they will read their mention here as a metonym for the world they mean to me.

Sebastian Matzner

King's College London
November 2015

TABLE OF CONTENTS

"Metonymic. One of the fundamental tools of semiotics is the distinction between metaphor and metonymy. D'you want me to explain it to you?"
"It'll pass the time," he said.

David Lodge, *Nice Work* (1988)

1 Introduction

Metonymia at Aulis

Iphigenia overlooks the shore of Aulis. Her father, Agamemnon, has eventually submitted to the seer Calchas' prophecy and has ordered that she be sacrificed to Artemis so as to appease the goddess and obtain safe passage for the Greek fleet on its way to Troy. His henchmen drag and lift Iphigenia, bound and gagged, to the altar where she will soon be killed—and amidst the ensuing commotion her robe starts to come undone. The chorus in Aeschylus' *Agamemnon* describes this dramatic moment in powerful poetic language. The elders of Argos conjure up a vision of Iphigenia at Aulis, brutally restrained

> ... by force and by the silent power of a bridle.
> As she poured saffron dye toward the ground
> she cast on each of her sacrificers a glance darted from her eye,
> a glance to stir pity, standing out as if
> in a picture, wanting to address them...

In the original Greek, this passage reads:

> ... βίᾳ χαλινῶν τ' ἀναύδῳ μένει.
> κρόκου βαφὰς δ' ἐς πέδον χέουσα
> ἔβαλλ' ἕκαστον θυτήρ-
> ων ἀπ' ὄμματος βέλει
> φιλοίκτῳ, πρέπουσά θ' ὡς ἐν γραφαῖς, προσεννέπειν
> θέλουσ'...[1]

which Wilamowitz-Möllendorff in his 1885 translation of the play translates as:

> Die Fessel hielt. Stumm und starr lag sie da.
> Vom Busen riss rohe Faust das Safrankleid.
> Auf jeden ihrer Schlächter schoss sie Gnade flehend Blick um Blick,
> schön wie ein Bild, wie ein Bild der Sprache bar
>
> The shackles held tight. Mute and stiff she lay there.
> The raw fist tore the saffron robe from the bosom.

[1] A. *Agam.* 238–43; trans. Sommerstein (adapted).

She shot at each one of her slaughterers glance after glance, begging
for mercy,
beautiful like an image, like an image without voice[2]

The Prussian philologist displays a surprising poetic flair in his rendition of this passage, particularly unexpected given that his translation, as he emphasizes in its preface, sets out to be clearer and easier to understand than the notoriously dark original, whose diction is so intensely poetic that it sometimes verges on the brink of obscurity. Yet a closer look at the Greek and German passages reveals that the centre of poetic gravity in the passage has shifted. In fact, the philologist-translator Wilamowitz seems to have become something of a poetic scene painter himself here: the raw fist tearing at Iphigenia's robe and the shackles holding her tight—these are *his* additions. The Greek text contains neither these dramatic details nor the powerful repetition of 'like an image' ('schön wie ein Bild, wie ein Bild der Sprache bar'). This final line's chiasmus, which lets the sentence swing calmly back and forth like a pendulum, marks the transition of Iphigenia's presence—now motionless, speechless, helpless—from being a character with agency to being the centrepiece of a tableau. The rather more stationary aspect introduced here contrasts sharply with the dramatic action earlier, expressed in 'Vom Busen riss rohe Faust das Safrankleid' ('The raw fist tore the saffron robe from the bosom'), where the r-alliteration of 'riss rohe', the omission of the article before 'Faust', and the metonymic focus on the henchman's fist create an extremely pointed, fast-paced, and dynamic impression of the movement in this scene. The much more 'literal' translation published by Wilhelm von Humboldt in 1816, on the other hand, conveys that the Greek original itself contains *another* metonymic expression at *another* point in this passage. Humboldt translates:

mit Zaum, und sprachlosen Zwanges harter Kraft.
Des Safrans Tünchung zum Boden gießend
und sanft des Mitleids Geschosse
vom Blick der Opfrer jedem sendend,
erschien sie bildähnlich dort, verlangend noch,
wie sonst, nach Anrede

with bridle, and speechless coercion's hard force.
Pouring down to the ground the saffron dye,
and softly sending from her gaze missiles of pity
to each of the sacrificers,
[thus] she appeared there, like an image,
still longing to be spoken to as usual

[2] Unless otherwise indicated, all translations are mine.

A relatively minor difference between the two translations lies in the fact that Wilamowitz and Humboldt each preserve in their translation a different component of a metaphor contained in the Greek original. Drawing on the image and terminology of an armed struggle, Aeschylus uses both the verb ἔβαλλ᾽ ('cast', 'hurled', 'shot') and the noun βέλει ('missile') to metaphorically describe Iphigenia's final gaze which desperately seeks to move her sacrificers to mercy—'shooting a missile at someone' being a metaphor for 'casting a glance at someone'. Wilamowitz's translation retains only the verb of this metaphor, 'schoss' ('shot'), Humboldt's translation only the noun, 'Geschosse' ('missiles'). The two different terminologies—the literal terminology of an emotional engagement through a pity-stirring gaze and the metaphorical terminology of a physical attack through a launched missile—are therefore much more closely and intensely intertwined in Aeschylus' text than in the two translations: ἔβαλλ᾽... ἀπ᾽ ὄμματος βέλει φιλοίκτῳ ('she shot from her eye a pity-stirring missile')—Iphigenia fights for her life with her eyes as the only weapon left at her disposal. While both translators thus slightly reduce the intensity of this metaphor in their versions of this passage, their translations differ more significantly when it comes to the presence of metonyms. Where Wilamowitz adds—of his own accord—a metonymic representation of the brutal sacrificer (the mentioned 'raw fist' being a metonym that points to the henchman as a whole), the Greek original and Humboldt's translation of it contain an altogether different metonym, which Wilamowitz omits. In these texts, the tableau-like, quasi-ecphrastic atmosphere of the scene—the chorus describes Iphigenia in her last moments as πρέπουσά θ᾽ ὡς ἐν γραφαῖς ('standing out *as if in a picture*')—is emphasized by a striking metonymic expression: the most prominent *visual* element of the picture painted here, Iphigenia's saffron-coloured *robe*, is transformed—metonymically—into a liquid *colour* as we see her 'pouring down to the ground the saffron *dye*' (κρόκου βαφὰς δ᾽ ἐς πέδον χέουσα/'Des Safrans Tünchung zum Boden gießend'). As Lebeck has shown, kindred images and recurrent imagery of liquids and of flowing and dipping constitute an important structuring feature of the *Oresteia*. Through the deployment of such imagery and images, key scenes are subtly connected with each other. Thus, when Clytemnestra convinces Agamemnon to step onto the fateful carpet which, dyed in deep purple, flows into the palace and leads Agamemnon to his violent end, she herself explicitly associates this carpet with the sea as the source of all purple: ἔστιν θάλασσα... τρέφουσα πολλῆς πορφύρας... κηκῖδα ('there is the sea... nourishing much purple... that gushes forth'; vv. 958–60). Clytemnestra's image here eerily anticipates the imminent murder of Agamemnon who, stabbed to death in the bath, will soon be gushing much purple-coloured blood himself. The metonymic use of 'saffron dye' (κρόκου βαφάς/'Des Safrans Tünchung') in the very scene that portrays the murder of Iphigenia, therefore, not only adds to the intense visuality of this particular scene, but also facilitates a direct, imagistic connection between the crime committed by Agamemnon in this moment at Aulis and its subsequent punishment with his own murder later on the play.

Metonymy—the forgotten trope?

Aeschylus' portrayal of Iphigenia's final moments at Aulis thus revolves around a metaphor and a metonym as the two key poetic devices that give shape to his dramatic expression and contextualization of this significant event. Yet despite metonymy's capacity to create such aesthetically impressive and structurally important effects as in this example, it has hitherto received so little attention in literary stylistics and rhetorical tropology—especially in comparison with the attention that has been lavished on metaphor—that it may well be called 'the forgotten trope'. If metonymy is deemed worthy of any discussion of its aesthetics at all (which is rarely enough the case), it is usually quickly dismissed as a rather more boring variant of metaphor. The poetic effects of metonymy are, admittedly, indeed consistently different from those created by metaphor—but precisely this makes it problematic to consider metonymy a 'variant' of metaphor: whether boring or not, *variants* are after all by definition based on *the same* fundamental principle, yet whether this is in fact the case for metaphor and metonymy is still very much an open question. On the one hand, metonymy is often taken to be a sort of metaphor, especially in discussions of literary style; a view that owes much to (post-)Romantic notions of poetic language as fundamentally and universally metaphorical. Yet this view is not without alternatives: Jakobson and many structuralists and post-structuralists in his footsteps conceive of metaphor and metonymy as two *diametrically opposed* poles of language, thus postulating the exact opposite relationship between metaphor and metonymy—not variants of the *same*, but radically different *opposites*. Ever since Jakobson set out this latter view in seminal essay 'Two Aspects of Language and Two Types of Aphasic Disturbances' (1956), it has sparked (and continues to spark) large numbers of far-reaching semiotic-structural analyses in countless disciplines—from narratology, anthropology, and psychology to performance, film, and media studies—which draw on and appeal to 'metonymy' to discuss a near-infinite variety of phenomena. Yet *these* discourses have detached themselves almost entirely from literary aesthetics and stylistic analyses, and thus from concrete metonyms in the original sense, as developed in the context of rhetoric and poetics. Jakobson's suggestion that contiguity is for metonymy what analogy is for metaphor seemed to offer a sound logical basis for both tropes, which would guarantee the comparability of semiotic structures even when extending the terms to non-verbal discourses. But what is 'contiguity'? In the fields of poetics, rhetoric, and stylistics as well as in structuralist and post-structuralist studies this term and concept has remained largely underdetermined, if not undetermined: a semantic placeholder whose logic can at best be circumscribed as 'something that has something to do with something'—which is why attempts at defining metonymy have often remained limited to 'something somewhat like metaphor, but not metaphor'. Already the oldest surviving 'definition' of metonymy, by the Greek grammarian Trypho (first century BC), is marked by this problematic vagueness. Trypho explains, if one wants to call it an explanation, μετωνυμία ἐστὶ λέξις ἀπὸ τοῦ ὁμωνύμου τὸ συνώνυμον δηλοῦσα ('metonymy is an expression that explains a synonym by a homonym')[3]—a statement that is not only bewilderingly obscure, certainly on first reading, but one that also, on reflection, turns out to assert little more than that metonymy is some sort of indirect expression that draws on terms which are somehow related. Two millennia later, the same predicament is still with us and bedevils in more or less the same way more recent definitions of metonymy; compare, for instance, Evans and Martin's formulation, 'Metonymy...A trope in which one word is substituted for another on the basis of *some* material, causal, or conceptual relationship',[4] or Lausberg's definition:

> *Metonymia*...consists in the replacement of the *verbum proprium* by another word whose actual meaning stands *in a real relationship*...to the intended meaning in the particular instance—*not in a comparative relationship*...as in metaphor.[5]

Describing the fundamental principle of metonymy as being based on 'some' relationship that is 'real' and 'not comparative' may not be wrong, but it is hardly particularly insightful either. The felt need to contradistinguish metonymy from metaphor even after a positive definition of metonymy has been given, as in Lausberg, is a telling indicator of just how underdetermined and insufficiently specific the existing positive definitions themselves are. Thus the first part of Lausberg's definition

[3] Trypho, *Trop.* 739, 20–1.
[4] Evans/Martin 1986, 144; italics added.
[5] Lausberg 1960, 257; italics added.

('consists in the replacement of the *verbum proprium* by another word whose actual meaning stands *in a real relationship*...to the intended meaning in the particular instance') could be said to apply to metaphor just as well as to metonymy—provided one is prepared to accept that similarity or analogy also constitute a 'real' relationship of sorts. The same is true for Evans and Martin's definition, for here, too, it seems reasonable to acknowledge that similarity and analogy surely constitute the basis of '*some*...conceptual relationship'; and if one were to specifically rule out these two conceptual relationships (effectively by way of adding a 'not metaphor' contradistinction *à la* Lausberg in the guise of an added 'not based on analogy or similarity'), then we are back to where we started: *what* sort of relationship *exactly* are we talking about for metonymy when stating that it is based on *some* relationship (material, causal, or conceptual)? Existing definitions such as these, then, may (just about) suffice as operational definitions that allow us to tentatively localize *prima facie* metonyms in literary texts. For this, they offer the following parameters: an indirect expression/trope; not a metaphor; based on the substitution/replacement of one word for another; operative on the basis on some sort of relationship between two words (but not one that involves analogy or similarity). They do not, however, adequately *explain* the phenomenon of metonymy in poetic action, that is, as a poetic device in literary texts, since they fall short of truly clarifying metonymy's core principle, have little to say about the shape of metonymy's concrete manifestation (or manifestations) in language, and remain silent on its aesthetic effect (or effects). In fact, the parameters that can be deduced from currently available definitions raise more questions than they answer: if both metaphor and metonymy are tropes, then what do they have in common that makes them both recognizable as tropes, and in what respects do they differ so as to be recognizable as distinct tropes (if indeed they really are two distinct tropes and not just two variants of the same phenomenon)? Furthermore, if metonymy is based on a substitution or replacement of words, are there always only two words involved, as these definitions suggest? As we have seen, the metaphor in the *Agamemnon* passage, 'she shot from her eye a pity-stirring missile', involved two words—a verb and a noun—which jointly constitute a metaphorical expression. Are metonyms, by contrast, always based on just one word, as the above definitions seem to imply? And does this one word always unambiguously refer to just one other word that it replaces? And what sort of word are we talking about here? The examples for metonymy given in rhetorical handbooks—both ancient and modern—as well as the subsets into which these examples are often grouped (e.g. 'cause for effect', 'container for contained', 'producer for product', 'material for object') always seem to point only to nouns (e.g. 'Athens' for 'the citizens of Athens', 'bronze' for 'sword', 'Hephaestus' for 'fire', or indeed 'saffron dye' for a 'saffron-coloured robe'). Does this mean that verbs, adjectives, and adverbs, which can be used metaphorically, cannot be used metonymically? And if so, why? A related consideration arises regarding the different conformations that metaphorical and metonymic expressions may take. Metaphors appear in many different forms, not only concerning the different parts of speech they involve, but also the different grammatical and syntactical means they draw on. Thus, when Wallenstein mourns the loss of his dear Piccolomini with the words 'Doch fühl ich's wohl, was ich in ihm verlor. | Die Blume ist hinweg aus meinem Leben' ('Yet I truly feel what I have lost in him. | The flower has vanished from my life'),[6] then it is the parallelism of the two lines that creates the metaphor which implicitly compares Piccolomini (and what he brought to Wallenstein's life) to a flower—with all the concomitant connotations of youth, beauty, joy, and flourishing. By contrast, when Plangus says about Erona that 'the world the garden is, she is the flower',[7] then it is the copula 'is' that creates the two metaphors of this line. Is the same true for metonymy? Does it, too, manifest itself (*sc.* its core principle) through various different linguistic means? Or does metonymy always appear in one and the same form?

These may seem fairly detailed and specific (or, as one might also say, fairly basic) questions, yet finding answers for them is not only important for developing a better appreciation and understanding of the literary-aesthetic effects of metonyms in poetic texts; it is also necessary for addressing the fundamental yet still unresolved question of the exact nature of the relationship that links the (two?) words involved in metonymy, which is itself key to grasping metonymy's seemingly elusive core principle. Providing an answer to this fundamental question, in turn, makes it possible to clarify the still disputed relationship of metaphor and metonymy and also to productively engage with metonymy's peculiar and problematic double life as a literary trope in stylistics on the one hand, and as a semiotic pattern in structuralist studies on the other. Ironically enough, metonymy's great success as a tool of structuralist criticism seems to be owed to a good extent precisely to its hitherto rather vague and underdetermined status within its original context of stylistics, which has endowed it with an appealing and convenient openness and malleability that allows it to fit a wide range of phenomena

[6] Schiller, *Wallensteins Tod* Act 5, Scene 2, ll. 2686–7.

[7] Sir Philip Sidney, *The Countess of Pembroke's Arcadia*, Book 2/The Second Eclogues, Poem 30, l. 98.

(given, again, its largely negative definition as 'something structured in a way that is not metaphorical/based on similarity or analogy'). Yet once a clearer, deeper, and more comprehensive understanding of metonymy in its original conception as a literary trope has been established, it becomes possible to ask how this kind of metonymy, as manifest in concrete metonyms in literary texts, relates to the various more recent conceptions of metonymy as a structural-semiotic pattern in various verbal and non-verbal discourses. In other words, it then becomes possible to ask what, if anything, the structures and phenomena described as 'metonymic' by structuralists—such as metaphorical and metonymic cuts in films or metaphorical and metonymic structures in drama—have to do with actual metonyms *stricto sensu* and to assess what has been gained (and lost) by structuralist appropriations of this term and concept.

This book sets out to confront these questions by going back to the basics: on the basis of concrete metonyms found in literary texts, it develops a new theory of metonymy—of its fundamental principle, its different types, aesthetic effects, and poetic functions—and then ponders the implications of the insights gained in this process for appeals to 'metonymy' in the critical practice of various fields—from translation studies to stylistic criticism and (post-)structuralist analysis. The major questions addressed in this book, therefore, are: what is the one general principle that underlies all forms of metonymy? What types of metonymy are there, and how does their form (*a*) relate to the general principle and (*b*) affect their aesthetic effect? What is the relationship between metaphor and metonymy (and the remaining other tropes and figures), and how do they compare and differ in structure and effect? And, crucially, how does the new theoretical understanding of metonymy developed to answer these questions enable us to read differently, see more, understand better, and argue more clearly when put to work in the analysis of the stylistic texture of literary works, of tendencies of literary translations, or of structural patterns in verbal and non-verbal discourses?

At the heart of this book lies the aim of providing a more precise understanding of the contiguity principle as the key characteristic of metonymy, which, I propose, should be understood as lexical—not logical—contiguity. By way of revising the theory of semantic fields, I suggest that metonymy is best understood as a lateral shift within the terminology of one semantic field, considering such semantic fields themselves as pragmatically determined, that is, as the result of regular collocation in ordinary language usage. This suggestion makes it possible to explain why the defamiliarizing effects of metonymy typically appear weaker than those of metaphor, to elucidate the relevance of grammatical categories for metonymic expressions, and to unequivocally clarify the relationship between metaphor and metonymy. By offering these explanations, I hope to achieve two things in particular: to raise awareness and increase sensitivity for the importance (and beauty) of metonymy as a poetic device in literary texts, particularly in the context of complex imagery and often in intense interaction with neighbouring metaphors; and to help safeguard the immense potential of structuralist and post-structuralist approaches in interdisciplinary research and inter-arts criticism against the risk and pitfalls of 'incomparability creep'. Such 'incomparability creep' results from imprecision and slippage in the use of central concepts and terms across different disciplines: *different* phenomena are referred to by the *same* critical term—here 'metonymy'—which is, however, understood *differently* in each context; this gradually erodes the shared point of reference and thus undermines the actual comparability of the phenomena under discussion. To achieve both these ends, my study mobilizes, in close engagement with literary texts, the methodologies and frameworks developed by formalist critics and, in doing so, emphatically advocates—both *expressis verbis* and *ipso facto*—the usefulness of descriptive poetics as a valuable and insightful perspective in literary studies and beyond. The remainder of the present chapter will soon turn to such matters of methodology, offering a critical assessment of the place of tropology in contemporary scholarship and discussing in more detail the potential and limitations of formal-aesthetic approaches to the study of poetry before commenting on the texts chosen for analysis and on some further practical matters such as the notion of 'the reader' put to work in the subsequent close readings, the use of typesetting throughout this book, and the particular challenges that arise when studying defamiliarized, poetic language in a dead language and in contradistinction to ordinary language usage.

Chapter 2, 'Contiguity and its (dis-)contents: metonymy in theory', then gives a full account of the paradoxical status of metonymy in current literary theory (and critical practice) and of why a theory of metonymy based on the evaluation of actual metonyms in poetry is indeed a *desideratum*. It traces how metonymy became 'the forgotten trope' and shows how the study of metonymy ties in with important broader questions in the theory of poetic language, such as the distinction between figures and tropes or the relationship between metaphor, metonymy, and the other tropes. A subsequent review of major theoretical advances in the study of metaphor and a survey of existing theories of metonymy then draws on currently available theorizing to sharpen the focus on the contested issue of 'contiguity' and to formulate a preliminary set of markers for the analysis of metonymic occurrences in the text corpus examined in the following chapter.

In Chapter 3, 'Forms and effects: metonymy in poetic action', the discussion moves firmly into the realm of close readings and inductive theorizing based on concrete metonyms in literary texts. It explores different conformations of metonymic expressions and develops a taxonomy of different types of metonymy, proceeding from relatively straightforward examples to increasingly complex scenarios. The exploratory design of this chapter is aimed at keeping the process of identification and classification transparent as the discussion gathers cumulative insights into the different manifestations and recurring characteristics of metonymy through the analysis of individual examples, which allows for the development of a progressively more and more refined and comprehensive understanding of metonymy regarding both its unifying core principle and the diversity of its manifold expressions. The first three subsections of this chapter are each dedicated to a major type of metonymy—'index metonymy', 'amplification metonymy', and 'grammatical metonymy'—while the fourth subsection, 'Metonymic presences', looks at a range of several phenomena in which it is less clear whether or not they are in fact to be considered cases of metonymy (examples discussed here include expressions that are merely suggestive of associations along the lines of metonymy; cases where a word may, or may not, be taken as a metonym, depending on how other words in its context are interpreted; as well as the question whether instances of personification and synecdoche can be seen as instantiations of either metaphor or metonymy). The typology of metonymy developed and offered in this chapter serves four main purposes, namely: (*a*) to draw out and deepen our understanding of the shared principle fundamental to all forms of metonymy; (*b*) to comprehend the linguistic parameters that govern the variations of this core principle's textual realization; (*c*) to showcase the rich variety, unexpected frequency and significant poetic efficacy of metonymy in poetic texts; and (*d*) to illustrate (in the process) the importance and value of descriptive poetics for a nuanced appreciation of literary texts.

With this new theoretical understanding and critical framework thus established, Chapter 4, 'Beyond theory: metonymy in critical practice', makes explicit the stakes in the argument advanced here. In three cases studies, it demonstrates how rethinking metonymy in its original context of poetics and rhetoric sets an agenda for far-reaching (re-)considerations in several fields of literary scholarship. The first section of this chapter, 'Metonymy and translation criticism', offers a comparative evaluation of five translations of Aeschylus' *Agamemnon* (into German and English; each committed to different translation ideals), focusing specifically on their respective treatment of metonyms in the Greek source text. It extends current perspectives in the field of translation criticism by (*a*) offering reflections on the translatability of metonyms and metaphors in general, (*b*) extrapolating a range of translation strategies in response to tropes encountered in source texts, and (*c*) problematizing the dichotomy of 'domesticating' versus 'foreignizing' translation from the perspective of poetically defamiliarized language usage. The discussion of these literary translations as literary texts in their own right also adds further to the study of the aesthetic effects of metonymy begun in the preceding chapter. The following section, 'Metonymy and stylistic criticism', centres on an assessment of the poetic devices used to constitute the distinctive 'hellenizing' style in Housman's 'Fragment of a Greek Tragedy' and Schiller's *The Bride of Messina*, highlighting in particular the crucial role metonymy plays in it. The stylistic evaluation of these two texts serves as an illustrative example for how the *general* theory and typology of metonymy offered in this book makes it possible to conduct author-/period-/genre-*specific* tropological analyses and evaluations with much greater insight and precision. The last section of this chapter, 'Metonymy and (post-)structuralist criticism', is dedicated to a critical re-examination of (post-)structuralist reappropriations of 'metonymy' in the light of the insights gained over the course of this study, conducted by way of a comparative-contrastive discussion of the use and conceptualization of 'metonymy' in works by de Man, Lodge, and others. By rendering visible some troublesome tacit suppositions and contradictions that frequently blight (post-)structuralist usages of 'metonymy', it commends the new theory of metonymy advanced here as a point of reference and an aid to best practice in transdisciplinary structuralist scholarship and inter-arts criticism. A brief conclusion then draws the discussion to a close.

With the road ahead thus mapped out, it is time for some methodological remarks.

Tropology and the formal method: a reappraisal of descriptive poetics

Tropology, the study of tropes, and stylistics, the study of literary devices more generally, occupy a peculiar place in modern scholarship. Landfester points out that

as a study of the ways in which language is used and shaped, stylistics is situated within the disciplines of languages and literature ['Philologie'] at the border between literary and linguistic studies. Insofar as it is concerned with the linguistic elements of a specific language, it is considered a sub-discipline of linguistics; if, on the other hand, individual texts become the object of enquiry, it becomes associated with literary studies.[8]

Landfester suggests that this interdisciplinarity has potential advantages, which are all too often lost. Instead of drawing simultaneously on both branches of scholarship, scholars of different languages and literatures have parted company by giving preference to one over the other. Scholars of modern languages and literatures have entrusted stylistic studies to linguistics, following the discipline's surge in theoretical sophistication and popularity between the 1960s and 1980s, while most classicists have been less than responsive to the new developments in linguistics and, instead, have continued to consider style as the province of literary criticism,[9] largely pursued in a mode that conserves and perpetuates the tradition of classical rhetoric.[10]

Yet even within Classics, the traditional home of 'rhetoric' at universities, research dedicated exclusively to specific categories of literary style (as opposed to studies into the specific style of individual authors) has become increasingly rare. In his book on Pindar's style, now ninety years old, Dornseiff suggested a cultural-historical explanation for this phenomenon:

The diligent reader will see in each and every poet all such tropes as metonymy, synecdoche, hypallage, but for fear of seeming pedantic—who would want to have counted a poet's rhetorical figures?—they are covered up in bashful silence wherever Romanticism has had an influence. The period from about 1750 until [the triumph of] Romanticism did away with normative poetics. But apprehension about the fatal authoritative power of these ancient-roman(ce) norms ['antik-romanische Normen'] has exercised a long-enduring influence. The fear of being taken for a 'Magister' *à la* Opitz has largely precluded any objective

[8] 'Die Stilistik als Wissenschaft von der Art und Weise der Sprachverwendung oder Sprachgestaltung ist innerhalb der Philologie eine Wissenschaft an der Grenze zwischen Literaturwissenschaft und Sprachwissenschaft. Sofern sie die sprachlichen Elemente einer Einzelsprache erforscht, versteht sie sich als eine Teildisziplin der Sprachwissenschaft; wenn dagegen einzelne Texte ihr Objekt sind, gerät sie in den Bann der Literaturwissenschaft.' Landfester 1997, 1.

[9] See Landfester 1997, 1.

[10] '[Research in s]tylistics... is rarely conducted systematically. Within Classics, it takes its cues from, and continues more or less directly, the system of categories established for stylistics by ancient rhetoric' ('Die Stilistik... wird nur selten systematisch betrieben. Innerhalb der Klassischen Philologie knüpft sie mehr oder weniger direkt an das Kategoriensystem der antiken rhetorischen Stilistik an.' Landfester 1997, xi). Landfester goes so far as to argue that '[t]he "Handbook of Literary Rhetoric" by Heinrich Lausberg of 1960 has sanctioned this position to the present day and has thereby prevented [the emergence of] a linguistics-based stylistics' ('Das "Handbuch der literarischen Rhetorik" von Heinrich Lausberg aus dem Jahre 1960 hat diese Stellung bis in die Gegenwart hin sanktioniert und damit eine sprachwissenschaftlich gestützte Stilistik verhindert.' Landfester 1997, 1).

engagement (with a clear conscience) with the various artistic means of heightened idiom, that is, with the maligned surface. After all, it had taken such a profound revolution for our literature to rid itself of didactic poetics . . . Since [the rise of] Symbolist poetry we have more aware and sharper senses for this side of poetic expression.[11]

Landfester's and Dornseiff's acute remarks may serve as a starting point to set out the nature, scope, and perspective of this book.

The fundamental conviction at the heart of this study is that theorizing literary phenomena should be inductive and based on the evaluation of empirical evidence. That is to say, the theory of metonymy offered here will be developed on the basis of actual metonymic occurrences isolated from a corpus of poetic texts. Given that we are dealing with a range of isolated examples from different sources, we are neither interpreting specific individual texts in the traditional sense of literary scholarship, nor studying specific linguistic elements from the traditional perspective of linguistics. In other words, the literary scholar should not expect to find a comprehensive interpretation of each and every passage in the light of its literary and historical context, nor should the linguistician expect a full, quantitative corpus study that includes every metonym in all the texts examined. My aim is neither to offer exhaustive interpretations of the selected passages nor to submit elements of ordinary language to linguistic explication. My concern is with *literary aesthetics*, with a specific phenomenon of *poetic language*. The aim is to establish how metonymy, as a trope, functions—in its structural mechanisms and in its poetic effects. As such, this study stands in intimate connection with both conventional literary studies and linguistics but does not, or not exactly, share the customary interests or methods of either. Among much else, I have not attempted a comprehensive, quantitative evaluation of the entire corpus but instead offer a selection of revealing examples; these examples are then qualitatively analysed. At times, this analysis reaches out to, and draws on, the broader context of a work in

[11] 'Alle die τρόποι wie Metonymie, Synekdoche, Hypallage wird der genaue Leser bei jedem Dichter sehen, aber aus Furcht, pedantisch zu erscheinen—man will doch einem Dichter nicht seine rhetorischen Figuren nachgerechnet haben—, werden sie überall, wo die Romantik eingewirkt hat, schamhaft verschwiegen. Die Zeit von etwa 1750 bis zur Romantik hat die Regeln gebenden Poetiken beseitigt. Aber die Scheu vor der lebentötenden autoritativen Kraft jener antik-romanischen Normen hat lange nachgewirkt. Die Angst, für einen Magister der Opitzzeit zu gelten, hat es weithin verhindert, daß man sich sachlich und ruhigen Gewissens mit den verschiedenen Kunstmitteln der gehobenen Sprache, d.h. mit der verpönten Oberfläche beschäftigte. Es hatte eben einer so tiefen Umwälzung bedurft, bis unsere Literatur sich der erlernbaren Poetik entledigt hatte . . . Seit der symbolistischen Dichtung haben wir bewußtere, geschärftere Sinne für diese Seite des dichterischen Ausdrucks.' Dornseiff 1921, 70–1.

order to illustrate, paradigmatically, the potential wider ramifications of individual instances; more often, the discussion stays focused on short sequences. It would have been impossible to do justice to the full potential of each passage cited *and* to adduce sufficient material to support all the theoretical claims made *and* to maintain a focused argument. My ambition here is nothing more (and nothing less) than fundamental research: the aim is to formulate the basic principle of metonymy, to distinguish its fundamental varieties, and to provide a nuanced framework which will enable readers to interpret literary texts in which metonyms occur with greater precision and insight.

This book, then, is focused precisely on 'the maligned surface', as Dornseiff called it, that is, on verbal particularities of poetic texts, and it is indeed indebted to a particular post-Symbolist way of thinking about poetry: Russian formalism.[12] At the height of the Symbolist movement in Russia, when criticism had exhausted itself in divining the mystical meanings of poetic words, both poetry and theory took a turn towards language in its materiality. Futurist poetry dismissed not only realistic modes of art but the entire referential side of language, considering words as self-sufficient and self-validating artistic entities regardless of any spiritual or social message.[13] Inspired by this new approach, formalist critics turned their attention to artistic effects created by phonetic, rhythmic, morphological, and syntactic structures as the primary carriers of a literary work's aesthetic value. Shklovsky's essay *Art as Technique* (1917) is often seen as the founding manifesto of this school of criticism since it was the first to elaborate its core principle: defamiliarization (*ostranenie*; literally: 'making things strange'). According to Shklovsky, the use of unfamiliar, unexpected, striking expressions and formulations 'removes objects from the automatism of perception'[14] and presents whatever is at issue in a fresh, new way. In his view, what distinguishes poetry from other discourses is a formal criterion, namely the stylization of language beyond and against the conventions that govern its ordinary, daily usage: '[t]he language of poetry is . . . a difficult, roughened, impeded language . . . [W]e can define poetry as attenuated, tortuous speech. Poetic speech is formed speech.'[15] Consequently, it was considered

[12] Erlich 1981 and Steiner 1984 and 1995 offer comprehensive accounts of the historical development and key tenets of Russian Formalism.

[13] Symbolism itself did, of course, already carry the seeds for these developments; a good example is Mallarmé's (reported) dictum: 'One does not write poems with ideas, but with words' ('Ce n'est pas avec des idées qu'on fait des vers, c'est avec des mots', Delacroix 1927, 93).

[14] Shklovsky 1917, 16.

[15] Shklovsky 1917, 19–20.

to be the primary task of literary criticism to elucidate the different ways in which 'speech' can be 'formed', that is to say, what the aesthetic effects are of different forms of defamiliarized language. In Eichenbaum's words: 'the object of literary science, as literary science, ought to be the investigation of the specific properties of literary material'.[16] These 'specific properties', usually referred to as 'literary devices', can only be understood when contrasted with ordinary language use. Accordingly, the formalist movement saw the interface of linguistics and aesthetic analysis as the quintessential *locus* of literary studies:

> Formalists came up with their own characteristic orientation toward linguistics, a discipline contiguous with poetics in regard to material under investigation, but one approaching that material from a different angle and with different kinds of problems to solve... Formalists simultaneously freed themselves from the traditional correlation of 'form-content' and from the conception of form as an outer cover or as a vessel into which a liquid (the content) is poured. The facts testified that the specificity of art is expressed not in the elements that go to make up a work but in the special way they are used.[17]

The exclusive focus on the structural modalities of literary aesthetics at the expense of all other elements soon provoked criticism. As early as 1928, critics like Bakhtin would reprimand formalists for inattention to the sociological and ideological context of literary works.[18] Moreover, even within the broader formalist movement the pioneering members of OPOJAZ in Petrograd/Leningrad,[19] including Shklovsky, Eichenbaum, and Tynjanov, soon found that their insistence on the autonomy of artistic forms and their reduction of artworks to a collection of devices was deemed problematic by their Muscovite colleagues.[20] The Moscow Linguistic Circle, including Bogatryev, Jakobson, and Vinokur, moved away from this absolutist position. In particular, Jakobson, soon to become a central figure in the development of structuralism, insisted that equating a poetic work with its aesthetic dimension was erroneous. Instead, he argued that 'a poetic work is not confined to aesthetic function alone, but has in addition many other functions... often closely related to philosophy, social didactics etc.'.[21] And Jakobson and Tynjanov

[16] Eichenbaum 1926, 7.
[17] Eichenbaum 1926, 8–9.
[18] See Bakhtin/Medvedev 1928.
[19] OPOJAZ: *Obshchestvo Izucheniia Poeticheskogo Jazyka* ('Society for the Study of Poetic Language').
[20] For the notion that poetry is a sum of literary and artistic devices that the artist manipulates to construct his work, see, for instance, Shklovsky 1917, 5.
[21] Jakobson 1935, 83.

duly agreed that, though literary criticism should be a 'systematic science' and not an 'episodic and anecdotal genre', the pursuit of a 'scholastic "formalism" which replaces analysis by terminology and the classification of phenomena' was equally misguided.[22]

Rehearsing these developments and debates serves to clarify both the potential and the limitations of a study like the present one. By way of bridging the gap between approaches to stylistics in Classics (on the one hand) and Modern Literatures and Languages (on the other), we shall draw both on the classical tradition of rhetoric and on linguistics as well as on key concepts of Russian formalism. Inevitably, categorization and attempts to develop a precise terminology will feature prominently—the following pages may indeed at times recall the work of a '"Magister" *à la* Opitz'. It should, therefore, be stressed at the outset that these classifications are not offered as an end in themselves but rather intended to be an aid to future critical practice. Again, as I seek to establish a better understanding of a distinctive phenomenon in poetic language, it is necessary to privilege and foreground the formal-aesthetic dimension of literature at the expense of the content or historical context of individual works. This decision is pragmatic, not dogmatic. The theoretical understanding of metonymy established here is intended, among other things, to enlarge the toolkit available to literary scholars so that future studies of literary works will be able to elaborate the formal-aesthetic dimension of texts more precisely and more concisely, alongside discussions of substance and context. For this purpose, however, no theoretical framework is more relevant than Russian formalism and, in this sense, I can only agree with Steiner's verdict:

> Russian Formalism was without a doubt a transitional and transitory period in the history of literary study. But insofar as the literary-theoretical paradigms it inaugurated are still with us, it stands not as a mere historical curiosity but as a vital presence in the critical discourse of our day.[23]

Accordingly, throughout this book, the discussion of metonymy is conducted, whenever appropriate, in terms of the central formalist concept of defamiliarization.[24]

[22] Jakobson/Tynjanov 1928, 79. [23] Steiner 1984, 280.

[24] Which is not to say that the case might not be made in other terms or that defamiliarization is the definitive feature of poetry *tout court*.

Finding metonyms in poetic action: the text corpus

While grounded in the tradition of classical rhetoric and informed by formalist theory, the fundamental basis of my theorizing will be concrete, empirical evidence from literary texts. The texts chosen for evaluation and analysis in the process of conducting the research for this book were taken from ancient Greek lyric and tragic poetry, due to their extraordinary richness in poetic imagery, further supplemented by a range of literary translations of these texts into German from the eighteenth and nineteenth centuries. I have also drawn on further examples from English and German poetry, as and where appropriate, for further illustration, comparison, and contrast. The selection of authors and texts has been guided by two *desiderata*: first, a range of metonymic instances and, second, a range of literary translations. The resulting corpus, therefore, consists of texts with a high degree of defamiliarized language, which have been particularly popular among German philhellenists. I have undertaken full assessment of the following texts: Sophocles' *Oedipus Tyrannus* and *Antigone*, Aeschylus' *Agamemnon* and *Eumenides*, Euripides' *Iphigenia among the Taurians*, and Pindar's *Olympian Odes* and *Pythian Odes*. I have conducted further selective readings of other Pindaric odes and Greek tragedies as prompted by critical observations on the main texts and by discussions of the style of individual authors in the secondary literature. In addition, I have examined translations and adaptations of the main texts by Jenisch, Goethe, Schiller, Hölderlin, Humboldt, Droysen, Gedike, Solger, Stolberg, Boeckh, and Wilamowitz—both in comparison with the Greek originals and as literary works in their own right.

However (to restate the point), although this entire corpus has been assessed, my discussion makes no attempt at any comprehensive coverage, but confines itself to particular instructive samples. While the most illustrative and insightful cases of metonymy in the above-mentioned works by Pindar, Euripides, Sophocles, and Aeschylus, along with poems from Hölderlin and Goethe, constitute the main body of empirical evidence discussed in Chapter 3, Aeschylus' *Agamemnon* occupies a particularly prominent place in this study since it not only informs some of the theorizing in Chapter 3 but also features as the sole source text for the translations studied in Chapter 4. The *Agamemnon* was chosen as the primary source text for the study of metonymy in translation because of (*a*) the availability of a particularly wide range of translations with intensely different translatorial agendas, and (*b*) the particular challenge this play's dense and complex imagery poses to translators (as explicitly acknowledged by them). While many other texts could have been chosen for this part of the study (for instance, a comedy rather than a tragedy, given comedy's extensive employment of metonyms involving objects and body parts for comic effect), none meets both of these two criteria simultaneously to the same high degree as Aeschylus' *Agamemnon*.

The mixed corpus, combining ancient Greek and 'modern' German texts, may seem peculiar, but the choice is quite deliberate: this study is tentatively universalist in the sense that it aims at extrapolating mechanisms and structures of non-ordinary language usage that can be found in any language.[25] In other words, the principles I am interested in are inherent possibilities of language in general; where properties and features specific to a particular language appear to arise, this is noted. Meanwhile, the comparative approach and the combination of material from a classical and a modern language serve both a methodological and a disciplinary purpose. In terms of methodology: they extend the variety of metonymic instances available for analysis; they enable us to cross-check arguments and validate any theoretical hypotheses developed on the basis of the Greek texts; and they add a further dimension to the present enquiry, by raising the question of what happens to metonyms in translation. In disciplinary terms, I hope that the mixed corpus will also contribute to closing the gap between discussions of style in Classics on the one hand, and in Modern Literatures and Languages on the other. After all, 'Literary-theoretical debates are debates that concern language and literature as a whole; as such, they are debates to which a specialist in Greek language and literature should feel able to make a contribution.'[26]

Moreover, this book's 'tentative universalism' not only relates to its ambition to theorize metonymy beyond the confines of a single, specific language and literary tradition, but also entails a sidelining of author-/period-/genre-specific considerations. This is not to suggest that the use of metonymy in all authors, periods, and genres would be the same. To the contrary: many studies on the use of individual tropes or figures in individual authors, periods, or genres provide ample evidence for the interest and potential insight of such enquiries. While issues of stylistic and generic variation are important ones and while such studies are therefore certainly desirable, they raise a logical problem insofar as metonymy is concerned: to ascertain the *specificities* of metonyms in

[25] Or, at the very least, in any Indo-European language. To comment on linguistic details in languages from other language families is beyond my competence. However, it is hard to imagine convincing arguments that would undermine the potential applicability of the theory developed here to non-Indo-European languages.

[26] Silk 1995, 115.

particular authors, genres, periods, and their styles is surely only possible *after* an understanding of the functional principle and aesthetics of the trope *in general* has been established. This is the fundamental task that this book sets itself. It is very much hoped that future stylistic studies will take the first principles established here further, by examining how metonymy features and is used in specific writers and texts. Yet what is needed first, and is offered here, is a general understanding of the trope metonymy, and while the formalist methodology and framework of this study ensure that the distinct forms and types identified in the chosen text corpus are indeed such general possibilities of poetic language *tout court*, the criteria according to which the texts have been chosen ensure that they are bound to contain concrete realizations of an exceptionally wide range of such general possibilities.

Standard usage, literary aesthetics, and literary lexicography

General issues apart, particular and important complications arise when one confronts instances of presumed tropical usage in a 'dead' language such as ancient Greek. How are we to *know* that a term is used tropically, that we are dealing with actual defamiliarization in ancient Greek, as opposed to expressions that merely appear unfamiliar to us as non-native speakers? Methodologically, 'Sprachgefühl', the intuitive sense of what is linguistically appropriate, is a highly questionable criterion here. A soundly based discussion of non-ordinary, tropical usage must be based on a reliable knowledge of ordinary usage. In spoken languages, ordinary usage is determined pragmatically by native speakers in terms of the predominant daily usage of these and other native speakers at a given time. Owing to the lack of native speakers of ancient Greek, it is necessary to reconstruct ordinary usage on the basis of extant literature and general principle. The discussion of metonymic occurrences in ancient Greek texts, therefore, must subsume the establishment of the ordinary usage of the term/s in question in order to demonstrate and analyse (metonymic) deviance from it. This reconstruction of normal usage in classical Greek is based primarily on the principle of distribution:[27] normality can be established positively by the citation of evidence which

[27] On the concept of and procedures for such 'literary lexicography', see Silk 1974, 33–56 and 82–4 as well as Silk 1983 for further illustration.

(*a*) comes from 'reliable' authors, i.e. authors whose general language usage makes them least likely to contain defamiliarized, poetic expressions,[28] and (*b*) is available in sufficient quantity (or distributional variety) to be deemed significant. Unavailability of such evidence indicates, *ex silentio*, deviant, non-ordinary usage.[29]

Two more clarifications are in order. Unlike the vast majority of those who have contributed to the literature currently available on the topic, I am not concerned with the cognitive-conceptual aspect of metonymy. Needless to say, concepts and words are intricately linked, but here my concern is with aesthetic effect. The discussion will therefore be centred on 'usage' and 'terminology' rather than on 'concepts' and 'meaning'.[30] By the same token, my interest in aesthetic effect means that this study will be focused on 'live' metonyms, as opposed to 'dead' metonyms and clichéd metonyms. As with 'dead' metaphor, in any language there are innumerable expressions which can be traced back to an extension of a term's earlier semantic scope along the lines of metonymy but which have long since entered general, ordinary usage. 'Buckingham Palace announced this morning...' or 'I'll have another glass' will hardly strike any contemporary English speaker as remarkable cases of metonymy. In current English, 'Buckingham Palace' effectively denotes 'the sovereign' (when not denoting a residence), just as 'a glass' effectively denotes 'a drink' (when not denoting a container). Similarly, developed literary traditions abound in metonyms that occur so frequently in poetic texts that their aesthetic effect is significantly reduced. From 'sword' evoking military force to 'crown' implying royal prerogative, there are manifold examples of expressions that are etymologically metonyms but *effect*-ively not tropical in the strict sense of deviant, unfamiliar language usage.[31]

[28] The most reliable writers in this respect are authors of non-literary prose such as Aristotle or the Hippocratic corpus. Making due allowance for the possibility of individual instances of 'poetic' expressions, we can also draw on literary-prose authors such as Thucydides, Xenophon, Lysias, and Herodotus (the last-named best used only as corroborative evidence). Because of its fundamental and foundational place in the development of Greek literary idiom, we can also include Homeric usage as, effectively, a standard in its own right; see Silk 1974, 41–4.

[29] In principle, such issues might arise for a native speaker of modern German (which the author of the present study is), when faced with literary German texts from two centuries ago. In practice, problems arising (discussed where appropriate) are few and marginal.

[30] Where this dimension needs to be reflected in the discussion, I will speak of the 'conceptual content' of words, following the suggestion by Silk that '[t]he term "conceptual" is convenient, although the antithesis could be misleading. Concepts and words are not opposites nor happily separable.' Silk 1974, 9.

[31] This is not to say that such expressions have no poetic force at all. Choosing such an expression over alternative denotative expressions *without* a metonymic etymological background is a choice with consequences—but these consequences are different in kind

My concern is with synchronic aesthetics rather than historical linguistic developments. Therefore, while examination of metonymic clichés will sometimes be a relevant adjunct to my theorizing, I omit any discussion of metonymy in a diachronic perspective.[32] However, the (sometime) relevance of metonymic clichés, as well as the frequent contextual embeddedness of metonyms into other, non-tropical forms of stylized language, makes it essential to distinguish between two different kinds of deviance from the economy and norm of ordinary language. To that end, I will differentiate poetic 'elevation' from 'heightening', by which it is understood that '[e]levation is in general a matter of conventional stylization and formal dignity, heightening of ad hoc intensification and enhanced meaning'.[33] In other words, I will speak of poetic elevation and elevated language when referring to instances in which the register of expression is raised above that of ordinary language usage and displays a certain poetic texture (constituted by familiar formal elements indicative of the register of poetic idiom), whereas I will speak of poetic heightening and heightened language when referring to the startling and intense effects created by a bold use of poetic language that contravenes the expectations (and rules) set by ordinary language usage and endows words with fresh and new meanings.

Enter the reader

A few words should also be said about an entity of fundamental methodological importance to this study: 'the reader'. The formalist notion of tropes as literary devices is grounded in perceptible deviance from ordinary usage, and perceptibility implies a perceiving subject. Culler, citing Genette, summarizes this fundamental proposition concisely:

> The rhetorical figure, says Genette [in *Figures*], 'is nothing other than an awareness of the figure, and its existence depends wholly on the reader being conscious,

from the startling, abrasive effects created by new metonyms. Using terms such as 'palace', 'crown', or 'sword' to denote the exercise of state authority can, for instance, give an expression an air of material concreteness and physicality it might otherwise lack. Yet from the perspective of semantics and aesthetics, this is a matter of purposefully choosing words of a suitable register and colouring from a language's ordinary, standard vocabulary, and not a matter of poetic deviance from it (which would constitute proper, intensely effective tropical usage).

[32] For an exemplary study of 'dead' metaphor and metonymy, together with an up-to-date introduction to recent cognitive-conceptual approaches and corpus linguistic studies in the field, see Allan 2008.

[33] Silk 2010, 435. For a discussion of the two concepts in more detail, see *ibid.*, 434–9.

or not being conscious, of the ambiguity of the discourse before him'. One has a rhetorical figure when the reader perceives a problem in the text and takes certain rule-governed steps to devise a solution.[34]

What this study seeks to establish is not so much *what* exactly readers understand when they encounter the metonyms chosen for discussion, but *how* these metonymic occurrences deviate from ordinary usage and *how* readers make sense of them. That is to say, we are not concerned with the consciousness of individual readers, past or present, but with the general potential inherent in a distinct form of language use.[35] In these terms, 'the reader' is in no sense a historical entity nor should his or her 'readings' or his or her way of reading be taken as an accurate representation of what concrete readers experience on encountering a metonym. My 'reader' is a deliberate construction, a heuristic tool for exploration, which lays open in full the processes that may (or may not) occur, consciously or unconsciously, in concrete reading acts. Rather than being an external entity that approaches a text, this 'reader' is constructed by the potential inherent in language. Just as the 'author' as a historical entity with a cultural and biographical background has been complemented in recent literary criticism by the concept of the 'author function', understood as a function of a written work which ultimately forms part of its determinative structure, so my 'reader' is more akin to a 'reader function'. Stripped of race, gender, sexual identity, class, and any other criteria that are bound to affect concrete historical acts of reading, this 'reader' is the abstraction and sum of the possible readings that readers with full linguistic competence in the given language might conduct in their attempt to make sense of the text.[36] The central point

[34] Culler 1975, 180.

[35] In this sense, my 'reader' is similar to the one that forms the basis of Budelmann's study of the language of Sophocles. Budelmann explains: 'I do not... try to develop a detailed and universally valid psychological, behavioural or other kind of model of audience or reader response, as, in their different ways, narratologists following Gérard Genette, reception theorists like Wolfgang Iser or Hans Robert Jauss, students of semiotics like Umberto Eco, anthropologists like Victor Turner, scholars in the semiotics of theatre or psychoanalytic critics have done... my emphasis throughout this book will be on Sophoclean language and kinds of possible response, rather than on detailed accounts of the spectators' and readers' precise reactions. There is too much that is different from one spectator or reader to the next to make the latter a worthwhile project.' Budelmann 2000, 10–11.

[36] Compare, again, Budelmann: 'I will... refrain not only from trying to account for the processes in the spectators' brains, but also from claiming that anything I say is true for all spectators in the same way. When I speak, for instance, as I will, about certain spectators "being surprised by" or "wondering about" certain features of a sentence, I do not suggest that each of them is in a state of shock or that they all have the mentality of crossword-solvers... Everything I say about the spectators' possible reactions... should

of reference that guides my 'readings' is the linear movement of the text and the expectations which are built up and then fulfilled or frustrated in this process, including in particular an expectation of grammatical and semantic coherence.[37]

The 'reader' (or 'reader function') that appears in this study thus operates, for strategic methodological reasons, at a remove from the concrete experiences of individual flesh-and-blood readers, just as this study with its rigorous formalist methodology, emphasis on descriptive poetics, and decided focus on literary aesthetics operates at a remove from most existing engagements with metaphor and metonymy: while Lakoff and Johnson's *Metaphors We Live By* (1980) revitalized research into metaphor and also, albeit somewhat later, into metonymy, it was above all their view that metaphor and metonymy are conceptual in character and pervasive in daily usage that researchers found inspiring. Recent publications on metonymy, mostly essay collections, have therefore almost exclusively adopted the perspective of cognitive linguistics,[38] or, less frequently, historical linguistics.[39] While cognitive science has been enjoying a growing interest in the humanities for some time now, the questions raised in this book call for a different approach. It may be interesting to see if poetic tropical language is processed by a reader's brain differently from 'plain' ordinary language, or if metaphor and metonymy affect the brain in different ways—but the insights gained in this way do not readily address the questions that are to be dealt with

be understood as tentative and should be granted a certain margin of variation.' Budelmann 2000, 22.

[37] Linear movement, however, need not necessarily correspond to strict 'linearity' in the sense of a reader's rigidly word-by-word and line-by-line progress. Actual reading of course can and does include both the retrospective revision of larger passages as well as prospective glances ahead. But such reading acts are still 'linear' in the sense that they remain fundamentally progressive: they follow, overall, a directed forward movement and progressively incorporate new information into a previously established framework. Neither the fact that (*a*) this framework is itself subject to readjustment as the reading progresses (including the revision of earlier passages) nor that (*b*) information pertinent to a sequence may come from words that do not immediately follow the sequence poses a problem for my theorizing per se. As and where necessary, the discussion of individual passages will reflect this suitably broad notion of 'linearity'.

[38] A helpful account of the shift in the study of metonymy from structuralist semantics to cognitive linguistics is offered in Steen 2005. Key works in the cognitive-linguistic study of metonymy include Goossens et al. 1995, Panther/Radden 1999, Barcelona 2000, Dirven/Pörings 2002, Stefanowitsch/Gries 2006, Kosecki 2007, Panther et al. 2009, Handl/Schmid 2011, Bierwiaczonek 2012, Wojciechowska 2012.

[39] In addition to individual essays in the collections mentioned in the above footnote, see especially Allan 2008. Nerlich and Clarke perfectly capture these shifts of emphasis in approaches to the study of metonymy with their remark: 'Metonymy has been studied for at least two thousand years by rhetoricians, for two hundred years by historical semanticists, and for about ten years by cognitive linguists.' Nerlich/Clarke 2001, 245.

here, nor do they offer much of substance for the enhancement of literary critical practice. Cognitive science might be able to comment further from its own perspective on the descriptions of 'reading' processes offered in this book, and such an engagement with the arguments advanced here could well be a promising avenue of future research, but in order to find answers to the questions set out above, I will be following a decidedly different approach and shall leave the exploration of possible cross-fertilizations between descriptive poetics and cognitive approaches to others.

Finally, two points of guidance on issues of practical concern to the flesh-and-blood reader of this book. The first concerns the obvious difficulty that comes with discussing the poetic idiom of a foreign language. Throughout, I quote all passages under discussion in the original language (using the edition of each text referenced in the bibliography along with abbreviations for Greek authors and their works following the LSJ standard), together with a standard translation (with the translator referenced in the accompanying footnote). I have supplied additional 'literal' translations where I felt that no available translation adequately represents the poetically relevant specifics of the respective passage; these are placed in square brackets and marked '[lit.: . . .]'. Where no translator is referenced in the footnote, I have supplied a translation of my own. The fact that an entire section of this book is specifically dedicated to the problem of metonymy in translation makes it seem almost facetious to point out that none of the translations is intended to replace the original but rather to offer some guidance to the reader. Secondly, I make use of various typographical means to highlight the tropically used terms of a sequence. *Metonymic elements* of a sequence are set in italics, metaphorical elements are underlined. A dashed line indicates terms that may under certain interpretative conditions be read metaphorically, whereas a dotted line draws attention to an altogether different phenomenon that requires independent discussion.

2 Contiguity and its (dis-)contents

Metonymy in theory

Between forgotten trope and master trope—why metonymy matters

Poetic language is a key area of investigation in literary studies, usually in the close reading of individual texts but also as an area of theory in its own right. Even so, to single out the phenomenon of metonymy and to dedicate an entire study to understanding its structure, functions, and poetic effects may seem arbitrary. A look into any handbook from the rhetorical tradition reveals a plethora of tropes and figures that have not received any analytical treatment by literary critics beyond a brief description and a handful of stock examples. Yet even a quick glance at the history of tropology in poetics and rhetoric shows that from the earliest reflections on poetic language some forms of non-ordinary language usage have been deemed more significant and worthy of more extensive treatment than others. Genette has noted in his essay 'La rhétorique restreinte'[1] ('Rhetoric Restrained') that the history of rhetoric is marked by a movement of contraction: from a comprehensive art of oratory (in classical antiquity) to a mere science of tropes and figures, from which then, in a further process of 'tropical reduction',[2] an ever smaller set of key phenomena is singled out and credited with a greater structural significance in the organization of the ramified system of tropes and figures. This set of what one might call 'master tropes'[3] initially comprises metaphor, metonymy, synecdoche, and irony; then a triad emerges in which either of the last two is no longer present, followed by a binary model in which metaphor and metonymy stand

[1] Genette 1970a. [2] Genette 1970a, 105.

[3] The term was coined, albeit for rather different purposes, by Burke (see Burke 1941 and 1945, 503–17). Here and in what follows, I will use the term to refer to tropes which are seen as paradigmatic in terms of their inner structure to the extent that other tropes can be subsumed under them as specific variations of that structure.

out as polar opposites with synecdoche subsumed under one or other of them.[4] Finally, Genette notes,

> The age-old tendency of rhetoric to reduction seems . . . to have culminated in an absolute valorization of metaphor, bound up with the idea of the essential metaphoricity of poetic language—and language in general.[5]

Genette's observations highlight the fact that metonymy has already been foregrounded by rhetoricians and literary critics for some time, even if it has never attracted anything like the degree of interest or analytical penetration that marks the study of metaphor. More importantly, however, Genette's study points to two developments in earlier and current thinking about tropes and figures which are formative for the position of metonymy in scholarly discourse, which shape the initial framework of any closer investigation into the phenomenon of metonymy in poetic action, and which explain why a systematic study is indeed called for: the structuralist turn in tropology, on the one hand; and the question of the organization and conceptualization of the tropical space, the 'black box' of the poetic function of language, on the other.

Genette's analysis indicates that despite the rhetorical tradition's lack of interest in metonymy as a trope in its own right, it has long featured as a 'master trope' and has been increasingly recognized as central to a general understanding of tropical language, particularly in association with and counter-distinction from metaphor. The developing sense of a binary opposition between metaphor and metonymy at the centre of poetic language can be traced among formalist and structuralist scholars. Arguably inspired by Eichenbaum, who was the first to extend this primary opposition between metaphor and metonymy to a structural paradigm by associating the former with poetry and the latter with prose,[6] Jakobson widened the application of the terms metaphor and metonymy to various non-verbal discourses.[7] Jakobson claimed that metaphor characterized lyric poetry, Romanticism, Chaplin's films, and Freudian dream symbols, while metonymy was embodied in epic poetry, realist novels, Griffith's films, and Freudian dream projections. His identification of substitution, paradigm, and metaphor on the one hand, and of combination, syntagm, and metonymy on the other,[8] has

[4] Cf. Genette 1970a, 104–18. I shall return to the issue of synecdoche's affiliation in Chapter 3; see below, pp. 154–65.

[5] Genette 1970a, 118.

[6] Eichenbaum 1923.

[7] In his seminal article 'Two Aspects of Language and Two Types of Aphasic Disturbances' (Jakobson 1956).

[8] Jakobson 1956, 243–4.

led to an extension of the understanding and scholarly use of the two terms from specific modes of language usage to a universal structural schema in which metaphor and metonymy represent patterns of interrelation between elements in any one given semiotic system.

Heeding Jakobson's advice, scholars from virtually all disciplines of the humanities have applied his theory to one symbolic system after another—from language and literary narratives to film, dramaturgy, advertisements, visual art, historiography, folklore, and psychoanalysis.[9] While this development has, for the first time, brought metonymy under the spotlight of scholarly interest, it is fair to say that the outcome for literary study has been negligible. After the initial blow of being deemed unworthy of explicit acknowledgement by Aristotle, and having consequently been treated only marginally through the centuries by his literary-theoretical successors, metonymy's reinvention as a tool of structuralist analysis after a bimillennial sleep in the rhetorical handbooks has turned out to be effectively a death sentence for any prospects of close attention to its status as a literary trope. If there was hardly any tropological criticism of metonymy before, it now ceased almost entirely, and every critical discussion of the term took place under the new notion of metonymy as a structural-semiotic paradigm. The outcome is a stark discrepancy between (*a*) the pervasiveness of the new technical (in fact, *horribile dictu*, metaphorical) usage of the term 'metonymy' in structuralist studies—as inspired by Jakobson both within and beyond the field of literary studies—and (*b*) the continuing absence of any theoretical conceptualization of the structure, function, and effects of actual metonyms in literary texts. Metonymy may have gained more significance and a wider usage but the transfer of the term from rhetoric to semiotics has left it as insufficiently defined and analysed as ever: 'To date, despite a number of studies, there is no widely accepted definition of metonymy which distinguishes it clearly from metaphor, and attempts to clarify the relationship between the two... have proved inconclusive.'[10]

Even though this book is predominantly concerned with literary applications, rather than discarding this currently dominant strand of thinking about metonymy as irrelevant to my purposes, I shall revisit the topic towards the end of this study by contrasting the theoretical insights gained from my analyses of metonymic occurrences in literary texts with the implicit and explicit notions of metonymy as a semiotic pattern in Jakobson-inspired structuralist studies.[11] Suffice it to say at this stage that

[9] For a bibliography of works that 'develop, apply or challenge' Jakobson's theory, see Bohn 1984.

[10] Allan 2008, 11.

[11] See below, pp. 266–79.

it is, at the very least, ironic that this transfer should have taken place *prior* to a sustained investigation into metonymy in its original signification as a phenomenon of tropical language. What matters for now is to note that, although long earmarked as (in one way or another) of central relevance to tropology as a whole, metonymy has had its most extensive discussion to date in the context of its structuralist redefinition, and on the basis of an assumed bipolar opposition of metaphor and metonymy as structural-semiotic paradigms. While the problems resulting from this broadening of the term's scope can be postponed for the time being, the notion of a bipolar opposition of metaphor and metonymy requires closer attention before we can approach metonymy in its own right.

Jakobson's bipolar model of metaphor and metonymy as structural opposites and Genette's observations on the new perception of metaphor as the only true 'master trope' which essentially represents the whole of poetic language are startling in their incompatibility. They do, however, represent the two general views that pervade the literature on poetic usage and in their incompatibility contribute to the general impression of fuzziness in this field;[12] for what is hardly ever explicitly addressed is the question how the whole field of operations that constitutes the poetic function of language is structured and organized. It would seem that almost two millennia after Quintilian's dry remark on the unending battle fought by grammarians and philosophers on the genera, species, number, and classification of the tropes,[13] there is now less rather than more clarity on this topic in literary criticism. On the contrary, the confusion about the classification and number of tropes and 'master tropes' is now made worse by an indiscriminate use of 'trope' and 'figure' in the discussion of linguistic creativity. Sojcher, for instance, cited by Genette as a proponent of metaphor monism, writes:

[12] Compare and contrast Stanford's notion that 'in none of its contexts does μετονομάζειν suggest any of the significance of the term μετωνυμία as afterwards applied to metonymy, *a particular kind of* metaphor' (Stanford 1936, 4; italics added) and Goheen's view that 'the classical distinction of metaphors and similes from synecdoches and metonymies . . . involves chiefly a difference of degree in *the same kind of* effect and is largely a matter of intensity in the specific instance' (Goheen 1951, 108; italics added) with Wellek and Warren's assertion that 'we may *divide the tropes* of poetry most relevantly into figures of contiguity and figures of similarity. The traditional figures of contiguity are metonymy and synecdoche' (Wellek/Warren 1949, 199; italics added) as well as Ullmann's position that '[t]wo objects or ideas may be associated with one another in two ways: by similarity or by "contiguity" . . . Simile and metaphor arise from the former *whereas* metonymy and allied figures spring from the latter' (Ullmann 1964, 177; italics added).

[13] *circa quem inexplicabilis et grammaticis inter ipsos et philosophis pugna est quae sint genera, quae species, qui numerus, quis cuique subiiciatur.* Quint. *Inst.* 8.6.1 ('An endless battle has raged round this, both by the *grammatici* among themselves and by the philosophers, as to the genera, species, number and classification of Tropes.' Trans. Russell).

If poetry is a space that opens up in language, if through it words speak again and meaning becomes significant again, it is because there is between everyday language and rediscovered speech a shift of meaning, metaphor. Metaphor is no longer, from this point of view, *a* figure among others, but *the* figure, the trope of tropes.[14]

Deguy, also cited by Genette, argues similarly in an article entitled 'Pour une théorie de la figure généralisée' that 'metaphor and metonymy belong, beneath their secondary difference, to the same dimension—for which the term metaphoricity may generally serve'.[15] What happens here, and in many other works on the topic, is a twofold confusion of categories and levels of discussion: one resulting from the (relatively modern) failure to distinguish between figure and trope, the other from the (relatively ancient) failure to distinguish different levels of structural analysis in non-ordinary language usage. Both of these failures—innocuous though they may seem—play an important part in creating the problems and opacities that bedevil this field of literary studies and literary theory, since they introduce false assumptions and problematic misconceptions at the most fundamental level of literary-critical discussion and give rise to a slippery and misleading usage of central critical terms which, in turn, further exacerbates and proliferates the ensuing confusion in both critical practice and theoretical reflection. Carefully avoiding these pitfalls by scrutinizing (and rectifying) the underlying misapprehensions will go a long way towards putting the theory of metonymy developed here on a sure footing. Let us begin, then, by addressing the (relatively modern) failure to distinguish between figure and trope, prevalent even in Genette's own polemic on the decline of rhetoric,[16] which causes confusion over what kind of phenomenon of stylized speech metonymy and metaphor are and how they relate to other modes of expression and other forms of stylized speech.

[14] Sojcher 1969, 58; italics in the original. [15] Deguy 1969, 861.

[16] Genette uses both terms indiscriminately in his discussion, sometimes calling metonymy a figure, sometimes a trope. Thus he writes, for instance, that '[t]o reduce every metonymy (and a fortiori every synecdoche) to a pure spatial relation is obviously to restrict the play of these *figures* to their physical or sensory aspect alone' (Genette 1970a, 109–10; italics added) and then 'By definition, every *trope* consists of a substitution of terms... [T]o say "sail" for "ship" [i.e. use a metonymy/synecdoche] is to make the sail the substitute, and therefore the equivalent of the ship.' (Genette 1970a, 120; italics added). For a discussion of the French 'tradition' of blurring the lines between tropes and figures (including Fontanier, Dumarsais, and Genette), see Ricoeur 1975, 52–5.

Tropes and figures

If poetic language as a whole can be understood in a formalist way as defamiliarized language, then this defamiliarizing deviation from ordinary language usage can occur on various levels and in different ways. When coining the term and developing the concept of defamiliarization, Shklovsky sketched the different areas in which this poetic activity can take place:

> In studying poetic speak [sic] in its *phonetic and lexical structure* as well as in its characteristic *distribution of words* and in the *characteristic thought structures* compounded from the words, we find everywhere the artistic trademark—that is, we find material obviously created to remove the automatism of perception; the author's purpose is to create the vision which results from that deautomatised perception.[17]

From the beginning, ancient criticism was sensitive to this 'artistic trademark' of deviance from ordinary usage but also sought to establish systematically the different forms such deviation could take.[18] The differentiation between tropes and figures is an important analytical achievement of the ancient critics and should not be discarded by casual and indiscriminate usage of 'figurative' and 'tropical', as is all too common among modern critics. The precise development of the distinction cannot indeed be traced for lack of surviving textual evidence.[19] The distinction is not present in early theory but appears more or less clearly defined in the rhetorical writings of Cicero and Dionysius of Halicarnassus;[20] it then features as a critically discussed orthodoxy in Quintilian.[21] It must be admitted that, in their choice of examples, the ancient critics themselves repeatedly blur the lines which they are themselves drawing,[22] and the proliferation of technical terminology triggered by rhetoric's *translatio* from Greece to Rome adds further to this impression

[17] Shklovsky 1917, 19; italics added.

[18] The terms most frequently used in ancient criticism evincing this sensitivity are κύριος/κυρίως (e.g. Arist. *Rhet.* 1404b6, 1410b12; Arist. *Poet.* 1457b3; D.H. *Comp.* 21) and κυριολογία/κυριολεξία (e.g. Trypho, *Trop.* 728.5; Longin. *De Subl.* 28.1), all of which denote ordinary, standard language usage as the backdrop for the discussions of deviant usages at issue.

[19] 'We have only fragmentary knowledge of literary and rhetorical theory between Aristotle and authors of the first century B.C., a period including Theophrastus' *On Style* (περὶ λέξεως) and the development of the theories of styles, tropes, and figures, which we see in the works of Cicero and his contemporaries' (Innes 1995, 313–14). The theory of tropes is likely to be a Hellenistic development; see Barwick 1957, 88–111 and Russell 1981, 143–7.

[20] See Schenkeveld 1964, 147.

[21] See Quint. *Inst.* 9.1.1–18.

[22] See e.g. Silk 1974, 218.

of blurriness. The Greek term σχῆμα, for instance, which is reasonably consistently used in Greek rhetoric to denote what the later rhetorical tradition will call a 'figure', is variously translated and/or referred to by Roman rhetoricians as *forma* or *conformatio*, *exornatio*, or *figura*. As Mankin notes, 'In Cic. *figura* is used in connection with "figures of speech and thought" only at *Opt. Gen.* 14.23; it would not become a standard rendering of Gk *schema* in this sense until Quintilian.'[23] Notwithstanding these terminological variances, what the Roman rhetoricians' observations consistently highlight is the difference between what might be called the internal and the external generation of a semantic surplus achieved through stylized language usage. Cicero's definitions of tropes and figures run as follows:

Ornari orationem Graeci putant, si verborum immutationibus utantur, quos appellant τρόπους, *et sententiarum orationisque formis, quae vocant* σχήματα...

The Greeks consider that language is embellished if such changes [*immutationibus*] of words are employed as they call tropes [τρόπους], and such formations [*formis*: 'appearance', 'forms', 'patterns', 'shapes'] of thought and language are used as they call figures [σχήματα]...[24]

σχήματα *enim quae vocant Graeci, ea maxime ornant oratorem eaque non tam in verbis pingendis habent pondus quam in illuminandis sententiis.*

For what the Greeks call figures [σχήματα] are the greatest ornaments of oratory. They are not so important in heightening the colour of words, as in throwing ideas into a stronger light.[25]

Formantur autem et verba et sententiae paene innumerabiliter, quod satis scio notum esse vobis; sed inter conformationem verborum et sententiarum hoc interest, quod verborum tollitur, si verba mutaris, sententiarum permanet, quibuscumque verbis uti velis.

Now there are countless ways to give form [*formantur*] to both words and thoughts, as I am well aware that you know. But between a formation [*conformationem*] of words and of thought there is this difference, that the formation of words disappears if you change the words, while that of thought remains no matter what words you choose to employ.[26]

What are the crucial differences? Tropes are based on some sort of 'change' that affects individual words (*verborum immutationibus*) while

[23] Mankin on Cic. *De Or.* 3.199.

[24] Cic. *Brut.* 69; trans. Hendrickson (adapted). Here and elsewhere Cicero uses *forma* and *conformatio* as Latin equivalents to the Greek σχῆμα to denote figurative usage that depends on the specific form, shape, or pattern given to an expression; see Douglas *ad loc.* and Mankin on Cic. *De Or.* 3.200 and 201.

[25] Cic. *Brut.* 141; trans. Hendrickson. Cf. also the similar definition in 275.

[26] Cic. *De Or.* 3.200; trans. May/Wisse (adapted).

figures, subdivided into figures of thought (*sententiarum... formis*, in Greek σχήματα τῆς διανοίας) and figures of speech (*orationis formis*, in Greek σχήματα τῆς λέξεως), are all about the arrangement of a given idea into a specific form, shape, or pattern (*conformatio*). Figures of thought do this in a way that concerns the meaning of a larger unit, a sentence or comparable sequence, without being dependent on individual words in their linguistic materiality; they are abstract, intellectual structures.[27] Figures of speech, on the other hand, depend entirely on the precise word used, since the conformation is achieved by exploiting verbal properties (phonetic, syntactic, etymological, and so on).[28] Tropes differ from both of them. Quintilian defines a trope as *verbi vel sermonis a propria significatione in aliam cum virtute mutatio* ('a shift of a word or phrase from its proper meaning to another, in a way that has positive value')[29] and distinguishes it specifically from the figure:

> *Est igitur tropos sermo a naturali et principali significatione tralatus ad aliam ornandae orationis gratia, vel, ut plerique grammatici finiunt, dictio ab eo loco in quo propria est tralata in eum in quo propria non est: 'figura', sicut nomine ipso patet, conformatio quaedam orationis remota a communi et primum se offerente ratione.*
>
> A Trope, then, is language transferred from its natural and principal meaning to another for the sake of embellishment, or (as most *grammatici* define it), 'an expression transferred from a context in which it is proper to one in which it is not.' A Figure [*figura*: 'form', 'shape'], on the other hand, as its very name shows, is a configuration [*conformatio*: 'shape', 'arrangement'] of language distinct from the common and immediately obvious form.[30]

Quintilian thus likewise indicates that the key characteristic of tropes lies in a shift or change in the meaning of words resulting from their usage outside their normal context, which precludes an interpretation

[27] Cf. Auct. ad Her. 4.18: *sententiarum exornatio est quae non in verbis, sed in ipsis rebus quandam habet dignitatem* ('A figure of thought derives a certain distinction from the idea, not from the words.' Trans. Caplan; or rather: 'Embellishment of ideas is that kind of embellishment which involves a certain distinction not in the words used but in the content itself').

[28] Cf. Auct. ad Her. 4.18: *verborum exornatio est quae ipsius sermonis insignita continetur perpolitione* ('It is a figure of diction if the adornment is comprised of the fine polish of the language itself.' Trans. Caplan). As already indicated above, neither this passage nor the one quoted in the note above has the technical term *figura* ('figure') in the Latin original, which instead speaks of *exornatio* ('embellishment') of either *sententiae* ('ideas') or *verba* ('words'); however, these variations in terminology do not affect the principle which lies behind the distinction and is what matters for my argument here. On this author's particular preference for *exornatio* where Cicero uses *forma* and *conformatio*, see Mankin *ad* Cic. *De Or.* 3.201.

[29] Quint. *Inst.* 8.6.1; trans. Russell.

[30] Quint. *Inst.* 9.1.4; trans. Russell.

according to their standard usage (*dictio ab eo loco... in eum in quo propria non est*). Figures, on the other hand, characteristically transform the mode of expression; the given expression differs from ordinary forms of unstructured or unstylized usage but does not affect the meaning of the words it contains.[31] Quintilian makes it clear that, unlike tropes, figures are not a subversion of the normal semantic order of language but rather assume the natural properties of words. This is made clear by how he frames his discussion of figures, which includes an acknowledgement of the increasing confusion that already in his day surrounds the meaning of the term.[32] In order to clarify the matter, Quintilian traces how two different notions of what constitutes a figure (*nam duobus dicitur*; 9.1.10) equally look to the fact that figures of speech are operative on the interface of grammar and stylistics. On the one hand, figures (*figurae*) as stylistic devices are concerned with the specific form (*figura*) of an expression, yet on the other hand all expressions necessarily consist of words that occur in a specific form, namely their specific phonetic and rhythmic structure and, where applicable, the form they receive through their inflection:

Itaque cum in eosdem casus aut tempora aut numera aut etiam pedes continuo quis certe nimium frequenter incurrit, praecipere solemus variandas figuras esse vitandae similitudinis gratia: in quo ita loquimur tamquam omnis sermo habeat figuram. Itemque eadem figura dicitur 'cursitare' qua 'lectitare', id est eadem ratione declinari. Quare illo intellectu priore et communi nihil non figuratum est.

So when a speaker falls continually, or at least often, into the same cases, tenses, rhythms, or even feet, we usually advise him to vary his 'Figures' so as to avoid monotony. Here we are speaking as if all language has a 'Figure.' Again *cursitare* and *lectitare* are held to be in the same 'Figure', that is to say, be inflected in the same way. Thus, according to the first and usual interpretation of the word, there is nothing that is not 'figured' [*figuratum est*].[33]

Quintilian's example hinges upon the interrelatedness of grammar (or linguistics) and rhetoric (or stylistics), which coincide in the notion of *figura* as 'form' or 'formation': in Quintilian's scenario it is impossible to separate the grammatical-morphological *form* of the frequentative infinitive ending from the *form* of poetic expression that constitutes the device

[31] Cf. Quint. *Inst.* 9.1.7: *nam et propriis verbis et ordine conlocatis figura fieri potest* ('A Figure can be formed out of words used in their proper sense and in a normal order.' Trans. Russell).

[32] Quint. Inst. 9.1.10: *Est autem non mediocris inter auctores dissensio et quae vis nominis eius et quot genera et quae quamque multae sint species* ('There is however a considerable difference of opinion among the authors as to the meaning of the name Figure, and the number of genera and the nature and number of species.' Trans. Russell).

[33] Quint. *Inst.* 9.1.12; trans. Russell (adapted).

of the homoioteleuton. The logic of this first and extremely broad notion of *figura* thus runs as follows: a figure is a specifically shaped verbal expression, but all words have a shape, therefore all verbal expression is somehow shaped, hence all language is figurative. This view is both insightful and misleading. It is important and helpful to point out that it is the natural, linguistic properties of words that are key to distinctively *figurative* modes of stylization. However, to go so far as to conclude from the valuable insight that figures are, as opposed to tropes, operative on the basis of the properties of ordinary language that *all* language is figurative is not only a logical fallacy but one which renders the entire category of figurality useless for criticism. This is avoided in the second notion of figurative language, which defines a figure in the narrower sense as *a strategic exploitation of the natural properties of words.* Rather than merely using words which, inevitably, come with their own shape, figures of speech purposefully foreground and use their specific shape (*sc.* linguistic properties) in a way that goes beyond the economy of ordinary, unstylized language (while leaving them unchanged in their meanings):

Sed si habitus quidam et quasi gestus sic appellandi sunt, id demum hoc loco accipi schema oportebit quod sit a simplici atque in promptu posito dicendi modo poetice vel oratorie mutatum.

If on the other hand we are to give the name [of 'figure'] to specific attitudes and gestures, as it were, then we must limit the scope of *schema* ['figure'] in this context to that which is poetically or rhetorically varied from the simple and immediately available means of expression.[34]

On the basis of these ancient attempts to come to terms with the two main modes of poetic language, 'tropes' and 'figures' might be defined as follows:

Figures prominently deploy a given word or group of words while assuming their current meaning, whereas tropes redefine their meaning, since they entail a 'turn' away from their meaning in ordinary usage to an unforeseen, new meaning that must be inferred to render the sequence comprehensible.[35] While both of these two modes of poetic usage tend

[34] Quint. *Inst.* 9.1.13; trans. Russell.

[35] For this eponymous 'turn' cf. Trypho's observation that tropes are not just any manner (τρόπος) of speaking that differs from the daily usage of language but one that is marked by a characteristic turn (τροπή): τρόπος δέ ἐστι λόγος κατὰ παρατροπὴν τοῦ κυρίου λεγόμενος (Trypho, *Trop.* 728.12f.; 'a trope is an utterance of speech that involves a turning away from the ordinary'). The notion of this turn as a deviance from ordinary usage has remained the essential defining feature of tropicality: 'A trope is deviant usage—that is, a known word or phrase used, in context, deviantly from any normal usage of that word or phrase.' Silk 2003, 122.

towards defamiliarization through deviance from ordinary language usage, the semantic surplus of figures is external to the meaning of the words in question; it is generated by exploiting, and thereby rendering visible, their given properties (phonetic structure, syntactic position, and so on) in correspondence with their context and in amplification of the ordinary meaning of these words. The semantic surplus of tropes, on the other hand, is internal; it affects the meaning of the words, and is generated by using words in a way and context that invests the ordinary word with a new, extraordinary meaning without which no sense can be made of the sequence.[36]

Maintaining such a distinction between figure and trope is a necessary first step, whereby we avoid the recent tendency, rightly criticized by Genette, to reduce every phenomenon of poetic language to metaphor. Even if the ancient critics who first introduced this differentiation are deficient in terms of coherence of definitions or consistency of examples, the field of poetic language is far too complex to justify its abandonment. Its importance for the present enquiry is fundamental, and it requires us to reject the absolutism of statements such as Sojcher's 'Metaphor is no longer *a* figure among others, but *the* figure, the trope of tropes'[37] or Deguy's efforts to establish a 'théorie de la figure généralisée'[38] ('generalized theory of the figure') which would include the tropes metaphor and metonymy. In particular, it is inconceivable that metaphor could be both the figure of figures and trope of tropes. Such a status can be granted to metaphor only if it is perversely understood as encompassing every imaginable deviance from ordinary language usage.[39]

The classification of metaphor and metonymy as tropes and an awareness of their characteristic features and their difference in kind from figures—all this is a necessary prerequisite for any more specific theorizing

[36] Stanford suggests a similar differentiation between tropes and figures, and distinguishes metaphor clearly from figures along the lines suggested above; see Stanford 1936, 19. However, he privileges metaphor so much that he then goes on to suggest that it should be seen as different in kind from tropes as well, thereby casting metaphor as a phenomenon *sui generis*: 'Tropes on the other hand are superficial and artificial manipulations of uninspired words and have little imaginative or emotional force. Tropes are arbitrary devices of style: metaphors are necessities of expression. True metaphors are essentially of one indivisible order—the order of strokes of genius. They cannot be categorized like tropes; they can hardly even be analysed like tropes for the manifestations of genius are inscrutable.' Stanford 1936, 21. The neo-Romantic prejudice that pervades Stanford's discussion of metaphor is as unmistakable as its unhelpfulness for any attempt at illuminating phenomena of poetic language for the purpose of practical criticism.

[37] Sojcher 1969, 58; italics in the original. [38] Deguy 1969.

[39] Which seems to be what Sojcher effectively does when he equates the entire space of poetic language opened up by deviance from ordinary language usage with metaphor; see Sojcher 1969, 58.

(as well as for literary critical practice).[40] However, the basic distinction between ordinary and deviant usage, and the consequential subdivision of poetic language into figurative and tropical usage, are only the first steps in mapping the field. While the order of the figural space—that is, the further differentiation of various individual forms of figurative usage into figures of speech and figures of thought—has at least been sketched by the ancient critics,[41] the structural organization of the different forms of tropical usage is still largely unclear and seldom addressed. This continuing obscurity of the tropical space has seriously handicapped attempts to understand metaphor, metonymy, and their relationships with all other tropes, from Aristotle up to the present.

Tropicality, the tropical space, and the tropes

Given, now, the elementary distinction between ordinary and deviant/poetic usage and the structural differentiation between figurative and tropical language, we need to distinguish further the different levels on which the structural analysis of tropical usage takes place. It is precisely the recurrent failure to do so which has not only led to the *inexplicabilis pugna* that Quintilian deplored but ultimately also to the current unproductive co-existence of the incompatible views of metaphor monism criticized by Genette and the metaphor-metonymy binarism of Jakobson. The three levels that need to be distinguished are:

1 The level of tropicality
  What is under discussion here is the question of what makes a trope a trope: that is, what qualities and characteristics define the general nature of the tropical space as such and all of its constituent tropes.

2 The level of the tropical space
  Here the question of the order and structure of the tropical space is addressed. The various phenomena of poetic usage that differ structurally from figurative language, and that are to be identified as tropes, can stand in various possible relations to each other; they can all be thought of as independent and distinct tropical phenomena,

[40] For a discussion that fleshes out the significance of maintaining and mobilizing this differentiation in stylistic criticism, see below, pp. 261–6.
[41] For further elucidation of the difference between figures of speech and thought see e.g. Quint. *Inst.* 9.1.15–18 and 9.2–3.

or they can be seen as revealing cognate traits which bring them into some sort of hierarchy according to their structural relatedness.

3 The level of tropes
Finally, metaphor and metonymy and all the other tropes can, and should, be discussed in their own right as distinct, specific, individual tropes.

Awareness of these three distinct levels of theorizing about tropes makes it obvious that when Deguy suggests that 'metaphor and metonymy belong, beneath their secondary difference, to the same dimension—for which the term metaphoricity may generally serve',[42] he is using the partial and privileging term 'metaphoricity' to describe a characteristic of a higher order, one that is common to both metaphor and metonymy. The 'same dimension' to which both individual tropes belong is the tropical space (second level), whereas what metaphor and metonymy have in common 'beneath their secondary difference' on that tropical space is therefore their 'tropicality' (first level). From the false equation of 'tropicality' and 'metaphoricity'[43] a confused argument is constructed: the order of the tropical space (second level) is that of a pyramid, with metaphor (third level) as the purest embodiment of the structural principle (second level) that underlies all other tropes (first level).

The originator of this confusion is Aristotle in his discussion of metaphor in the *Poetics*. In his initial classification of eight categories of words, Aristotle gives the impression that μεταφορά here comprises more than metaphor as one particular trope.[44] This is confirmed later, in the much-discussed passages on the four different kinds of metaphor,[45] where he defines metaphor as ὀνόματος ἀλλοτρίου ἐπιφορά ('the transference of a term from one thing to another'),[46] a definition so broad that it covers all phenomena of the tropical space and thus defines tropicality (first level) rather than metaphoricity (third level). More specifically, under μεταφορά Aristotle subsumes examples of metaphor in its narrow sense as one particular trope alongside instances of other tropical phenomena that later ancient criticism would classify as hyperbole and

[42] Deguy 1969, 861.
[43] Deguy's case is representative for most theorists who hold a metaphor monist view based on 'the idea of the essential metaphoricity of poetic language' (Genette 1970a, 118).
[44] See Arist. *Poet.* 21, 1457b1–3; this categorization is in itself problematic since it equates modes of usage (ordinary, κύριον, and metaphorical, μεταφορά) with status in usage (marginal, γλῶττα, and ornamental, κόσμος) and formal status (made-up, πεποιημένον, lengthened, ἐπεκτεταμένον, shortened, ὑφῃρημένον, and adjusted, ἐξηλλαγμένον).
[45] See Arist. *Poet.* 21, 1457b7–32.
[46] Arist. *Poet.* 21, 1457b7; trans. Halliwell.

metonymy;[47] to this extent, he seems to imply indeed a notion of metaphor as the 'master trope' that structures the entire tropical space (second level). Famously, however, he identifies (and commends) metaphor's logical basis in resemblance, which in the philosopher's eyes makes it a token of genius;[48] and this characterization is too specific to subsume any other trope but metaphor in the narrow sense (third level). Aristotle's treatment of metaphor in the *Rhetoric* is also geared to explicating metaphor as a particular trope.[49] What follows from all of this is that Aristotle's praise of metaphor, largely based on the philosopher's admiration of its logic, elevated it right from the start to a predominant position in any discussion of tropical language, while his own confusing use of the same term, μεταφορά, for different phenomena on different levels has bedevilled the study of tropes and the tropical space throughout the centuries.

Mapping the tropical space

The discussion above has shown that Genette's analysis of the development of tropology needs to be amended in the sense that the ruling tendency is not, in fact, linear reduction but rather a circular movement of inflation and deflation in conceptualizing the tropical space: a movement from Aristotle, who discussed tropes and tropicality under the generalized notion of metaphor, to the diversification of the tropical space by the rhetorical tradition, to modern attempts to reduce the multitude of tropes by subsuming them under an ever-decreasing set of 'master tropes', to the eventual metaphor monism in which tropicality, the tropical space, and the individual tropes are again, as in Aristotle, ultimately all metaphorical. After two millennia, one might say, tropologists are back to where they started. Levin summarizes the contemporary situation as follows:

> This problem of definition and hence of scope is one that has troubled and embarrassed theorists and rhetoricians for over two millennia and is perhaps

[47] Cf. Silk 2003, 116–18; see also below, p. 155.

[48] πολὺ δὲ μέγιστον τὸ μεταφορικὸν εἶναι. μόνον γὰρ τοῦτο οὔτε παρ' ἄλλου ἔστι λαβεῖν εὐφυΐας τε σημεῖόν ἐστι· τὸ γὰρ εὖ μεταφέρειν τὸ τὸ ὅμοιον θεωρεῖν ἐστιν. Arist. *Poet.* 1459a5–8 ('by far the most important point is facility with metaphor. This alone is a sign of natural ability, and something one can never learn from another: for the successful use of metaphor entails the perception of similarities'; trans. Halliwell).

[49] See Arist. *Rhet.* 1405a8–10 and 1410b17–20.

> inescapable given the number and complexity of possible figurative relations. Playing major contributory roles in this complexity are the figures [sic] of metaphor, metonymy, and synecdoche. Although the relations subsisting among them are not entirely clear, it is generally agreed that they cluster at the center of the figural space. That they are central needs no urging. That they are proximately related is evidenced by attempts that have been made to effect reductions among them... Finally, how shifting and open to arbitrary definition are the boundaries between the various major tropes [sic] is amply attested in the essay of Genette.[50]

While the systematic study of tropes is undoubtedly one of the most intricate areas of literary theory, it seems defeatist to capitulate in the face of problems of definition and scope. As I have argued, establishing and maintaining a clear distinction between figurative and tropical language (*pace* Levin) is needed to promote a better understanding of poetic language in general. Likewise, if we are to resolve this age-old *inexplicabilis pugna*, it is essential to move beyond arbitrary redefinitions and the speculative shifting of boundaries and begin a systematic analysis of the order and structure of the tropical space.

The main obstacle here is the fact that scrutiny of individual tropes has always focused almost exclusively on metaphor, leaving metonymy (and indeed all other tropes) largely as metaphor's counter-distinct but underdetermined and ill-defined Other, and thereby making metaphor the seemingly obvious yet ultimately arbitrary paradigm for all attempts to theorize tropical language as a whole. What is required above all is a mapping of the tropical space on the basis of the general criteria of tropicality that establish this space along with a comparative assessment of the individual tropes that fill this space. The earlier discussion of the difference between tropes and figures has pointed to the framing criterion of tropicality as the neutral foundation for all subsequent theorizing on individual tropes. The question now is: how far can we identify similarities and differences between the individual tropes that exceed their common trait as non-ordinary usage involving a re-semanticization of a word's conventional meaning? It is only through an empirically supported, structural comparison of different tropes that we can shed light on the relations subsisting among them. The case studies of metonymic occurrences later on in this book will provide empirical evidence for just such a contrastive comparison, and will, in particular, be offered as a definitive point of reference for a worked-out theory of metonymy,

[50] Levin 1977, 80.

which is itself, in turn, a prerequisite for a proper assessment of the relationship between metaphor, metonymy, and the other tropes.

At this stage of the enquiry, however, the first need is to consolidate a directional notion of metonymy and to formulate a set of operational criteria and preliminary questions to guide the specific analyses of concrete examples in Chapter 3. In this connection, further theoretical reflection is in order before we can to turn to examining the tropes themselves.

As suggested earlier, the order of the tropical space can be conceptualized in different ways according to the various possible relations in which the individual tropes can stand to each other: they might be distinct and independent tropical phenomena; alternatively, they might reveal cognate traits which bring them into some sort of hierarchy based on a structural relatedness. This hierarchy itself might prove to be either multipolar, bipolar, or monistic. It follows that an adequate theory of metonymy will show whether metonymy is indeed a subordinate trope to metaphor: that is, whether metonymy is ultimately to be seen as structurally similar to but more limited and less effectual than metaphor while still being describable with the same terms and concepts that are used to characterize metaphor.[51] Alternatively, metonymy will be shown to function in an essentially different way, which requires a different descriptive and analytical framework; should this be the case, the corollary will be that metonymy has to be understood either as metaphor's bipolar counter-trope or else (simply) as one distinct trope amongst others. On this second scenario, the question whether the tropical space is bipolar or multipolar can then be answered by a further determination: do the remaining tropes show a structural affinity that would allow us to subsume them to either metonymy or metaphor?

It follows, again, that we can properly make use of analytical tools and frameworks already developed by theorists of metaphor as provisional guides for theorizing metonymy. The seeming applicability of theory developed for the study of metaphor would imply structural similarities between the two tropes, whereas inapplicability would serve to characterize metonymy *ex negativo* and thereby highlight relevant starting points for further investigations into the specific idiosyncrasies of metonymy. The following survey of major theoretical advances in the study of metaphor should thus yield a preliminary set of markers for the analysis of metonymic occurrences in the text corpus studied in the next chapter.

[51] A view implied, for instance, in Johnson/Lakoff 1980, 37.

Developments in theory of metaphor

From Aristotle's definition of metaphor (and tropical language in general) as ὀνόματος ἀλλοτρίου ἐπιφορά ('the transference of a term from one thing to another') onwards,[52] metaphor and indeed all tropes have essentially been conceived of as linguistic substitutions. On this view, metaphorical and all tropical language is seen as a secondary order to the general linguistic system of signs which repeats the relationship between *res* and *verbum* (*aliquid stat pro aliquo*; 'something stands for something'); in Quintilian's words: *in tropis ponuntur verba alia pro aliis, ut in* μεταφορᾷ, μετονυμίᾳ... ('In Tropes... words are substituted for words, as in metaphor, metonymy...').[53] The concept of metaphor as a more or less mechanical replacement of one word by another on the basis of their similarity or an underlying analogy was first decisively challenged by Richards's introduction of 'tenor' and 'vehicle' as analytical tools to identify the components that constitute metaphor. Richards defines the tenor as (referring to) the underlying idea and principal subject in a metaphorical compound, that which is at issue, while the vehicle denotes the element which is related by similarity or analogy to whatever is at issue but is in itself extraneous to the subject.[54] It is the development of these terms that enabled Richards to characterize the implicit bipartite structure of metaphor beyond simply calling metaphor an elliptical simile,[55] and allowed him to make a key observation, namely that:

> in many of the most important uses of metaphor, the co-presence of the vehicle and tenor results in a meaning (to be clearly distinguished from the tenor) which is not attainable without their interaction. That the vehicle is not normally a mere embellishment of a tenor which is otherwise unchanged but that the vehicle and tenor in co-operation give a meaning of more varied powers than can be ascribed to either.[56]

Richards's theory led to a paradigmatic shift from the age-old substitutional view of metaphor to a new interactional view, which has since become predominant in understanding metaphor's mechanisms and dynamics.

[52] Arist. *Poet.* 21, 1457b7; trans. Halliwell.
[53] Quint. *Inst.* 9.1.5.
[54] Richards 1936, 96–7.
[55] ἔστιν γὰρ ἡ εἴκων, καθάπερ εἴρηται πρότερον, μεταφορὰ διαφέρουσα προθέσει· διὸ ἧττον ἡδύ, ὅτι μακροτέρως· καὶ οὐ λέγει ὡς τοῦτο ἐκεῖνο· οὐκοῦν οὐδὲ ζητεῖ τοῦτο ἡ ψυχή. Arist. *Rhet.* 1410b, 17–20 ('A simile is, as was said earlier, a metaphor differing in what is put first. Thus, it is less pleasing because longer and because it does not say that this *is* that, nor does (the listener's) mind seek to understand this.' Trans. Kennedy; italics in the original). In Aristotle, as in much later theory of metaphor, these principles of comparison and substitution coexist; see, for instance, Black 1962, 35.
[56] Richards 1936, 100.

On the basis of Richards's model, albeit in his own terminology of 'frame' (Richards's 'tenor') and 'focus' (Richards's 'vehicle'), Black sought to further illuminate the nature of the 'interplay between focus and frame'.[57] Richards had rejected the assumption of a mere substitution and, with it, the necessary implication of a one-to-one equivalence of the two elements involved, stressing instead the irreducible newness of the meaning emerging from the interaction of the two. Black goes further and argues that, as far as this new meaning brought forth by interaction is concerned, it is often closer to the truth 'to say that the metaphor creates the similarity than to say that it formulates some similarity antecedently existing'.[58] Black postulates that every word is part of a 'system of ideas'[59] and that metaphor exploits patterns of implications which make it possible 'that the principal subject is "seen through" the metaphorical expression—or, if we prefer, that the principal subject is "projected upon" the field of the subsidiary subject'.[60] However, seeing the principal subject (tenor) through the lens of the subsidiary subject (vehicle) automatically reorganizes the system of ideas of both subjects: 'If to call a man a wolf is to put him in a special light, we must not forget that the metaphor makes the wolf seem more human than he otherwise would.'[61] The relationship between tenor and vehicle, in short, is one of real and mutual interaction in which both are equally affected. In Black's view 'metaphor selects, emphasises, suppresses, and organises features of the principal subject by implying statements about it that normally apply to the subsidiary subject'.[62]

This last statement makes clear that Black's view of interaction in metaphor is essentially conceptual and is concerned with the reactions and modifications between the conceptual content of the two constitutive elements. It is Brooke-Rose's merit to have drawn attention to hitherto disregarded philological aspects of the study of metaphor by emphasizing that 'metaphor is expressed in words, and a metaphoric word reacts on other words to which it is syntactically and grammatically related'.[63] Through a systematic evaluation of a representative corpus of English poetry, Brooke-Rose develops a plethora of categories that describe the various formal configurations in which the interaction between tenor and vehicle can occur and illustrates how it is different grammatical and syntactical operations that establish the link between both elements and thereby structurally shape their interaction. In so doing, she disproves Black's claim that '"metaphor" must be classified

[57] Black 1962, 28. [58] Black 1962, 37. [59] Black 1962, 40.
[60] Black 1962, 41. [61] Black 1962, 44. [62] Black 1962, 44.
[63] Brooke-Rose 1958, 1.

as a term belonging to "semantics" and not to "syntax"—or to any physical inquiry about language'[64] and shows that metaphor in fact occupies a space between syntax and 'semantics'.

A concern to move away from a conceptual discussion, with its focus on conceptual content, towards a verbal orientation focusing on words and their micro-context also characterizes Silk's formulation of interaction as a critical concept.[65] His assessment of examples from Greek and English poetry adds to Brooke-Rose's observations on the importance of grammatical and syntactical linkages but, more importantly, shifts the focus to terminology as the key area of interaction. While grammar clearly facilitates the linkages that effect the interaction of tenor and vehicle, Silk stresses that it is the interruption of an otherwise terminologically coherent sequence by terminologically extraneous material that is essential to the phenomenon of metaphor.[66] As opposed to Black's conceptual notion of the vehicle as a different, subsidiary 'system of ideas' through which the principal subject is seen, here the vehicle is understood as a word or sequence of words that is terminologically incongruous with the terminology used in ordinary language for the subject at issue, and which therefore stands out in the micro-context of the metaphor in question. Metaphors involve a 'terminological barrier... between tenor and vehicle'.[67] Silk's terminological interaction theory allows him to integrate the primary criterion of metaphor as a literary trope, namely its deviance from ordinary language usage, with its much-discussed logical basis:

> In metaphor, the deviant item or sequence (the vehicle) is distinct from the non-deviant sequence in its vicinity (the tenor) terminologically, and the relation between the two terminologies, in whole or part, is one of analogy, comparison or similarity. As an operational definition of metaphor, I suggest: a deviantly used word or sequence of words whose adequate explication (*sc.* explanation by paraphrase or expansion) into non-deviant usage involves overt analogy, comparison or simile).[68]

While the study of metaphor has thus seen a fundamental change in the paradigm that traditionally governed its conceptualization,[69] namely the replacement of the substitutionalist view by the interaction theory, in the general perception of metonymy, *faute de mieux*, the outdated

[64] Black 1962, 28. [65] See Silk 1974, 8. [66] See Silk 1974, 12.
[67] Silk 1974, 22. [68] Silk 2003, 124.
[69] Another major strand of recent thinking about metaphor, which has almost come to dominate the field, is represented by the cognitive school, whose approach, however, as explained in the introduction, is geared less towards the kind of literary-aesthetic questions pursued here and is, therefore, of rather limited relevance to this study; see above, pp. 23–4.

substitution theory still widely prevails. In order to capitalize on the theoretical advances in the study of metaphor for the development of a theory of metonymy and also to elucidate the relationship between metaphor and metonymy by assessing the transferability and applicability of these theoretical tools and concepts, a series of questions will be kept in mind when we consider metonymic occurrences from the text corpus: how can metonymic deviance from ordinary language usage be characterized? Do metonyms display an implicit bipartite structure like metaphor? Can the terms 'tenor' and 'vehicle' be used to analyse the structure and mechanisms of metonyms? Do the different components at play in metonymy, if there is indeed a plurality of components, interact? If so, do they interact in a way similar to that observed in metaphor? On which level or levels does any such interaction take place? How and by what means would the components then be linked and brought into interaction? Are there patterns of grammatical linkages to be observed that are comparable to the categories elaborated by Brooke-Rose?[70] What is the logical relation between the constituent components (if indeed there are two or more components) of a metonym?

'Contiguity' and its (dis-)contents: characterizing metonymy

So far no attempt has been made to quote or provide any definition of metonymy, which is, after all, the principal object of this study. This is not an oversight. It is important to adopt a largely inductive approach as a safeguard against developing a theory of metonymy on the basis of unchallenged, traditional preconceptions. But as the present enquiry is now about to move from establishing a theoretical framework to contextual analysis, and thus to move from speaking about metonymy essentially *ex negativo* (in its potential opposition to metaphor) to the concrete analysis of actual metonyms in literary texts, the time has come to introduce (and problematize) positive characterizations of metonymy from the rhetorical tradition and modern scholarship. However inductive the approach pursued here may be, we do need at least a provisional notion of metonymy in order to identify examples in the text corpus.

[70] Such as link through genitive case, use of possessives and demonstratives, groups of linking verbs, apposition, etc.

Although discussion of examples which one might consider to be prima facie metonyms regularly occurs under various headings in ancient criticism,[71] metonymy is only rarely discussed explicitly in its own right by the ancients. As noted earlier, Aristotle does not distinguish clearly between 'tropical' and 'metaphorical', and while some of his remarks are obviously directed at metaphor as a particular trope he never focuses on metonymy. Trypho, who writes in the first century BC, is the first to use μετωνυμία in extant Greek literature, but he clearly uses it as an already established term.[72] Trypho's discussion of metonymy begins with the words μετωνυμία ἐστὶ λέξις ἀπὸ τοῦ ὁμωνύμου τὸ συνώνυμον δηλοῦσα ('metonymy is an expression that explains a synonym by a homonym').[73] This 'definition' is barely worth the name: given the indeterminate nature of all the three key terms used, it is hardly more than a serial tautology of the substitution view and says nothing more than that metonymy is somehow conceived of as being based on the replacement of one word by another to which it is effectively fully equivalent. If one had no preconception of metonymy and was given nothing but this definition it would be virtually impossible to identify concrete examples of metonymy; it is only the examples which follow Trypho's definition that give a vague idea of what he is talking about: οἷον 'σπλάγχνα δ' ἀμπείραντες ὑπείρεχον *Ἡφαίστοιο*'·"Ηφαιστος γὰρ ὁ εὑρὼν τὸ πῦρ· καὶ ὅταν τὸν πυρὸν *Δήμητραν* εἴπωμεν ('... such as in "having fixed the inner parts on a spit, they held them over *Hephaestus*"; for Hephaestus is the inventor of fire; and likewise when we call wheat *Demeter*').[74] The same vagueness marks the majority of definitions provided by other Greek rhetoricians,[75] as also, for instance, Quintilian's description: *metonymia, quae est nominis pro nomine positio* ('metonymy, which is the substitution of one name for another').[76] By way of modest qualification, Quintilian goes on to offer examples of metonymic expression which are, rather superficially, classified as either widely used (*vulgo audimus*) or as adjusting the level of expression by rendering

[71] For instance, under 'figure' in Longin. *De Subl.* 24.1, and under 'metaphor' in Arist. *Rhet.* 1411a26f. and 31–3.

[72] The term μετονομάζειν is used by Isocrates, Herodotus, Thucydides, and Plato to mean 'to call by a new name', 'to change something's name'. However, it always refers to a change in denotative, ordinary language usage and in none of its contexts suggests *tropical* language usage (as the term μετωνυμία does in Trypho); see Stanford 1936, 4.

[73] Trypho, *Trop.* 739, 20–1.

[74] Trypho, *Trop.* 739, 21–5; the example is taken from *Il.* 2.426.

[75] See e.g. Anon. *De Trop.* (717.8–9), Greg. Cor. *De Trop.* (770.9–12), Choerob. *De Trop.* (811.14–21).

[76] Quint. *Inst.* 8.6.23; trans. Russell.

it more learned (*eruditus est sermo*) or more socially acceptable (*magis decet*):[77]

Nam ut 'Vulcanum' pro igne uulgo audimus et 'uario Marte pugnatum' eruditus est sermo et 'Venerem' quam coitum dixisse magis decet, ita 'Liberum et Cererem' pro uino et pane licentius quam ut fori seueritas ferat. Sicut ex eo quod <continent id quod> continetur: usus recipit 'bene moratas urbes' et 'poculum epotum' et 'saeculum felix'...a possessore quod possidetur, ut 'hominem deuorari', cuius patrimonium consumatur: quo modo fiunt innumerabilis species.

We can hear 'Vulcan' meaning fire in common speech; "They fought with varying Mars" is an educated turn of phrase, and it is more decent to speak of 'Venus' than to speak of coitus; yet 'Liber' and 'Ceres' for 'wine' and 'bread' are too bold for the seriousness of the courts. Similarly, <a container> may stand for what it contains. Usage permits 'cities of good character,' 'a cup drunk up,' and 'a happy age'... [there is also the case of] 'possessor for the possessed,' like 'the man is being eaten up,' meaning that his estate is being used up.[78]

What remains obscure in all these attempted definitions is the nature of this alleged substitution and in particular the relationship between the elements involved in it. This is especially true for mythological metonyms, based on the names of gods, which are often used as stock examples for metonymy in rhetorical handbooks (the 'god-for-sphere-of-operation'-type metonym, as it were). From a modern perspective, an additional complication arises here out of the difficulty to assess whether or not, in any particular case, Greek religion treats divinities as 'actually' subsuming their sphere of operation—which makes it impossible to determine the exact semantic range of what is denoted, or else metonymically implied, by the name of a god (and for exactly this reason such mythological metonyms have been excluded from the main body of my discussion in Chapter 3).[79] But even this particular issue aside, what appears to be generally assumed is an equivalence of the substitute and the substituted that effectively amounts to synonymy. This assumption invites at once objections: why should such a device of poetic diction be noticed by the reader? And indeed, why should it be used by the poet in the first place? Cicero's treatment of metonymy in *De Oratore* illustrates the point. Cicero distinguishes metonymy from the creation of new words (neologism) and the transfer of old words (metaphor) and is then left to 'define' metonymy rather paradoxically as *ornandi causa proprium proprio commutatum* ('for the sake of imparting distinction, one proper word is substituted for another').[80] But, how would anyone

[77] Quint. *Inst.* 8.6.24.

[78] Quint. *Inst.* 8.6.24–5; trans. Russell.

[79] For an ancient discussion of mythological metonymy, see Plut. *De Aud. Poet.* 23a–c.

[80] Cic. *De Or.* 3.167; trans. May/Wisse.

notice that one proper term has been exchanged for another? How would this differ from the choices in vocabulary that lie behind every ordinary non-tropical utterance? The confusion follows inevitably from the coexistence of mutually exclusive conceptualizations of metonymy: as a substitution, with the implicit claim of synonymity, and at the same time as a trope, with the implicit claim of non-ordinary, deviant, and therefore, perceptibly im-proper usage—*non ut dictum est in eo genere intellegitur, sed ut sensum est* ('a word is understood not as said, but as supposed'),[81] as Cicero himself goes on to remark.

Cicero gets closer to tackling this issue in his *Orator* where he distinguishes metaphor (*tralatio*) and metonymy (*immutatio*) by describing the former in the Aristotelian manner as a transfer by resemblance from one thing to another and the latter as a substitution in which the proper word is replaced by another word, which has the same meaning (*idem significet*) but is 'taken from some other matter that follows on [from what is at issue]' (*sumptum ex re aliqua consequenti*).[82] The Auctor ad Herennium goes further in his definition: *denominatio est quae ab rebus propinquis et finitimis trahit orationem qua possit intellegi res quae non suo vocabulo sit appellata* ('Metonymy is the trope which draws from an object closely akin or associated an expression suggesting the object meant, but not called by its own name').[83] Here at last an ancient theorist moves away from the assumption of synonymity and, after asserting the tropical trait of deviation from terminologically normal usage (*non suo vocabulo*), characterizes the relationship between the terms deviantly used and the ones one would expect to be used in normal usage as a relationship of proximity (*propinquis et finitimis*).

Consequens ('following on', 'accompanying'), *propinquus* ('near', 'neighbouring'), *finitimus* ('bordering', 'adjoining'): these key terms used by Roman rhetoricians to describe the relationship between the 'substituting' and the 'substituted' element in metonymy find their echo in the modern term used wherever definitions of metonymy are attempted: 'contiguity'. This term, made particularly popular through

[81] Cic. *De Or.* 3.168.

[82] Cic. *Or.* 92: *tralata dico, ut saepe iam, quae per similitudinem ab alia re aut suavitatis aut inopiae causa transferuntur; mutata in quibus pro verbo proprio subicitur aliud quod idem significet sumptum ex re aliqua consequenti* ('By "transferred" I now mean, as often before, words transferred by resemblance from another thing in order to produce a pleasing effect, of because of lack of a "proper" word; by "borrowed" [lit.: "changed"] I mean the cases in which there is substituted for a "proper" word another with the same meaning drawn from some suitable sphere [lit.: from some other matter that follows on (from what is at issue)].' Trans. Hubbell).

[83] Auct. ad Her. 4.43; trans. Caplan (adapted).

the structuralist reappropriation of metonymy,[84] also features prominently in what is arguably the most comprehensive attempt to date to define metonymy as a phenomenon of poetic language:

> Metonymy may be defined as a trope whose logical basis is one of association or contiguity. An operational definition might be: a word or sequence of words whose explication can be made to use all the tropical items untropically but without any similarity marker ('like', 'as' or whatever). If you are faced with a deviant usage wherein each word is literally possible in an expanded context in a sense approximating to that of its given use, you have metonymy.[85]

This operational definition, by Silk, highlights metonymy's tropical nature in characterizing it as deviant usage, introduces a notion of discourse compression at play in this trope equivalent to the widespread understanding of metaphor as a compressed simile,[86] and distinguishes metonymy from metaphor as not being logically based on analogy or similarity. It seems to be generally acknowledged that 'contiguity' is for metonymy what 'analogy' is for metaphor; a comparison of Silk's definition of metonymy with his definition of metaphor cited above also suggests this. Yet, while 'analogy' as a logical relation is a readily definable term, 'contiguity' seems almost as elusive a notion as metonymy itself. On reflection, it soon becomes obvious that 'contiguity' is nothing more than an umbrella term for the various notions floated by the Roman rhetoricians (*consequens*, *propinquus*, *finitimus*), albeit with the reassuring flavour of academic abstraction. So what is meant when the 'logical basis' is described as being one of 'association or contiguity'? Is there any one logic of association? Genette rightly asks: 'what kind of "contiguity" could be maintained by the heart and courage, the brain and intelligence, the bowels and mercy?'[87]

It is striking that there has not yet been any sustained attempt to explain what exactly can be meant by 'contiguity'. Philosophers speak of contiguity when referring to two events or objects that lie directly side by side in space and time without being connected by causality or any other principle.[88] In psychology, association by contiguity refers to the principle that ideas, memories, and experiences are linked when one is frequently experienced with the other.[89] How can 'contiguity' then be defined in a literary-linguistic context? While philosophy and psychology

[84] See Jakobson 1956, 244.
[85] Silk 2003, 132.
[86] See e.g. Arist. *Rhet.* 1406b20.
[87] Genette 1970a, 109.
[88] See Prechtl 1999, 300.
[89] Theorizing on contiguity in this context goes back to Guthrie's behaviourist theory of learning which stresses the contiguity between stimulus and response (see Guthrie 1952 and 1959); theorizing on the psychology of association more generally dates back (at least) to Locke's *Essay Concerning Human Understanding* (1690).

are concerned with conceptual and actual entities, that is, thoughts, experiences, (perceptions of) things that may occur together in space and time and are thereby associated (spatial and temporal contiguity), contiguity in the field of language and literature can best be understood as lexical contiguity: thoughts, experiences, (perceptions of) things that occur together as words in language. On reflection, it seems clear that, as in philosophy and psychology, the link between whatever is in contiguity with something else can be nothing but that contiguity itself: this is a relation based solely on frequently experienced togetherness, without the necessary involvement of *any* logical principle as such. Ancient criticism tried to come to terms with this relation of contiguity by creating countless sub-classifications of various different causal-logical relationships between the two elements involved in the alleged metonymic 'substitution': place and inhabitant, individual and group, producer and product, container and contained, cause and effect, and so forth. Most of the classical authors who address the issue produce a more or less extensive list of this kind but the varying selection of categories chosen by each of them makes these lists seem both arbitrary and limitless—characteristics that usually imply the inadequacy of a classificatory system.[90] The categories of the ancients and of the rhetorical handbook tradition remain on the superficial level of a purely content-based taxonomy and fail to formulate a structural principle which would adequately describe a verbal phenomenon such as metonymy.[91] In literary and linguistic scholarship the closest one gets to such a word-oriented concept of contiguity is the theory of semantic fields.

Lexical contiguity: metonymy and the theory of semantic fields

The concept of semantic fields was developed by German and Swiss scholars, within twentieth-century descriptive linguistics, as a way of coming to terms with the structuring of vocabulary and the interrelations

[90] A fact of which the Auctor ad Herennium is clearly aware—Auct. ad Her. 4.43: *Harum omnium denominationum magis in praecipiendo divisio quam in quaerendo difficilis inventio est, ideo quod plena consuetudo est* ('It is harder to distinguish all these metonymies in teaching the principle than to find them when searching for them, for the use of metonymies of this kind is abundant.' Trans. Caplan).

[91] This conceptual content-based approach also continues to inform current cognitive approaches to metonymy; see, for instance, Kövecses 2002, 143–61, with further bibliographical references to recent cognitive-linguistic research.

of its constituent elements. A semantic field is constituted by a set of words defined by semantic proximity and joint occurrence. Of the two pioneers in the development of this approach, Trier's conception of the organization of vocabulary is largely focused on the referential element of vocabulary organization and hence is too conceptual to be of much help in developing an understanding of lexical contiguity.[92] Porzig,[93] on the other hand, takes the observation that 'lexemes vary enormously with respect to the freedom with which they can be combined in syntagms with other lexemes'[94] as his starting point.[95] With this more intralingual approach he develops theories of 'encapsulation' and 'collocation'. Porzig observes that words have what he calls 'essential meaning-relations' with other words. Lyons offers some straightforward examples:

> one could hardly hope to explain the meaning of the verb 'bark' without mentioning dogs or of 'blond' without mentioning hair . . . The sense of 'with the foot' is encapsulated in the sense of 'kick', as the sense of 'with teeth' is encapsulated in the sense of 'bite'.[96]

While *encapsulation* represents the most intimate of essential meaning-relations between words (one cannot be explained without mentioning the other), *collocation* more openly defines the restrictions governing the legitimacy of the combination of two words (one can be explained without the other but they regularly occur together and implicitly contain aspects of one another). Firth specifies the phenomenon as follows:

> Meaning by collocation is an abstraction at the syntagmatic level and is not directly concerned with the conceptual or idea approach to the meaning of words. One of the meanings of *night* is its collocatability with *dark*, and of *dark*, of course, collocation with *night*.[97]

Firth's example makes the relevance of collocation in semantic-field theory to contiguity in the theory of metonymy obvious: the link of contiguity that holds together a potential metonym (say, 'darkness') and its virtual, inferred, non-tropical counterpart (say, 'night') is established not actually by any extralingual reality or logical principle but by their pragmatic lexical collocatability. What follows is that whatever is said, when something is expressed through a metonym, must always be

[92] Despite his Humboldtian belief in the powers of language as structuring an a priori unstructured extra-lingual 'reality'; see Trier 1934, 429.

[93] Porzig 1934.

[94] Lyons 1977, 261.

[95] This theory was initially known as 'Wortfeldtheorie' ('lexical field theory'), suggesting a focus on words, which progressively became sidelined by a focus on 'meaning', as implied by the now conventional name 'semantic-field theory'. In the redefinition of 'semantic fields' proposed below (see pp. 51–2 and 91), I return to the original conception.

[96] Lyons 1977, 262.

[97] Firth 1951, 196.

contained and implicitly said in a hypothetical non-tropical version because of the 'essential meaning-relation' between the two words or sequences of words in question: each one is encapsulated or at least contained in the semantics of the other one by virtue of their collocatability in ordinary language. If the term 'semantic field' is not understood from a concept-centred point of view ('all things to do with night') but from a lexical point of view ('all the words that could ordinarily be used in a meaningful way in some sort of collocation with the word "night"'), then a semantic field can be defined as the sum of all words that are collocatable with any one chosen term in ordinary usage. If, furthermore, the 'contiguity' that characterizes metonymy has to be understood as lexical contiguity then one can reasonably expect that it must be a precondition for a term *x* to be a potential metonym of *y* that both belong to the same semantic field: that is, that they are collocatable in ordinary usage. Such collocatability of the terms involved is ultimately the condition on which Silk's litmus test of expanding metonyms into literal expressions cited above is based:[98] all the terms involved—both the actually present ones ('what is said') and the virtual, inferred ones ('what is meant')—can potentially stand next to or near to each other in a coherent sentence without the need to introduce any explanatory conjunctions or logical markers to bind heterogeneous elements together.

This clarification of contiguity as the principle that governs metonymy has two consequences. The first follows from a dilemma of semantic-field theory itself, which has been subjected to criticism over the criteria that define the borders of semantic fields. Lyons remarks: 'What is lacking so far, as most field-theorists would probably admit, is a more explicit formulation of the criteria which define a lexical field than has yet been provided.'[99] Unnerving as this state of affairs may be, it seems as though this blurriness quite accurately describes the fluidity of actual language usage. The notion of metonymic contiguity as developed above with reference to contiguity in philosophy and psychology makes this fluidity almost a corollary: if lexical contiguity is based on the frequent experience of togetherness, that is, on the regular joint occurrence of words, without the involvement of any causality or other logical principle, then ultimately the legitimacy of any word combination that constitutes collocatability is determined not by semantics but by pragmatics. In this sense we can reply to Genette's question that the 'contiguity' between heart and courage, brain and intelligence, bowels and mercy, is ultimately maintained by the establishment of their frequent

[98] See above, p. 48. [99] Lyons 1977, 267.

joint usage in general discourse which makes them form part of the same semantic field.[100] Metonymy, as it emerges, is thus predicated not on an abstract logic, but on pragmatically determined association.[101] No wonder it did not take Aristotle's fancy.

The second consequence concerns the question whether the theoretical framework of interaction theory as developed for the description and analysis of metaphor can also be used to describe and analyse metonymy. If metaphor involves a 'terminological barrier... between tenor and vehicle',[102] then one might press this line of thought further and suggest that metaphor is characterized by an interaction of heterogeneous terminologies, that is, of verbal sequences from disparate spheres that are related by analogy or similarity at certain points. The precondition of metaphor is thus a logical contact on the level of the signified while its various poetic effects stem partly from the lexical contact of the interacting signifiers and the evocative powers of the connotations and associations that come with them; in other words, from the interaction of their terminologies.[103] If metonymy were to work in a way structurally similar to metaphor, then there should be a similar pattern observable there. However, if metonymy is based on contiguity as its defining characteristic, then the lexical proximity thereby implied means that contact on the level of the signifier is already a given. Metonymic contiguity itself, it would seem, thus precludes the very possibility of terminological interaction since both terms are by definition in a pre-established relationship, defined by their terminological proximity. This obviously has consequences for the status of poetic metonyms: if tropical speech is understood strictly as a deviation from standard usage, and if metonymy is defined by contiguity within a semantic field, and if such contiguity is determined by the combinatory rules of standard usage, then paradoxically it might seem to follow that metonymy is seriously limited in its ability to produce the striking effects of deviance from ordinary language that are the hallmark of tropicality (and that metaphor achieves through facilitating a clash of different terminologies).

[100] For a more detailed discussion of the complex issue of corporeal organs representing abstract faculties, see below, pp. 192–202 and 259–60.

[101] This is not to say that an association enabling a metonymic expression may not involve some sort of logic; quite the contrary: because the number and kinds of logical connections that can be perceived behind metonymic expressions are virtually limitless, it is not possible to ascertain *one abstract logical principle* as the basis of metonymy per se, whereas the pragmatic fact of collocation in language usage (however motivated) is something common to all metonyms.

[102] Silk 1974, 22.

[103] But partly also from the physical immediacy associated with the metaphorical leap.

Once again, as with the ancient substitution theories,[104] metonymy appears to be hovering elusively between ordinary and deviant usage, between being and not quite being a trope. If to be or not to be is the question, then it is doubtless time to turn to analysing the tropes themselves in the light of the theoretical perspectives suggested so far, and to defer fuller theorizing until some examples are before us.

[104] See above, pp. 41 and 45–7.

3 Forms and effects

Metonymy in poetic action

Index metonymy

In order to develop a clearer understanding of the mechanisms at play in metonymy (and of the paradoxes associated with the conflicting notions of substitution and contiguity), let us start by examining a first selection of metonyms, from the poetry of Pindar and Hölderlin,[1] which resemble, more or less, the stock examples in the handbooks of the rhetorical tradition.[2] We shall then move on from these to a second set of less straightforward instances, whose greater complexity problematizes the idea of substitution and replacement. To begin with, consider εὐναί ('beds') in the following verses from Pindar's *Second* and *Ninth Pythian Ode*:

a) ἔμαθε δὲ σαφές. εὐμενέσσι γὰρ παρὰ Κρονίδαις
γλυκὺν ἑλὼν βίοτον, μακρὸν οὐχ ὑπέμεινεν ὄλβον, μαινομέναις φράσιν
Ἥρας ὅτ' ἐράσσατο, τὰν Διὸς *εὐναὶ* λάχον
πολυγαθέες·

He [Ixion] learned this clearly, for having won a pleasant existence
among Kronos' beneficent children, he could not sustain his happiness for
long, when in his maddened mind
he fell in love with Hera, who belonged to Zeus for joyous acts of love
[lit.: whom the joyous *beds* of Zeus had won][3]

b) *εὐναὶ* δὲ παράτροποι ἐς κακότατ' ἀθρόαν
ἔβαλον.

Aberrant acts of love [lit.: *beds* mis-turned] cast one into the thick of trouble.[4]

[1] The joint appearance of Pindar and Hölderlin in this chapter is, of course, anything but coincidental: Pindar's poetry has been famed since antiquity for its bold use of poetic language (and lends itself, for this very reason, particularly to the study of metonymy in poetic action). Pindar, in turn, is of immense importance to Hölderlin, not least with regards to the development of the latter's own daring use of poetic language—as illustrated powerfully by his poem 'Wie wenn am Feiertage', discussed below, which marks a breakthrough for him as a crafter of poetic language (in which metonyms play, again, a significant part).

[2] Which no doubt sparked the notion of substitution in the first place.

[3] Pi. *P.* 2.25–8; trans. Race.

[4] Pi. *P.* 2.35–6; trans. Race.

c) ὑπέδεκτο δ' ἀργυρόπεζ' Ἀφροδίτα
Δάλιον ξεῖνον θεοδμάτων
ὀχέων ἐφαπτομένα χερὶ κούφᾳ·
καί σφιν ἐπὶ γλυκεραῖς *εὐναῖς* ἐρατὰν βάλεν αἰδῶ,
ξυνὸν ἁρμόζοισα θεῷ τε γάμον μιχθέντα κούρᾳ θ' Ὑψέος εὐρυβία·

Silver-footed Aphrodite welcomed
her Delian-born guest
as she laid a gentle hand on his divinely wrought chariot,
and shed loving reverence over their sweet acts of love
[lit.: and shed loving reverence over their sweet *beds*],
joining together in a marriage of mutual consent the god and the daughter of mighty Hypseus.[5]

d) ...'κρυπταὶ κλαΐδες ἐντὶ σοφᾶς
Πειθοῦς ἱερᾶν φιλοτάτων,
Φοῖβε, καὶ ἔν τε θεοῖς τοῦτο κἀνθρώποις ὁμῶς
αἰδέοντ', ἀμφανδὸν ἁδείας τυχεῖν τὸ πρῶτον *εὐνᾶς*.'

...'Hidden are the keys to sacred lovemaking
that belong to wise Persuasion,
Phoebus, and both gods and humans alike
shy from engaging openly for the first time in sweet love [lit.: in sweet *bed*].'[6]

It is immediately clear that εὐναί in these verses does not mean 'beds', as the word would in ordinary usage. Gildersleeve comments accordingly: '*eunai*: pl. of the joys of love'.[7] But what makes it so clear? There is obviously something that marks the word out as not being used here to convey its primary meaning, and indicates that its usage is non-ordinary. The reception process is somewhat slowed down when εὐναί makes its appearance; it obstructs smooth, linear progress and creates a hitch in the hermeneutic process of making sense of what is being heard or read—the trademark of a trope.[8] This felt obstruction occurs here when εὐναί is

[5] Pi. *P.* 9.9–13; trans. Race. [6] Pi. *P.* 9.39–41; trans. Race.

[7] Gildersleeve on Pi. *P.* 2.27; likewise Gentili on Pi. *P.* 9.12: 'usato spesso (in Omero in associazione con φιλότης) per indicare il "letto d'amore". Il plurale εὐναί per il singolare si ritrova nell' uso tragico' ('often used (in Homer in association with φιλότης) to indicate the "bed of love". The plural εὐναί for the singular is found in tragic usage'). This spread of the term's usage, however, effectively renders the expression normal usage (albeit normal usage as a literary cliché in elevated language) so that it no longer exemplifies metonymy proper, i.e. striking, palpable metonymic deviance from normal usage. Bearing this caveat in mind, we can nevertheless use these examples to establish some basic principles of metonymic deviation before moving on to more decisively tropical examples.

[8] In any discussion of archaic Greek lyric it is hard to avoid the question of its performative nature. For my purposes here, however, listeners and readers follow the same principle of linear reception: a hermeneutic curve that is constantly readjusted as

collocated with adjectives with which it is incongruous in any coherent, non-tropical sequence. Literal 'beds' are neither 'joyous' (πολυγαθέες)[9] nor 'sweet' (γλυκεραῖς, ἀδείας);[10] one can hardly imagine any non-tropical sequence in which these words could jointly occur. Literal 'beds' might just be literally 'mis-turned' (παράτροποι) but the preceding context of Ixion's attempt to rape Hera strongly suggests that it was not disarranged furniture (παράτροποι in a spatial sense) but illicit intercourse (παράτροποι in a moral sense) that brought him trouble. Similarly, in addition to the peculiar 'sweetness' of the beds on which Aphrodite sheds lovely reverence, the development of the scene into a marriage ritual in the next verse retrospectively situates the preceding verse in the wedding night—and

the reception process continues and new 'information' is integrated into the framework established by the preceding context.

[9] The adjective can be read, as LSJ suggests, as if used actively (*sc.* 'much-rejoicing', 'much-cheering') in the majority of its (earlier) occurrences as an epithet, mainly of Dionysus (see Pi. *Fr.* 29.5, 153, Hes. *Th.* 941, *Op.* 614, *Fr.* 70.6; the same is true for Orph. *H.* 10.10, 44.3, 51.3, 74.1, 68.4, though we must bear in mind the uncertainties in dating these latter texts and that we are probably dealing here with post-classical usage). A further instance, in which the word is not used as a divine epithet, also supports this reading: πᾶς δὲ δόμος θάλλει πολυγηθὴς εἵνεκα σεῖο (Orph. *H.* 68.4; 'the whole house, much-rejoicing, flourishes because of you'). West on Hes. *Th.* 941, however, draws parallels with *Il.* 14.325, where Dionysus is given the epithet χάρμα βροτοῖσιν ('joy for the mortals'), and Hes. *Sc.* 400, which tells of Dionysus' gift of grapes as ἀνδράσι χάρμα καὶ ἄχθος ('to men a delight and a burden'). On this account, one might consider the possibility of a more transitive usage of the adjective: 'bringing much joy', as indeed Dindorf 1831–65 suggests (s.v. πολυγηθής: *multum laetitiae afferens*). The usage at Orph. *H.* 50.3–4: Βάκχε... πολυγηθέα κάρπον ἀέξων ('Bakchos... growing the fruit that brings much joy'; cf. similarly Orph. *H.* 26.10) supports this proposition, and all instances of the term as a divine epithet are perfectly compatible with both suggestions. If we take the Homeric usage as fundamental, noting especially *Il.* 21.450–1: ἀλλ' ὅτε δὴ μισθοῖο τέλος πολυγηθέες ὧραι ἐξέφερον ('But when at length the glad seasons were bringing to an end the term of our hire'; trans. Murray/Wyatt), it becomes clear that it is necessary to broaden the term's scope in this way. The remaining extant instances of the word in (later) Greek, namely *Anth. Pal.* 9.189.5: ὄλβιαι ὀρχηθμοῦ πολυγηθέος ('blessed in a dance that brings much joy') and Man. *Apo.* 2.158: ἀτὰρ πολυγηθέος ὄλβου ('without riches that bring much joy'), though not immediately pertinent to the establishment of classical usage, also point the same way. Further corroborative evidence can be drawn from other compounds of -γηθης: while ἀγηθής (S. *Tr.* 869; 'joyless') and ἐριγηθής (Orph. *L. Prooem* 24; 'very joyful') are fairly straightforward in denoting the absence and degree of presence of joy, the structurally more similar compounds appear to come with the same potential for a broader semantic scope. Consider: ἥξετ' εὐγαθεῖ κελάδῳ (E. *Her.* 793; 'you come with joy-bringing clamour', 'you come with joyous clamour'), μελιγαθὲς... ὕδωρ (Pi. *Fr.* 188; 'water enjoyable like honey', 'water bringing joy like honey'), and πλουτογηθῆ μυχὸν (A. *Ch.* 800–1; 'an inner chamber delighting in/by riches', 'an inner chamber bringing joy in the form of riches'). However, even in the light of these lexicographical reconsiderations, and bearing in mind that there is no ordinary prose usage available as a solid point of reference for this verse word, we can still safely assume that it is not the beds which are πολυγαθέες but whatever takes place in them.

[10] In ancient Greek, just as in contemporary English, 'sweet' is a stock 'metaphor', but even in its secondary ('metaphorical') sense it is only applicable to abstracts (e.g. love, fame, sleep) but not to beds in the literal sense.

Aphrodite's blessing is clearly aimed at the act which creates the matrimonial bond, and not at the furniture on which it takes place. The same is true for the understanding of Cheiron's advice on how 'sweet beds' are to be touched openly for the first time: the 'sweetness' signals a non-ordinary usage of the following 'beds' since they constitute an unexpected and non-ordinary collocation; the move towards a tropical meaning, which the listener (or reader) is likely to establish, is prompted not only by failing to find a meaning for 'beds' that makes sense together with 'sweet' but also by the context, in the shape of Apollo's preceding question to Cheiron:

> 'ὁσία κλυτὰν χέρα οἱ προσενεγκεῖν
> ἦρα καὶ ἐκ λεχέων κεῖραι μελιαδέα ποίαν;'
>
> 'Is it right to lay my famous hand upon her
> and indeed to reap the honey-sweet flower from the bed of love?'[11]

Both explicitly and then metaphorically, Apollo's question makes it unambiguously clear that he is not concerned with beautiful bedroom furnishings.

What is gained by all this analysis? Quintilian, as we have seen, identified *decorum* as one of the functions of metonymy and it is easy to see from the above examples how he came to this opinion. But are we to think of metonymy just as a form of *variatio* that embellishes the text and keeps the poet out of trouble for being too explicit? *Variatio* and the effect of embellishment that follows from it is no doubt one of metonymy's poetic functions. Sometimes, it can be, or can on the surface appear to be, the only one. Take the following lines from Hölderlin's poem 'Wie wenn am Feiertage', which contain a seemingly unremarkable metonymic *variatio* involving 'Abend' (evening) for 'Abendland' (occident):

> Jetzt aber tagt's! Ich harrt und sah es kommen,
> Und was ich sah, das Heilige sei mein Wort.
> Denn sie, sie selbst, die älter denn die Zeiten
> Und über die Götter des *Abends* und Orients ist,
> Die Natur ist jetzt mit Waffenklang erwacht...
>
> But now it dawns! I waited longingly and saw it coming,
> And what I saw, the numinous be my word.
> For she, she herself, who is older than all times
> And who is above the gods of the *evening* and orient,
> Nature has now wakened with weaponry sound...[12]

[11] Pi. *P.* 9.36–7; trans. Race. Note that 'of love' is not in the Greek text but added by the translator to clarify the preceding metaphor for lovemaking—and thereby gives an example for the joint occurrence of 'love' and 'bed' in a non-tropical sequence.

[12] Hölderlin, 'Wie wenn am Feiertage', 19–23.

A superficial rhetorical analysis would focus on the inconsistency here. The 'gods of the evening' (Götter des Abends) and 'gods of the orient' (Götter des ... Orients) are obviously parallel—but not described in parallel. The analyst might then formulate the thought that while there are different pantheons in Eastern and Western cultures, neither of them has a prominent set of deities responsible for various aspects of the evening which might be literally referred to as 'gods of the evening', and conclude that 'evening' stands here as a 'substitute' for the actual opposite of orient, 'occident', which is not used. And why is it not used? In order to add some *variatio* to the line by avoiding the formulaic cliché of 'orient and occident' as equivalent for the whole of the globe. The outcome, then, would be a 'metonymic substitution' with no change in meaning and little impact on the rest of the poem, just enough to be noticed.

Yet what happens in the actual process of reception goes far beyond this. In the (micro)context of the line itself, in which the metonym 'Abends' ('evening') occurs, the metonymic and the literal elements, 'evening' and 'orient,' interact. A first obvious symptom is the occurrence of the slight hermeneutic hitch observed in the earlier discussion of εὐναί in Pindar: the reader will be familiar with the expression 'gods of the orient' but unfamiliar with the collocation 'gods of the evening' and in the reception process will seek to make something of this counter-ordinary lexical collocation by semantically readjusting the meaning of 'evening'; that is, the reader will understand it not literally but metonymically. The establishment of a metonymic meaning thus follows the criteria of collocatability with the microcontext ('gods of' + x) and semantic suitability with the wider context (something compatible with 'gods of the orient'). Here, the process is fairly straightforward, which is why, at first, one might toy with the idea of a substitution taking place, but the discussion of more complex examples later on will show that this is not always the case. In the present instance, however, the reader, guided by the criteria of contextual suitability and collocation rules, will quickly move from the present term 'evening' to the inferred term 'occident' as the hermeneutic process of reception continues.

Yet this resolution of the hermeneutic hitch is not the end of the matter here. The opening up of meaning, rather, leads to a further interaction on a different level: if the literal 'evening' is now evoking a parallel, inferred term, 'occident', then the literal 'orient' that follows also seems to imply a parallel inferred term, 'morning', which bears significantly on the stanza as a whole. The stanza is dominated by two interlocking themes: sunrise and the supreme rule of nature. As the sun rises majestically to the zenith where it transcends everything that is, so does nature and its rule transcend any other ordering force in the world. This theme of the supremacy of nature, first obscurely hinted at ('das Heilige', 'the numinous'; l. 22) and then overtly established through the emphasis on nature's sovereignty over time, gods and space in ll. 23–4, is connected with the event of dawn ('Jetzt aber tagt's!') and interwoven with the theme of sunrise from the stanza's dramatic opening onwards. Through the interaction of 'evening' (subsuming 'occident') with 'orient', 'orient', in turn, is implicitly made to subsume 'morning'—and thereby reveals its etymology as 'Morgenland' ('land of the morning') and land of the rising sun (*sol oriens*): the juxtaposition with the deviantly used 'evening' creates a heightened awareness for a chain of connected (and metonymically interchangeable) elements in the semantic field (West-sunset-evening, East-sunrise-morning) and thus reactivates semantic properties (*virtual* properties) of the literally used 'orient' as the land of the rising sun. The metonymically reactivated etymology binds the line back to the theme of sunrise in the first line of the stanza and to nature's awakening in the following line and thereby increases the stanza's cohesion. Moreover, the deviant use of 'evening' also allows for another linkage, namely between the twofold assertion of nature's supremacy over time and space. The two orders do not just stand separately or self-contained next to each other in linear sequence, but are linked through 'Abend' ('evening') in its initial perception as literally denoting a time of day and its subsequently established metonymic usage as implying the space of the western hemisphere. The metonym 'Abend[-land]' ('evening'/'occident') thus functions as a polyvalent semantic pivot, as a locus of multiple intratextual correlations and consonances between different parts of the stanza. The trope yields both cohesion and force, and significantly contributes to the textual representation of the stanza's central conceit: the sun-like rise of nature to its due supremacy.

With this cohesive potential of metonymy in mind, let us revisit Pindar's metonymic use of εὐναί. In the light of the above analysis of Hölderlin's stanza, the verse

> καί σφιν ἐπὶ γλυκεραῖς *εὐναῖς* ἐρατὰν βάλεν αἰδῶ
>
> and shed loving reverence over their sweet acts of love [lit.: their sweet *beds*][13]

emerges as another example of this pivotal function that metonyms can now be seen to exercise. The whole verse hovers between the concrete and the abstract, the physical bed as the place of sexual intercourse and

[13] Pi. *P.* 9.12; trans. Race.

the sexual morals and attitudes of the lovers. Aphrodite's interaction with the lovers belongs to the abstract sphere: she adds αἰδώς (a moral feeling of respect) to their lovemaking. This non-physical supplement, which qualifies their physical intercourse, is expressed by the very physical verb βαλλεῖν ('to throw, to cast, to shed'). Since the goddess's act of bestowing an abstract quality is expressed by analogy to the physical act of putting something on top of something else, the usage of βαλλεῖν here is metaphorical. This invests the sequence with two levels of meaning which are both active at the same time: a concrete level (something is thrown on a bed) and an abstract level (a moral feeling is added to the attitude of the lovers in their lovemaking). The metonymic implication of 'beds' (εὐναῖς)—lovemaking—is compatible with the abstract concept denoted by αἰδώς, whereas 'beds' in its primary sense accommodates and facilitates the metaphorical usage of βαλλεῖν (expressing here the bestowal of an abstract quality) by providing a material object on which something can be literally 'thrown'. 'Throwing something onto beds' (ἐπὶ... εὐναῖς... βάλεν) constitutes a coherent, non-tropical collocation of words conforming to ordinary usage, onto which an abstract level of meaning is superimposed: the non-physical moral quality that is ascribed to the lovers' attitude. Here, then, the polyvalence of metonymy, enabled by the co-presence of the present term's properties and its virtual semantics, reconciles heterogeneous elements and enhances the semantic and aesthetic cohesion of the passage.

This potential of polyvalence can also be exploited within the semantics of the metonym itself as the last verses of Pindar's *Sixth Pythian Ode* show:

> γλυκεῖα δὲ φρὴν
> καὶ συμπόταισιν ὁμιλεῖν
> μελισσᾶν ἀμείβεται *τρητὸν πόνον*.
>
> And his sweet spirit,
> in company with his drinking companions,
> surpasses the *perforated labor* of bees.[14]

A straightforward substitutionalist reading, triggered not least by the abrasive tonal clash between μελισσᾶν ('bees') and τρητόν ('perforated'), would simply state that 'perforated labour' stands for 'honeycomb': in rhetorical handbook-speak, the action (πόνον, 'labour') for the result ('honeycomb', as established through the contextual qualifications of sweetness, γλυκεῖα, and bees, μελισσᾶν, as well as the collocation with

[14] Pi. *P.* 6.52–4; trans. Race.

'perforated', τρητόν).[15] In addition, however, we have interaction between the metonym and its context that shapes the mini-scene sketched here. On the one hand, 'sweet' is used once again in its stock 'metaphorical' sense of 'delightful', and the virtual term implied by the metonym, 'honeycomb' (and, by extension, 'honey'), forms part of an implicit comparison (flagged by ἀμείβεται, 'surpasses') that brings together a literally sweet and a metaphorically sweet element. The metonymically inferred term, 'honeycomb' (/'honey'), engages with the stock 'metaphor' 'sweet', thus reinforcing its literal dimension. At the same time, the present, literal term of the metonym, 'labour', juxtaposes the socializing of the symposiasts and the activity of the bees: it contrasts the leisure of the symposiasts and the labour of the bees—their joyful gathering is obviously 'sweeter' than any work. We might be inclined to see the famous harmony of the beehive introduced into the comparison through the bees' labour, a harmony which via this juxtaposition would then reflect on the gathering of the symposiasts. In this reading, the shared spirit of harmony in the beehive and among the symposiasts would implicitly emerge as a secondary *tertium comparationis* between the two components alongside the primary notion of sweetness. The sweetness itself would thereby become, in turn, invested with overtones of an ideal of delightful harmony. However, the beehive as a social-political metaphor representing an orderly and harmonious society is fully developed only in Roman literature.[16] Although bee terminology is also used in political contexts in Greek literature,[17] similes and metaphors there tend to stress the opposition between hard-working bees and parasitic drones, who consume the labour of others, within the beehive.[18] With this in mind, Pindar's assertion of the superiority of the aristocratic victor's social graces at the leisurely symposium over the labour of bees acquires entirely different overtones within the framework of the aristocratic value system of Pindar's epinician poetry.[19] None of these layers of further associations and connotations would have been created if the sequence had ended non-metonymically on 'honey' in its ordinary form.

Occasionally, such polyvalence can even have narrative significance, as in another stanza of Hölderlin's poem 'Wie wenn am Feiertage':

[15] A relatively moderate tropical expression, perhaps, but still more noticeable in Greek than in comparable expressions in English or German where words such as 'work' and 'Werk' denote both labour and its result.

[16] See e.g. Varr. *R.R.* 3.16.4, Cic. *Off.* 1.157, Verg. *Geor.* 4 *passim*, Sen. *Ep.* 121.22.

[17] See e.g. Pl. *Resp.* 293d.

[18] See e.g. Hes. *Th.* 594, Pl. *Resp.* 552c.

[19] 'Pindar's attitude to humbler people differs from the hatred and contempt which Alcaeus and Theognis pour on them; he is hardly conscious of their existence, and they play no part in his scheme of things.' Bowra 1964, 100–1.

> So fiel, wie Dichter sagen, da sichtbar sie
> Den Gott zu sehen begehrte, sein Blitz auf Semeles Haus
> Und die göttlichgetroffne gebar,
> Die Frucht des *Gewitters*, den heiligen Bacchus.
>
> Thus, as the poets say, his lightning fell
> Onto Semele's house, for she desired to see the god undisguised,
> And the divinely struck gave birth
> To the fruit *of the thunderstorm*, the sacred Bacchus.[20]

These lines renarrate the myth of Semele, a mortal lover of Zeus, who asked him to reveal himself to her in his true divine nature, with the fatal consequence of her immediate death when he granted her wish and revealed himself in the form of the lightning, though the god was able to rescue his child, Dionysus (Bacchus), which she was carrying. The last line refers to Dionysus as the son of Zeus by calling him 'fruit of the thunderstorm' ('die Frucht des Gewitters').[21] In the particular context of this myth, this is more than just a metonym of the remit-for-godhead type ('thunderstorm' for 'Zeus'). The contiguity between Zeus and thunderstorm that lies behind this metonym encapsulates the whole myth in a nutshell: for Dionysus is *in fact* (metaphorically speaking) the 'fruit' of the thunderstorm, which is the very reason for his mortal mother's death. Note that it is only thanks to this metonym that there is no need to explain that the unnamed god is Zeus and that the reason why he struck Semele's house with his lightning is that he essentially *is* the lightning (this is not made clear in the preceding lines; it might as well have been a divine punishment for the hubris of making such a request). The trope, with its abrasive tonal clash between 'Frucht' ('fruit') and 'Gewitter' ('thunderstorm'), functions as a *mise en abîme* of the mythological narrative.[22]

[20] Hölderlin, 'Wie wenn am Feiertage', 50–3.

[21] The expression is also in part a metaphorical cliché, based on the extended metaphor 'fruit of one's loins/womb'.

[22] This instance, however, is also a reminder that even in classicizing modern poetry, written in a post-pagan context that operates against the backdrop of an altogether different world view and metaphysical reference system, establishing 'the literal' is never straightforward when divinity is involved (on this issue, see also above, pp. 45–6, and below, pp. 202–7): in the present case one could say, for instance, that in the abstract sphere of divinity, the thunderstorm constitutes Zeus' phallic, generative power, so that Semele was 'in fact' impregnated by Zeus' thunder (just as elsewhere he impregnates by rain); on this reading, it would be difficult to argue for the presence of a metonym here. Yet this reading would require a very specific perspective and the concomitant very specific understanding of the terms involved here. According to standard language usage at the time, it seems safe to posit a case of metonymy here, but we ought to be sensitive to the fact that in and through its particular phrasing the poem invites these lines of thought and poses them as a question and/or possibility.

What follows from these first observations? In particular, can Richards's concept of tenor and vehicle be used to describe and analyse metonyms? Throughout my analyses so far, we have observed that, as in metaphor, there are two elements at work in every metonym: the present term and a virtual, inferred term which the listener or reader is forced to establish as soon as a literal reading of the term in question is felt to be impossible in the given context. To an extent, this does indeed resemble Richards's tenor (what is at issue) and vehicle (what is being said). There are, however, also considerable differences, most notably the absence of any interaction between tenor and vehicle. As predicted theoretically at the end of Chapter 1, textual evidence thus far confirms the assumption that the relationship between metonymic vehicle (the present term) and metonymic tenor (the virtual term inferred in the act of reception) is stable and pre-established. This relationship is neither introduced through the metonym nor negotiated in the metonym—both characteristics of metaphor. When Hölderlin in his poem 'Buonaparte' writes

> Heilige Gefäße sind die Dichter,
> Worin des Lebens Wein, der Geist
> Der Helden sich aufbewahrt
>
> Sacred vessels are the poets
> In whom the wine of life, the spirit
> Of heroes, finds a container[23]

a whole set of new connections is introduced, each one determined by analogy or similarity and established by various grammatical and syntactic means: between 'vessels' and 'poets' (through equation by means of the copula), between 'the wine of life' and 'the spirit of heroes' (through equation by means of apposition), and between 'wine,' 'life,' and 'the spirit of heroes' (by means of genitive link and apposition: what wine is to an individual, the spirit of heroes is to life in general—a gift of nature, an intoxicating luxury, etc.). Nothing of this kind is observable in any of the metonymic occurrences examined above. What can be observed instead is that the relationship between metonymic tenor and metonymic vehicle is in fact pre-existing: no link needs to be created; on the contrary, the link is the given which the metonym is, precisely, exploiting. It is instructive to note that although no interaction is taking place between metonymic tenor and metonymic vehicle, there is often a significant interaction taking place between both of them jointly and the context in which the metonym is embedded. And, crucially, it is because of this polyvalence of metonymy,

[23] Hölderlin, 'Buonaparte', 1–3.

that metonymic replacement is far from being a mere substitution. However, the enhanced contextual cohesion that arises from associative interconnections in the examples discussed above does not categorically distinguish metonymy from metaphor. Metaphor can and often does function in a similar way, and this function should rather be characterized as a feature of tropical language in general: wherever language deviates from ordinary usage in a way that affects the semantics of a given word, it opens up a space between the present term in its literal meaning and a virtual term whose inference is enforced by the context and indispensable for the sequence to mean anything. The duplication of semantic agents (present *and* virtual) and, consequently, the multiplication of the trope's potential for interactive contact with the context is observable in both metaphor and metonymy; the difference between the two tropes lies in the relationship between the present and the virtual terms, that is, within the relationship of tenor and vehicle.

The metonyms discussed so far have all been of the same structure, with one noun seemingly 'replacing' another noun, analogous to Brooke-Rose's category of metaphor by 'simple replacement'.[24] This is arguably the most widespread type of metonymy and is presumably what led Quintilian to his definition of metonymy as a noun replacing another noun. It has, however, already become clear that the term 'replacement' must be used very carefully in this context to avoid any confusion with misleading notions of 'substitution'. As has been demonstrated above, there is nothing like a poetic or semantic equivalence between the lexically present metonymic vehicle and the virtual metonymic tenor as inferred from the context, nor should one imagine the productive poetic process from which a metonym originates as one in which poets straightforwardly 'replace', 'substitute', what they 'mean' by another word for the sake of superficial embellishment. Creative writing is indeed, as Harding once noted, more plausibly seen as a process in which the poet, in his case the Great War poet Isaac Rosenberg, is 'reworking phrases and images again and again, developing out of them meanings which were

[24] 'Simple replacement: the proper term is replaced altogether by the metaphor, without being mentioned at all. The metaphor is assumed to be clear from the context or from the reader's intelligence.' Brooke-Rose 1958, 24. An example of this type of metaphor would be '. . . sie kömmt gewiss die Stunde, | die das Göttliche vom Kerker trennt (Hölderlin, 'Griechenland', 38–9; 'The hour will surely come, which separates the divine from the prison'). The following critique of the term 'replacement' for the study of metonymy applies *mutatis mutandis* also to Brooke-Rose's study of metaphor in general. Despite her perceptive elaboration of the different formal categories of interaction in metaphor, her overall substitutionalist approach ('In my study, any identification of one thing with another, any replacement of the more usual word or phrase by another, is a metaphor'; Brooke-Rose 1958, 17) is outdated in the light of interaction theory.

not "the" meaning he had originally wanted to "express" with them'.[25] In poetic usage, it is fallacious to conceive of words as servants of ideas. 'Replacement', therefore, can only be a provisional term and it will be desirable to develop a more adequate understanding and find a more appropriate term to describe and categorize this type of metonym. Meanwhile, the observations and preliminary results of my analysis of 'replacement type metonyms' so far can be summarized as follows:

'Replacement metonyms' consist of two elements: a present term (metonymic vehicle—MV) and a virtual, inferred term (metonymic tenor—MT), together with which the present term is rendered compatible with the context but which deviates from the MV's semantic range in ordinary usage. 'Replacement type metonyms' are identifiable as such because the MV in its context constitutes an illegitimate collocation of words. Since the MV cannot be understood literally in the given context as a consequence of this breach of collocation rules, its semantics have to be readjusted ad hoc in a hermeneutic loop that leads from the MV to the MT and allows the process of reception to continue. The reader's (or listener's) comprehension of the MV in the light of its MT is guided by the MV as the starting point, by the context as the framework, and by the microcontext as the immediate determinative. The relationship between the MV and the MT is one of lexical contiguity, that is, both terms can be and are collocated in ordinary usage; they belong to a shared semantic field. Because of this pre-established link of lexical contiguity between MV and MT, no interaction takes place between them nor is there any need to employ grammatical or syntactical links to bind them together. MV and MT can, however, interact individually with the context and thereby contribute to the cohesion of the surrounding text and to the multilayeredness of potential intratextual cross-reference. MV and MT, therefore, are not mere substitutes of one another but have different properties, connotations, and associations, that can gain significance in the interplay between the context and the MV–MT compound.

In this first set of examples, the hermeneutic distance between MV and MT has been relatively short and in every case the inferred, virtual MT can be formulated relatively easily. In Pindar's εὐναὶ δὲ παράτροποι[26] the MV εὐναί (beds) is immediately understood to 'mean' acts of lovemaking in the given context. The relationship between the MV (beds) and the MT (acts of lovemaking) is fairly straightforward, involves no ambiguity, and leads to no interaction with the context. This example surely

[25] Harding 1963, 101; notwithstanding the explicit rhetoric of some poetic traditions, in the medieval West in particular.

[26] Pi. *P.* 2.35: 'Aberrant acts of love [lit.: mis-turned *beds*]'; trans. Race.

represents the type of metonym Quintilian must have had in mind: it is a *variatio* for the sake of *decorum*, and the absence of any further poetic effect or function makes it understandable how metonymic occurrences such as this could lead to the erroneous generalization that all metonyms are based on 'replacements' with such straightforward equivalence that they could be seen in effect as substitutions. Examples like this, however, only prove that some of the most basic metonyms of the 'replacement type' come under the heading of *variatio* since their poetic function is a matter of elevating language without heightening it;[27] that is to say, they indicate the register of poetic idiom through fairly conventional stylization, without creating the intense effects and enhanced meaning achieved by deviating palpably from any form of familiar language usage.

A second set of examples of 'replacement metonyms' shows greater complexity. Consider first these verses from Pindar's *First Pythian Ode*:

> ... ἔσχον δ' Ἀμύκλας ὄλβιοι
> Πινδόθεν ὀρνύμενοι, λευκοπώλων
> Τυνδαριδᾶν βαθύδοξοι
> γείτονες, ὧν κλέος ἄνθησεν *αἰχμᾶς*.

> ... Blessed with prosperity, they came down
> from Pindos and took Amyklai, to become much acclaimed
> neighbours of the Tyndaridai with white horses,
> and the fame of their spears flourished.
> [lit.: and the fame of the *spear* flourished][28]

The collocation κλέος αἰχμᾶς ('fame of the spear') is in itself aberrant and deviates from ordinary usage in so far as κλέος customarily refers to humans or their deeds and achievements, but not to things; it is always κλέος ἀνδρῶν with regards to something to be specified.[29] Thus it is *both*

[27] On the difference between the two, see above, p. 21.

[28] Pi. *P.* 1.65–6; trans. Race. The singular of αἰχμᾶς ('of the spear') makes the metonym more obvious in the Greek than Race's translation suggests.

[29] Where a genitive construction is used to describe the fame of someone in something, it is still an implied action, not an object, that stands in the genitive; cf. οἱ δὲ τῆς μελλοῦς κλέος πέδοι πατοῦντες (A. *Agam.* 1356–7; 'they are trampling the much-touted virtues of delay into the ground [lit.: the fame of delay]'; trans. Sommerstein). A. *Agam.* 1098: τὸ μὲν κλέος σοῦ μαντικὸν ('your fame as a seer'; trans. Sommerstein), on the other hand, has the person, Cassandra, in the genitive and the specific kind of fame expressed in the form of a qualifying adjective. Although desirable for the purposes of literary lexicography, more authoritative examples of ordinary usage in prose are not available since κλέος is used there (*a*) less frequently and (*b*) almost always in a comprehensive rather than particularizing manner, i.e. denoting fame as such rather than fame for a specific reason or in a specific area (cf. Hdt. 7.220, 9.78, Pl. *Leg.* 1.625a, 2.663a, and *Smp.* 208c, X. *Cyn.* 1.6, and Lys. 2.5). Note, however, that Th. 1.25: κλέος ἐχόντων τὰ περὶ τὰς ναῦς ('having fame in nautical matters') uses the accusative of respect, not the genitive, to indicate the specific area within which the fame arises. All available evidence taken together allows us to take Homeric usage as

the breach of ordinary collocation rules *and* the context, notably the capture of Amyklai reported in the preceding verse, that prevent the hearer from understanding 'spear' as a literal weapon and invite a metonymic understanding instead.[30] This may at first seem to be a straightforward case of metonymic 'replacement' again, the 'fame of the spear' 'replacing' 'fame earned by showing excellence in fighting with the spear', but though αἰχμᾶς ('of the spear') is contextually marked as a metonymic vehicle, the initial specification of 'spear' is not definitive enough to determine one virtual, metonymic tenor: neither context nor microcontext give the reader (or listener) sufficient grounds for assuming that it is the Dorians' skills in fighting with the spear in particular that 'flourish'. Rather, the metonym can be understood to refer to their flourishing reputation for excellence in warfare in general, the MV 'spear' corresponding to an MT 'military prowess'. There is no clear indicator in context or microcontext that would privilege either of these understandings; they are both contained in the semantic field opened up by metonymy.

A similar indeterminacy in the MT can be observed in the famous opening of Pindar's *First Olympian Ode*:

> ... ἀλλὰ *Δωρίαν* ἀπὸ *φόρμιγγα* πασσάλου
> λάμβαν', εἴ τί τοι Πίσας τε καὶ Φερενίκου χάρις
> νόον ὑπὸ γλυκυτάταις ἔθηκε φροντίσιν
>
> Come, take the *Dorian lyre* from its peg,
> if the splendor of Pisa and of Pherenikos has indeed
> enthralled your mind with sweetest considerations[31]

A literal reading of Δωρίαν φόρμιγγα ('Dorian lyre') as a musical instrument made by Dorians in a traditional Dorian manner is theoretically possible but, as Race points out,

> since we have no evidence for a specifically Dorian lyre and since the meter of the ode is Aeolic, the reference may apply to the Dorian character of Syracusae (cf. *Pyth.* 1.61–65) and, perhaps, to the presence of the Doric dialect in Pindar's choral lyric.[32]

The potential for virtual metonymic tenors is thus rather broad: the 'lyre' could 'stand for' a 'lyrical performance in Dorian style'—the Dorian style

fundamental (cf. *Od.* 1.344, 8.73, and *Il.* 9.189, 524) in the sense that κλέος there is indeed always κλέος ἀνδρῶν.

[30] The one famous Dorian spear: note how the (metonymic!) use of the singular too hinders a literal understanding.

[31] Pi. O. 1.17–19; trans. Race.

[32] Race *ad loc.*

referring to either the musical mode accompanying it or the dialect of the lyrics—but it could also refer to 'a lyric performance with Dorian contents', namely the Dorian Hieron, king of the Dorian settlement in Syracusae, whose victory in the horse race is the topic of the ode. Again, neither the surrounding (literary-textual) context of the ode as a whole nor the microcontext of this passage rule out any of these possible metonymic tenors, and the metonymic vehicle appears to encompass all of them, thereby significantly increasing the verse's semantic potential.[33] In passing, though, it should be noted that this passage also exemplifies a phenomenon we might call 'conditional tropicality', in the shape of the necessary correspondence of the tropical or non-tropical status of terms, here λάμβαν' ('pick up') and φόρμιγγα ('lyre'). Only a literal lyre can literally be picked up, which means that any metonymic understanding of lyre as 'lyrical performance' requires a metaphorical understanding of 'pick up' as 'begin'.[34]

This indeterminacy of the MT in 'replacement metonyms' coexists with further complexities within the MV–MT relationship in Hölderlin's poem 'Gesang des Deutschen'. Here, Hölderlin evokes the decay of the civilization of classical Greece:

> Wenn Platons frommer *Garten* auch schon nicht mehr
> Am alten Strome grünt und der dürft'ge Mann
> Die *Heldenasche* pflügt, und scheu der
> Vogel der Nacht auf der Säule trauert.
>
> Even if Plato's pious *garden* no longer blossoms
> By the old stream and the indigent man
> Ploughs the *heroes' ashes*, and the
> Bird of the night mourns shyly on the top of the column.[35]

[33] Unsurprisingly, all these possible interpretations have been put forward *individually* by various Pindarists, see Gerber *ad loc.* The conclusion that remains largely unconsidered is that it is precisely the point of this metonym (and many others) that it does not have one denotative meaning but is open to *multiple* references *simultaneously*. In addition, the qualification of the lyre as specifically 'Dorian' also bears significance for the ode's intertextual self-positioning in this passage: given the very clear allusion to Demodocus' appearance and performance in *Od.* 8, which likewise involves a phorminx being placed on and taken from a peg as the performance of a desired song takes place, the qualification 'Dorian' serves here to highlight a divergence from the Odyssean hypotext and thus as a marker for the independence and specificity of this ode within the broader literary tradition to which it allusively connects itself.

[34] I shall revisit this phenomenon in the discussion of 'tropical clusters' and 'conditional metonymy' in this chapter; see pp. 123–34 and pp. 135–40 below, respectively.

[35] Hölderlin, 'Gesang des Deutschen', 29–32.

'Platons frommer Garten' ('Plato's pious garden') follows the pattern of Pindar's metonymic use of εὐναί. 'Gardens' cannot literally be 'pious', so a different understanding of the term is elicited, distinct from any that would follow the normal usage of this word but coherent with 'pious'. In itself, the collocation 'Plato's garden' suggests a reference to the philosopher's school rather than to a horticultural site, since his school, the academy, was in fact situated in a sort of garden, the grove of Academus, a park used for gymnastics from the sixth century BC. Yet in terms of collocation rules 'Plato's garden', understood as 'the grove of Academus', still clashes with 'pious'. A grove can be thought of as 'heilig' ('sacred') but in ordinary usage 'fromm' ('pious') is reserved for persons or their actions. This would lead the reader's thoughts to the Platonic philosophers philosophizing in the grove of Academus; or, just as plausibly, to Platonic philosophy as such, since 'fromm' ('pious') as an abstract concept could perfectly well be attached to Platonism as a world-view and a spiritual-intellectual exercise.[36] Indeed, in the context of the poem's vision of the rebirth of the ancient Greek spirit in Hölderlin's Germany, 'Plato's pious garden' might even be understood as epitomizing the entirety of ancient Greek culture, no longer alive or 'blossoming by the old stream' but perhaps destined for a rebirth in Germany, as the poet indicates a few lines later:

> Doch, wie der Frühling, wandelt der Genius
> Von Land zu Land.
>
> But the spirit of genius, like spring,
> Wanders from land to land.[37]

Again the reader is left not with one 'equivalent' MT that can be set alongside the MV, but with a range of associations that all inform the semantic potential, and the colouring, of the passage.[38]

[36] Additionally, both these inferred meanings work just as well for another locality that might inform such inferences, namely the setting of Plato's *Phaedrus* (Pl. *Phaedr.* 229a–230c), which reinvents the poets' rural spaces of inspiration and becomes itself a (metonymic) trope for philosophical remove more generally (as well as a metaphor for what Cicero deems the 'soft and shady' style of rhetoric: see Cic. *De Or.* 1.28). While this locality's association with several deities (Socrates invokes nymphs, Pan, the Muses and, in his main speech, Zeus) connects perhaps even more readily to the religious dimension of the formulation 'Platons frommer Garten', all of the above qualifications and inferential moves would also be triggered in a reading that takes the garden as referring (primarily) to this dialogue's setting rather than to the Academy's location.

[37] Hölderlin, 'Gesang des Deutschen', 37–8.

[38] An alternative approach to reading this passage and to elucidating the perception of defamiliarization in it would focus not on possible nouns that could be inferred from a metonymically used *noun* here, but rather on the *adjective* 'fromm' ('pious') as deviantly used, namely as transferred away from a noun it would ordinarily describe (a poetic device

In this Hölderlin passage, polyvalence and conditional tropicality are observable once again. The vision of a garden with all its associations of flowers and cultivation pervades the stanza, notably through the alliterative centrepiece of the first two lines 'Garten... grünt' ('garden... blossoms [lit.: greens]'). The terms are co-dependent in their tropical status: if 'Garten' ('garden') is understood metonymically with an MT that conforms with 'fromm' ('pious'), then 'grünt' ('blossoms') must be understood metaphorically in the sense of 'thrives'. On the lexical level the first two lines thus create an impression of the rich, green, cultivated place of the past which is then markedly contrasted with the ploughing of the dry remainders of this past ('Heldenasche', 'heroes' ashes') in the present,[39] while on the level of tropical semantics it is the metonym on which the potential metaphorical understanding of 'grünt' ('blossoms') entirely depends. Again, the correlation of metonym and metaphor enhances the cohesion of the individual words and the different layers of meaning that they entail.

Here, then, we have a tropical effect that depends on a particularly stark breach of ordinary collocation rules in the combination of adjective ('fromm', 'pious') and MV noun ('Garten', 'garden') which, in turn, produces the sense of a wide gap between MV and MT and a significant hermeneutic detour. Quite differently, the second metonym in the stanza, 'Heldenasche' ('heroes' ashes'), exploits the specifying properties of a compound word to increase the effect of defamiliarization. What happens in 'Heldenasche' is that in a further move, from 'Asche' ('ashes') to 'Heldenasche' ('heroes' ashes'), the 'replacing' term ('ashes' for 'soil') is additionally specified, and this specification reduces the directness of the connection between MV and MT. The link of lexical contiguity between 'Asche' ('ashes') and earth is established through collocation in ordinary usage, notably in funerary contexts, but the specification of ashes as heroes' ashes undermines the ordinariness of the collocation and introduces an additional element of defamiliarization: the soil ploughed by the ploughman is not simply mixed with the mortal remains of its former inhabitants, but is completely saturated with the sacred relics of a glorious past. This additional specification strongly affects both the semantics of the metonym and the intensity of its defamiliarizing effect. This is an example in which a metonymic

the rhetorical tradition refers to as 'enallage' or 'transferred epithet'). I will turn to this line of thought and to the question whether adjectives can be used metonymically later in this chapter, see below, pp. 92–121.

[39] Cf. the aural link in 'grünt... pflügt', further supported by their parallel word-positioning.

'replacement' involves multiple shifts within a single semantic field. The inadequacy of a substitutionalist understanding of metonymy becomes once again apparent.

A particularly insightful example for the directional yet open semantics of this type of metonymy is the following extreme case of a metonym whose polyvalence is so intense that it remains—to us—obscure. It occurs in Pindar's *Tenth Pythian Ode*, in a passage that describes how Perseus once witnessed the sacrificial offering of donkeys to Apollo at the halls of the Hyperboreans, where the god was traditionally thought to spend the three winter months:

κλειτὰς ὄνων ἑκατόμβας ἐπιτόσσαις θεῷ
ῥέζοντας· ὧν θαλίαις ἔμπεδον
εὐφαμίαις τε μάλιστ' Ἀπόλλων
χαίρει, γελᾷ θ' ὁρῶν *ὕβριν ὀρθίαν* κνωδάλων.

when he came upon them sacrificing glorious hecatombs
of asses to the god. In their banquets
and praises Apollo ever finds greatest delight
and laughs to see the beasts' braying insolence
[lit.: and laughs to see the beasts' *upright/high-pitched insolence/violation*][40]

The collocation of ὕβρις ('insolence, violent transgression') and ὄρθιος ('standing straight up, upright, steep, high-pitched') breaches ordinary collocation rules. Yet what is it about the donkeys that constitutes a violent transgression, that can be characterized as standing straight up or being high-pitched, and causes Apollo's amusement? Ancient scholiasts and modern scholars have interpreted this passage as referring to either the donkeys' outrageous leaping, to their high-pitched braying, or to the immodest size of the donkeys' erect phalli that make the god laugh.[41] In any case, it is clear that ὕβρις, denoting a transgression of some sort that violates the divinely ordained boundaries of what is proper in the moral and natural sphere, is a qualification of a phenomenon but not the phenomenon itself ('attribute-for-object' in rhetorical handbook-speak). As such, ὕβρις both contains and 'replaces' the actual source of Apollo's laughter: something is funny because it constitutes an outrageous case of ὕβρις, but what? Due to a lack of contextual information that might narrow down the options that present themselves here by rendering some of them implausible (or, at least, less plausible), it is not possible for a modern reader of these verses to establish one single (or even one main) MT for the MV: the donkeys are doing something amusingly

[40] Pi. *P.* 10.33–6; trans. Race.

[41] See Gentili *ad loc.*

hubristic, but what this something is, is deferred out of reach by the metonym.[42]

With these (admittedly preliminary and selective) readings in mind, a more comprehensive theoretical assessment of 'replacement metonyms' can now be attempted. The transferability of Richards's tenor–vehicle model from metaphor to metonymy has proven to be practicable and instructive in concrete critical analysis, albeit with certain qualifications. The qualifications themselves—the observed absence of any interaction between tenor and vehicle and the importance of context and micro-context for the establishment of the tropical understanding of the metonym—can now be conceptualized with greater precision. The attentive reader may already have noted that after the initial introduction of the terms metonymic vehicle (MV) and metonymic tenor (MT), the former has always been used unambiguously to refer to the metonymically used term or terms in a given passage, whereas the usage of the latter has hovered between reference to a virtual but distinct *term* and more loosely to a vague *meaning* that emerges from the context but cannot be pinned down to any one concrete term or even a set of terms. Understanding the reasons for this oscillation of the metonymic tenor between 'term' and 'meaning' will lead to a further clarification of the tenor–vehicle relationship in metonymy and thereby of the applicability of interaction theory as a tool to understand and theorize metonymy.

The examination of 'replacement metonyms' has made it evident that the relationship between tenor and vehicle in metonymy is *neither* one of substitution of equivalent terms *nor* one of interaction of logically related terms. It is helpful to adopt a reception aesthetic point of view to describe their real relationship: in the actual process of reception of a metonym, the metonymic tenor is called forth through an abrasive (illegitimate) collocation of the present terms, which instigates a hermeneutic process that leads to the resolution of this incompatibility on a virtual, semantic level by amending the literal meaning of the MV to the MT. The micro-context, however, not only negates the positive meaning of the MV in ordinary usage and thus establishes its status as a metonym; it is also determinative in the process of reaching the MT. The MV, the present term whose literal meaning has been negated and suspended, is thus designated as a starting position for a hermeneutic search process: the semantic field of this term is opened up and now constitutes the framework within which an MT is to be located. This hermeneutic search is

[42] Whether the point (or points?) of this metonym could be grasped more easily by ancient audiences is difficult to ascertain, though the different suggestions offered by the scholiasts indicate that similar ambiguities were felt here, too.

not arbitrary but restricted (and governed) by context and microcontext, since it is a prerequisite for the MT to be semantically compatible with the context and collocatable with the specific microcontext.

The essential importance of context-determination for the MT also marks a crucial difference between metaphor and metonymy: metaphor is always ultimately based on the logical relationship of analogy or similarity that holds tenor and vehicle together. Metaphors can therefore usually be isolated from their wider context and still function and maintain their meaning; metaphorical meaning is contained within the metaphorical compound, within its logic of analogy and similarity. In metonymy, on the other hand, tenor and vehicle have no such internally negotiated and stabilized relationship, either in the sense that their relationship would ever be established *in situ* through grammatical or syntactic links or in the sense that they could be isolated from their context and still function.[43] The comprehension of a metonym is always initially framed by the semantic field of its vehicle but determined (or not) by its context and microcontext.

However, this notion of the metonymic tenor as a vehicle-based but contextually determined virtual entity conflicts with the basic assumptions of interaction theory as developed in the theory of metaphor. The initial experience of abrasiveness in the reception process of both metaphor and metonymy makes it appear likely that similar dynamics take place between tenor, vehicle, and context in both tropes, but it follows from my analysis that the configurations are distinctively different: in metaphor, a passage in tenor terminology (or, with hindsight, in neutral terminology)[44] is interrupted by the appearance of extraneous vehicle terminology. The two terminologies, linked by the logic of analogy or similarity, interact through the immediate, extraordinary collocation of the present terms and through the conceptual associations that come with them. It is this interaction between tenor and vehicle which creates the surplus of meaning characteristic of metaphor. In metonymy, on the other hand, the poetic effect of the trope does not result from an interaction of tenor and vehicle (there is none) but from the movement of tracing the tenor which takes the vehicle as the starting position and is guided by the context and thus interacts with it. The relationship between tenor and vehicle in metonymy might therefore be described as in itself directional but open; it is the context and microcontext that

[43] This claim readily finds support in word-for-word translations which tend to destabilize coherence of syntax and context, for instance in Hölderlin's translations of Pindaric odes; see below, p. 254.

[44] See Silk 1974, 16–18.

do, or do not, determine the point (or points) of closure on the trajectory of tracing the MT. It follows that while in both metaphor and metonymy the initial impression of tropicality stems from an abrasive juxtaposition of terms which are not collocatable in ordinary usage, interaction in metonymy takes place between vehicle and context/microcontext and has a constitutive significance for the tenor, whereas interaction in metaphor takes place between tenor and vehicle and does not constitute either but leads to the emergence of a new meaning from the interaction of their properties. While the semantics of metaphor thus result from the explosive consequences of the terminological collision between tenor and vehicle, the semantics of metonymy result from the emergence of the tenor from the vehicle's semantic field as a second active (though virtual) component of the metonym.

If metonymy is indeed characterized by the hermeneutic process of tracing a metonymic tenor which arises from the metonymic vehicle's semantic field, then it is no wonder that the more complex and obstacle-ridden this process is, the more rich and multilayered the poetic effect of the metonym is likely to seem. In other words, metonymy involves an illegitimate collocation of two (or more) words out of whose tension a metonymic understanding of one emerges; and the more abrasive the collocation and the more open and under-determinative both context and microcontext are, the greater the semantic potential. As the examples have shown, the extremes seem to range from a virtual one-to-one equivalence in the case of Pindar's εὐναί to effective indeterminability in the case of his ὕβριν ὀρθίαν. This is a first indication that metonymy subsumes degrees of tropicality that range from the elevated language of poetic *variatio* to the heightened language of striking metonyms.[45] However, it would seem that *every* MV is in principle capable of a multitude of significations, namely all the terms it is associated with by contiguity in its semantic field. Apart from the boundaries of the semantic field, the semantic potential of a metonym is capped as and where context and microcontext narrow it down, at times to one specifiable tenor term—which is where the impression of a mere substitution of terms is created. Conversely, the breadth of metonymy's semantic potential shines through wherever the restrictive criteria set by context and microcontext are loose. And wherever these criteria are so loose that no single MT can be established, the reader or listener is left with a string or set of associated potential MTs from the MV's semantic field. Rather than speaking of a 'replacement metonym', therefore, we might do better

[45] On the difference between the two, see above, p. 21.

to think of it as an *index metonym*: just as individual words listed in the index of a book point the reader to one or several different contexts in which the word in question occurs, so a metonymically used word (the MV) points the reader to this word's semantic field, which is essentially the sum of all contexts in which it can and does occur—or in terms of lexical contiguity: the sum of all words it can be collocated with in ordinary usage. The mechanism at work in this type of metonymy is thus comparable to the index of a book insofar as both devices exploit and rely on pre-established links, and specifically links pre-established through actual collocation in ordinary usage; tracing these links ultimately leads to the points of interest: the relevant page numbers and text passages on the one hand, and the metonymic tenor on the other. The comparison holds true also for cases with multiple MTs: as with words in an index that refer to several different pages/contexts, all instances to which the word in question points are linked together in a chain of unbroken contiguity through their shared connection with the original, lexical starting point.[46]

As we have seen, one of the major poetic functions of index metonymy is the duplication of the potential for intratextual cross-references which makes index metonyms potential focal points of a web of associations and intratextual relations on both the level of the present metonymic vehicle and the inferred, virtual metonymic tenor. This externally directed poetic function, however, is complemented by an internal poetic effect, arising from the characteristic shift within the semantic field which occurs during the hermeneutic movement from the MV to the MT. In particular those index metonyms whose MT cannot be established with such immediate accuracy that they border on one-to-one equivalence with the MV, but which instead only point directionally to several possible MTs, reveal with great clarity the intrinsically directional character of the semantics of index metonyms. Theoreticians and literary critics, who have often been tempted to dismiss the poetic potential of the allegedly 'simple' metonymic shift, might do well to remember the way the Great War poet Rosenberg characterized 'simple poetry' in one of his letters from the trenches, calling it 'an interesting complexity of thought [that] is kept in tone and right value to the dominating idea so that it is understandable and still ungraspable'.[47] His critic Harding interprets this characterization in a way which, *mutatis mutandis*, magnificently

[46] To prevent any misunderstanding it should be noted that my category of index metonymy is unrelated to the concept of 'indexicality' as developed in semiotics, in particular in Peirce's second trichotomy of signs (see Peirce 1903).

[47] Rosenberg 1916, 317.

describes my point here, since index metonyms, just like Rosenberg's 'simple' poetry, leave 'every idea partly embedded in the undifferentiated mass of ideas from which it has emerged'.[48]

Amplification metonymy

Both my introductory theoretical reflections and the first case studies on index metonymy might seem to have provided reasons for assuming that grammatical categories, whose relevance as facilitators of linkage in metaphor has been stressed by Brooke-Rose, are not in the same way relevant for metonymy as a whole. Metonymy is not based on the intratextual connection of heterogeneous terminology. The contiguity that 'links' the components of a metonym and is the precondition of 'replacement' in index metonyms is a given and does not require additional grammatical and syntactical linkages. There are, however, recurrent types of metonymy that are defined precisely by their grammatical structure. The examples classified and discussed as instances of 'index metonymy' in the first section of this chapter all centred on just *one noun* as the metonymic vehicle present in the text. In this section on 'amplification metonymy' we will look at metonyms that involve a specific *constellation of several nouns* before pondering in the next section, on 'grammatical metonymy', whether or not metonymy as a phenomenon of poetic language *is indeed exclusive to nouns*—as the definitions, examples, and discussions of the rhetorical treatises seem to suggest—or whether there are also metonyms based on verbs and adjectives.

Consider the following examples from Pindar's *Pythian Odes*:

> κατέκλασε γὰρ *ἐντέων σθένος* οὐδέν.
>
> For he broke none of his strong equipment
> [lit.: For in no way did he break the *strength of the equipment*][49]

> ... ταύτας δὲ μή ποτε τιμᾶς
> ἀμείρειν *γονέων βίον πεπρωμένον*.
>
> ... and never to deprive of like honor
> one's parents during their allotted lifetime
> [lit.: *the allotted lifetime of one's parents*].[50]

[48] Harding 1963, 100.
[49] Pi. *P.* 5.34; trans. Race.
[50] Pi. *P.* 6.26–7; trans. Race.

Both examples involve divergence from the economy of ordinary language usage. Both are recognizable as examples of stylized language that exceed in length a more direct mode of expression: 'he broke none of his equipment' or 'one must never deprive one's parents of such honour' respectively. In both cases, the term that could have been used on its own in a more direct and simple expression occurs in the genitive and is joined by another term together with which it forms an extended complex. In substitutionalist terms one might say that in the first example 'strength of the equipment' *replaces* 'equipment' and in the second example 'the allotted lifetime of one's parents' *replaces* 'one's parents'. The inadequacy of the substitutionalist view, however, is once again revealed when we consider the implications of the terms actually chosen. In the first case, this genitive extension from ἔντεα ('equipment') to ἐντέων σθένος suggests an implicit metaphorization of the verb: 'equipment' can literally be broken; 'strength of equipment' can only be broken metaphorically. In the second case, the shift to a compound based on genitival extension results in a breach of the rules of collocation in ordinary usage: the verb ἀμέρδω, 'deprive', is ordinarily constructed with the accusative of the person and the genitive (or accusative) of the object (here ταύτας τιμᾶς, 'of such honour'). The persons left 'deprived' or 'bereft' here, however, stand in the genitive and it is instead the persons' 'allotted lifetime' that takes the ordinary grammatical position of the person in the accusative. These formulations no doubt recall the earlier observations on illegitimate collocation and conditional tropicality which emerged as characteristic traits of index metonymy in the previous set of examples. The crucial difference between these two types, however, is that in index metonymy the tenor (MT) must always be traced in the semantic field of the vehicle (MV), guided by context and microcontext, whereas in this type of metonymy the MT is already co-present in the tropical compound which in its entirety forms the MV. In κατέκλασε γὰρ ἐντέων σθένος οὐδέν, for instance, the MT, the equipment (ἔντεα) which the chariot-driver literally did not break, is co-present in the MV, the 'strength of the equipment' (ἐντέων σθένος). Likewise, the MT, the persons who are literally not to be deprived of honours are the parents (γονεῖς) who are co-present in the MV (γονέων βίον πεπρωμένον).

The character and structure of this type of metonymy determine its poetic effect. In the first example, the shift from physical 'equipment' to its abstract 'strength' presents the charioteer as a victor who can manage great physical forces and the strain they cause. He does not simply own exceptionally sturdy equipment (and was not so incompetent as to break it); rather, he controlled all the forces at work in the chariot race and steered himself and the chariot through them without any harm to either. The impression this metonym creates is noticeably less static (something is broken or not broken) and more dynamic (something has emerged from a battle of conflicting forces).[51] In the second example, the broader context needs to be taken into account to appreciate the poetic effect more fully:

> . . . ὀρθὰν
> ἄγεις ἐφημοσύναν,
> . . .
> . . . μάλιστα μὲν Κρονίδαν,
> βαρύοπα στεροπᾶν κεραυνῶν τε πρύτανιν,
> θεῶν σέβεσθαι·
> ταύτας δὲ μή ποτε τιμᾶς
> ἀμείρειν *γονέων βίον πεπρωμένον.*
>
> . . . you uphold the precept
> . . .
> . . . above all gods
> to revere Kronos' son, loud-voiced lord
> of lightning and thunder,
> and never to deprive of like honor
> one's parents during their allotted lifetime
> [lit.: *the allotted lifetime of one's parents*].[52]

In the context of this precept, with its dual imperative of piety towards the gods and one's parents, the metonym creates a potential to connect the two commandments: one must honour Zeus who is the supreme ruler and one must honour one's parents in the lifetime (*which Zeus has*) allotted for them. Read in this way, Zeus remains implicitly present in the second precept, as the metonym carries the overtone that not to fulfil one's duty of achieving glory through honourable deeds ultimately means both to fail one's parents and to set oneself against the will of Zeus. As with index metonymy, both enhanced cohesion and intratextual cross-referencing are apparent.

Another example can be found in Hölderlin's poem 'Wie wenn am Feiertage':

> Drum wenn zu schlafen sie [die Natur] scheint zu Zeiten des Jahrs
> Am Himmel oder unter den Pflanzen oder den Völkern

[51] A predictable objection to this analysis is the formulaic nature of such expressions in the epic tradition which Pindar here reflects and, more precisely, the metrical restraints that might be thought to influence the employment of such expressions. Any such objection is methodologically false. The poet's chosen diction may be traditional and accommodate metrical requirements but it is still potentially *effect*-ive diction. Cf. e.g. Vivante 1982, vii–x and 151–91, as well as Silk 2004, 14–22, for the principle.

[52] Pi. *P.* 6.19–27; trans. Race.

So trauert *der Dichter Angesicht* auch,
Sie scheinen allein zu sein, doch ahnen sie immer.
Denn ahnend ruhet sie selbst auch.

Thus when she [nature] seems to sleep at [certain] times of the year
In the sky or among/underneath the plants or peoples,
So does the *poets' countenance* mourn,
They seem to be alone, yet they are always full of premonition.
For full of premonition she rests herself.[53]

The central line in this passage, l. 16, contains a restrained but noticeable breach of ordinary collocation rules: in ordinary usage only persons can mourn, not their countenances, which can merely bear outward signs of it. The effect of this violation is softened through the co-presence of the metonymic tenor ('poets') in the genitive. Although not directly governing 'trauern' ('mourning') as required by ordinary usage, its presence limits the repercussions of this deviant language usage by interrupting and thereby softening the otherwise more abrasive collocation of the verb, 'mourning', and its subject, 'countenance'. While the tropical impact of this metonym is thus restrained in terms of defamiliarized usage, the conceit of the entire passage, the likening of poets to nature, depends on it. The simile is one of outer appearance and inner spirit: the 'face of nature', its visible appearance in the sky and the lives of plants and peoples which may be resting and subdued in winter, is but a reflection of the spirit of nature which, although hidden underneath, is alive and full of foreboding. Likewise, the 'face of the poets' may appear to be showing outward signs of melancholy and mourning, but the poets' spirit, like the spirit of nature, is, rather, premonitory. It is surely apparent that the parallelism between the faces of nature and of poets, and the spirits of nature and of poets, would not have the clarity and pungency that it has were it not for the metonym: if we had, simply, 'so trauern auch die Dichter' ('and so mourn the poets too'), the reduced parallelism between nature and poets would, for instance, foster an understanding of 'so' in a largely causative sense, introducing the poets' mourning as a mere consequence of nature's sleep. Thereby much of this passage's semantic activation would be lost.

While in index metonymy, then, the metonymic tenor is only virtual and arises as a separate entity from the metonymic vehicle, in this second type of metonymy the MT is itself present in the text and forms part of the MV. This means, in other words, that the pre-existing link between MT and MV is invisible in index metonymy, but visible in the genitival

[53] Hölderlin, 'Wie wenn am Feiertage', 14–18.

co-presence of the MT in the MV compound in this type. However, the visible presence of this link has an effect that needs careful formulation. Rather than juxtaposing two heterogeneous terminologies and linking them together by means of the genitive, thus facilitating their interaction (a mechanism analysed by Brooke-Rose for some forms of metaphor),[54] the MT present in the genitive of this type of metonymy always constitutes the backdrop against which the specifying extension of the MV is set: it is the *strength* of the equipment and the *allotted lifetime* of the parents which are in focus; they are the highlighted aspects of the broader MT. Metonyms of this type operate on the basis of a 'partitive' genitive: the MT in the genitive opens up a field and the MV extension specifies which aspect of it is put in the spotlight.[55] Again, there is no interaction between MV and MT; they are not *being* linked, they *are* linked. What both index metonymy and this second type of metonymy have in common, therefore, is the fact that the relationship between tenor and vehicle is a relationship of selection from a field established by the trope. The peculiarity of the second type is that it renders the link that exists between MV and MT manifest, by incorporating it in the form of the genitive that holds the two components of the new compound together. Index metonymy explores a semantic field that lies (implicitly) behind the MV and remains virtual to it. In these second cases, on the other hand, the MV focuses on a specific segment of a semantic field which is itself present in the text; the semantic field thus appears within the text as a two-dimensional segment of which the specifying genitive extension highlights a particular aspect. As a result, metonymy's characteristic contiguity is here operative between the semantics of one present term (MT) and the collective semantics of a series of present terms (MV) to which the MT term itself contributes but within which, for grammatical reasons, another term

[54] See Brooke-Rose 1958, 146–205; an example used by Brooke-Rose is the opening of the poem 'Ah, Sunflower' from William Blake's *Poems of Experience*, 'Ah, Sun-flower! weary of time, who countest the *steps of the sun* [i.e. hours, or minutes]' (see Brooke-Rose 1958, 150).

[55] My usage and understanding of 'partitive genitive' here and thoughout this book is broader than that usually found in grammatical contexts. I take it to refer to instances where a noun in the genitive denotes the whole of which the governing noun is *a constitutive element*—be it as a distinct part, an aspect, or a quality (whereas the more narrow grammatical notion of the partitive genitive requires the governing noun to specifically indicate a quantifiable *portion* of the whole expressed in the genitive); on the related issues of synecdoche, meronymy/holonymy, and hyponymy/hypernymy, see below, pp. 154–65.

is more prominent. The contiguous relationship between the two terms is one in which the latter is focused on one single aspect of the former.

It has to be said that metonyms of this type are often more smoothly embedded into their context, even to the extent that there is little or no abrasiveness felt but merely some impression of stylization stemming from a (seemingly superfluous) over-specification. In such cases, metonyms of this type can seem to hover between a tropical and a literal signification, as in the following three examples:

> ... Εὐρυσθῆος ἐπεὶ κεφαλὰν
> ἔπραθε *φασγάνου ἀκμᾷ*...
>
> ... after he cut off Eurystheus' head with *the edge of his sword*...[56]
>
> ἦλθες ἤδη *Λιβύας πεδίον*...
>
> and now you have come to *the plain of Libya*[57]
>
> *Διός* τοι *νόος* μέγας κυβερνᾷ
> δαίμον' ἀνδρῶν φίλων.
>
> Truly *the* great *mind of Zeus* steers
> the fortune of men who are dear to him.[58]

In all of these cases, the term in the genitive is itself sufficient for a literal statement: one would expect from a formulation in normal usage that it was the whole sword, and not just its edge, that completed the beheading; that the charioteer has returned to Libya, rather than particularly to Libya's plain; and that it is Zeus who is the metaphorical navigator of human affairs and not just his mind.[59] All these specifications serve to highlight aspects that flesh out and colour the scene, yet nowhere is there an actual breach of collocation rules or an unmistakable deviation from ordinary usage.

I propose to refer to this category of metonymy as *amplification metonymy* because this term captures the two key characteristics of metonyms of this type: first, metonyms of this type are in their structure characterized by an amplification of the number of words used; the noun-with-noun-in-genitive compound, which constitutes the metonymic vehicle, is considerably larger than the co-present metonymic tenor, which

[56] Pi. *P.* 9.80–1; trans. Race.
[57] Pi. *P.* 5.52; trans. Race.
[58] Pi. *P.* 5.122; trans. Race.
[59] Yet again the presence of a deity complicates matters for tropological analysis: in the context of anthropomorphic polytheism, it seems plausible to assume metonymic usage here (albeit only on the basis of an assumed consistent and comprehensive analogy between gods and humans); a reader like Anaxagoras, however, whose cosmic νοῦς–Zeus *can* act in the world, may well read this statement in a perfectly literal way. On the general problematic of mythology and metonymy, see above, pp. 45–6, and below, pp. 202–7.

in itself constitutes only a part of the metonymic vehicle. Secondly, the poetic effect of this type of metonym is likewise one of amplification. The main aesthetic consequence of its deployment, as my discussion of selected examples has shown, is additional emphasis and focus. Amplification metonyms give an intensified impression of what is at issue while at the same time adding to 'the bigger picture' in the metonymic tenor which is co-present in the partitive genitive.

Grammatical metonymy

The previous two sections of this chapter have shed light on the mechanisms and effects of metonymic tropes by focusing initially on two types of metonymy that were both based on nouns: *index metonymy* (based on one noun) and *amplification metonymy* (based on a specific constellation of several nouns). In this section, we will probe whether there are also forms of metonymy that are based on verbs and adjectives. Pondering the different ways in which different parts of speech collocate in ordinary language as well as the concomitant implications for their respective ability to develop links of lexical contiguity—which, as I have argued, constitute the basis for (potential) metonymic usage—I propose that metonymy is indeed a noun-based phenomenon. I will suggest that verbs are for linguistic reasons much less capable of being used metonymically, so much so that hardly any examples for potential verb metonymy can be found, whereas adjectives, precisely because of their (comparatively) closer association with nouns, can be seen to form metonymic expressions (which, however, rely heavily on nouns for their semantic and poetic efficacy). These adjective-based expressions constitute a third type of metonymy, classified here as *grammatical metonymy*, whose different manifestations reflect the structural differences that emerged between the two noun-based expressions of metonymy in index and amplification metonyms. Developing a sound understanding of this third, adjective-based type of metonymy will involve a critical engagement with discussions of hitherto separately theorized phenomena of poetic language, notably enallage and transferred epithets, which, I suggest, can be better understood precisely as adjectival forms of metonymy. It seems helpful, therefore, to begin this section with a brief restatement of the definitive features of the first two types of metonymy (on the basis of some new examples) so as to consolidate the state of the discussion up until this point.

Index metonymy features in this verse from the prophecy on the Greek victory over Troy in Aeschylus' *Agamemnon*:

> χρόνῳ μὲν ἀγρεῖ Πριάμου πόλιν ἅδε *κέλευθος*
> In time this *expedition* will capture the city of Priam
> [lit.: In time this *path/journey* will capture the city of Priam][60]

Here, one word (κέλευθος, 'path, journey') appears in a direct collocation with other words (in particular the verb ἀγρεῖ, 'to capture, seize'), which is illegitimate and nonsensical in ordinary usage and which marks it out as a trope. In any attempt to make sense of the passage, this word will be read as a metonymic vehicle and serves as a starting point for a hermeneutic process that reconciles the abrasive collocation of the present words by supplementing the present metonymic vehicle (MV) with an inferred metonymic tenor (MT) which is compatible with the microcontext. The establishment of this metonymic tenor is directional and in itself open-ended: the present MV serves as a starting position which indicates the semantic field within which one or more MTs are traced that comply with the restrictions of collocatability within the given context (here, for instance, 'expedition' or 'army' or 'those soldiers beginning their journey here'). Index metonymy thus leads to the unfolding of a second, co-present dimension: on the one hand, the present term in the text (metonymic vehicle), and on the other the term/s inferred from it (metonymic tenor).[61]

[60] A. *Agam.* 126; trans. Sommerstein. We have no evidence in extant Greek for κέλευθος in prose texts which would allow us to reliably establish the term's ordinary usage. However, the available evidence in the elevated vocabulary of epic and tragic poetry makes it clear that the word's usage in the above example deviates significantly from its general elevated use to denote 'way, path' or 'journey'. LSJ, for instance, gives 'expedition' as a further 'meaning' of the term but lists, in addition to the passage under discussion, only one more instance, namely A. *Pers.* 757–8: τοιάδ' ἐξ ἀνδρῶν ὀνείδη πολλάκις κλύων κακῶν | τήνδ' ἐβούλευσεν κέλευθον καὶ στράτευμ' ἐφ' Ἑλλάδα ('Having heard again and again such taunts from evil men, he prepared this journey and an army against Greece'; trans. Sommerstein). It is clear that in this latter case the term still conforms to its general elevated usage, literally denoting the *journey* of an army (note the unproblematic collocatability with the verb). This is markedly different from ἀγρεῖ... πόλιν ἅδε κέλευθος ('this κέλευθος will capture the city'), since here the collocation with the verb, which requires *human agents*, is abrasive and makes its 'ordinary' sense impossible. As far as Sommerstein's translation of this line is concerned, one might say that the English 'expedition' is also metonymic insofar as it points to the *agents* who undertake the expedition.

[61] On the large scale of this play, this metonymic shift from the army and its Trojan expedition to the initial journey runs deep with significance—after all, it is neither the army nor the war against Troy but the events on the army's *journey* which are of crucial importance to the events of this play. True enough, the army's journey will eventually lead to the fall of Troy, but it is the journey itself that entails the sacrifice of Iphigenia, which will bring about the fall of Agamemnon. Placed early on in this play, in v. 126, this metonym

In amplification metonymy, on the other hand, the metonymic tenor itself is present in the sequence. In a pleonastic compound the metonymic tenor here stands in the genitive case while the governing noun specifies the compound to a degree which, if read literally, makes it incompatible with the context. Take, for instance, the way that the means of silencing Iphigenia before her sacrifice are described in Aeschylus' *Agamemnon* as

> βίᾳ *χαλινῶν τ' ἀναύδῳ μένει*
> by force and by the *silencing* [lit.: *silent*] *power of a bridle*[62]

In the economy of ordinary language, a simple dative χαλινῷ/χαλινοῖς ('with a bridle') would have been used here. Instead, this direct, more economic term appears in the genitive (χαλινῶν, 'of a bridle'), while a specific aspect of it, namely the abstract μένει ('strength'), is isolated and given, in its stead, as the genitive's governing noun.[63] The resulting compound constitutes an amplification in two ways: first, in that it pleonastically enlarges the expression used to express what is at issue, and secondly, in that, when read as a compound, it conversely reduces the semantic scope and narrows it down to emphasize and focus on only one specific aspect. The potential abrasiveness of the resulting non-ordinary collocation caused by this 'spotlight' or 'zoom' effect (to use theatrical/cinematic metaphors) is mitigated by the co-presence of metonymic vehicle (the compound as a whole) and metonymic tenor (the noun in the genitive): the metonymic tenor is present in the partitive genitive, the whole from which one specific aspect is brought into focus. The shift in the semantic field, implicit and inferential in index metonymy, is now explicit and occurs within a sequence of present words that form a semantic and syntactic unit.

subtly shifts the focus into this direction and thereby not only prepares the narration of this all-important event a hundred verses later but also heightens the atmosphere of doom by focusing on the very journey whose destructive consequences will bring ruin to both the captured city and the returning king.

[62] A. *Agam.* 238; trans. Sommerstein (adapted).

[63] The adjective ἀναύδῳ ('silent', 'unable to articulate') is also used tropically here, since it is Iphigenia who is speechless, and not the μένει ('power', 'strength') that causes her to be speechless (on the denotative meaning of ἄναυδος as 'silent' rather than 'silencing', see below, n. 159, p. 246). Such tropical usage of adjectives, based on the grammatical reaffiliation of the adjective away from what would be its actual governing noun in ordinary language to another noun present in the sequence, is discussed later on in this chapter in full detail; see below, pp. 92–121.

Both index metonymy and amplification metonymy, as studied and defined thus far, appear to be noun-based phenomena, and as such they form a suitable starting point for the analysis of metonymy as a whole, which in virtually all discussions is exclusively illustrated by and associated with nouns. This presupposition is already, for better or worse, implicit in the name μετωνυμία itself which, after all, contains within it the technical term used by ancient grammarians to denote the noun: ὄνομα. Yet, as Brooke-Rose has shown for metaphor, tropes formerly thought of as 'substitutions of one word for another' are by no means restricted to nouns; in fact, as every reader of poetry will know, some of the most striking metaphors are verb-based. The question arises, then: are there any forms of metonymy that display the characteristic metonymic shift, within a virtual semantic field as observed in index metonymy or within a present syntactic field as in amplification metonymy, but involve verbs, adjectives, or adverbs? A good starting point for engaging with this question is to think about the role and status of verbs in metaphorical expressions before examining some putative examples for verb metonymy in the light of these considerations and against the backdrop of the theory of metonymy developed thus far.

WHAT'S IN A VERB? VERB-CENTRED METAPHOR VERSUS NOUN-BASED METONYMY

Although Brooke-Rose's discussion of the 'grammar' of metaphor follows a division into noun metaphor, verb metaphor, and adjective metaphor, she suggests that behind this grammatical division the general tenor–vehicle relationship in metaphor is inherently verb-centred: 'the relationship between the metaphor and the third term is verbal'.[64] Reflecting on the logical element of similarity or analogy that is constitutive of metaphor, she describes the verb-centred nature of this logical element as follows:

> Very broadly speaking, metaphors can be divided, from the point of view of idea-content, into functional metaphors (A is called B by virtue of what it does), and sensuous metaphors (A is called B by virtue of what it looks like, or, more rarely, sounds like, smells like, feels like, tastes like).[65]

In this spirit, she concludes her discussion of noun-based metaphors by arguing that '[t]he various grammatical links, in fact, stood for a verb,

[64] Brooke-Rose 1958, 153.   [65] Brooke-Rose 1958, 155.

and sometimes contained or consisted of a verb'.[66] In other words, the element of similarity and analogy that enables terminological interaction in metaphor does not merely consist of a suppressed, implicit 'like' but of an implicit '(verb) + like'. Consequently, Brooke-Rose argues that the 'chief difference between the noun and the verb metaphor is one of explicitness'.[67]

From the demonstration that metonymy is not based on any logical relationship, but instead on lexical contiguity within a semantic field, it should follow that metonymy does not share this intrinsic verb-centred characteristic of metaphor. The empirical evidence vindicates this assumption. An assessment of metonymic occurrences in poetry soon shows that there are hardly any instances which can be understood as verb-based metonyms at all. Consider the following line from Hölderlin's translation of Sophocles' *Antigone*:

> Und auch ein Kind von einem andern Manne,
> wenn diesen ich *umarmt*
>
> And even children [lit.: a child] by another man
> If I *embraced* that man . . .[68]

Here, 'umarmt' ('embraced') will be read in this context of procreation as 'had sexual intercourse with'. This would appear to be a rare case of verb-based index metonymy, albeit one with little poetic effect: the immediate context makes the metonymic tenor very clear and neither leaves room for ambiguity nor provides contact points for any interactions with surrounding words. In fact, it is hardly felt as tropical at all since the reference to a child conceived from another man is already made in the preceding words; although the verb attracts a readjusted reading in this particular context, which constitutes to an extent a deviation from ordinary usage, it occurs in a conditional clause which merely illustrates what has already been said—the verb is *not* the sole conveyor of the action at issue.[69]

[66] Brooke-Rose 1958, 210; to illustrate this point: in her analysis of noun-metaphors based on a 'genitive link' Brooke-Rose 'found that *of* can most successfully express complete identity of the two linked nouns ['the fire of love'] when the metaphor can very easily be turned into a verb: if love burns, it is a fire' (Brooke-Rose 1958, 155; italics in the original).

[67] Brooke-Rose 1958, 206.

[68] Hölderlin, *Trauerspiele des Sophokles: Antigonä*, l. 945; trans. Constantine. Hölderlin diverges here from the Sophoclean text, which has καὶ παῖς ἀπ᾽ ἄλλου φωτός, εἰ τοῦδ᾽ ἤμπλακον ('a child from another man, if I became bereft of this one here', S. *Ant.* 910; trans. Lloyd-Jones). This does not affect my argument: for now, I am concerned with the tropical effect in the German passage in its own right.

[69] While this alone does not constitute sufficient evidence to dispute that what we are dealing with here is a genuine metonymic expression based on a verb—after all, the same

In other cases, the situation is even less straightforward, as in the following verse from Sophocles' *Antigone* itself:

> πλεκταῖσιν ἀρτάναισι λωβᾶται βίον
> she *did* [lit.: *does*] *violence* to her life with twisted noose[70]

The collocation λωβᾶται βίον ('to mutilate one's life') violates ordinary collocation rules: λωβᾶσθαι in ordinary usage denotes the *concrete* mutilation or damaging of a person, a body, or any other material object, while βίος denotes the *abstract* concepts of 'manner of life', 'means of living', or 'lifetime'. In the given context of the passage, where Ismene recalls her mother's suicide, it is clear that Jocasta's (biological) life was not damaged or mutilated, but altogether destroyed and ended. Yet the word that stands out most in this verse is arguably βίον, since πλεκταῖσιν ἀρτάναισι ('with twisted ropes') belongs, together with λωβᾶσθαι, to a much more concrete terminology. The opening words πλεκταῖσιν ἀρτάναισι λωβᾶται, then, focus on the neck of Jocasta, thus setting up an expectation of a physical object in the accusative. In βίον, this expectation is unfulfilled; instead, the narrow focus is now opened up: the act of suicide by hanging becomes a perversion of the normal way of life, as indeed all the acts of familial bloodshed listed in the immediate context are. While λωβᾶται thus forms an elegant mediator between the concreteness of the rope and the abstractness of 'living', the abrasiveness of the verse is most strongly felt in βίον which, given the collocation with λωβᾶται, and the expectations raised by it, is read as an index metonym. There are, then, two items in the verse that can appear as tropical, one fixed, the other conditional: λωβᾶται can be read metonymically as 'terminated, ended' if βίον is read, metonymically again, as 'biological life' (in the sense of ζωή). Alternatively, λωβᾶται can be read literally with βίον understood, still metonymically, as 'body' or 'herself (*sc.* Jocasta)'; this reading would, in turn, lead those with independent knowledge of the mythical plot to a metonymic reading of the entire verse as a whole: she mutilated her body/herself with a rope, that is, she killed herself. In such a case of what I suggest we call 'conditional metonymy'—a phenomenon that will be discussed in more detail later on in this chapter—it is virtually impossible, and arguably counterproductive, to seek a definitive decision on which part of the verse is

might be said of some of the noun-based examples discussed earlier—the observation still matters because it highlights the fact that the very few instances that can be cited at all as possible cases of verb metonymy never carry anywhere near as much weight, significance, and ambiguity as the more striking manifestations of index or amplification metonymy.

[70] S. *Ant.* 54; trans. Lloyd-Jones.

tropical.[71] What can and should be noted, however, is that in the micro-context of the verse the noun is unequivocally metonymic, the verb only conditionally so (namely when certain interpretative conditions regarding the understanding of other terms in the sequence are met).

Complications also arise in the following lines from Hölderlin's poem 'Hyperions Schicksalslied':

> Schicksallos, wie der schlafende
> Säugling, *atmen* die Himmlischen
>
> Fateless[ly], like the sleeping
> baby, the immortals *breathe*[72]

Again, at first glance, this appears to be a straightforward case of a verb-based metonymy: 'atmen' ('breathe') is to be read metonymically for 'to be, to live'. However, the precondition of this reading is the adverb 'schicksallos' (literally 'fatelessly'), which itself appears to be tropical: fatelessness, being without or beyond the remit of fate, is surely always an attribute of a given state, but never of a single action; above the rule of fate, 'the heavenly ones' thus may *be* 'fateless' but one cannot think of any single action, or hence any verb, that could, in ordinary language, be modified by the adverb 'fatelessly'. Reading this passage, one immediately connects the adverb with the subject of the sentence—and thereby reads it, in effect, as an adjective. Given that this adverb also stands in a doubly emphasized position (it heads the sentence, and thus sets its tone, and renders explicit the *tertium comparationis* of the simile), the verb as a potential metonym is itself rather overshadowed. 'Schicksallos', being the odd adverb that it is, effectively converts itself by default implicitly into an adjective, supplies the copula 'to be', and makes a statement about the subject of the sentence ('the gods are fateless') rather than modifying the action described in the present verb. Consequently, the predicate 'atmen' ('breathe') has hardly any semantic value as a governing verb in its own right but rather serves to colour the atmosphere of the preceding simile: the comparison of (*a*) a baby's obliviousness to the worries and fears of the world of mortals and (*b*) the gods' state of perpetual calm is sharpened by focusing on the peaceful, undisturbed, quiet *breathing* of the sleeping baby which encapsulates the state of tranquil serenity at issue here. Yet, while this observed effect of 'focusing' may appear to be reminiscent of noun-based amplification metonymy, it should be noted that the usage of the verb 'atmen' ('breathe') here is not tropical: presumably, anthropomorphic gods can literally breathe. If we

[71] See the discussion of 'conditional metonymy' below, pp. 135–40.
[72] Hölderlin, 'Hyperions Schicksalslied', 7–8.

remove the adverb from the sequence, we have a perfectly non-tropical, ordinary sentence. Moreover, the adverb in question is unusually restricted in terms of rules of collocation in ordinary language: it would lead to structurally similar tropical readings with any verb other than the copula 'to be'.

While we can observe certain readjustments taking place when reading the sequences in which these verbs occur, closer observation shows that in all three cases the potential candidates for verb metonymy are weak and undermined or eclipsed by their literal and tropical context: the sequence is either altogether resemanticized as a result of conditional metonymy, or else the context is so definitive that the potential verb metonym is effectively reduced to a mere apposition which, if read as an independent clause, would not appear tropical at all. In fact, the tropical status of all the verbs can be called into question. Certainly, in their respective contexts they seem to be saying more than they denote in ordinary usage, yet they can still be read as they would be in ordinary usage; something beyond their ordinary denotation seems to be at issue but the literally made statement remains valid in its own right, the expressions do not forcefully negate an understanding of the verb in its usual meaning in ordinary usage (as would be indicative of proper tropical usage strictly speaking): the anthropomorphic gods do literally breathe (though what is at issue is their existence); Jocasta did literally mutilate her body (though what is at issue is her death); Antigone would literally embrace another man in lovemaking (though what is at issue is procreative sexual intercourse). While they display a semantic surplus in their respective contexts, which one would intuitively read as metonymic, these instances are problematic when it comes to identifying them as tropes because they do not involve unequivocal deviation from ordinary usage. There is no need to categorically rule out the possibility of verb metonymy or to deny that the examples discussed above are somehow metonymic, but the evidence derived from the evaluation of the substantial text corpus that informs this study strongly suggests that verbs have drastically less metonymic potential than nouns. Given that the cases discussed above constitute the only examples of (potential) verb metonymy that have emerged in my corpus studies, there is all the more reason to wonder whether there is some structural impediment to the possibility of striking verb metonyms; my reflections on Brooke-Rose and metaphor have already pointed in this direction.[73]

[73] See above, pp. 86–7.

The answer to the question lies once again, I suggest, in the way that metonymy relies on links pre-established through lexical contiguity within a shared semantic field. As already noted, the theory of semantic fields has long been criticized for being intuitive rather than being based on objective parameters,[74] in particular when it comes to defining the actual boundaries of a semantic field.[75] This is indeed a problem for anyone who takes a Neohumboldtian approach that focuses on the organization of conceptual content in the vocabulary of a given language.[76] In order to understand the poetic effects of tropical language, however, what matters is non-ordinary usages and abrasive collocations. Rather than conceptualizing semantic fields as static entities based on conceptual content,[77] which indeed leads to arbitrary boundaries drawn within the vocabulary of a given language, I have been using the term 'semantic field' to denote an entirely usage-based phenomenon: I propose that we understand as a word's semantic field the sum of all other words with which it can be, and is, collocated in ordinary usage.[78] It is this collocatability, the actual lexical contiguity of words in ordinary language, which lies at the heart of metonymy and its lexical-semantic shifts.

On the basis of this understanding, we can reconsider the issue of verb metonymy by assessing the implications of the different parts of speech for their participation in semantic fields. If lexical contiguity is based on semantic fields—that is, on words associated with each other by collocations within ordinary language—it naturally follows that nouns are in a privileged position: nouns frequently group together in sentences and enter various relations with each other, linked (according to the language) by their cases or prepositional connections; verbs, on the other hand, tend to appear in distinct and discrete constructions. Even where they occur together in the same sentence in ordinary usage, they are either subordinated to one another in hypotaxis or comparable constructions, or else separated by conjunctions in parataxis—either way, their normal usage in ordinary language keeps them apart from each other, to a certain degree, and leaves them to form discrete sequences in a way which is markedly different from the more coequal

[74] See Homberger 2000, 632. [75] See Pelz 1996, 195.

[76] See, for instance, Weisgerber 1962.

[77] Such as 'the mind', as in Trier 1931, the seminal study for the development of this theory.

[78] This broad definition is essential to avoid arbitrariness in drawing boundaries for semantic fields: after all, it *is* true that in any given language any given word can be used to head an area which is then labelled a semantic field, just as it is true that there are necessary overlaps caused by words belonging to various semantic fields at the same time. While this constitutes a taxonomical problem for approaches based on conceptual content, it is wholly unproblematic within the usage-based approach taken here.

and less segregated way in which nouns appear jointly in ordinary language clauses. To illustrate the point in the light of our putative examples for verb metonymy discussed above: possible ordinary language sentences, in which the verb present in these passages could appear together with the verb a reader would be inclined to infer (as a supplement to the present one), might be: 'Antigone could meet another man and fall in love with him and embrace him in passionate love and have sexual intercourse with him and so conceive a child from him' ('embrace' and 'have sexual intercourse' appear in separate clauses that stand in parataxis, the verbs are separated from each other by 'and'); 'Jocasta mutilated her body so badly that she died from the wounds she inflicted on it' ('mutilate' appears in the main clause, 'die' appears in the subordinate result clause, the verbs are separated from each other by 'so...that'); 'the immortal gods, although they breathe like men, are in fact fateless' ('be' appears in the main clause, 'breathe' in the subordinate concessive clause, the verbs separated from each other by 'although'). It would appear that it is this kind of lexical contiguity of nouns in ordinary language, characterized by collective semantic engagement without mutual subordination or paratactic separation, that is fundamental to the suitability of nouns for index metonymy. Conversely, verbs appear to be structurally incapable of forming striking index metonyms, precisely because they lack this kind of pre-established link (based on cooperative and coequal collocation) in ordinary language usage.[79]

ADJECTIVES IN DEVIANT USAGE—EVIDENCE FOR ADJECTIVAL METONYMY?

If there are such structural impediments in the way of verbs being used in a metonymically defamiliarizing way, what about adjectival forms of metonymy? Consider the following two examples, the first from the graphic description of a besieged city in enemy hands given by the chorus in Aeschylus' *Seven Against Thebes*, the second from the praise of Apollo as bringer of the athlete's victory in Pindar's *Eighth Pythian Ode*:

[79] Needless to say, amplification metonymy with its reliance on a compound established through a genitive link is a category of metonymy that is by definition not open to verbs.

βλαχαὶ δ' *αἱματόεσσαι*
τῶν ἐπιμαστιδίων
ἀρτιτρεφεῖς βρέμονται

loud, *bloody* screams
rise up from infants [lit.: rise up from those at the breast]
fresh from the nourishing breast[80]

τὺ δ', *Ἑκαταβόλε*, πάνδοκον
ναὸν εὐκλέα διανέμων
Πυθῶνος ἐν γυάλοις,
τὸ μὲν μέγιστον τόθι χαρμάτων
ὤπασας...

And you, *Far-shooter* [lit.: far-shooting], who govern
the all-welcoming famous temple
in the vales of Pytho,
it was there that you granted the greatest
of joys...[81]

In both instances, it is adjectives which command our attention, albeit for different reasons and in very different degrees of intensity. In the first case, the agreement of βλαχαί and αἱματόεσσαι is startling because it drastically breaches ordinary collocation rules: in ordinary usage, these two words cannot be found in a close semantic unit as expressed here. The abrasiveness of this collocation is mitigated only once the next verse comes into view: the genitive τῶν ἐπιμαστιδίων ('of infants', 'of those at the breast') supplies a term which is collocatable with αἱματόεσσαι ('bloody', 'covered in blood').[82] Taken together, and disregarding grammatical allegiances, the two verses now do create a sequence that conforms with the rules of collocatability in ordinary speech (infants—covered in

[80] A. *Sept.* 348–50; trans. Sommerstein. Note that the translation given here does not fully represent the fluidity of syntactic-semantic relationships between the individual words in the original Greek; it does, however, adequately capture the terminological clash under discussion here. On this point see also below, pp. 119–20.

[81] Pi. *P.* 8.61–5; trans. Race.

[82] Whether or not ἐπιμαστιδίων is itself used metonymically is hard to decide. The word is not only an elevated verse word but also very rare. In addition to the passage under discussion, it only occurs in E. *IT* 231–2: σύγγονον, ὃν ἔλιπον ἐπιμαστίδιον, | ἔτι βρέφος, ἔτι νέον, ἔτι θάλος ('my brother, whom I left at his mother's breast, still a tender shoot, a young babe'; trans. Kovacs) and in S. *Fr.* 793: ψακαλοῦχοι | μητέρες αἶγες τ' ἐπιμαστίδιον | γόνον ὀρθαλίχων ἀναφαίνοιεν ('...mothers with young, and may the goats display a brood of young ones at the breast!'; trans. Lloyd-Jones). In both of these cases we note the grammatically 'proper' adjectival usage of the term as qualifying a noun, whereas in its usage in the passage above the term itself effectively serves as a noun. While this points to another grammatical metonym, the lack of 'reliable' ordinary usage compels us to withhold final judgement.

blood—screams). The deviation lies precisely in the grammatical allegiance of the adjective within the given elements of this sequence.[83]

In the second example, far less abrasive and not at all startling, a deviation (if one wants to call it that) is hardly perceptible and can perhaps only be construed as such by the grammarian. The verse, though an apostrophe, lacks any explicit specification of an addressee. It follows a sequence on the poet's encounters and the motivations behind the present ode, which is followed by praise of the presiding deity of the Pythian games. Given this turn, the personal pronoun τύ ('you'), which opens the new sequence, is initially underdetermined, and indeed is not fully determined by any noun in the remaining part of the sentence. Needless to say, it is impossible to miss the fact that Apollo is the addressee of this eulogy. The larger context of the ode, the preceding verses about a meeting γᾶς ὀμφαλὸν παρ' ἀοίδιμον ('near the earth's famed navel') and the subsequent mention of ναὸν εὐκλέα...Πυθῶνος ('the famous temple of...Pytho'), make it abundantly clear that it is Apollo who is evoked (and invoked) here. And yet 'evoked' remains the right word since the name 'Apollo' itself is absent. It is (together with the context) an adjective (ἑκαταβόλε, 'far-shooting') and a periphrastic participle construction (ναὸν εὐκλέα διανέμων | Πυθῶνος ἐν γυάλοις, 'governing the famous temple in the vales of Pytho') that make the reader infer the subject and implicitly supply the present sentence with it. Classifying ἑκαταβόλος as an adjective is not without problems: in terms of morphology, a more or less equally good case could be made for seeing it either as a noun or as an adjective. That there is at least some residual ambiguity at play here is implicit in the presentation of the text offered by different editors: Bowra, Turyn, and Puech, prudently, leave

[83] This particular usage of an adjective like αἱματόεσσαι ('bloody', 'covered in blood') raises the question of whether there is a certain slippage between nouns and adjectives. In the expression 'screams full of blood', for instance, does the metonymy attach to the adjectival phrase, 'full of blood', or just to the 'noun', 'blood'? It would seem that, in terms of poetic effect, it is the nominal element in the adjective (*αἱμα*-τόεσσαι) that generates the abrasion felt here, yet it is less clear whether this would be equally true for all adjectives: a nominal element in the adjective is, for instance, fairly visibile in 'blood-y'/ 'blood-covered' or 'resource-ful', but not in 'fast' or 'sweet', which suggests that there may be slippage between nouns and *some* adjectives but not others, or at least that there may be *relatively more* slippage between nouns and some adjectives than others). The question thus shifts to probing the extent to which compound adjectives differ from simplex adjectives; for further discussion of the (as it turns out) limited role that compound formations play for tropical effect, see below, pp. 241–3 and 252. Ultimately, however, while it may well be true that it is (in some cases) a nominal element where the abrasion is felt, it is nonetheless the adjectival reaffiliation through grammatical (in-)congruence that constitutes the mechanism which achieves the abrasive juxtaposition. In other words: the perceived effect may be located at the nominal element, but the mechanism that generates this effect (and constitutes this type of metonymy) remains tied to the adjectival nature of the word.

ἑκαταβόλος uncapitalized, thereby leaving open the possibility to take the word, grammatically speaking, as an adjective—yet Snell-Maehler and Race, for instance, capitalize the word in their editions, thereby indicating that they read it as a proper name and, hence, as a noun. The above suggestion of a shift between the present part of speech (taken to be an adjective) and the one assumed in reading the passage (read as a noun) is made explicit by Slater, who refers to the usage as 'pro subst. as epithet of Apollo',[84] and this use of ἑκαταβόλος as a noun is indeed highly conventional, particularly in the context of ritual invocations where epithets can (and often do) substitute for names. One might nonetheless stop short of considering the word a proper noun (in strictly grammatical terms), given that there is also evidence for usage of the word as qualifying a noun in the manner of an adjective, for instance in Pindar's *Ninth Olympian Ode* or in the Homeric *Hymn to Artemis*:

> ἀλλὰ νῦν ἑκαταβόλων Μοισᾶν ἀπὸ τόξων
>
> but now, from the far-shooting bows of the Muses[85]
>
> ...ὅθ' ἀργυρότοξος Ἀπόλλων
> ἧσται μιμνάζων ἑκατηβόλον Ἰοχέαιραν
>
> ...where silver-bowed Apollo
> sits waiting for the far-shooting pourer of arrows [i.e. Artemis][86]

In these cases, the usage of the word is grammatically consistent with the function and syntactic behaviour of an adjective. At the same time, in terms of poetic effect, the usage of the (potential) adjective ἑκαταβόλος as an epithet for Apollo is so widespread in the epic and hymnic tradition that the impression of straightforward denotation almost eclipses any sense of defamiliarization.[87] However, this instance, along with the Aeschylean example, may serve as a heuristic starting point for a structural analysis of adjective-based defamiliarizations.

In the Aeschylus, then, we have a non-literal reading prompted by an adjective which, in breach of ordinary collocation rules, has shifted its grammatical allegiance from one noun to another within a sentence;[88] in

[84] Slater 1969 s.v. ἑκαταβόλος, 160. [85] Pi. *O.* 9.5; trans. Race.

[86] *h. Hom.* ix. 6; trans. Shelmerdine.

[87] Consider for the Homeric tradition alone the following instances where ἑκαταβόλος is used immediately before the name 'Apollo': *Il.* 1.370, 5.444, 16.711, 17.333, and *Od.* 8.339, 20.278, as well as *H. Apoll.* 134, 140, 215, 222, 229, 239, 277, and *H. Merc.* 234.

[88] In the rhetorical tradition, this phenomenon is usually referred to as 'transferred epithet', 'hypallage', or 'enallage'. I reconsider this poetic language usage in the light of my reflections on metonymy later on in this chapter; see below, pp. 100–21.

the Pindar, a non-literal reading of an adjective as a noun, prompted by the lack of a fully determined noun as subject of the sentence.

The first thing to note is that the tropical status and effect of the adjectives in question depends on nouns. These adjectives (one might say) are only part-tropical in their own right, insofar as they have not changed their semantics compared to their ordinary usage. The assessment of metonymic occurrences in the text corpus has, in fact, not yielded any example of a purely adjective-based index metonymy; that is to say, I know of no instance where a literal reading of an adjective is rendered impossible by its given context (thus marking it as an adjective in tropical usage) and where this abrasive collocation can be reconciled by supplying another adjective, inferred from the present one, that would meet the requirements of collocatability and compatibility with the context and lead to a plausible reading. Instead, it is grammatical deviations of the kind discussed above which constitute non-ordinary (and non-metaphorical) usages of adjectives. In other words, while verbs seem to be structurally precluded from metonymic defamiliarization, adjectives are only to a certain extent open to metonymic shifts—by virtue of their association with nouns. Again, I would argue, this ultimately stems from differences in the way that different parts of speech collocate in ordinary language: adjectives always qualify nouns or, in predicative construction, nouns and verbs, and are therefore, in terms of lexical contiguity, primarily associated with nouns rather than with other adjectives. If several adjectives occur in the same sentence one of two things happens. *Either* they qualify different nouns and then do not semantically engage with each other. Thus, in 'the white sail of the swift ship', 'sail' and 'ship' are in semantic engagement by virtue of the genitive link; 'white' and 'swift', on the other hand, remain entirely unrelated. *Or* they qualify the same noun, but even then are only linked with the noun individually and do not engage with each other, even if linked paratactically. Thus, in 'the swift, old, wooden ship', the ship is qualified as swift *and* old *and* wooden, without any semantic engagement between the adjectives within the sentence. Like verbs, adjectives do not associate with other adjectives, in ordinary language, in the way necessary to create the link of lexical contiguity which is a prerequisite for index metonymy. The connection thereby established between instances of a given part of speech, which is exploited in index metonymy, simply does not exist in verbs and adjectives. It would seem, however, that this specific form of collocation in ordinary language constitutes a necessary though not sufficient requirement for index metonymy: after all, not all nouns that can legitimately occur together in a sentence in ordinary speech form any durable link that can be drawn upon in metonymy. Instead, both the actual regularity of collocation in ordinary language (which facilitates a strengthened pre-existing link) and a capacity for contextual framing (which facilitates a strengthening of the metonymic link by a given context) would seem to be further prerequisites here.

With these principles in mind, how are we to understand the sort of adjective-based deviation seen in the examples above? Are they indeed to be classified as metonymic, and if so, how are we to understand the relationship of noun-based and adjective-based forms of metonymy? To begin with the second example, Pindar's use of ἑκαταβόλος ('far-shooting'): if we assumed a straightforward analogy to noun-based index metonymy, one would expect that in the process of reading this sequence another *adjective* would emerge as a metonymic tenor, inferred from the present one, whose co-presence would lead to a plausible reading of the sequence. But this is not the case. Instead, either an *additional noun* is inferentially supplied ('But you, far-shooting [Apollo],...') or the adjective itself is *read as a noun* (as Race suggests by translating 'But you, Far-shooter,...'). This implicit adjustment of the present term points to tropical usage, and (sure enough) it is based on collocation: the epithet ἑκαταβόλος is so closely associated with Apollo (even if also, to a lesser degree, associated with Artemis) that a pre-existing link exists which can be exploited in metonymical usage. Because of its frequent and specific use as an epithet, the adjective has itself gained, through lexical contiguity, almost the denotative value of a name, and hence virtually assumed the status of a noun. As mentioned earlier, precisely this degree of conventional collocation becomes an issue in assessing the actual tropical status of such usage. For the record: in addition to the passage under discussion there are only two more attested instances where the adjective ἑκαταβόλος is used *without* an accompanying noun and is consequently read as a noun-substitute.[89]

It is worth noting that there are other epithets which likewise suppress and only evoke a proper name. Modern translations tend to give pleonastic paraphrases for these terms by supplying a lordly title ('god of', 'lord of', and the like) and turn the present term into a subordinated genitive attribute, but in Greek poetry the actual usage is often far more

[89] Cf. σοὶ δ' αὐτῷ μελέτω, ἑκατηβόλε, φαίδιμος Ἕκτωρ (*Il.* 15.231; 'And for you yourself, god who strikes from afar [lit.: <the> far-shooting <one/Apollo>], let glorious Hector be your care'; trans. Murray/Wyatt) and ὁ δ' ἐθέλων τε καὶ δυνάμενος ἁβρὰ πάσχειν | τὰν Ἀγαμήδεϊ Τρεφωνίῳ θ' Ἑκαταβόλου | συμβουλίαν λαβών (Pi. *Fr.* 2; 'He who is willing and able to live luxuriously by taking the advice of the Far-Shooter [lit.: <the> far-shooting <one/Apollo>] given to Agamedes and Trephonios'; trans. Race).

compressed, for instance in these two examples from Pindar's *First Olympian Ode*:

> τότ' Ἀγλαοτρίαιναν ἁρπάσαι
> δαμέντα φρένας ἱμέρῳ χρυσέαισί τ' ἀν' ἵπποις
>
> It was then that the Lord of the *Splendid Trident* seized you,
> his mind overcome by desire, and with golden steeds[90]
>
> ... ἐγγὺς ἐλθὼν πολιᾶς ἁλὸς οἶος ἐν ὄρφνᾳ
> ἄπυεν βαρύκτυπον
> *Εὐτρίαιναν* ...
>
> He approached the grey sea alone at night
> And called upon the deep-thundering
> Lord of the *Fine Trident*[91]

Again we are dealing with words that are, grammatically speaking, adjectives but which are uncontroversially used as nouns (since there is no evidence for usage of these terms as adjectives actually qualifying a noun, and in particular no evidence for them qualifying a noun other than the name of the god with whom they are usually associated). In a sense, such epithets that suppress the proper name, both the quasi-nouns here and the adjective above, are metonymic and resemble index metonymy; yet one would be reluctant to call them tropical because they impinge as conventional literary clichés and lack the sense of abrasiveness which is characteristic of tropical, defamiliarizing usage.[92]

There are, however, cases of adjective-based defamiliarization which follow the same mechanisms as discussed here for ἑκαταβόλος but are less clichéd. Consider the following passage from Pindar's *Second Olympian Ode*:

[90] Pi. *O.* 1.40–2; trans. Race. [91] Pi. *O.* 1.71–3; trans. Race.

[92] Although both terms are *hapax legomena*, the principle behind the formation of these two compounds connects them with other, more widely used epithets of Poseidon: ὀρσοτρίαινα ('wielder of the trident', cf. Pi. *O.* 8.48, *P.* 2.12, *N.* 4.86, *Pae.* 9.47) and χρυσοτρίαινος ('with golden trident', cf. Arion 939.2 *PMG* and Ar. *Eq.* 559). In the majority of these instances, the grammatical adjective is used as if a noun, that is to say, it stands in its own right without qualifying a governing noun; the exceptions are Pi. *P.* 2.12, where the adjective qualifies θεόν, and Arion *loc. cit.*, which is the only instance where a τριαινα-compound adjective appears in direct collocation with the name 'Poseidon'—in all other cases, the name of the god is only implied. The available evidence thus suggests that these terms virtually denote Poseidon. Ancient rhetoricians classify usage of this type as 'antonomasia'; see, for instance, Trypho, *Trop.* 757, 24–30 or Quint. *Inst.* 8.6.29–30. The value of this category is doubtful: on the one hand, we are dealing with metonymic shifts and this separate category does not add to our understanding of the mechanism or the poetic effects of the phenomena it includes; on the other hand, such antonomasia is by definition confined to literary clichés and as such does not describe tropical but ordinary, albeit elevated, usage.

λείφθη δὲ Θέρσανδρος ἐριπέντι Πολυνείκει, *νέοις* ἐν ἀέθλοις
ἐν μάχαις τε πολέμου
τιμώμενος...

but Thersandros, who survived the fallen Polyneikes, gained honor
in *youthful* contests
And in the battles of war...[93]

Contests cannot literally be called νέοι ('young, youthful') in ordinary language (unless they were 'newly' established, which is ruled out by the context), but those participating in them can be called 'young'. As with ἑκαταβόλος, an implicit change in grammatical form and status of the present term is involved, namely a shift from actual dative to implied genitive and an implied shift from adjective to noun: νέων ἐν ἀέθλοις ('in contests of young [ones; i.e. of youths, young men]'). Such a reading is then reinforced by the next phrase, which in parallel structure (note the connection with τε) offers a sequence of the same type that conforms with ordinary usage (note that πολέμου is a noun in the genitive case).

Similar in structure is the poetic usage of an adjective in the following verses from the description of the sacrifice of Iphigenia in Aeschylus' *Agamemnon*:

λιτὰς δὲ καὶ κληδόνας *πατρῴους*
παρ' οὐδὲν αἰῶνα παρθένειον τ'
ἔθεντο φιλόμαχοι βραβῆς

Her pleas, her cries of *'father!'* [lit: her *fatherly* cries]
and her maiden years, were set at naught
by the war-loving chieftains[94]

Comparable prose constructions that express such exclamations have the exclaimed word as a noun in the genitive case.[95] Instead, this passage has the exclamation as an adjective in the accusative case, πατρῴους ('fatherly'), where in ordinary usage one could expect τοῦ πατρός ('of [the] father').[96] While the adjustment of the case of an exclamation

[93] Pi. *O.* 2.43–5; trans. Race. [94] A. *Agam.* 228–30; trans. Sommerstein.

[95] 'The commentators seem uneasy: Fraenkel states that πατρῴους "to some extent [represents] an objective genitive", but Page's remark, "an extraordinary expression for 'her cries of "father"', shows a better understanding. Syntactically, κλῇδων functions here like ὄνομα, to which a prose writer could add a suitable word in the genitive case, e.g. τὸ μέγα ὄνομα τῶν Ἀθηνῶν (Thuc. 7.64). The point here is that the Aeschylean expression would be easily understood by an audience for whom the adjective had a particularly strong association with the genitive case of the noun.' Bers 1974, 38.

[96] An alternative translation of κληδόνας πατρῴους that would follow Fraenkel's perception of the adjective as used *in lieu* of an objective genitive not denoting an exclamation would be 'her invocations of her father'. What matters for my argument here is that on this reading, too, it is a *noun* that emerges from the metonymically used

to fit a sentence's grammar appears to be permissible in ordinary usage,[97] the use of an adjective here in lieu of a noun is clearly poetic. Once again, a reading that seeks to make sense of this use of the adjective does not lead to the emergence of another adjective as a suitable metonymic tenor but to a shift in the case and grammatical status of the present adjective-based metonymic vehicle.

A MATTER OF GRAMMAR AND SHIFTING ALLEGIANCES: ENALLAGE AND/AS METONYMY

Deviations of this type, that is, deviations based on changes in grammatical status and syntactic dependency, have been discussed by ancient rhetoricians (and modern scholars) under various headings, but where adjectives are concerned the discussion has centred on 'enallage', 'hypallage', and 'transferred epithet'. As so often in tropology, variations in terminology have led to more confusion than differentiation: terminological usage is often unclear or inconsistent or changes from writer to writer. Thus, for the Greek rhetoricians, hypallage seems to denote a completely unrelated figure of postpositive correction and clarification,[98] while Cicero, remarkably enough, uses the term ὑπαλλαγή in his *Orator* as a technical term for noun-based metonymy, thereby providing a first, albeit perfectly arbitrary, indication that these adjective-based phenomena should indeed be understood as metonymic types.[99] Apollonius Dyscolus appears to be the first to highlight the grammatical nature of such shifts by speaking of ἐναλλαγὴ πτώσεως ('enallage of the case').[100] Modern scholars tend to refer to the syntactic reorientation of adjectives

adjective, and not another adjective (though the frequency with which comparable expressions occur in poetry would then suggest elevated poetic usage rather than an instance of striking poetic heightening).

[97] Groeneboom on A. *Agam.* 47–54.

[98] Zonaeus' definition is representative: Ὑπαλλαγή ἐστιν, ὅταν ἐπιτιμήσαντες τῷ ὀνόματι ἕτερον προσλάβωμεν, οἷον 'οὐκ ἔστι τοῦτο φιλανθρωπία, ἀλλ' ἔρως', καὶ 'οὐκ ὠργίζετο, ἀλλ' ἐμαίνετο.' (Zonae. *Fig.*, 689, 7–10; 'Hypallage occurs whenever, by way of objecting to a word, we add another one to it as in "it is not philanthropy, it is desire," and "he was not angry, he was furious"'); in Alex. *Fig.* 486, 21–31 and Anon. *Fig.* 712, 22–7, though seemingly based on Zonaeus' examples and definition, the term seems to indicate metonymy.

[99] A connection of this adjective-based phenomenon with metonymy is also suggested by Genette, who describes the expression 'le papier *coupable* de Boileau' ('the *guilty* paper of Boileau') as 'hypallage métonymique' (Genette 1970b, 156; italics in the original). The nature and modalities of the connection between metonymy and hypallage/enallage, however, remain unexplained.

[100] See A. D. *Pron.* 54.13.

as *enallage adiectivi* or *hypallage adiectivi*.[101] Landfester summarizes the current *communis opinio* in the following definition:

> Enallage/hypallage of the adjective. Enallage consists in the relocation of an adjective away from a genitive attribute to the governing noun. As an important aesthetic means of defamiliarization it is particularly prominent in Greek lyric (Pindar) and tragedy; it abounds in the tragedies of Euripides. It became naturalized in Latin poetic language under the influence of the Greek model: νεῖκος ἀνδρῶν ξύναιμον ('kindred strife of men'), instead of: νεῖκος ἀνδρῶν ξυναίμων ('strife of kindred men'), Soph. *Ant.* 793f.; *iratos* <...> *regum apices* ('irate helmets of kings'), instead of: *iratorum regum apices* ('helmets of irate kings'), Hor. *Carm.* 3, 21, 19f.[102]

In order to assess whether such 'adjective-based defamiliarizings' are indeed a form of metonymy, we can now take into account the potential of different parts of speech to form metonymy, and the way adjectives relate to nouns. That is to say, it appears that we must focus on the nouns upon which one has to draw in order to arrive at a reading that semantically rectifies the abrasive breach of ordinary collocation rules which these adjectives effect.

This way of approaching the issue presents us with two different types of adjective-based defamiliarization. In the first type, the noun qualified by the tropical adjective is entirely absent (or can only be found, virtually, in the tropical adjective), as in Pindar's ἑκαταβόλε, 'far-shooting' ([ἑκαταβόλε <Ἀπόλλωνα>], 'far-shooting <one/Apollo>'), and νέοις ἐν ἀέθλοις, 'in young contests' ([ἐν ἀέθλοις νέων], 'in contests of young <ones/men>'), or in Aeschylus' κληδόνας πατρῴους, 'fatherly cries' ([κληδόνας < πατρός >], 'cries <of "Father!">'/'invocations <of her father>'). In the second type, the noun qualified by the tropical adjective is present in the microcontext but is dissociated from the adjective by a lack of grammatical agreement, as in Aeschylus' βλαχαὶ δ' αἱματόεσσαι τῶν ἐπιμαστιδίων, 'blood-covered screams of infants' ([βλαχαὶ δ' <αἱματοέσσων> τῶν ἐπιμαστιδίων], 'screams of blood-covered infants'), and Sophocles'

[101] For proponents of both usages see Lausberg 1960, 306.

[102] 'Enallage/Hypallage des Adjektivs. Die Enallage besteht in der Versetzung eines Adjektivs von einem Genitivattribut zum regierenden Nomen. Als ein wichtiges ästhetisches Mittel der Verfremdung ist sie vor allem für die griechische Lyrik (Pindar) und Tragödie charakteristisch; in den Tragödien des Euripides wuchert sie geradezu. In den lateinischen Dichtersprachen ist sie unter dem Eindruck des Griechischen heimisch geworden: νεῖκος ἀνδρῶν ξύναιμον (der blutsverwandte Streit der Männer), statt: νεῖκος ἀνδρῶν ξυναίμων (der Streit blutsverwandter Männer), Soph. Ant. 793f.; *iratos* <...> *regum apices* (die zornigen Helme der Könige), statt: *iratorum regum apices* (die Helme der zornigen Könige), Hor. carm. 3, 21, 19f.' Landfester 1997, 112.

τόδε νεῖκος ἀνδρῶν ξύναιμον, 'this kindred strife of men' ([τόδε νεῖκος ἀνδρῶν <ξυναίμων>], 'this strife of kindred men'). In the first type, the governing noun which the tropical adjective would qualify in ordinary usage is inferred from the adjective and implicitly supplied; in the second type, the tropical adjective's abrasiveness follows from the shift of grammatical allegiance within the present sequence which is reversed in the hermeneutic process of reading such occurrences.

If we compare these findings with the now established categories of noun-based metonymy, index metonymy, and amplification metonymy, we must surely acknowledge that the resemblance between the two categories of noun-based metonymy and the two types of adjective-based metonymy is striking. In noun-based index metonymy, just as in the first type of adjective-based metonymy, a noun emerges as metonymic tenor and virtually supplements the present tropical term (for adjectives this includes the possibility of the adjective itself becoming this metonymic tenor by changing its part of speech and becoming a noun). In noun-based amplification metonymy, just as in the second type of adjective-based metonymy, all the elements for a literal reading are available in the sequence as it stands, but an intrasequential shift occurs: in noun-based amplification metonymy, a shift into over-specification within the semantic field of the noun in the genitive case which, if it stood on its own in a different syntactic position, would pass as literal usage in ordinary language; in adjective-based metonymy, a shift of grammatical allegiance on the part of the adjective, away from a present noun which one would expect to be its governing noun in ordinary usage. It seems clear that the same phenomenon is occurring here, modified only by the inherent differences between these two parts of speech: the dependency of adjectives on nouns in order to exercise metonymic defamiliarization contrasts with their incapacity to do so in and of themselves.

These theoretical reflections find their vindication in the most extensive study of 'enallage' in Greek literature to date, offered by Bers, and also allow us to take his theorization of the phenomenon further.[103] Bers's approach to enallage is largely that of a historical linguist and textual scholar; the discussion of poetic effects is given significantly less attention. A methodological difficulty arises when historical linguistics and literary criticism are conflated, as is the case when Bers speculates about the 'origin', 'history', and 'development' of enallage:

[103] Bers 1974.

If my theory on the origin of enallage is correct, the non-possessive type arose directly by analogical imitation of the syntactical form, through an intermediate type employing an adjective whose meaning was both possessive and descriptive, or by a combination of these developments.[104]

Such claims imply a problematic notion of tropes as historically contingent phenomena that develop organically and are constructed and willed into being by poets in the course of the development of a language. While it is certainly true that individual tropes may gain greater prominence at different times in the literary culture of any given language, tropes are properly seen as possibilities of defamiliarization inherent in language. They are ahistorical in the sense that they embody structural patterns of defamiliarization which may or may not pertain to a specific language at a specific stage of its development, but (unlike, say phonetic or morphological features of a language) tropes do not 'develop' by themselves.[105]

With these qualifications and caveats in mind we can profitably assess the value of Bers's study for the aims pursued here. The main thrust of his argument is that (*a*) enallage is indeed a tropical phenomenon and not just a function of ordinary usage in ancient Greek, and that (*b*) enallage is an archaizing device which is connected with syntactically conservative contexts and 'originated' in the coexistence of possessive adjective and genitive in the early stages of the Greek language. Moving on from these arguments, Bers surveys a broad range of enallages in Pindar and the tragedians, but confines himself to defending these passages against attempts by commentators and textual critics to emend or deny the tropicality of these passages. In these attempts to see enallage as a phenomenon of *ordinary* language, Bers extrapolates a succession of theoretical positions and disproves them on grounds of demonstrable deviance from ordinary usage. While rightly rejected by Bers, these attempts are nonetheless revealing for my purposes, since they shed light on different reading strategies designed to make sense of the non-ordinary usage that occurs in these instances. Bers's first

[104] Bers 1974, 27.

[105] Likewise, it does not appear helpful to speculate on stylistic or metrical restraints if one is seeking to illuminate the aesthetics of poetic language. Note, for instance, Bers's remark that 'enallage allows a poet to accumulate adjectives without resorting to an ungainly crowd of genitive endings', Bers 1974, 51; an earlier study on enallage by Headlam also approaches the topic largely from the perspectives of historical linguistics and textual criticism and is troubled by the same methodological problems, as Headlam's opening sentence already shows: 'Transference of epithets was *in its origin* a *metrical device* for dealing conveniently with proper names, especially geographical' (Headlam 1902, 434; italics added).

observation is that enallage is particularly prone to normalizing emendation by scribes and textual critics, which confirms the general tendency to re-align grammatical allegiance of deviant adjectives as outlined above. More interestingly, Bers discusses critically what he calls 'the "compound" theory', according to which 'many apparent instances of enallage are explained as noun + adjective combinations in which the two substantives have merged into an *ad hoc* "compound"'.[106] Bers successfully shows that the use of adjectives in ordinary language disproves this theory as well as the hypothesis of enallage as a mere attraction of case (as ordinarily occurs in relative pronouns). Yet although he demonstrates that such reaffiliation of the adjective is indeed tropical, we should not entirely dismiss other critics' impression of a felt 'compound' effect in such passages.[107] It is right to insist with Bers that the adjective's reaffiliation constitutes an abrasive shift, and is therefore tropical; however, it is worth noting that this is a shift within a semantic unit—and therefore not unlike the shift within a semantic field that characterizes noun-based metonymy, either within a virtual semantic field (as in index metonymy) or, even more clearly, within the present semantic unit (as in amplification metonymy).

Interestingly, the analogy between the two types of noun-based and adjective-based metonymy suggested here also finds support in Bers's study. Bers proposes a clear distinction between 'enallage', 'quasi-enallage', and 'transferred epithet'. He confines enallage to

> the transfer of a term to the governing substantive of an adjective which by logic, or at least convention, belongs with *an expressed* dependent genitive... Phrases in which the inflections do not satisfy this definition, though the semantical outcome is similar, will be called 'quasi-enallages'.[108]

Bers justifies this differentiation with reference to the frequency of occurrence in (Greek) poetry:

> Examples in which the writer includes the word from which the adjective is transferred but puts the noun in a case other than the genitive... are... very rare. The switch in concord of adjective away from the genitive is so much more frequent that we are entitled to select precisely this inflectional category as the distinguishing feature of a discrete phenomenon in Greek.[109]

While this quantitative difference is undoubtedly noteworthy, it does not seem to warrant the presumption of a qualitative difference, a difference in kind, in respect of the defamiliarizing usage of adjectives under

[106] Bers 1974, 5. [107] See Bers 1974, 5–8.
[108] Bers 1974, 1; italics added. [109] Bers 1974, 2–3.

discussion here. Consider for instance some further examples from Aeschylus' *Agamemnon* in the light of those discussed above:

> ... μηδὲ βαρβάρου φωτὸς δίκην
> *χαμαιπετὲς* βόαμα προσχάνῃς ἐμοί
>
> do not *fall on the ground* before me and utter open-mouthed cries
> in the manner of a barbarian
> [lit.: do not, in the manner of a barbarian, open your mouth to me
> with a cry *that falls to the ground*][110]

For this usage, Denniston and Page give the following interpretation: '"fallen on the ground" suggests that the poet thought of his Clytemnestra as actually prostrating herself, with oriental προσκύνησις, in Agamemnon's path'.[111] On this interpretation, the adjective χαμαιπετές ('falling on the ground') is transferred away from Clytemnestra, that is, from the subject in the nominative as implicit in the predicate. Compare a sequence uttered by Clytemnestra herself earlier in the same play:

> ἐν *ὀψικοίτοις* δ' ὄμμασιν βλάβας ἔχω
>
> I have damaged those eyes *by lying awake*
> [lit.: I have damage in my eyes *that go to sleep late*][112]

Again it is Clytemnestra, the subject, who goes to sleep late and the transfer of the adjective to the dative of ὄμμασιν ('eyes') is a transfer away from an implicit nominative.

That another mode of analysis is required becomes all the more obvious as soon as one widens one's perspective and examines instances of transferred adjectives in languages other than Greek, where the spread of the cases of the nouns involved is not as heavily centred on the genitive case as appears to be the case in Greek. Consider the following two examples from Hölderlin's poetry, the first from his poem 'Im Walde', the second taken from 'Griechenland':

> Aber in Hütten wohnet der Mensch, und hüllet
> Sich ein ins *verschämte Gewand* ...
>
> But man lives in huts, and wraps himself
> Into *bashful garments* ...[113]
>
> Und die schönste der Begeisterungen
> Lächelte vom *trunknen Auge* dir
>
> And the most beautiful enthusiasm
> Smiled from your *drunken eye*[114]

[110] A. *Agam.* 919–20; trans. Sommerstein.
[111] Denniston/Page *ad loc.*
[112] A. *Agam.* 889; trans. Sommerstein.
[113] Hölderlin, 'Im Walde', 1–2.
[114] Hölderlin, 'Griechenland', 19–20.

In the first case, the transfer of 'verschämte' ('bashful') is from the subject of the sentence, 'Mensch' ('man'), to his garments, 'Gewand'; in the second, the transfer of 'trunknen' ('drunk') is from the person in the dative ('dir') to that person's eye.[115] It is evident, however, that, despite the difference in language and cases involved, the mechanism and effect of these transferred adjectives is essentially the same as in the Greek examples involving nouns in genitive. It follows that there are no grounds for any categorical differentiation of transferred adjectives based on grammatical case.[116]

Accordingly, I am inclined to abandon Bers's inflection-based distinction between 'enallage' (transferred adjective involving a noun in the genitive) and 'quasi-enallage' (transferred adjective involving a noun in a case other than the genitive). However, his differentiation between enallage and quasi-enallage on the one hand, and 'transferred epithets' on the other, is more illuminating. By 'transferred epithet', Bers refers to usages like Euripides, *Alcestis*, v. 261, ὀφρύσι κυαναυγέσι ('dark-gleaming eyebrows'), where the epithet is 'more naturally used of the eyes [which are not specified as such] than of the brows'.[117] Bers adds:

[115] '[T]runknen' ('drunk') itself is used metaphorically: the 'you' is not literally 'drunk' but filled with an enthusiasm that is intoxicating and exhilarating *like* wine. However, in addition to the metaphorical usage, the adjective is also shifted away from its proper noun: persons, as present in the pronoun 'dir' ('you'), can be drunk, eyes cannot. Note also the metonymic singular-for-plural of 'Auge' ('eye') which implies both eyes while pointing to the facial expression as a whole. For a more detailed discussion specifically dedicated to the complications that arise from clusters of interacting tropical usages, see below, pp. 123–34. A further metaphorical element in this sequence is the personification of 'Begeisterung' ('enthusiam') through the attribution of human agency via the verb 'lächelte' ('smiled'); on personification as metaphor, see below, pp. 147–54.

[116] Speculations on an affinity, historical or structural, between the wide-ranging semantics of the Greek genitive and the Greek adjective are for the same reasons unlikely to lead to a better understanding of the phenomenon of transferred adjectives as such. Bers draws on this debate in his own discussion, in particular on the claims in Wackernagel 1908 for the historical precedence of the possessive adjective over the genitive case, a view rejected by Miller who nevertheless holds that the 'genitive and the relational adjective are identical in semantic content' (Miller 1969, 150, as cited in Bers 1974, 21). This 'identity in semantic content' refers to the similarity between adjective-based qualifications and some functions of the genitive in denoting the sphere, milieu, or environment in which a noun is placed (see Palmer 1962, 132–4, and, more generally, Meillet/Vendryes 1927, 510). Yet even if such a similarity between the semantic scope of the Greek genitive and the Greek adjective exists, this would prove only that, as elements involved in a transfer within a given sequence, they are more akin to one another; it would not explain the actual mechanism or poetic effects of that transfer.

[117] Dale, cited by Bers 1974, 1.

in the first [*sc.* enallage/quasi-enallage], a poet transfers an adjective away from *a word which appears in the utterance*, he places far greater emphasis on the manipulation than if he *omits the word* to which the adjective belongs in ordinary language, as in the second [*sc.* transferred epithet]. One way he compels the audience to notice the *switch*; the other he permits them to understand the phrase as being a *metaphor* of the usual type, viz. that in which the literal meaning is implicit.[118]

Once more, 'enallage' (including 'quasi-enallage') emerges as the adjective-based counterpart of amplification metonymy: the tropical effect of both depends on a modification that involves a noun which is *present* in the sequence and drawn upon to resolve the abrasiveness caused by this deviance from ordinary usage; no inference of a noun as metonymic tenor is required. 'Transferred epithets', on the other hand, just like index metonymy, prompt the supplementation of the sequence in question with an *inferred* noun as metonymic tenor.

GRAMMATICAL METONYMY: TYPES, AESTHETICS, AND POETIC EFFECTS

I propose that we refer to all these adjective-based phenomena collectively as *grammatical metonymy*. This seems appropriate given that the characteristic shift of metonymy manifests itself in this category as a grammar-based shift.[119] At the same time, it seems advisable to maintain a significant subdivision into *grammatical index metonymy* (metonymic adjectives which point to nouns that need to be inferred, or become the inferred noun themselves by changing their grammatical status), and *grammatical amplification metonymy* (metonymic adjectives which

[118] Bers 1974, 2; italics added. On the surprising reference to metaphor in this context, cf. below, pp. 109–11.

[119] In suggesting this term, I also draw on Jakobson's differentiation between 'lexical tropes' and 'grammatical tropes and figures' (Jakobson 1960, 375). While Jakobson does not elaborate this distinction further, he rightly observes that '[t]he poetic resources concealed in the morphological and syntactic structure of language, briefly the poetry of grammar, and its literary product, the grammar of poetry, have been seldom known to critics and mostly disregarded by linguists but skilfully mastered by creative writers' (Jakobson 1960, 375). Metonymy, as discussed here, subsumes both grammatical and lexical variants, depending on whether the characteristic metonymic shift is based on grammar or lexis. On this basis, we note that (*a*) the potential and relevance of grammar for metonymy further undermines any substitutionalist understanding which is inevitably restricted to lexis, and that (*b*) the resources for defamiliarization provided by syntax are not limited to facilitating figurative usage (a notion implicit in Jakobson 1968, 602) but tropical usage too.

amplify the intensity of a sequence by shifting their grammatical allegiance within a semantic unit).

On the basis of these structural observations on grammatical metonymy, we can analyse its aesthetics in greater detail. The two critics cited on 'enallage' comment only briefly on its poetic effects. In the passage just quoted, Bers initially observes that in grammatical amplification metonymy, the transfer of the adjective between elements present in the sequence 'compels the audience to notice the *switch*'. However, he then associates grammatical index metonymy with metaphor, arguing that it will prompt readers 'to understand the phrase as being a *metaphor* of the usual type, viz. that in which the literal meaning is implicit'. These remarks are both problematic and unsatisfying. In the first place, for a reader to notice the occurrence of a 'switch' in grammatical amplification metonymy means no more than awareness of (the mechanism behind) this device, but it does not fully describe its poetic effect(s). The insufficiency of such analysis is similar to the shortcomings of the now outdated notion of metaphor as mere 'embellishment' and 'replacement': while the reader of a metaphor surely notices that the present word is not the/a word which one would expect in ordinary usage, the poetic effects of metaphor are hardly explained by this. Likewise, the 'switch' that occurs in grammatical amplification metonymy surely characterizes this trope, but this says little about the aesthetic consequences. Secondly, when Bers describes the reading strategy prompted by grammatical index metonymy as understanding it 'as being a metaphor', he is evidently using 'metaphor' (like Aristotle) in the broad, undifferentiating sense of 'tropical, non-literal'. After all, in grammatical index metonymy, there is clearly no element of similarity or analogy which would be a prerequisite for metaphor. Instead, the way 'in which the literal meaning is implicit' is not characterized by logic—but by lexical contiguity.

Compare and contrast Bers's initial assessment with Headlam's suggestions on how to understand the aesthetic effects of 'enallage'. Headlam quotes the 'bloody screams' (βλαχαὶ... *αἱματοέσσαι*) at Aeschylus, *Seven Against Thebes*, v. 348, and remarks that

> [t]he inaccurate attachment of the epithets has that further value that I spoke of, producing an effect intentionally confused, *impressionistic*. Infants at their mothers' breast, besmeared with blood, and passionately crying in their bleating voice; if you wish to convey the impression vaguely flashed upon the eye and ear, you dab the various colours in among the substantives.[120]

[120] Headlam 1902, 435; italics in the original.

In a similar vein, he cites a choral passage from Aeschylus' *Persians* to support this characterization:

> ὀτοτοτοῖ, φίλων
> ἁλίδονα μέλεα *πολυβαφῆ*
> κατθανόντα λέγεις φέρεσθαι
> *πλαγκτοῖς* ἐν διπλάκεσσι.
>
> Otototoi, you are saying
> that the dead limbs of our loved ones,
> are floating, dipped in the sea and *dyed in many colours*,
> In their *wandering* cloaks.[121]

And he comments:

> The sober sense is ἁλίδονα μέλεα καταθανόντα λέγεις φέρεσθαι πλαγκτὰ ἐν πολυβαφέσι διπλάκεσσι; but this is one of those pictorial descriptions; their imagination shows them dead and mangled limbs tossed on the waves adrift in many-coloured garments; and the scattered way in which they jot the details in conveys the impression more effectively than if it were more accurately phrased.[122]

Although sharing Headlam's appreciation of the passage from *Seven Against Thebes*, Bers rejects his generalization about the effect of enallage on that basis. Bers maintains that 'this enallage is among the most startling and impressive in Greek: the impressionistic effect is not characteristic'.[123] Whereas Headlam's description of these poetic effects points us to the passage as a whole, Bers's own analysis of the effect of 'enallage' in general is centred on the reading of the tropical adjective itself:

> Enallage bridges the figurative and prosaic. The effect is paradoxical. On the one hand, if a reader or listener takes an enallage literally, i.e. if he follows the grammatical concord and fails to notice the transfer, he is forced to make metaphorical sense of the expression, find an *ad hoc* logical relation between the adjective and noun in agreement, or remain baffled. On the other, if he detects enallage he can perceive the prosaic sense at once, and so is in danger of leaving his poetic faculty unexercised... The majority of modern readers... either follow the grammar without observing... a problem, or they transfer the adjective back to the genitive and regard the standard expression and the deviation as equivalents.[124]

[121] A. *Pers.* 274–7. Headlam's reconstruction of the passage largely follows the manuscripts, whereas e.g. Sommerstein accepts Prien's emendation of 277 (my changes to Sommerstein's translation as provided in the text reflect this); this textual complication, however, does not affect the point: the passage, as Headlam takes it, contains the phenomenon under discussion. Sommerstein's editorial decision nevertheless reminds us of Bers's remark about the vulnerability of enallage to emendation.

[122] Headlam 1902, 435.

[123] Bers 1974, 52.

[124] Bers 1974, 3. Note, again, the imprecise, broad usage of 'metaphorical'.

The two critics' positions, however, are not as far away from each other as they may seem to be at first. After all, the two reading acts that Bers constructs in his analysis as 'either-or' are, in fact, simultaneous: it is precisely the simultaneity of (*a*) a possible literal reading based solely on terms present in the sequence and requiring only the smallest grammatical rectification *and* (*b*) the startling, abrasive, illegitimate collocation that produces the 'paradoxical' effect and leads to the impression of a hovering between literal and tropical usage. While Bers arguably goes too far in drawing such a black-and-white distinction (*either* a baffling, tropical reading *or* an unnoticed, rectified literal one), his observation points in the right direction: the intensity of the tropical effect of grammatical metonymy does not lie in the adjective itself but in the nature of its interaction with the context. That is to say, once the adjective has been shifted away from its corresponding noun in ordinary language, *different effects* can occur (depending on the nouns involved) which determine how the adjective and the nouns in question themselves are read. In other words, in grammatical metonymy we find the tropical effect depending on context in the same way as with the two forms of noun-based metonymy: the poetic effect does not occur, as is the case in metaphor, within the tropical word or compound, but in the new potential for interaction between the tropically used word and its context.

This issue of context-dependency is important for the broader question of the multi-, bi-, or monopolar structure of the tropical space. In the passages just discussed, Bers associates the effect of 'enallage' with metaphor, and he is not the only one to do so: by its very title ('Metaphor, with a Note on Transference of Epithets'), as also by its juxtaposition of analyses of metaphors and 'enallages', Headlam's article suggests a certain relatedness of the two—although he never explicitly makes a connection between them. Among more recent critics, Richards, despite some initial reluctance, draws on enallages to develop his theory of metaphorical interaction.[125] Brooke-Rose, too, while acknowledging that in many cases a transfer of the adjective is taking place, nevertheless

[125] See Richards 1936, 106–8. Richards discusses the examples 'giddy brink', 'jovial wine', and 'daring wound' taken from the eighteenth-century rhetorician Kames. He notes the 'impressionistic' squashing that takes place as well as the lack of metaphorical analogy behind these terminological juxtapositions but eventually drops such caveats and proceeds, without real explanation, to subsume the phenomenon under metaphor: '... we may doubt for a moment whether there is metaphor here at all—until we notice how this whirling that infects the world as we grow giddy comes to it by a process which is itself radically metaphorical.' Richards 1936, 108.

discusses various examples of enallage as metaphors in her chapter on adjective-based metaphor.[126] Williger, however, is more cautious, arguing that

> the ... exchange of terms, the ... artificial interlacing with an expression is more related to metaphor. At best, enallage has in common with it that both phenomena presuppose the possibility of constructing words purely grammatically while leaving their logical relation open to guesswork.[127]

Are there any good reasons for these critics' association of transferred adjectives with metaphor? Or does their unquestioned and unexplained association of this form of deviant expression with metaphor merely reflect the modern bias of literary critics towards metaphor as the ultimate trope beyond and behind all other tropes? Williger's and Bers's assessments implicitly point to the crucial interface from which poetic effects of 'enallage' emerge: it is the constructive potential stemming from the unexpected collocation of the transferred adjective and its new corresponding noun. To understand the poetic effects of grammatical metonymy, we must understand the different kinds of interaction that can occur at this interface. My argument suggests that in addition to the *primary metonymic shift*, which is felt as *a poetic effect in its own right*, the increased potential for engagement with the context caused by the transfer of the adjective can trigger *several different types of secondary effects*: it can engender *metonymic readings of neighbouring terms*, it can lead to *metaphorical interaction*, it can cause *ambivalence* within the sequence, and it can produce effects of *verbal collage*.

According to Bers's assessment above, 'enallage' leads either to a purely literal reading following the rectification of the adjective-based grammatical deviation or to a metaphorical reading ('forced to make metaphorical sense of the impression') or to a collapse of the hermeneutic process ('remain baffled'). It remains unclear whether he takes the reading strategy of finding 'an *ad hoc* logical relation between the adjective and noun in agreement' as a further explanation of the process of making metaphorical sense (implying perception of analogy or similarity), or as an additional, separate reading strategy (perhaps erroneously assuming other kinds of logical relation as constitutive for

[126] 'Besides being often very verbal, many of these are in fact simple transfers from one mentioned or unmentioned part of the sentence to an object': Brooke-Rose 1958, 240; for her full discussion of adjective metaphor see ibid., 240–9.

[127] 'die ... Vertauschung der Begriffe, die ... künstliche Verschränkung des Ausdrucks, die eher der Metapher verwandt ist. Mit ihr hat die Enallage allenfalls das gemeinsam, daß bei beiden Erscheinungen die Möglichkeit vorausgesetzt wird, die Worte rein grammatisch zu konstruieren und ihren logischen Zusammenhang erraten zu lassen.' Williger 1928, 11.

metonymy). Although he concedes that 'in the vast majority of examples one can make some sense of the adjective taken with the governing substantive',[128] he does assume that there are cases in which a literal reading of the transferred adjective in collocation with its new governing noun is entirely impossible, as it would lead to a meaningless, nonsensical expression: 'Occasionally the literal reading of an enallage makes the expression meaningless, as in Aesch. *Ag*[*am*]. 504: δεκάτῳ ... φέγγει ... ἔτους.'[129]

This last example belongs to a verse from Aeschylus' *Agamemnon*, which is often emended by editors:

> δεκάτῳ σε φέγγει τῷδε ἀφικόμην ἔτους
>
> on this *tenth* daylight of the year I have come back[130]

The broader context of the Achaeans' return from Troy makes it clear that the speaker (the herald) is talking about the long-awaited day of return in the tenth year of the Trojan expedition, and the reader will quickly mitigate the grammatical affiliation of δεκάτῳ accordingly. Yet is Bers right to assume that the collocation δεκάτῳ ... φέγγει is 'meaningless' and merely leaves the reader 'baffled'? In the course of a linear reading of the verse, there appears to be interaction between the adjective and its new corresponding noun: one will be inclined to read φέγγει, 'daylight', as an index metonym, and hence as 'day', and this reading is prompted not least by the numeral δεκάτῳ, 'tenth', which is essential in creating an abrasive collocation with φέγγει, thus giving it MV status and co-defining the MT. The metonymic reading that emerges, of course, still leaves the genitive ἔτους, 'of [the] year', unintegrated, so that the continuing reading process will entail a realignment of the deviantly used adjective. Nevertheless, in its tropical position, δεκάτῳ exercises a semantic function in emphasizing and delineating the metonymic usage of one of the two nouns of the semantic unit to which the transfer of the adjective belongs. A similar interaction occurs in the lines from Hölderlin's poem 'Gesang des Deutschen', discussed in a previous chapter:

> Wenn Platons *frommer* Garten auch schon nicht mehr
> Am alten Strome grünt ...
>
> Even if Plato's *pious* garden no longer
> blossoms by the old stream ...

[128] Bers 1974, 3. [129] Bers 1974, 3.

[130] A. *Agam.* 504, with the manuscript reading, rather than Jacob's emendation of δεκάτου for δεκάτῳ, accepted by e.g. Sommerstein and Page, which does away with the enallage.

Within the semantic unit 'Platons frommer Garten' ('Plato's pious garden'), 'fromm' ('pious') is undoubtedly closer to 'Plato' than to 'garden' in terms of the collocation rules of ordinary language; accordingly, we see this as an instance of enallage. And though 'pious garden' may be literally nonsensical, the collocation (rather than leaving the reader 'baffled') triggers an index metonymic reading of 'garden' as already discussed.[131] While the Aeschylean example represents a case of grammatical amplification metonymy (the numeral has suffered a shift, but the noun which it would qualify in ordinary usage is present in the sequence), in the Hölderlin it is less obvious that 'frommer' ('pious') has been shifted away from 'Platon's' ('Plato's'); the two words are closer in ordinary usage, but the context of the passage, in particular the subsequent index metonym, makes it difficult to ascertain whether the adjective literally qualifies the metonymic tenor of its corresponding, tropically used noun or has been transferred away from 'Plato'. In another *Agamemnon* passage, on the other hand, a grammatical index metonym, arguably, involves a degree of metonymic cross-fertilization:

> εὖτ' ἂν δὲ *νυκτίπλαγκτον* ἔνδροσόν τ' ἔχω
> εὐνὴν ὀνείροις οὐκ ἐπισκοπουμένην
>
> But while I keep this night-walker's bed, wet with dew,
> [lit.: But while I keep this bed *that causes wandering at night* wet with dew],
> This bed of mine not watched over by dreams[132]

νυκτίπλαγκτον, 'causing to wander by night, rousing from the bed', appears to be an Aeschylean coinage as it does not occur anywhere outside of his plays. In the three other instances of its occurrence, however, it is used to qualify a task, experience, or action which brings this state about.[133] If we take this as the word's 'ordinary' usage, then the

[131] See above, pp. 69–72. [132] A. *Agam.* 12–13; trans. Sommerstein.

[133] Even the underlying simplex, πλαγκτός ('wandering, roaming'), is attested only in epic and tragic poetry (viz. *Od.* 21.363, A. *Agam.* 593, *Pers.* 277, E. *Supp.* 961) so we cannot establish any ordinary usage for the term in the strict sense. It is noteworthy that Aeschylus (including the 'Aeschylean' *Prometheus Vinctus*) displays a particular fondness for new compound variations based on πλαγκτός (viz. A. *Pr.* 838: παλίμπλαγκτος, 'back-wandering', 'back-driven'; A. *Pr.* 467: θαλασσόπλαγκτος, 'made to wander over the sea', also in E. *Hec.* 782; A. *Agam.* 303: [ὄρος] αἰγίπλαγκτον ('[mountain] wandered over by goats'; probably a proper name), while other compounds also appear in Homer (πολύπλαγκτος, 'much-wandering', at *Od.* 17.425, 511 and *Il.* 11.308, also in A. *Supp.* 572, S. *Ant.* 615, *Aj.* 1186, E. *HF* 1197), Sophocles (ἁλίπλαγκτος, 'wandering the sea', viz. S. *Aj.* 695), and Aristophanes (ὀρείπλαγκτος, 'wandering on mountains', at Ar. *Th.* 326). However, it is difficult to draw any conclusion about νυκτίπλαγκτος from these compounds since they all differ in the way the simplex and the additional element of the compound relate to each other in the compound's semantics: in some cases the prefix designates the place or manner

collocation with εὐνήν ('bed') constitutes a breach of ordinary collocation rules. The sentence, however, does not contain a noun denoting a task, experience, or action from which νυκτίπλαγκτον might have been dissociated. It is, therefore, a grammatical index metonym which is either to be read as a noun itself ('I have that which causes wandering by night', *sc.* the duty of night guard) or from which a missing noun has to be inferred and implicitly supplied ('I have <the duty of night guard> that causes me to wander at night'). The neighbouring adjective, ἔνδροσον ('dewy, wet with dew'), on the other hand, can literally qualify εὐνήν ('bed'); however, given the metonymically active adjective that precedes it, the reading of the rest of the sequence is changed: the reader will not assume that it is literally the dew-induced wetness of the guard's bed that keeps him from sleeping.[134] Instead, it is again the duty of being on guard until the small hours when the morning dew appears that informs the adjective (though seemingly used literally) and modifies the way it is understood. The bed, unvisited by dreams but covered in morning dew, is the bed not slept in by someone whose duty is νυκτίπλαγκτον ('causing him to wander by night') and thus keeps him from getting any sleep, by keeping him out of his bed. We have, then, an artful compression of an entire scene into no more than two verses, thanks to the metonymically used adjective νυκτίπλαγκτον, which, to use a musical analogy, states the key in which the rest of the passage is heard.

In all of the above examples, a primary metonymic shift, namely the transfer of an adjective into a position of illegitimate collocation, has prompted further metonymic readings of the immediate context. This is markedly different from the following cases where the same phenomenon of an initial metonymic shift leads to secondary metaphorical interactions. Consider to begin with the following verses from Euripides' *Bacchae*:

of the wandering and in others the agent; in some cases the simplex conveys an intransitive notion of 'wandering', in others a transitive notion of 'making wander'. Consequently, the only remaining frame of reference for any kind of 'ordinary' usage of this term in elevated poetic diction are the other instances in Aeschylus' plays: νυκτίπλαγκτος... πόνος (A. *Agam.* 330; 'toil that causes to wander by night', *sc.* nocturnal patrolling), νυκτιπλάγκτων δειμάτων πεπαλμένη (A. *Ch.* 524; 'shaken by terrors that cause to wander by night'), and νυκτιπλάγκτων ὀρθίων κελευμάτων (A. *Ch.* 751; 'shrill commands that cause to wander by night')—all three trans. Sommerstein.

[134] This lack of sleep is itself expressed metonymically in the personification of dreams watching over the bed (εὐνὴν ὀνείροις οὐκ ἐπισκοπουμένην): the bed not visited by dreams is the bed not visited by sleep.

ἆρ' ἐν παννυχίοις χοροῖς
θήσω ποτὲ λευκὸν
πόδ' ἀναβακχεύουσα, δέραν
αἰθέρ ἐς δροσερὸν ῥίπτουσ',
ὡς νεβρὸς *χλοεραῖς* ἐμπαί-
ζουσα λείμακος ἡδοναῖς...

Shall I ever in the nightlong dances
move my white feet
in ecstasy? Shall I toss
my head to the dewy heaven
like a fawn that plays
amid *green* meadow delights...[135]
[lit: in the *green* joy of a meadow]

Dodds remarks that 'a colour word applied to an abstract noun is bold for a Greek poet' and then seeks to mitigate the abrasiveness of this collocation by suggesting that the passage 'has perhaps the effect of a compound, "green-meadow-joy"'.[136] Following the rules of ordinary collocation, χλοεραῖς ('green') is, of course, felt to have a closer connection with λείμακος ('meadow') than with ἡδοναῖς ('delight, joy'), but Dodds's reading of the sequence as a compound does not do justice to the actual effect of the abrasive collocation. In this context of a simile concerned with the energy and exuberance of life, the adjective χλοερός/χλωρός ('green') carries metaphorical overtones: the energy behind nightlong ecstatic dances is *like* the energy behind a young deer's movements which itself is *like* the energy behind the sprouting plants that fill the meadow with green vegetation. 'Green joy' metaphorically captures this very energy with which the passage is concerned.

An even more intense example of secondary metaphorical interaction triggered by grammatical amplification metonymy occurs in a passage from Aeschylus' *Seven Against Thebes*:

σὺ δ' ὥστε ναὸς κεδνὸς οἰακοστρόφος
φάρξαι πόλισμα, πρὶν καταιγίσαι πνοὰς
Ἄρεως· βοᾶι γὰρ κῦμα *χερσαῖον* στρατοῦ

Be like a good ship's captain
and make the city tight, before the squalls of war assail her
—for this army is like a roaring land-wave—
[lit.: for this *land*-wave of an army is roaring][137]

[135] E. *Ba*. 862–7; trans. Kovacs.

[136] Dodds *ad loc.*; Dodds's suggestion exemplifies the reading strategy that Bers refers to as the 'compound theory' of enallage; see above, p. 104.

[137] A. *Sept*. 62–4; trans. Sommerstein.

κῦμα … στρατοῦ ('wave of an army') as a description of the approaching enemy forces constitutes a metaphor, consistent (in typical Aeschylean mode) with the preceding imagery of a captain's leadership, the city as a ship, and the squalls of war. The qualification of this metaphor's vehicle, κῦμα ('wave'), as χερσαῖον ('from/of/on dry land') not only constitutes a stark clash of terminologies,[138] it also leads to further metaphorical interactions: referring to the approaching army as a land-wave (κῦμα χερσαῖον) evokes the image of the cloud of dust whirled up by and preceding the approaching forces as seen from afar. Once the noun στρατοῦ ('of the army') comes into the picture, which χερσαῖον would qualify in more ordinary (albeit poetically elevated) usage, the reaffiliated adjective serves to underscore the terminological difference between the two elements linked by analogy in the primary metaphor, κῦμα … στρατοῦ ('wave of an army'): this army, in its speedy movement, destructive power, and terrifying sound (βοᾶι, 'it roars'), is the *terrestrial* equivalent of a wave on the sea. Another example of such an enhancement of an existing metaphor as a secondary effect of grammatical amplification metonymy occurs in the concluding verses of the same play:

> ὅδε Καδμείων ἤρυξε πόλιν
> μὴ 'νατραπῆναι μηδ' *ἀλλοδαπῷ*
> κύματι φωτῶν
> κατακλυσθῆναι τὰ μάλιστα
>
> he did most to prevent the city of the Cadmeans
> being destroyed and overwhelmed
> by the human wave of *foreigners*
> [lit.: by the *foreign* wave of men][139]

Once again, κύματι φωτῶν ('wave of men') constitutes a metaphor in its own right but, once again, the reaffiliated adjective enhances the poetic effect: for the wave to be literally ἀλλοδαπῷ ('foreign' or, closer to the Greek, 'from another land') it has to have travelled quite a distance; hence, even in itself ἀλλοδαπῷ κύματι ('wave from another land') metaphorically points to the enemies marching against the city.

Contrast the situation in grammatical amplification metonymy when the adjective in question suits *both* nouns of the semantic unit. In such cases, an effect of ambivalent semantic openness rather than a secondary

[138] In the terms used by Silk 1974, this is presumably an example of an 'intrusive tenor' in the form of 'tenor adjective + vehicle noun' (ibid. 142, 144)—though Silk does not cite the passage and identifies the structure as 'purely Pindaric' (ibid. 144).

[139] A. *Sept.* 1075–8; trans. Sommerstein. Greek text here according to Sommerstein's edition instead of Page's.

effect of metaphor (or metonymy) is the outcome. Bers discusses a prime example in Pindar's *Tenth Olympian Ode*:

> ... ὦ Μοῖσ', ἀλλὰ σὺ καὶ θυγάτηρ
> Ἀλάθεια Διός, ὀρθᾷ χερί
> ἐρύκετον ψευδέων
> ἐνιπὰν *ἀλιτόξενον*.
>
> ... O Muse, but you and Zeus' daughter,
> Truth, with a correcting hand
> ward off from me the charge of *harming a guest friend*
> with broken promises
> [lit.: ward off from me the charge of lies
> *which is a sin against a guest friend*][140]

Here, Gildersleeve interprets ἀλιτόξενον ('sinning against one's friend') as transferred to ἐνιπὰν ('rebuke, charge') from ψευδέων ('lies'), with which one would expect collocation in ordinary usage. He classifies this usage as 'hypallage' but merely remarks that this is 'much more poetic than ἀλιτοξένων with ψευδέων'.[141] Bers notes the ambivalence caused by this grammatical shift of the adjective and offers a more perceptive reading:

> Perhaps the enallage is deliberately equivocal. Taken as a transferred epithet it means that Pindar has been rebuked for deceits that sin against his friends; but following the grammatical concord, the meaning is that the rebuke itself sins against Pindar, who a few lines later observes that payment with interest satisfies a debt (9–12).[142]

Another instance of such ambivalence occurs in a simile from Sophocles' *Ajax* in which Athena compares Odysseus to a Spartan dog:

> ... εὖ δέ σ' ἐκφέρει
> κυνὸς Λακαίνης ὥς τις *εὔρινος* βάσις
>
> moving like a Spartan hound *with keen scent*
> [lit.: like a Spartan hound's *well-nosed* movement]
> you travel quickly to your goal[143]

On an interpretation that reaffiliates the adjective according to ordinary usage, the verse only compares Odysseus to a Spartan dog, proverbial for

[140] Pi. *O.* 10.3–6; trans. Race.
[141] Gildersleeve *ad loc.*
[142] Bers 1974, 47.
[143] S. *Aj.* 8, trans. Lloyd-Jones; this interpretation takes εὔρινος (following Jebb and Pearson *ad loc.*) as nominative singular and not as genitive singular of εὖρις as suggested by Stanford *ad loc.*, on which basis there would be no reaffiliation of the adjective here.

its especially keen scent. Such a reaffiliation, however, leaves the amplification metonym κυνὸς Λακαίνης... βάσις ('movement of a... Spartan dog') as a clumsy pleonasm. Yet as Bers observes, the juxtaposition of εὔρινος βάσις 'elegantly suggests the way a hunting dog's nose determines his posture and gait... and it neatly combines the dog's movement and sniffing to balance Odysseus' movement and scanning'.[144]

A particularly striking example of ambivalence as a secondary effect of grammatical amplification metonymy can be found in a simile in Aeschylus' *Agamemnon* where the chorus compares the Greek expedition against Troy under Menelaus and Agamemnon to birds circling over their nest:

> τρόπον αἰγυπιῶν οἵτ' *ἐκπατίοις*
> ἄλγεσι παίδων ὕπατοι λεχέων
> στροφοδινοῦνται
>
> like birds of prey who, *crazed*
> *by* grief [lit.: in *out-of-their-path* grief] for their children, wheel around
> high above their eyries[145]

In the context of this human–animal simile the semantic range of ἐκπατίοις is significantly exploited: the word has a concrete spatial dimension applicable to the animal sphere (ἐκ-πατίοις, 'out of the way', hence 'missing [from the nest]') but also suggests an abstract dimension applicable to human emotions (ἐκ-πατίοις, by analogy with ἔκ-τοπος, 'out of the common path', hence, 'extreme').[146] In the first case, ἐκπατίοις is taken as having been transferred from παίδων ('children'): the nestlings are missing from their nest; in the second case, ἐκπατίοις is taken with the noun that it overtly qualifies, ἄλγεσι ('grief, pain'): the birds are in extreme grief over their nestlings. Seeking to determine one 'correct' reading of the verses obstructs an appreciation of their full poetic quality which lies precisely in the expression of an entire scenario, cause and

[144] Bers 1974, 59. [145] *A. Agam.* 49–51; trans. Sommerstein.

[146] Satisfactory literary-lexicographical analysis of this word is complicated by its extreme rarity: it only occurs here. The adverbial form, ἐκπατίως, occurs only in Erotian's (first cent. AD) comment on Hp. *Mul.* 2. 171 where he discusses a variant of the Hippocratic text that has ἐκπατίως, which he explains as: ἐκτρόπως. καὶ... ὁδοῦ ἀγνοοῦντες. ἔνιοι δὲ γραφοῦσιν ἐκπάγλως ('"turning out of the way". And... not knowing the way. But some write "exceedingly"'). The Hippocratic text itself as transmitted in the MSS, however, has ἐκπάγλως (the variant that Erotian mentions: *Testimonien zum Corpus Hippocraticum*, ed. Anastassiou-Irmer 2006, 355) and therefore cannot be drawn upon as significant corroborative evidence for the suggested non-spatial notion. Given the scarcity of evidence, Fraenkel is right to state that '[a]s regards the meaning of ἐκπατίοις... we cannot get beyond conjecture' (Fraenkel *ad loc.*); we should, however, at least entertain the possibility that this is precisely the point of Aeschylus' usage of this (newly coined?) term here.

effect, compressed into three words, which is enabled by the ambivalence that grammatical amplification metonymy can engender.[147]

Finally, there are instances of grammatical metonymy where neither metonymic effects nor metaphorical interaction nor ambiguity arises from the rearrangement of the elements within a semantic unit. In these cases, however, the consequence is not a hermeneutic collapse nor is the poetic effect one of mere bafflement. In such cases, the grammatical modification still takes place within an otherwise coherent semantic unit, and it is such cases whose effect is indeed, as Headlam noted, 'impressionistic': the elements of the sequence are still felt as belonging together, since they do belong to the same semantic field, even though their concrete grammatical affiliation violates the collocation rules of ordinary language and does not allow for a meaningful reading of the terms in their grammatical order (even if adjusted by metonymic or metaphorical readings of neighbouring terms). While the words do not constitute a coherent, plausible, *linear* sentence (either literally or if read tropically), they do constitute a verbal collage which is all the more expressive for its stark juxtapositions of semantically related but grammatically incompatible elements. Headlam's term 'impressionistic' now has undesirable connotations, for instance of the art of Monet, which would be misleading here; however, his own 'impression' of the collage-like aesthetics of this type of grammatical metonymy is insightful. In this light, let us consider the passage from Aeschylus' *Seven Against Thebes* once again:

> βλαχαὶ δ' *αἱματόεσσαι*
> τῶν ἐπιμαστιδίων
> ἀρτιτρεφεῖς βρέμονται
>
> loud, *bloody* screams
> rise up from infants
> fresh from the nourishing breast[148]

The primary metonymic shift, which is felt in the abrasive juxtaposition of βλαχαί and αἱματόεσσαι, does not give rise to any secondary effect: no ambivalence arises, no metonymic reading of any term of the sequence is prompted, no metaphorical interaction occurs. Only the entire sequence taken together allows for an acceptable reading, and the acceptable reading is one which includes a rectification of the grammatical shift but is still coloured by the collage-like effect that results from squashing a

[147] Denniston/Page *ad loc.* succumb to the perennial temptation to simplify poetic ambiguity. Fraenkel discusses the possibility of ambiguity with greater openness but eventually prefers suspending his judgement rather than positively endorsing ambiguity: 'And so the summing up must be *non liquet*.' Fraenkel *ad loc.*

[148] A. *Sept.* 348–50; trans. Sommerstein.

linear narration into an expressive assortment of otherwise grammatically uncollocatable nouns and adjectives.[149] What is true for this case of grammatical amplification metonymy also holds for grammatical index metonymy, as in this example from Euripides' *Trojan Women*:

> σφαγαὶ δ' ἀμφιβώμιοι
> Φρυγῶν ἔν τε δεμνίοις
> *καράτομος* ἐρημία
> νεανίδων στέφανον ἔφερεν
> Ἑλλαδι κουροτρόφον,
> Φρυγῶν δὲ πατρίδι πένθος
>
> The slaughtering of Phrygians about the altars
> and, in our beds, desolation wrought by the headman's blade
> [lit.: and, in our beds, *beheaded* absence/loneliness]
> brought a victory garland of young women
> to Greece to bear them children,
> but grief to the land of the Phrygians[150]

The adjective καράτομος ('beheaded') is, in non-tropical (albeit poetically elevated) usage, collocatable only with human beings, but there is no noun in the sequence from which the adjective appears to be grammatically dissociated. Consequently, taken as grammatical index metonymy, the adjective would be read in a nominalizing way: 'and in our beds the absence of those who have been beheaded' or 'and in our beds the loneliness following the beheading'. On both readings, the effect is one of a verbal collage, of an expressive juxtaposition of different scenes—the killing around the altars, the beheadings, the empty beds as a consequence, and domestic symbol of the loss of life—which are not straightforwardly explicated but dramatically (as well as grammatically) conflated and left to be separated by the reader.

Our discussion has shown that various types of poetic effect can result from the grammatical reaffiliation of an adjective—instigation of metonymic readings, metaphorical interaction, introduction of ambivalence, and collage-like compression of narrative. But it is important to remember that these effects are themselves the result of a grammatical shift within a semantic unit. This grammar-based shift, as I have argued, is in itself similar in kind to the sorts of shift identified in Chapters 2–3 as

[149] A comparison of different available translations shows the range of possible reassociations (and supplementations); compare the above with 'For the babes at their breast resound the wailing cries of young mothers, all streaming with blood' (trans. Smyth) and 'new-born infants suckling at the breast are wailing and screaming in their own blood' (trans. Collard).

[150] E. *Tro.* 562–7; trans. Kovacs.

index and amplification metonymy, and the affinity entitles us to classify this phenomenon as grammatical metonymy. As the discussion has shown, it is arguably only a conflation of cause and (selected) effect, allied to the widespread tendency to describe all tropical usage as 'metaphorical', that has led many critics to associate 'enallage' with metaphor.

METONYMY IN POETIC ACTION: CATEGORIES AND CONCLUSIONS

Three main features of metonymy in poetic action thus emerge from my analysis of these three categories:

1) The central characteristic of metonymy is the occurrence of a *metonymic shift*, that is, a lateral shift within a given, pre-existing, stable semantic field and/or semantic unit, facilitated either by a grammatical or a lexical deviation from ordinary usage.
2) By contrast with metaphor (where startling poetic effects occur within the metaphorical compound of tenor and vehicle), the poetic effects of metonymy do not occur so much within (components of) the metonymic trope itself; rather, metonymically used words serve to create an *increased potential for engagement with the context* on the part of the metonymic vehicle. Such engagement can take various forms, but whatever the effects, they are epiphenomena of the primary metonymic shift; since that shift is ultimately based on linkages established by ordinary usage, it remains too close to ordinary usage to lead to stark effects in and of itself.
3) Insofar as metaphor can be understood (with Brooke-Rose) as an ultimately verb-centred phenomenon (the full implicit *tertium comparationis* always being an action or state of being), metonymy can be said to be *a noun-based phenomenon*, with the defamiliarization which it constitutes always ultimately relatable to nouns. Here, it would seem, we have literary-linguistic evidence to substantiate Jakobson's assertion of a bipolar order of the tropical space: the metaphorical and the metonymic poles as the basic principles of tropical language are in complementary distribution in their respective association with verbs and nouns, and correlate respectively with predicates and subjects as the basic principles around which ordinary language use is structured.[151]

[151] However, this binary opposition is not as neat as it may appear. If metaphor is verb-centred, then its verb-quality is of a semantic nature: metaphor is verb-centred insofar as

In analysing, differentiating, and characterizing the three types of metonymy studied in this chapter, we have also made substantial progress in clarifying the distinction between metonymy and metaphor by developing a better understanding of the distinctiveness of their respective internal structures, their core dynamics, and the poetic effects they each create. Yet as the discussion of grammatical metonymy in this section has shown, metonymic expressions can sometimes facilitate or contribute to after-effects that are themselves metaphorical. While the two tropes' different mechanisms remain clearly distinguishable, such co-occurrences, overlaps, and interactions of poetic effects can create an impression of them bleeding into each other—which has created a good deal of critical confusion. The theoretical framework established so far has proven valuable in dispelling some of this confusion and, building on these principles, the next and final section of this chapter will investigate further scenarios in which the tropical status of a word or a sequence of words is in various ways complicated, largely because of interactions and unclear distinctions between metaphor and metonymy.

Metonymic presences

Our starting point for this study was the paradoxical coexistence of two incompatible conceptualizations of the tropical space: Jakobson's suggestion of a bipolar order centred on an assumed opposition of metaphor and metonymy on the one hand, and the prevalent tendency of (modern) rhetoric towards metaphor monism as diagnosed by Genette on the other. The establishment of several distinct categories of metonymy and the comparison of my findings with theories of metaphor have confirmed that there is a fundamental difference in kind between the two tropes. Again and again we have seen confusion arise in the critical literature when 'metaphor'/'metaphorical' is used in a loose, indiscriminate way to denote deviant, tropical usage rather than metaphor proper; or else when secondary metaphorical effects overshadow less prominent, yet structurally more fundamental metonymic shifts which make such secondary metaphorical interactions possible in the first place. In this section, which concludes my proposal for a theoretical framework for the

verbs are the principle conveyors of action, and the similarity or analogy of actions lies at the heart of metaphor. Metonymy, on the other hand, is noun-based in the grammatical sense that nouns, as a part of speech, are always at the centre of its poetic mechanisms and effects.

analysis of metonymy, we shall examine a series of scenarios in which a metonymic presence is felt that eludes straightforward and unambiguous classification as an instance of metonymy proper. The following questions will be considered: how should we best theorize clusters of metaphorical and metonymic tropes in direct interaction and interdependence? How should we theorize instances of conditional metonymy? What are we to say of instances that are felt to carry a surplus of meaning along the lines of index metonymy but which are perfectly compatible with ordinary usage? How does personification relate to metaphor and metonymy and, likewise, is synecdoche to be understood as a subcategory of metaphor or of metonymy?

TROPICAL CLUSTERS

The attentive reader will already have noticed that in a fair number of examples discussed above metonyms occur jointly with metaphors.[152] In this section, we shall examine a selection of instances of this kind in order to assess how such joint occurrence impacts on the perception of both tropes and how they affect one another. An analysis of their engagement with each other will also help us distinguish such co-occurrences from cases of 'conditional metonymy', discussed further below,[153] where a metonymic understanding of a term or sequence of terms depends on the interpretation of other terms or sequences.

Let us begin with a straightforward example from Sophocles' *Antigone:*

> καὶ τοῦτον ἂν τὸν ἄνδρα θαρσοίην ἐγὼ
> καλῶς μὲν ἄρχειν, εὖ δ᾽ ἂν ἄρχεσθαι θέλειν,
> *δορός* τ᾽ ἂν ἐν χειμῶνι προστεταγμένον
> μένειν δίκαιον κἀγαθὸν παραστάτην.
>
> This is the man whom I would trust
> to be a good ruler and a good subject,
> and when assigned his post in the storm of the battle
> [lit.: and when assigned his post in the storm of *the spear*]
> to prove a true and noble comrade in the fight.[154]

Having outlined his conviction that the same strict principles need to govern both the private and the public sphere, Creon here describes the

[152] See above, pp. 56–8, 60–1, 63, and 105–6.
[153] See below, pp. 135–40.
[154] S. *Ant.* 668–71; trans. Lloyd-Jones.

ideal citizen's behaviour in both peace and war as the result of adherence to these principles. His particular attention is given to bravery, loyalty, and steadfastness in the heat of the battle, which is captured in v. 670 with the words δορός τ' ἂν ἐν χειμῶνι ('in the storm of the spear'). This sequence of words comprises both metaphorical and metonymic elements. The metaphorical vehicle, χειμῶνι, likens the chaos and assaults on the battlefield to a storm, with the effect that the principled citizen-soldier's steadfastness amidst such brutal, elemental forces shines out even more. However, the metaphor is not confined to this term alone. The full metaphorical sequence, which belongs to the type that Brooke-Rose classifies as metaphors based on a genitive link, also includes δορός. By means of this genitive link, the metaphor brings the tenor terminology of war, which is at issue here, into interaction with the extraneous terminology of a meteorological phenomenon. The effect is the characteristic surplus in meaning and associations introduced by metaphor, here especially the pointed contrast between the untamed, volatile forces of nature and the principled steadfastness of the good citizen. This δορός, however, involves a metonymic shift. While the tenor terminology in this sequence is the terminology of war, and δορός undoubtedly belongs to it, we note that the single spear effectively evokes various weapons (arrows, swords, etc.),[155] various combat actions, and hence the battlefield and battle in general. In other words, δορός is used as an index metonym and introduces via its semantic field a broad range of terms from the terminology of war. While the metaphor thus introduces extraneous terminology to convey what is at issue in a new light, the metonymic usage of a term from the metaphor's tenor terminology extends this term's semantic scope and thereby saturates the sequence with an array of further, implied terms from that terminology. The two tropes overlap as far as the terms involved are concerned but they remain autonomous in their mechanisms; that is to say, they co-occur but they do not depend on one another: the metaphor would still be a metaphor if we removed the metonym (for instance, 'stand his ground in the storm of war') and the metonym would still be a metonym if we removed the metaphor (for instance, 'stand his ground under the onslaught…of the spear'). Yet, while both tropes remain structurally independent, their poetic effects mutually influence each other and this interaction shapes the aesthetics of the tropical cluster as a whole. One notes, on distributional evidence, that χειμών of encounters with adverse forces gives every impression of

[155] In this sense, δορός is, in fact, a double metonym: the singular 'spear' implying a plural, and 'spears' implying various other weapons.

being literary cliché.[156] Juxtaposition with the metonymically used δορός, however, although in itself also clichéd,[157] reinvigorates (let us suggest) the defamiliarizing quality of both terms in their deviance from ordinary usage: by metonymically focusing the general actions and forces of the battlefield on a specific missile, some aspects of the metaphor's underlying analogy are strengthened and foregrounded. Even though χειμών ('winter, wintry and stormy weather, storm') does not denote rain in a direct way as, for instance, ὄμβρος ('rain, rain storm') does, it is frequently collocated with words denoting rain or snow so that, as a weather condition, it appears at least to imply the likelihood or possibility of some sort of precipitation.[158] The metonym supplies a term that enhances an aspect of the analogy on which the metaphor is based. With a more abstract term, say, 'the storm of battle' (as in Lloyd-Jones's translation of this sequence), the metaphor is centred on the comparability of the enormous, adverse forces which threaten to overpower the individual in both a hostile climate and on the battlefield. Thanks to the metonym, however, the focus shifts from abstract forces and a general threat to the more concrete exposure to damage, descent, and speed. Although the two tropes are independent in their mechanisms, their participation in a tropical cluster and the resulting dynamics of their interaction create a new (more heightened) effect overall.

For a more complex tropical cluster, involving multiple metaphors and metonyms, consider the allusion to the famous riddle of the sphinx in Aeschylus' *Agamemnon*:

> *τό θ' ὑπέργηρων* φυλλάδος ἤδη
> κατακαρφομένης *τρίποδας* μὲν ὁδοὺς
> στείχει
>
> While *extreme old age*, its leaves already
> Withering, walks its way
> On three feet
> [lit.: walks its *three-legged* path][159]

[156] Cf. A. *Ch.* 202, 1066, A. *Pr.* 643, and S. *Aj.* 207; also of battle *vel sim.* at Pi. *I.* 7.39 and B. 13.140. Its occurrence and usage at Hp. *Dent.* 12 ἐν τῷ ὀδοντοφυεῖν χειμῶνας ἔχει ('to have storms [*sc.* trouble] in cutting teeth') and Hp. *Flat.* 14 παύονται τῆς νούσου καὶ τοῦ παρεόντος χειμῶνος ('their disease and present affliction come to an end') suggests that we might even be dealing here with 'dead metaphor' which has already passed into ordinary usage—except that (*a*) the word is largely restricted to verse (see LSJ s.v.) and (*b*) Hp. *Dent.* may well be post-classical (see Silk 1974, 84).

[157] Cf. e.g. *Il.* 16.57, 708, Th. 1.128, A. *Eum.* 773, S. *OC* 1525; Dindorf et al. 1831–65 s.v. gives a list of the term's occurrences in this usage and summarizes: *frequentissimus apud Tragicos hic usus vocabuli, ut Pugnam aut Pugnantes s. Exercitium significet* ('this usage of the term is most frequent among the tragedians, to signify 'battle' or 'fighters' and 'army').

[158] Cf. *Il.* 3.4, *Od.* 4.566, 14.522, Hes. *Op.* 675, Th. 3.21.

[159] A. *Agam.* 79–81; trans. Sommerstein.

In these verses we find several separate but mutually illuminating tropes: τὸ ὑπέργηρων is an abstract term ('extreme old age') and is followed by a genitive absolute, φυλλάδος ἤδη κατακαρφομένης ('leaves already withering'), which metaphorically illustrates it: old age, in particular the physical decline that comes with it, is implicitly compared to a withered plant.[160] Next comes the unexpected collocation of τρίποδας and ὁδούς. τρίπους in ordinary usage mainly denotes objects with three legs but there is also evidence for its usage qualifying distances measuring three feet.[161] Only in one instance, in Hesiod's *Works and Days*, is it used in direct collocation with 'human' terminology:

> ... τότε δὴ τρίποδι βροτῷ ἶσοι,
> οὗ τ' ἐπὶ νῶτα ἔαγε, κάρη δ' εἰς οὖδας ὁρᾶται
>
> Then they are like the three-legged man
> whose curved back bends around—
> his head habitually is turned; he gazes on the ground[162]

The same metaphorical play on man leaning on a crutch as a 'third leg' in his old age stands behind both of these instances, but the Aeschylean passage integrates this metaphor into a larger, more complex image. While the first part of the sequence conjoins the abstract 'extreme old age' to a metaphorical illustration of that abstraction, the second part of the sequence features an adjective (τρίποδας, 'three-legged') that is terminologically incompatible with its governing noun (ὁδούς, 'paths') and introduces a verb (στείχει, 'walks') that is incompatible with the governing subject which opened the sentence (τὸ ὑπέργηρων, 'extreme old age'). In ordinary usage, στείχει assumes a human as its governing subject while τρίπους requires a material object (unless conceivably allusion to Hesiod permits extension to a person). The outcome of these abrasive collocations is that τὸ ὑπέργηρων is understood, retrospectively, as an index metonym ('abstract for concrete' in rhetorical handbook-speak): what is at issue turns out not to be old age but an old person. Once the verb στείχει prompts an index-metonymical understanding of τὸ ὑπέργηρων

[160] Note that, given the absolute construction, there is no grammatical or syntactical link between the abstract concept and the metaphorical vehicle—metaphor is established in the reading process (*a*) because a non-metaphorical reading would make it impossible to integrate the vehicle terms into the reading of the sequence, and (*b*) because of the perceptible underlying logic of analogy. With its prominent position at the beginning of the sentence, τὸ ὑπέργηρων sets the tone, and all subsequent information is aligned to the now designated tenor.

[161] Cf. for the former e.g. X. *An.* 7.3.21, Th. 1.132, Lys. 21.2, and Hdt. 9.81, and for the latter Hdt. 3.60, Pl. *Men.* 83e, *Tht.* 147d.

[162] Hes. *Op.* 533–4; trans. Schlegel/Weinfield. I give the Greek text according to the MSS and follow West *ad loc.* in seeing no need for emendation here.

and a compatible term such as 'old person/s' is implicitly supplied, the metaphorical adjective τρίποδας is reaffiliated to the implied governing subject: 'a three-legged old person', *sc.* 'an old person using a crutch'. As argued above, such a reaffiliation of an adjective is to be understood as grammatical metonymy: a shift in the grammatical status and/or affiliation of an adjective. The earlier discussion of this phenomenon prompted us to differentiate between grammatical amplification metonymy (the term from which the adjective has been transferred is present in the sequence) and grammatical-index metonymy (the term from which the adjective has been transferred needs to be inferred and supplemented). In the case under review, the term from which the adjective τρίποδας has been dissociated is both present and absent: in the form of the index metonym τὸ ὑπέργηρων, with the adjective transferred only from the implied metonymic tenor.

The outcomes of this complex cluster are complex in their turn. One is a greater cohesion of the passage in the sense that it integrates the more concrete notion of a person in old age (which is supported and indeed demanded by the tropes in the second part of the sequence) with the more abstract focus on old age as such. A further, and more important, consequence is the way the switch from abstract to concrete is 'timed' by the metonyms that follow. This is of particular importance for the metaphor that represents old age as a withered plant. By casting old age as a plant, the metaphor inevitably evokes the *static* aspect of ageing—which would seem incongruous and even comic, given the way the sequence (with the walking on three legs) continues. It is the retrospective reading of τὸ ὑπέργηρων as an index metonym which avoids this by allowing the genitive absolute to make a metaphorical statement about 'old age', in plant terminology, before moving on to the next metaphor, 'walking on three legs'; *this* metaphor now invites reference to the metonymic tenor 'old person/s' and thus averts any tonal clash between the two metaphors. The (retrospective) index metonym serves a function that I characterized in the earlier discussion of this type of metonymy as 'pivotal':[163] the term in question can be understood both literally and metonymically, and thereby allows a smooth transition between two terminological spheres in a given sequence. We will return to a related phenomenon, that of 'conditional metonymy' (that is, instances where a term may or may not be read as a metonym), below.[164] For now, let it suffice to note the way a tropical cluster creates a more protean and yet at the same time much more dense impression of what is at issue.

[163] See above, p. 60. [164] See below, pp. 135–40.

While the above example from Aeschylus' *Agamemnon* illustrated how metonyms in a tropical clusters can serve to hold together multiple metaphors, thereby facilitating the creation of an enormously condensed set of several integrated images on a very small scale, the parodos of Sophocles' *Antigone* contains a large-scale example that powerfully demonstrates how a seemingly insignificant metonym can be crucial in enabling and sustaining the effects of oscillation and condensation that typically arise from tropical clusters—with dramatic cumulative results. The chorus of Theban elders celebrate their victory and the retreat of the enemy, and a whole array of tropes (as well as other literary devices) is used in their description of the recent events:

> *ἀκτὶς ἀελίου*, τὸ κάλ-
> λιστον ἑπταπύλῳ φανὲν
> Θήβᾳ τῶν προτέρων φάος,
> ἐφάνθης ποτ', ὦ χρυσέας
> ἁμέρας βλέφαρον, Διρκαί-
> ων ὑπὲρ ῥεέθρων μολοῦσα,
> τὸν λεύκασπιν Ἀργόθεν
> *φῶτα* βάντα πανσαγίᾳ
> φυγάδα πρόδρομον ὀξυτόρῳ
> κινήσασα χαλινῷ·
> ὃς ἐφ' ἡμετέρα γῇ Πολυνείκους
> ἀρθεὶς νεικέων ἐξ ἀμφιλόγων
> ὀξέα κλάζων
> αἰετὸς ἐς γῆν ὣς ὑπερέπτα,
> λευκῆς χιόνος πτέρυγι στεγανὸς
> πολλῶν μεθ' ὅπλων
> ξύν θ' ἱπποκόμοις κορύθεσσιν.
> στὰς δ' ὑπὲρ μελάθρων φονώ-
> σαισιν ἀμφιχανὼν κύκλῳ
> *λόγχαις* ἑπτάπυλον στόμα
> ἔβα, πρίν ποθ' ἁμετέρων
> αἱμάτων γένυσιν πλησθῆ-
> ναί τε καὶ στεφάνωμα πύργων
> πευκάενθ' Ἥφαιστον ἑλεῖν.
> τοῖος ἀμφὶ νῶτ' ἐτάθη
> πάταγος Ἄρεος, ἀντιπάλῳ
> δυσχείρωμα *δράκοντος*.
>
> *Beam of the sun*,
> fairer than all that have shone before
> for seven-gated Thebes,
> finally you shone forth,
> eye of golden day,

coming over the streams of Dirce,
you who have moved off
in headlong flight
the man with white shield
that came from Argos in his panoply,
with a bridle of constraint that pierced him sharply,
him that was raised up against our land
by the contentious quarrels of Polynices,
and flew to our country,
loudly screaming like an eagle
sheathed in snow-white pinion,
with many weapons and with helmets,
ringing round the seven gates
with *spears* that longed for blood;
but he went before
his jaws had been glutted with our gore
and the fire-god's pine-fed flame had taken
the walls that crown our city.
Such was the din of battle
stretched about his back,
hard for the *dragon's* adversary to vanquish.[165]

The chorus opens emphatically with an apostrophe to the light of the day which sees the flight of the enemy. Already this opening sequence is rich in tropes: the day is addressed through what initially appears to be an amplification metonym (ἀκτὶς ἀελίου, 'beam of the sun'[166]—seemingly simply for 'sun') but emerges later, as the sequence continues, as an index metonym: at issue is the long-awaited (day of) victory, not the sunlight. This metonymic tenor, to which the opening apostrophe eventually points, reappears in the second apostrophe where 'day' appears as part of a familiar metaphor (ὦ χρυσέας | ἁμέρας βλέφαρον, 'eye of golden day'[167]). The multiple metonymic shifts effect a focus on the *splendour* of this day: all is radiance and light on this day of victory. In addition to the tropes, this emphasis is also supported by the assonance in φανὲν ... φάος ... ἐφάνθης ... βλέφαρον (vv. 101–4). The whole field of 'light' terminology (pointing to the radiant

[165] S. *Ant.* 100–26; trans. Lloyd-Jones.

[166] S. *Ant.* 100; trans. Lloyd-Jones. These opening words (literally) echo those of Pindar's *Ninth Paean*; see Griffith *ad loc.*

[167] S. *Ant.* 103–4; trans. Lloyd-Jones. Variations on sun and moon as the 'eye' of heaven are frequently used in poetry, cf. e.g. *Il.* 3.277: Ἠέλιός θ', ὃς πάντ' ἐφορᾷς ('Helios, who looks down on everything'), S. *Ant.* 879–80: λάμπαδος ... ὄμμα ('the eye of light'), E. *Phoen.* 543: νυκτός τ' ἀφεγγὲς βλέφαρον ('the sightless eye of the night'), Ar. *Nub.* 285: ὄμμα ... αἰθέρος ('the eye of the aether'). See also Davidson 1983, 41–3. For βλέφαρον (as metonymic cliché) for 'eye', see e.g. S. *Aj.* 85 and *Tr.* 107.

day of triumph) is then connected to the actual military triumph through the participle κινήσασα ('move', 'set in motion'): the day of victory is now personified and attributed agency, as if the day (or was it the sun?) itself had driven away the enemy, rather than the combating forces fighting on that day. Yet more important for what interests us here is the depiction of the enemy. The enemy is first introduced as

> τὸν λεύκασπιν Ἀργόθεν
> ἐκβάντα φῶτα πανσαγίᾳ
>
> *the man* with white shield that came from Argos
> in his white panoply[168]

and is, as such, markedly underdetermined. Commentators ponder: 'Has τὸν λεύκασπιν... φῶτα to be understood in a collective sense or is Polyneices himself (or Adrastus) meant?'[169] The sequence is clearly metonymic and implies a whole range of possible metonymic tenors. A few verses on, a relative clause qualifies 'the man' as ὃς ἐφ' ἡμετέρᾳ γᾷ Πολυνείκους | ἀρθεὶς νεικέων ἐξ ἀμφιλόγων ('[who] was raised up against our land by the contentious quarrels of Polyneices'[170]), which makes it retrospectively impossible that φῶτα refers to Polyneices (at least for now), but still leaves φῶτα hovering between Adrastus, king of Argos (persuaded by Polyneices to lead an army against Thebes) or (singular for plural) the whole army itself. Ambiguity is further increased when immediately after the relative clause a simile is introduced: vv. 113–14 compare 'the man' to an eagle, highlighting the loud cry (of the warrior and the bird) and the white colour (of the shield and the feathers) as particular points of comparison.[171] The subsequent verses are then marked by a constant movement back and forth between terminology compatible with *only* the tenor of the simile *or* the vehicle. Immediately after the eagle simile a further qualification is added through a prepositional construction: πολλῶν μεθ' ὅπλων | ξύν θ' ἱπποκόμοις κορύθεσσιν ('with many weapons and with helmets with horsehair plumes'[172]). The direct juxtaposition with the eagle creates a particularly abrasive effect since, owing to the plural, this additional description is not literally compatible with either constituent of the simile. The abrasiveness is reconciled *semantically* by our retrospectively understanding the ambiguous φῶτα ('man') as metonymically referring to the entire enemy army

168 S. *Ant.* 106–7; trans. Lloyd-Jones.
169 Kamerbeek *ad loc.*
170 S. *Ant.* 110–11; trans. Lloyd-Jones.
171 For the poetic tradition of comparing an army or individual warriors to birds or animals of prey, see Davidson 1983, 43–4.
172 S. *Ant.* 115–16; trans. Lloyd-Jones.

(which literally comes with many weapons and helmets); on the imagistic level, however, this juxtaposition sets the tone for a conflation of animal and military terminology that evokes a single monstrous, belligerent entity. By the time the simile clause comes to an end, the animal terminology has become metaphorical. Yet because it is so closely interwoven with the tenor terminology of the enemy army and because this interrelation is sustained for so long, the impression created is of an extended merging rather than a punctual similarity.[173]

This impression of a merging into a polymorphous monster allows for various terminological sleights, both in terms of further metaphorical deviations from the more specific vehicle terminology of the bird of prey (from the initial eagle simile), and in terms of metonymic specifications. Thus, v. 117 (στὰς δ' ὑπὲρ μελάθρων...) remains consistent with eagle terminology and can be read as describing a bird of prey hovering over the city and about to swoop down in attack; but the following verses introduce terminology that adds new complications:

> [φονώ]σαισιν ἀμφιχανὼν κύκλῳ
> *λόγχαις* ἑπτάπυλον στόμα
>
> he gaped around our sevenfold portals
> with *spears* thirsting for blood[174]

The complication arises from the abrasive juxtaposition of ἀμφιχανών ('gaping wide') and κύκλῳ (in effect 'surrounding') which are incompatible in any ordinary usage. Without ἀμφιχανών, the sequence more or less literally describes the army surrounding Thebes, the metonymic cliché 'spears' implying weaponry in general. With ἀμφιχανών, however, a continuing impression of animal terminology suggests the open mouth of an attacking beast. This impression is supported by the addition of στόμα ('mouth', 'entrance', 'opening'). Although the preceding epithet ἑπτάπυλον ('seven-gated') makes clear that the famous entrance gates of Thebes are at issue here,[175] the mere presence of the term στόμα reinforces a parallel impression of gaping jaws.[176] This, however, stretches the implicit analogy with the eagle: how far can a gaping mouth 'with bloodthirsty spears'

[173] Cf. Burton 1980, 93. The overall effect is akin to (though not entirely analysable in strict terms of) what Silk calls 'intrusion'; see Silk 1974, 138–49.

[174] S. *Ant.* 117–18; trans. Jebb.

[175] For this poetic code, see e.g. *Il.* 1.505, *Od.* 11.263, Hes. *Op.* 162, *Sc.* 49, A. *Sept.* 165.

[176] The usage of στόμα in the singular is of key importance for this association, alongside the word's literal-denotative function. Müller *ad loc.* also notes the relevance of the singular but goes too far when he argues that '[t]he metaphor requires that the bloodthirsty spears correspond to the bloodthirsty throat of the eagle. The metaphor also explains the singular of στόμα: it is the mouth of the bird.' ('Die Metaphorik will, daß dem blutrünstigen Rachen des Adlers die blutgierigen Speere entsprechen. Aus der Metaphorik erklärt sich auch der

still be comparable to an eagle's? In other words: within the context of a beast–army metaphor, the combination of 'spears' and 'mouth' more immediately suggests 'teeth', and thus a beast of a different kind. The rapid—clashing—progression from the image of an eagle pausing in mid-air above the city to the notion of an army surrounding the city seems indeed to give us a sudden impression of an approaching monster, growing and changing its form as it draws nearer.

A new complication arises a few verses later:

> ἔβα, πρίν ποθ' ἁμετέρων
> αἱμάτων γένυσιν πλησθῆναί
>
> but he went, before his
> jaws had been glutted with our gore[177]

Kamerbeek comments that '"jaw" remains within the imagery (but note that γένυς is also used of the "edge" of an axe)'.[178] The interpretation of γένυς as hovering semantically between 'jaw' and 'axe' is tempting, but problematic. If we follow Kamerbeek, we have here another instance of a movement between the metaphorical beast terminology and literal army terminology, this time within the ambiguity played out in a single word: depending on the interpretation, γένυσιν could be associated with either. We should note, however, that the usage of γένυς as '(the edge of) an axe' not only appears to be specifically Sophoclean but also is only attested in plays (probably) written after the *Antigone*, so that (if the lexicographical data are at least representative) this poet-specific usage cannot have informed the understanding of a contemporary audience.[179] Yet what can be safely assumed is that both in ordinary usage and elevated poetic usage, γένυς is always used of humans and other mammals; in no other attested instance in classical Greek is it used to refer to the beak of a bird.[180] Consequently, we have here too an extension of the initial eagle simile (and the eagle metaphor) to a broader monstrous enemy that acquires alarmingly unpredictable animal and human traits.

The key point for my assessment of metonymy in tropical clusters here is that the seemingly innocent oscillation of φῶτα ('man') between an

Singular στόμα: es ist das Maul des Vogels.'). It is not that στόμα 'is' the mouth of the eagle; rather, it facilitates its evocation.

177 S. *Ant.* 119–20; trans. Lloyd-Jones.

178 Kamerbeek *ad loc.*

179 This usage is only attested in S. *El.* 196 and *Ph.* 1205.

180 As confirmed by data in Dindorf er al. 1831–65, Bonitz 1870, Kühn/Fleischer 1986, and TLG (including -γενυς compounds as listed in Kretschmer/Locker 1963). The only (post-classical) instance in all of Greek literature where the term is used with reference to a bird's beak is Ar. Byz. *Epit.* 10.22.

individual warrior and the army as a collective entity is essential to the various conformations of the passage's main conceit. All the ambiguities that follow from the protean representations of the enemy would—one surmises—fall apart and become mere awkward contradictions, were they not held together by this opening metonym which, from the outset, introduces the co-presence of a single warrior and the entire army as simultaneously available points of reference. At the opening of the parodos the first metaphor is centred on the vehicle ὀξυτέρῳ κινήσασα χαλινῷ ('urging *him* with a swifter/sharper bit'[181]). Both the subject and the object of this participle are themselves metonyms: the 'beam of the sun' (and later the 'eye(lid) of day') on the one hand, and the 'man' on the other. The particularizing metonymic focus on a 'man', manoeuvred away by the sun, using a 'bit', creates a concentrated representation of what is at issue: the enemy army driven to retreat on the day of victory. The eagle simile, again, initially draws on the individualized 'man', and particular points of similarity (cries and white attributes) are highlighted to sharpen the comparison. Yet the simile is soon opened up to encompass the entire army, and the sustained animal terminology that follows also points to the army as a collective entity: it is the army's many spears and its ability, as a collective, to *surround* the city (κύκλῳ) that creates the resemblance to a gigantic monster set to devour the city which the various metaphorical terms exploit. While the 'man', as it were, expands into an army, the eagle expands into a shapeshifting monstrosity (although, as we have seen, both also move back to focus on particular points of contact that draw on the singular). After this remarkably vivid and detailed elaboration of the attack on the city, the passage moves in the opposite direction, towards emblematic abstraction, and it is again metonyms that facilitate both the shift into abstraction and the linking of those abstractions with the preceding imagery. The move towards abstraction occurs in the last sentence of the first part of the parodos and marks the end of the heightened sequence; after this point, the language becomes more direct again:

τοῖος ἀμφὶ νῶτ' ἐτάθη
πάταγος Ἄρεος, ἀντιπάλῳ
δυσχείρωμα *δράκοντος*.

Such was the din of battle
Stretched about his back,
Hard for the *dragon's* adversary to vanquish.[182]

[181] S. *Ant.* 107. [182] S. *Ant.* 124–6; trans. Lloyd-Jones.

In this concluding sequence, we observe a move back to the focusing singular, with δράκοντος ('dragon' or 'snake') representing one single opponent that has not been overcome by the attacker. The snake does not appear until the end of the antistrophe and receives none of the great elaboration which the eagle has been afforded in the preceding verses.[183] However, its occurrence here serves an important function in that it translates the animal terminology, first introduced by the simile and then maintained by various metaphors, onto a much more abstract level and thereby brings it to a conclusion. How is this achieved? Kamerbeek comments: 'δράκοντος as a metonymy for the Theban army is not strange and for a moment the battle is seen as a fight between eagle and δράκων ['snake'].'[184] Eagle and snake are traditional enemies in epic similes;[185] the association of Argos with the eagle has been impressively manufactured in the earlier verses; and the association of Thebes with the snake (or 'dragon') is traditional.[186] After unfolding the military confrontation in great detail and with sustained usage of animal terminology, the passage here 'zooms out' again, as it were, and presents the bigger picture, a confrontation between (the armies of) two cities, through their metonymic representatives. The Argive eagle's inability to overcome the Theban snake thus frames and concludes the first part of the parodos, and again we note that φῶτα ('man') is of central importance for this effect, as the element that first introduced a particularizing focus. Taken together, then, the various observations on this long passage demonstrate how a seemingly trivial metonym within a tropical cluster can create and facilitate poetic effects out of all proportion to the relatively unspectacular effect of the metonym taken by itself. They also highlight the importance of the grammatical categories of singular and plural for metonymy, to which we shall return shortly in the discussion of synecdoche.[187] For the moment, however, let us continue our reflections on the relationship of metaphor and metonymy through the assessment of more complex scenarios in which the two interact (or seem to interact) and turn to a phenomenon we have already encountered several times in examples discussed earlier on this chapter: the phenomenon of 'conditional metonymy'.

[183] Cf. Burton 1980, 93. [184] Kamerbeek *ad loc.*

[185] See Burton 1980, 92–3; the most prominent precedent is arguably *Il.* 12.200–7.

[186] It recurs later in the play in vv. 1124–5; Jebb *ad loc.* refers to S. *OC* 1534 and the mythical origin of the Thebans as having sprung from dragon's teeth sown by Cadmus.

[187] See below, pp. 154–65.

CONDITIONAL METONYMY

The metonymic presences discussed so far were marked by the joint occurrence of structurally independent metaphors and metonyms in tropical clusters, in which each trope's poetic effects and reverberations influence the perception of neighbouring tropes and of the cluster as a whole. I shall now examine such cases in which a term may or may not be read as a metonym, depending on the interpretation of another term (or other terms) in its context; that is to say, we will look at scenarios where the tropical status of a term—as used literally, metaphorically, or metonymically—is conditional on one of several possible interpretations of the sequence in which it occurs. Silk has observed a corresponding phenomenon in metaphor:

> By 'conditional metaphor' I mean metaphor whose existence is implied by one, and only one, of two possible interpretations, when by the other interpretation no metaphor is in question, but either some other trope (usually metonymy) or no trope at all. The metaphor is, therefore, not inescapably 'there' but conditional on a given interpretation. It is not characteristic of such instances that the alternatives are exclusive (*either/or*); rather that the fact of an alternative is the basic datum (*both/and*).[188]

In what follows, I shall seek to establish whether the same is the case with metonymy and consider what insights regarding the relationship between metaphor and metonymy can be gained from an examination of instances in which internal ambiguities or the presence of another trope determine the status of a given term as metonymic, metaphorical, or literal.

An example of such ambiguity can be found in Hölderlin's poem 'Griechenland'. The poem opens with a meditation on what it would have been like to live with the beloved, whom the poem addresses, in ancient Greece. The stanza quoted below marks the turning point where the poem's vision of a glorified past begins to be contrasted with perspectives on the present:

> Ist der *Stern der Liebe* dir verschwunden?
> Und der Jugend holdes Rosenlicht?
> Ach! Umtanzt von Hellas' goldnen Stunden,
> Fühltest du die Flucht der Jahre nicht,
> Ewig, wie der Vesta Flamme, glühte
> Mut und Liebe dort in jeder Brust,

[188] Silk 1974, 242.

Wie die Frucht der Hesperiden, blühte
Ewig dort der Jugend stolze Lust

Has the *star of love* vanished for you?
And the sweet rosy light of youth?
Alas! Surrounded in dance by Hellas' golden hours,
You did not [or: you would not] feel the flight of years,
Eternally, like the flame of Vesta, was the glow
Of valour and love there in every breast,
Like the fruit of the Hesperides, blossomed
Eternally there youth's proud joy.[189]

How are we to understand 'the star of love' ('der Stern der Liebe')? Two readings seem possible: we can take the genitive as a 'genitive link' in Brooke-Rose's sense and understand the sequence as a metaphor of the equation type; the star of love as a metaphorical representation of love itself. Alternatively, we can read the sequence as a metonymic paraphrase for 'Venus'—the 'star' of love. 'Venus' itself contains further metonymic potential: it evokes both Venus as the morning *star* and Venus as the goddess *of love*. The following lines support both the metaphorical and the metonymic reading. The phrase 'the sweet rosy light of youth' ('der Jugend holdes Rosenlicht') supplies a parallel '[light] of + abstract concept' construction, and one would be more inclined to understand this sequence as a metaphor based on a genitive link; read metaphorically, the two lines together can be understood as saying 'have love and youth vanished for you?'. However, the mention of Vesta and the Hesperides later in the stanza, each in the genitive and together with their characteristic attributes (the fire of Vesta, the fruit of the Hesperides), adds further divine figures, whose occurrence retrospectively confirms a metonymic reading of the first line of the stanza as referring to the gentle guidance of Venus. As noted by Silk, with reference to conditional metaphor, what we are dealing with here in terms of poetic effect is not an either/or but a both/and scenario. Even if we do understand 'the star of love' as metonymically referring to Venus the morning star, this is soon felt to be located in the metaphorical domain *as well* when 'youth' is introduced in the subsequent line: thanks to the two lines' parallelism, the light of the morning star appears analogous to the sweet rosy light of youth and consequently both lines evoke the light of dawn and the new day as a metaphor for youth.

[189] Hölderlin, 'Griechenland', 25–32.

A similar case of conditional metonymy, but one involving a different kind of metonym, can be found in Pindar's *Eleventh Pythian Ode*:

> τὰ μὲν ἐν ἅρμασι καλλίνικοι πάλαι,
> Ὀλυμπίᾳ τ' ἀγώνων πολυφάτων
> ἔσχον θοὰν ἀκτῖνα σὺν ἵπποις:
>
> With their chariots they were victorious long ago;
> at Olympia they captured the famous games'
> *swift* radiance with their horses.[190]

The term whose tropical status is ambiguous here is the adjective θοάν. Grammatically speaking, it is governed by ἀκτῖνα and thus forms part of a typical Pindaric radiance metaphor:[191] the ray (radiance/splendour) of the famous games at Olympia metaphorically represents the winner's glory obtained there. The qualification θοάν ('swift'), however, seems to hover between the metaphorical ray of light and the horses themselves insofar as both might be described as 'swift' in non-tropical usage. Farnell notes *ad loc.*: 'a vivid and effective phrase; "the light of victory flashes from the swift moving chariot"'.[192] θοός is, in fact, regularly collocated with means of transportation in Pindar's poetry, so that, while most commentators follow the metaphorical reading, Slater cites this instance s.v. θοός and explains it as '*speeding* brilliance: θοὰν transf. from ἵπποις'.[193] We have here, then, a case where it cannot be determined whether the word in question is a grammatical amplification metonym or part of a metaphor. Farnell's suggested translation adequately conveys the poetic effect: θοάν *effect*-ively operates as both. Note, however, that the noun which governs this conditional grammatical amplification metonym is itself unquestionably metaphorical.

[190] Pi. *P.* 11.46–8; I have amended the word order of Race's translation to bring it closer to the Greek.

[191] Other Pindaric instances of ἀκτίς as a metaphorical vehicle for 'glory' are Pi. *P.* 4.255 and *I.* 4.42.

[192] Similarly Gentili *ad loc.*: 'the ray of light metaphorically indicates the splendour which emanates from the contests, as in *Isth.* 4,42, and is defined as "swift" through the presence of the ἵπποις that follows (cf. ἱπποσόα θοάς as apposition to ἀκτὶς ἀελίου in *Pae.* 9,7)' ('il raggio di luce indica metaforicamente lo splendore che emana dagli agoni, come in *Isth.* 4,42, ed è definito "veloce" per la presenza del seguente ἵπποις (cfr. ἱπποσόα θοάς come apposizione di ἀκτὶς ἀελίου in *Pae.* 9,7)'. Although θοός is, as the evidence in TLG confirms, most frequently used to describe 'feet', 'ships', or 'horses', there is some (albeit limited) further evidence for its collocatability with 'light', cf. B. 3.55–6: θοὰν . . . ἀστραπάν ('swift . . . lightning') and, *per contrarium*, *Il.* 10.394, *Od.* 12.284, and Hes. *Th.* 482: θοὴν . . . νύκτα ('swift . . . night'). Cf. θοός of other natural phenomena as at E. *Tro.* 454: θοαῖς αὔραις ('swift winds').

[193] For straightforward collocations of θοός with horses (*vel sim.*) in Pindar's poetry, see *P.* 4.17, *Pae.* 9.7, and *Fr.* 80.

This is not the case in the following example from Aeschylus' *Agamemnon*:

> ... *οὐκέτ' ἐξ ἐλευθέρου*
> *δέρης* ἀποιμώζουσι φιλτάτων μόρον
>
> ... and *from throats [or: necks] that are no longer free*
> They cry out their laments for the death of their dearest.[194]

Verrall comments *ad loc.*:

> δέρης, both *neck* and *throat* (E. *Or.* 41 οὔτε σῖτα διὰ δέρης ἐδέξατο Wecklein), here combines the two meanings. With οὐκέτ' ἐλευθέρου it is the *neck*, the metaphor being that of the yoke, with ἀποιμώζουσι *throat*. No English word will exactly fit.

If we follow Verrall, we have a case where a conditional metaphor (δέρης) determines whether an adjective is read literally ('a [yoke-burdened, hence] unfree neck') or as a grammatical amplification metonym (ἐλευθέρου transferred from the implicit subject—'no longer free they cry out from their throat'). While the range of δέρη indeed covers both 'throat' and 'neck',[195] Verrall is too quick to move from metaphorical overtones of an English translation to claims about the tropical status of the Greek term—not least, because there is no evidence in extant Greek usage for δέρη of the neck of oxen or indeed any other animal, which would be a prerequisite for the alleged metaphor. Instead, the Greek term used to denote 'neck' in such a context is αὐχήν.[196] However, we should not discard Verrall's observation entirely but rather qualify it, for it is clear that the loss of freedom and, therefore, the 'yoke of slavery' are at issue in this passage. In fact, in the context of slaves captured during warfare we may well imagine the 'necks' of *human* captives being literally 'no longer free', but bound together for transportation to the slave market. At the same time, however, the force of δέρη/'throat' is also present, namely through the verb ἀποιμώζουσι ('cry out laments') in which connection the adjective ἐλευθέρου ('free') is transferred insofar as

[194] A. *Agam.* 328–9; trans. Sommerstein.

[195] See for the former, for instance E. *Or.* 41, for the latter E. *Phoen.* 166. Note that, with the sole exception of X. *Cyr.* 5.1.7, this word only occurs in Greek verse so that Homeric/epic usage is to be taken as determinative: for the former see, for instance, *h. Merc.* 133 and for the latter *Od.* 23.208, 240.

[196] See, for instance, Hes. *Op.* 815–16: ἐπὶ ζυγὸν αὐχένι θεῖναι | βουσὶ καὶ ἡμιόνοισι καὶ ἵπποις ὠκυπόδεσσι, ('to put yokes on the neck of oxen and mules and swift-footed horses') and Pi. *P.* 4.234–5: σπασσάμενος δ' ἄροτρον, βοέους δήσαις ἀνάγκας | ἔντεσιν αὐχένας ἐμβάλλων ('He grasped the plow, bound the necks of oxen by force in their harness'; trans. Race). The term's usage in prose at Arist. *HA* 493a5 and *PA* 691b29 refers to the entire part of the body between torso and head and thus subsumes both 'neck' and 'throat'.

it describes the subject rather than one specific body part of the subject. We can say, then, that at different stages in hearing or reading the sequence, different semantic properties of δέρη ('neck', 'throat') are foregrounded and that, depending on that, its adjective can, at first, be understood literally but will then, retrospectively, appear to be transferred and in need of reaffiliation. Tropical status, therefore, is conditional on the different ways in which the semantic range of the governing noun is exploited at different stages of the sequence.

How do these examples of conditional metonymy relate to my earlier discussion of tropical clusters? The accumulation of structurally independent tropes in clusters leads, as we have seen, to more complex tropical explorations. In terms of the intensity of poetic effect, it is metaphors in the various examples that are clearly dominant, though on closer examination it becomes clear that metonyms play a crucial role in facilitating transitions from one metaphor to the next and in lending cohesion to the cluster as a whole. Where clichéd tropes are reactivated through collocation in clusters, the effect of the metaphors is also stronger. Examination of tropical clusters in which metaphors and metonyms are co-present thus substantiates my earlier claim that the terminological extraneousness introduced by a metaphor's vehicle and the defamiliarizing effect resulting from this is likely to eclipse the more subtle metonymic shift within a semantic field which is in itself based on the combinatory rules of *ordinary* usage. On the other hand, in conditional metonymy, where both a metaphorical and a metonymic reading are possible, the effect that results from a metaphorical reading does not seem significantly more intense than that of the alternative metonymic reading.[197] Once again, this is explicable in terms of metonymy's dependence on semantic fields established by ordinary usage: if a sequence of terms can be read both as metaphor and as metonymy, the defamiliarizing potential of the metaphor within the context of the sequence is inevitably capped, because metonymy is based on the inference or reaffiliation of otherwise coherent and compatible terminology; the possible degree of felt abrasiveness caused by conflicting terminologies is inherently limited.

We can thus conclude that where metaphor and metonymy are co-present in clusters, metaphor 'trumps' metonymy in terms of poetic effect because of its stronger deviance from terminologically coherent usage. Where the same term or sequence of terms can be read both

[197] Cf. the instances discussed as 'conditional metaphor' which may also be read as (conditional) metonyms in Silk 1974, 242–3.

metaphorically and metonymically, however, metonymy's capped potential for abrasive collocations extends to the metaphor and limits the conditional metaphor's effect. We can now take these observations one step further by considering examples in which a term or sequence of terms may be read literally but seems to strongly invite a reading along the lines of metonymy.

METONYMIC ASSOCIATION

Whereas in conditional metonymy different interpretations of a term or terms in the immediate context trigger distinctively different readings of a term in question (either literal or metaphorical or metonymic), the situation lies slightly different in the case of metonymic association: here, a shift of understanding along the lines of metonymy is contextually compelling, but a literal reading is *also* possible and plausible. In such cases, there is a strong impression of a word being pregnant with a certain surplus in meaning that goes beyond its usual denotative power, but—crucially—without any negation of its usual meaning in ordinary language usage (as is the case in metonymy proper, where exactly this makes the inference of a metonymic tenor inevitable). Consider, to begin with, the following two examples, the first from Sophocles' *Oedipus Tyrannus* and the second from Aeschylus' *Eumenides*:

> εἰπὼν ἄπειμ' ὧν οὕνεκ' ἦλθον, οὐ τὸ σόν
> δείσας *πρόσωπον*...
>
> I shall go, now that I have spoken of things that brought me here,
> With no fear of your angry *countenance*...
> [lit.: with no fear of your *countenance*...][198]

> ἐς τὸ πᾶν δέ σοι λέγω,
> *βωμὸν* αἴδεσαι *Δίκας*,
> μηδέ νιν κέρδος ἰδὼν *ἀθέῳ ποδὶ* λὰξ ἀτίσῃς· ποινὰ γὰρ ἕπεσται
>
> I say to you, as a universal rule:
> respect *the altar of Justice*,
> and do not, with a view to gain, spurn and trample it *with godless foot*,
> for punishment will follow[199]

[198] S. *OT* 447–8; trans. Lloyd-Jones.

[199] A. *Eum.* 538–43; trans. Sommerstein.

In the first example, the reader will quickly assume that Teiresias' point here is not that he is undaunted by Oedipus' *face* but by the anger expressed by it.[200] Likewise, Aeschylus' choral ode, with its list of maxims on how to act righteously in various areas of life, invites an understanding of this passage as an admonition to have respect for justice in general rather than as a specific warning against desecrating altars of the goddess. In any case, the expectation of a summarizing, general statement raised by ἐς τὸ πᾶν makes any such specificity implausible. Does it make sense to understand these shifts—context-determined—as metonymic? Both readings seem to display the kind of shift that has emerged as the prime characteristic of metonymy. On the basis of the categories of noun-based metonymy established in previous chapters, we could classify the first example as an instance of index metonymy and the second as an instance of amplification metonymy. However, do such cases really constitute the kind of deviation from ordinary usage that makes it appropriate to identify them as tropical?

A case could be made that in the first example there is some deviation to guide us: Medusa aside, it would be hard to think of an instance where a countenance in and of itself can literally be said to be a cause of fear. However, as Lloyd-Jones's translation shows, the deviation is not so abrasive that another *noun* needs to be inferred to make sense of the sequence (as would be the case in index metonymy proper). But even given that one does have to make an inference—to infer that Teiresias' potential reason for fear would be Creon's anger and the harm that means for him—the actual source of this fear would *literally* be the expression of that anger on Creon's face. Thus, with these inferences arising as immediate associations, we seem to be within the territory of (albeit on the edge of) linguistic correctness—which makes the tropical status of this passage questionable. The passage, one might say, is elliptical ('angry' being suppressed) rather than metonymic; the effect, however, is still one of association along the lines of metonymy.

The same is true for the second example: while there is a focusing and specifying shift which takes the same syntactical form as is characteristic of amplification metonymy (from 'justice' to 'altar of justice'), the sequence itself does not violate any rules of collocation within ordinary language. In its given context, the overspecification goes against a reader's expectations; however, there is little concrete deviation from ordinary usage. Only the grammatical metonym ἀθέωι attached to ποδὶ

[200] Note that Lloyd-Jones's translation reveals a felt need to render this more explicit.

λάξ ('with *godless* foot') constitutes a real breach of ordinary collocation rules.[201] The passage as a whole does certainly create an image of the desecration of an altar, focused on the foot which tramples on it, and thereby expresses the more abstract idea of a violation of justice in concrete terms. Yet this is not achieved through any negation of ordinary usage but by a surplus in meaning: the words in context carry a greater significance than the present terms literally denote.

Another example of this phenomenon can be found in these lines from Aeschylus' *Agamemnon*:

> οὔ μοι φόβου μέλαθρον ἐλπὶς ἐμπατεῖ,
> *ἕως ἂν αἴθηι πῦρ ἐφ' ἑστίας ἐμῆς*
> *Αἴγισθος*, ὡς τὸ πρόσθεν εὖ φρονῶν ἐμοι
>
> no fearful apprehension stalks my house,
> *so long as the fire upon my hearth is kindled by*
> *Aegisthus* and he remains loyal to me as hitherto[202]

Clytemnestra's statement does not deviate from ordinary usage or, more precisely, from the habitual usage of tragic diction. However, it would be somewhat odd to read her words as meaning that she takes comfort, specifically, from the fact that Aegisthus lights the fire in her house. Not only is this a task one expects to be performed by the palace servants; even if Aegisthus did indeed light the fire in Clytemnestra's hearth, in the given context it is implausible that this action itself is literally at issue here. Instead, it is of course Aegisthus' presence in her house, and notably his presence as (stand-in) head of the household, that is evoked. The preceding personification (οὔ μοι φόβου μέλαθρον ἔλπις ἐμπατεῖ, 'no fearful apprehension stalks my house') creates an expectation that remains literally unfulfilled by the following verse. In order that this expectation be met, the words that follow must be given greater significance (retrospectively) than their mere denotative value merits. The clause that follows, ὡς τὸ πρόσθεν εὖ φρονῶν ἐμοι ('and he remains loyal to me as hitherto'), duly reinforces this reading. Again, we observe that a line of associations is prompted which *resembles* metonymy but is not based on deviation from ordinary usage, and hence is not strictly tropical.

A simile rather than a personification creates a potential for extended significance in the following lines from Hölderlin's 'Hymne an die Freiheit':

[201] With 'godless' being transferred from the subject and instead affiliated with 'foot'.
[202] A. *Agam.* 1434–6; trans. Sommerstein.

Glühend stehn, und stolz, die neuen Brüder,
Stehn und dulden für das Vaterland;
Wie der *Efeu*, treu und sanft umwunden
Zu der *Eiche* stolzen Höhn hinauf,
Schwingen, ewig brüderlich verbunden,
Nun am Helden Tausende sich auf.

Glowing, and proud, the new brothers stand,
Stand and endure for the fatherland;
Just as the *ivy*, faithful and soft/gentle, is twined around
The *oak* right up to its fine/proud heights,
So do thousands now, in brotherly bond,
Rise up alongside the hero.[203]

The simile itself contains no relevant deviation from ordinary usage:[204] the freedom-enthused masses, envisaged as rising up with 'the hero' as their support, are compared—literally—to the many-leafed ivy which rambles upward around the trunk of the solid oak. Yet the specific terms used here appear to be endowed with further significance, in terms of the ivy's association with ancient Greece (and Dionysus) and the oak's association with Germany (and Donar). On this secondary level, the rise of the masses, who find support in holding on to a hero, is implicitly linked with a resurgence of the spirit of ancient Greece, made possible through the vitality and strength of the German spirit. As before, a seemingly metonymic line of contiguity is perceptible (ivy-Dionysus-Greece, oak-Donar-Germany), yet no breach of ordinary collocation rules occurs and no ordinary usage is negated, so that no tropical usage is felt.

Such increased semantic investment of a term which is not metonymic, but *looks* metonymic, also occurs in this passage from Aeschylus' *Eumenides*:

...μέγα γὰρ δύναται πότνι' Ἐρινὺς
παρά τ' ἀθανάτοις τοῖς θ' ὑπὸ γαῖαν,
περί τ' ἀνθρώπων φανερ' ὡς τελέως
διαπράσσουσιν, τοῖς μὲν *ἀοιδάς*,
τοῖς δ' αὖ δακρύων
βίον *ἀμβλωπὸν* παρέχουσαι.

...for the august Fury has great power
among the immortals and among those beneath the earth;

[203] Hölderlin, 'Hymne an die Freiheit', 77–80.
[204] Though only by metaphor (personification) can a plant be described as 'faithful' ('treu'), in particular.

and as regards humans it is manifest how decisively
they effect their will, furnishing
to some *joyful song*
[lit.: *songs* to some]
to others a life *dim-eyed with tears*.[205]

The parallelism created by the τοῖς μέν... τοῖς δὲ construction ('to some... to others...') leads to an expectation of equivalence between the two clauses. Once βίον ('life') comes into view as the accusative object of the second clause, ἀοιδάς ('songs') as the accusative of the first clause is reinterpreted: the Erinyes distribute different kinds of life, either a life filled with joy or one filled with sadness. In both clauses, the present terms make sense in their literal usage but the syntactic structure and the broader context lead to associations on a more general level (constituting an instance of 'result-for-cause', in rhetorical handbook-speak). The associative leap is greater in the first clause than in the second since the latter contains βίον ('life') and the association is limited to the qualification of βίον: a life 'of tears' being a 'sad' life. The first clause, on the other hand, has only 'songs' which, owing to the syntactic parallelism, is retrospectively extended to 'a life of songs', that is, a 'happy' life. Note, however, that not only syntax and context but also a surprising collocation support this associative reading. In τοῖς δ' αὖ δακρύων βίον ἀμβλωπὸν ('and to others a life dim-eyed with tears') we have a grammatical amplification metonymy, for what is literally 'dim-eyed' is the 'others' (τοῖς δὲ) who have a life filled with tears, rather than their life itself.

While the examples discussed so far feature at least some form of defamiliarization, either through ambiguous tropical status or else collocation with an actual trope (*vel sim.*), we do also find cases in which an entire sequence is indisputably literal—*and yet* shows a similar surplus of meaning. In Goethe's *Iphigenia among the Taurians*, for instance, Iphigenia asks

...Sinnt er vom *Altar*
Mich in sein *Bette* mit Gewalt zu ziehn?

...Does he intend to drag
Me from the *altar* to his *bed* by force?[206]

A literal reading is possible, yet the reader is bound to infer that Iphigenia's anxiety consists not only, and not even primarily, in the fear that she will be violently dragged away from the altar in particular and placed in Thoas' bed in particular, but rather that she will be forced to surrender

[205] A. *Eum.* 950–5; trans. Sommerstein.

[206] Goethe, *Iphigenie auf Tauris. Ein Schauspiel*, 195–6. It is worth noting that the same phrasing occurs in Goethe's prose version of the play (Goethe, *Iphigenie auf Tauris*, p. 155, l. 14).

her role as priestess and coerced into assuming the role of Thoas' wife. 'Altar' and 'bed' encapsulate these two different roles and spheres and the broader context of the scene makes clear that this is what is at issue. Within the same sentence, however, no deviation from ordinary usage occurs, nor are there any tropical elements or ambiguities behind this semantic extension. Compare the following from Sophocles' *Oedipus Tyrannus*:

> ὡς εἴπερ ἄρξεις τῆσδε τῆς γῆς, ὥσπερ κρατεῖς,
> ξὺν ἀνδράσιν κάλλιον ἢ κενῆς κρατεῖν·
> ὡς οὐδέν ἐστιν οὔτε *πύργος* οὔτε *ναῦς*
> ἐρῆμος ἀνδρῶν μὴ ξυνοικούντων ἔσω.
>
> For if you are to continue ruling, as you govern now,
> better rule a land that has men than one that is empty,
> since a *wall* or a *ship* is nothing
> without men who live inside it.[207]

Again, within the sentence the sequence contains no violation of collocation rules, and yet the focus on πύργος ('wall', 'tower') and ναῦς ('ship'), as exemplary of the ruler's dependency on the civic body of the polis, are evocative beyond their denotative value. Highlighted by the οὔτε... οὔτε construction, they appear to point to two spheres, one internal (the defence of the polis) and one external (trade and war); without the support of his citizens, a ruler can neither defend his rule nor activate it in relation to the outside world. One might—just—wonder whether it makes sense to invoke a 'paratactic analogy',[208] that is, an analogy implied through the suggestively parallel syntactic arrangement of not (or not clearly) subordinate elements (in contrast to the explicit and more clearly hypotactic simile), but there is no formal or other pressure to do so.

A further point of kinship between this phenomenon and metonymy proper is its potential to involve cliché in the shape of elevated poetic language. Euripides' *Iphigenia among the Taurians* provides a good example. In the verse

> δοκοῦσ' Ὀρέστην μηκέθ' *ἥλιον βλέπειν*
>
> Thinking that Orestes no longer *looks upon the sun*[209]

[207] S. *OT* 54–7; trans. Lloyd-Jones.
[208] See e.g. Johansen 1959, 16–49 (where this passage is, however, not cited).
[209] E. *IT* 349; trans. Kovacs.

the reader will assume that 'looking upon the sun' is not what is at issue here, but whether or not Orestes is still alive. However, no breach of collocation rules occurs which would make this literal reading impossible. The literal reading's narrow scope is merely made implausible, though not impossible, by the context. Compare the following instances from the same play:

> οὐδείς γε, πλὴν θανοῦσαν οὐχ *ὁρᾶν φάος*.
> No, save that she is dead and does not *look on the light.*[210]

> ὃν οὐδὲν ἧσσον ἢ 'μὲ *φῶς ὁρᾶν* θέλω.
> and I desire that he should *look on the light* no less than I.[211]

> αἰσχρὸν θανόντος σοῦ *βλέπειν* ἡμᾶς *φάος*:
> It is disgraceful for me to *look on the light* with you dead.[212]

Comparable formulations can be found elsewhere, for instance in Sophocles' *Oedipus Tyrannus*:

> ὦ *φῶς*, τελευταῖόν *σε προσβλέψαιμι* νῦν
> O *light*, may I now *look on you* for the last time[213]

This same cliché also serves as the basis for subsequent literary appropriations, for instance in Goethe's *Iphigenia among the Taurians*:

> ...Und laß dir raten habe
> *Die Sonne* nicht zu lieb und nicht *die Sterne*;
> Komm, folge mir in's dunkle Reich hinab!

> ...and let me recommend you not to
> Love *the sun* too much or *the stars*;
> Come, follow me down into the dark realm![214]

Where such a formulation is so frequent, it effectively acquires denotative value in its 'extended' sense and in this regard resembles 'dead metonyms' which have entered ordinary usage.

How should we understand the examples discussed in this section? If we take the reading experience seriously, it cannot be denied that here too a shift occurs which resembles the metonymic shifts discussed in earlier chapters. At the same time, my opening argument about tropicality and the tropical space makes it inappropriate to consider these instances as metonymic *tropes*. If tropes are essentially characterized by

210 E. *IT* 564; trans. Kovacs.
211 E. *IT* 608; trans. Kovacs.
212 E. *IT* 674; trans. Kovacs.
213 S. *OT* 1183; trans. Lloyd Jones.
214 Goethe, *Iphigenie auf Tauris. Ein Schauspiel*, 1232–4.

the negation, in context, of a term's meaning in ordinary usage, none of the above cases can be deemed tropical. Instead, we are dealing with *associations* characterized by a specific conformation that might, still, be best described as 'metonymic'. What we see here, then, is a first extension of the term 'metonymy' and 'metonymic' beyond its original confines of tropology proper—but one that is warranted and, indeed, called for by literary analysis. I propose to refer to such instances as *metonymic association*. The distinction between metonymic association and metonymy proper (in all its various forms) is an important one, since it highlights, by comparison and contrast, the specific lexical-linguistic nature of metonymy proper. In metonymic association, a shift of understanding is contextually compelling; in metonymy proper, it is lexico-linguistically inevitable. The distinction also makes it apparent that any attempt to elucidate the structural organization of the tropical space can only be valid when based on metonymy proper. Failure to make the distinction must inevitably lead to confusion, once such associations are conflated with deviation from ordinary usage.[215] As we shall see, this distinction is also important when assessing complex literary devices which appear to have both a metonymic and a metaphorical dimension, such as (certain types of) personification and synecdoche to which we now turn.

PERSONIFICATION

Personifications involve applications of extraneous terminology (the terminology of humans and human agency) to non-humans, objects, and abstractions. And they are essentially metaphorical:[216] if an object or

[215] Confusion of precisely this kind tends to compromise structuralist reappropriations of tropology, for instance, several of De Man's close readings in his *Allegories of Reading*, which will be discussed in more detail below; see pp. 267–71.

[216] Ancient critics differentiate between personification of inanimate objects/concepts through attribution of speech or through other forms of personified behaviour, but they do not show any awareness of its structural similarity with metaphor (for a compilation of the relevant discussions by ancient critics see Lausberg 1960, 369–72 and Stafford 2000, 5–9). This is surprising given that Aristotle's subclassifications of metaphor are based on the possible combinations of animate and inanimate terminology (see Arist. *Rhet.* 1411b–1412a), one of which, treating inanimate objects or concepts as if alive, without doubt subsumes personification. The fourfold classification of metaphor (animate as animate, inanimate as animate, animate as inanimate, inanimate as inanimate) is maintained by the rhetorical handbook tradition (see e.g. Quint. *Inst.* 8.6.9 and Trypho, *Trop.* 730), but personification is generally discussed separately. Modern critics tend to continue this classification of personification as a distinct category in its own right rather than as a subcategory of metaphor, although they often associate the two. Landfester, for instance,

concept is said to (consciously) 'act' it is inevitably likened to humans and thereby displays metaphor's definitive characteristic of an underlying or implied similarity and/or analogy.[217] The object or concept is cast in another light by portraying it in the terminology of human agency which is alien to it and reconfigures the way it is perceived. An example from Goethe's poem 'Maifest' illustrates the point:

> Wie herrlich leuchtet
> Mir die Natur!
> Wie glänzt die Sonne!
> Wie lacht die Flur!
>
> How magnificently nature
> Shines for me!
> How the sun glistens!
> How the meadow laughs![218]

The metaphorically used verb 'lacht' ('laughs') expresses the exuberance and liveliness of the natural world in spring by analogy with the human activity of laughter.

If we accept this definition in terms of an implied analogy, it immediately becomes clear that personification is not a phenomenon of poetic language on the same level as metaphor and metonymy. Instead, among the countless terminologies which can be drawn on in metaphorical expressions, one specific terminology in metaphorical usage has been isolated here: personification is not *another* trope on a par with metaphor and metonymy, but rather a terminology-specific subcategory of metaphor. As such, it is equivalent, in taxonomic terms, to 'zoomorphization' (extraneous application of animal terminology) or 'nautification'

notes that 'personification... is frequently part of a metaphorical expression' ('[d]ie Personifikation... ist häufig Teil einer metaphorischen Aussage'; Landfester 1997, 194). Similarly, Lausberg concludes his discussion of *fictio personae* by stating that '[i]n general the personifying metaphor... and allegory... may, in the final analysis, be included under this heading' (Lausberg 1960, 372) and Knapp defines '[a]llegorical personification' as 'the endowing of metaphors with agency of literal persons...' (Knapp 1985, 2).

[217] This makes personifications an illustration par excellence of Black's point, cited earlier (above, p. 42), that the similarity which underlies metaphor is not necessarily a given which the metaphor exploits but may also be constructed by the metaphor itself. Coleridge, too, seems to be aware of this when he argues in his third lecture of 1818 (albeit in a discussion of allegory rather than individual personifications): '[w]e may... safely define allegoric writing as the employment of one set of agents and images with actions and accompaniments correspondent, so as to convey, while in disguise, either moral qualities or conceptions of the mind that are not in themselves objects of the senses, or other images, agents, actions, fortunes, and circumstances, so that the difference is everywhere presented to the eye or imagination while the likeness is suggested to the mind; and this connectedly so that the parts combine to form a consistent whole.' Coleridge 1818, 30.

[218] Goethe, 'Maifest', 1–4.

(extraneous application of nautical terminology) and so on.[219] While it is certainly useful in the critical analysis of individual pieces of literature to examine which particular terminologies are drawn upon in metaphorical usage, it is misleading to think of personification as different in kind from metaphor when theorizing poetic language.

There are, however, instances of personification which complicate this picture and make the differentiation between personification, metaphor, and metonymy less clear-cut. Landfester, for instance, defines personification as the 'introduction of a non-person (object, collective entity, animal, abstract concept) as a (speaking/acting) person',[220] and cites the following verse from Euripides' *Phoenician Women* as an example:

> βοᾶι δὲ *δῶμα* πᾶν…
>
> My whole *house* is wailing…[221]

Is 'house' here indeed personified, or should we rather understand it as an index metonym? That is: does 'house' metonymically imply 'the persons in the house'? The sequence undoubtedly meets Landfester's own definition of personification: an object, 'house', is introduced as a speaking/acting person; but, then again, one notes that his definition of personification significantly overlaps with traditional definitions of metonymy in the rhetorical handbook tradition. Content-based categories like 'container for contained' or 'city for inhabitant' must inevitably fall under Landfester's definition of personification if the metonymic

[219] When discussions of metaphor are based on classifications of vehicle terminology, personification naturally emerges as one of those groupings. Breitenbach, for instance, who proceeds in this fashion in his evaluation of Euripides' lyrical passages, lists in one chapter 'Metaphors and similes according to their subject areas' ('Metaphern und Vergleiche nach ihren Stoffgebieten'; Breitenbach 1934, 134–60), and then opens the following chapter by stating that 'the device of personification and of rendering the inanimate animate also belong to metaphor. Through attribution of human traits or activities…this trope gives life and soul to dead objects and makes abstract concepts sensually accessible to the imagination' ('[z]ur Metapher gehört auch das Kunstmittel der Personifikation des Unpersönlichen und der Belebung des Unbelebten. Durch Beilegung der Eigenschaften oder der Tätigkeiten von Menschen…gibt dieser Tropus leblosen Dingen Seele und Leben und bringt abstrakte Begriffe durch Verkörperung der sinnlichen Anschauung nahe'; Breitenbach 1934, 165). Despite this moment of good sense, however, Breitenbach maintains personification as a separate category with the status of a trope in its own right. In Pecz's collection of tropes in Aeschylus, Sophocles, and Euripides (Pecz 1886), on the other hand, a tripartite taxonomy—metonymy, synecdoche, 'proportion tropes' (metaphor, allegory, simile)—is maintained and personifications are listed, by and large, in the metaphor section under the heading 'The human' ('Der Mensch').

[220] 'Die Personifikation besteht in der Einführung von etwas Nicht-personhaftem (Gegenstand, Kollektivum, Tier, Abstraktum) als (redender/handelnder) Person.' Landfester 1997, 94.

[221] E. *Phoe.* 1317; trans. Kovacs.

term is attached to a verb denoting speech or (conscious) action. The key issue here is surely to determine what prompts a tropical reading of such a sequence and precisely which elements are understood in a way that deviates from ordinary usage. In his example, Landfester prints δῶμα ('house') in bold, thereby implying that this is the tropically used term. This seems right: given that the context of this verse is Creon's weeping and groaning over the loss of his son (cf. v. 1310), βοᾶι ('wails', 'cries') literally denotes what is at issue here. The terminology of humans and human agency—here crying or wailing—is not extraneous to the sequence, nor is any similarity or analogy implied between the sounds produced by human crying and the actual sounds at issue. On reflection it is apparent that personification too is a verb-centred phenomenon: what turns a term into a personification (or what 'introduces' it as a person, to use Landfester's phrasing) is collocation with verbs which in ordinary usage denote actions confined to the terminology of humans. We can therefore formulate the general rule, as follows: the tropical element in any *personification* is not the term which (as we tend to say) 'is personified' but the verb which personifies that term. Nouns can be *personified*, but *personification* is essentially concerned with a specific type of action, and thus depends on a specific usage of specific (implied or explicit) verbs.[222] In the instance under discussion, however, the verb is understood literally, and it is therefore misleading to base a tropological analysis of the sequence on it. Instead, the illegitimate collocation of βοᾶι ('wails') and δῶμα ('house') involves a metonymic shift in the understanding of the noun and the inference of some related but different expressions compatible with the literal verb: 'my entire household', 'all the people in the house'.

Yet if this argument serves to corroborate the view that personification constitutes a special case of metaphor, there are uses of personification that appear to point a different way. Consider an example from Hölderlin's poem 'Die Heimat':

> Ihr teuern *Ufer*, die mich erzogen einst,
> Stillt ihr der Liebe Leiden, versprecht ihr mir,
> Ihr Wälder meiner Jugend, wenn ich
> Komme, die Ruhe noch einmal wieder?

[222] Nouns and adjectives, insofar as they denote human action, can fulfil the same function thanks to the implicit verbal nature of any action. On the non-grammatical nature of metaphor's verb-centredness, see above, pp. 121–2, n. 151. The same is true (though for different reasons) for the different grammatical realizations of apostrophe, which constitutes—irrespective of whether or not it involves a verb in the second person—a speech act that interpellates a human counterpart insofar as it implies a scenario, real or imagined, in which the addressee can *hear* and *understand* the words of the apostrophe.

You dear *riverbanks*, who once raised me,
Will you soothe love's sorrow, will you promise me,
You forests of my youth, if/when I
Come, peace once more?[223]

The 'riverbanks' ('Ufer') are apostrophized and attributed with human agency when they are said to have 'raised ('erzogen') the poetic 'I', thus encouraging us to understand 'Ufer' ('riverbanks') here as personified and the sequence, *a fortiori*, as metaphorical. Yet there appears to be a difference between the personification of 'Ufer' ('riverbanks') in the first two lines and the personification of 'Wälder' ('forests') in the second two. With the 'forests', a natural phenomenon is apostrophized and personified by attribution of human agency ('versprecht ihr mir', 'will you promise me'), and the poetic effect goes no further. With the 'riverbanks', on the other hand, the metaphorically used verb seems simultaneously to evoke a metonymic understanding of the personified 'Ufer'. In addition to the landscape itself, the formulation also seems to evoke the people living at or around those riverbanks, who once literally 'raised' the poetic 'I'. Are we to understand 'mich erzogen einst' ('raised me once') literally, which means that we understand 'Ufer' ('riverbanks') as an index metonym (for the inhabitants of the area)? Or, conversely, are we to understand the verb as a metaphor, which implicitly compares the formative influence of the landscape on the childhood (and childhood memories) of the poetic 'I' with the formative influence of his parents, and personifies 'riverbanks' in the process of creating this analogy? Both readings seem perfectly plausible. The next verb, 'stillen' ('soothe'), does not eliminate the ambiguity either, since both the sight of the familiar riverbanks and of one's family may literally be said to be 'soothing'. This instance, then, constitutes a case of 'conditional metonymy' as discussed above. In the light of the unambiguous personification that follows, and given the general focus on landscape rather than persons, a reader may be more inclined to read this instance too as a case of personification; but that reading still coexists with a possible metonymic reading.

Compare these lines from Hölderlin's 'Hymne an die Freiheit':

Keck erhub sich des *Gesetzes Rute*,
Nachzubilden, was die Liebe schuf;
Ach! Gegeißelt von dem Übermute
Fühlte keiner göttlichen Beruf

[223] Hölderlin, 'Die Heimat', 5–8.

Brashly the *rod of law* rose up
To recreate what love had created;
Alas! Castigated by such hubris
Nobody felt a divine calling[224]

The passage contains a tropical cluster, and personification lies at its centre: the 'rod of law' ('des Gesetzes Rute') is personified (animated) by two verbs, 'rose up' ('erhub sich') and 'recreate' ('nachzubilden'), as well as by an accompanying adverb, 'keck' ('brashly'), all of which imply human agency. The verbs, and the accompanying adverb, can neither be collocated with 'rod of law' as their subject in ordinary usage, nor are they understood here in the sense which they would have in ordinary usage. What is at issue is the 'progression' from a lost Golden Age when love guided all human behaviour to the current age characterized by laws men have created and imposed on each other, which are enforced by threat of punishment. The emergence of this new law-and-order regime is defined by analogy with a person getting up and ready for action; the attempt to create a just society artificially by analogy with moulding or sculpting. While the 'rod of law' is thus personified, there is clearly more to it than just its personification. The parallel between the original 'creation' of a social order by love followed by a 're-creation' of a social order by law and punishment suggests that the equivalent to 'love' should be also an abstract concept: 'law', 'legal prosecution', 'fear of punishment', or whatever. Thus, even if the personifying verbs are understood metaphorically, 'the rod of the law' is understood as evoking, metonymically, more abstract concepts. Yet is 'the rod of law' in this particular context a straightforward metonym? The genitive structure of the compound alerts us to an amplification metonym: from law in general the focus is shifted to its punishing aspect, which is represented by an instrument used for such punishment. Then the third line picks up the image of the rod again and develops it further, though now in metaphorical usage, with 'gegeißelt von dem Übermute' ('castigated by such hubris'). Should we, all in all, invoke a personified amplification metonym here? My earlier discussions have shown that metonymy is more context-dependent than the relatively self-contained metaphorical tenor–vehicle compound. In a case like Hölderlin's here, the immediate syntactic context does not provide a sufficiently stable frame of reference of literally used terms from which a metonym could stand out in its deviant usage. While the context strongly suggests a metonymic understanding of a term, its meaning in ordinary usage is not negated or made

[224] Hölderlin, 'Hymne an die Freiheit', 49–52.

impossible by the microcontext. My analysis of tropical clusters has shown the tendency of metaphors to outdo metonyms in terms of poetic effect. Here, a fully metaphorical microcontext seems to undermine the conditions for metonymy proper so that the shift is better understood as a case of metonymic association.

Personifications appear to carry an increased potential for creating a context in which the tropical status of individual terms is hard to ascertain, either because they introduce possibilities for optional tropical readings or because they compel the reader to construct further associations. The fact that such ambiguities go beyond the primary effect of personification itself (the metaphorical attribution of human terms to non-human entities) is surely part of the attractiveness of this device and may be one of the reasons why theorists feel the need to classify it as an independent trope in its own right. Nevertheless, a structural analysis of the mechanisms at work in personification proper tends to confirm that it is based on a mode of defamiliarization along the lines of metaphor and constitutes a terminology-specific variant of metaphor. Retaining personification in critical practice, as a category to refer to this particular subset of metaphor, is surely helpful and legitimate as it allows us to highlight the specific *terminological* colouring of a literary work's tropological texture. The metaphorical attribution of human agency, specifically, can create, among other things, increased possibilities for embedding psychological motivations into narrative events and a greater proximity between the characters of a text and the narrative world they inhabit—in a way that is not open to metaphors which draw on other, non-human terminologies. But setting personification comprehensively apart from metaphor by treating it (unjustifiably and misleadingly) as an altogether different trope risks exaggerating the *differences* between authors, texts, and styles in terms of their (characteristic) use of metaphorical expressions by obfuscating actual *similarities* in their respective tropological texturing beneath the level of (predominant) terminology. That is to say, it inadvertently shifts the focus of analysis from tropology to vocabulary, to the implications of the words used rather than the mode of expression employed. The ensuing distortions are further compounded by the fact that metonymic components are, as we have seen, frequently overshadowed by metaphorical elements, due to the latter's more prominent poetic effects, and a perception of personification as a stand-alone trope is bound to concentrate critical attention on the more immediately apparent metaphorical elements of such expressions—at the expense of the more subtle metonymic elements that often occur in such contexts, adding further nuances and shades of meaning. A more finely tuned critical apparatus, by contrast, which recognizes the metaphorical nature of personification itself and its propensity to trigger further tropical readings in its context, makes it possible to discern these further elements and to discuss instances of personification in all their complex richness. Similar gains can be achieved by clarifying the contested tropological status of another poetic device: synecdoche—the last metonymic presence that needs addressing.

SYNECDOCHE

Closely related to the issue of personification is the question of synecdoche's position within the order of the tropical space. While personification is usually (if unhelpfully) understood as a trope in its own right, synecdoche's relation to both metaphor and metonymy has been subject to debate—and remains unresolved.[225] In critical practice, both classical scholars and literary scholars more broadly have tended to operate within the framework of the rhetorical handbook tradition, taking metaphor, metonymy, and synecdoche as three distinct phenomena of poetic language.[226] Within theories of rhetoric and poetics, however, synecdoche is subsumed under either metaphor or metonymy. The debates that continue to revolve around the uncertain status of synecdoche as well as the resulting inconsistencies and divergences in mobilizations of the term in critical practice bear a striking, conspicuous resemblance to those surrounding metonymy—not least because synecdoche, too, is invoked in both stylistic and (post-)structuralist analyses. The fact that we have here nothing less than a *mise en abîme* of the entire conundrum that the present study seeks to resolve, and one that simultaneously promises to provide us with a new angle to shed fresh light on many of the key problems at stake here, makes it desirable to briefly suspend the discussion of concrete examples and to return for a moment to earlier theorizations—now of synecdoche—before offering a positive argument for a better understanding of synecdoche in the light of the new theory of metonymy developed here.

[225] 'Confusion piles upon obscurity when we consider the treatment given to synecdoche... there is general disagreement on its relation to metonymy' (Bredin 1984, 45). This is particularly true of more recent, semiotic approaches to tropology. As Eco observes, 'It is very difficult indeed to consider... metaphor without seeing it in a framework that necessarily includes both synecdoche and metonymy—so difficult, in fact, that a trope that seems to be the most primary will appear instead as the most derivative, as the result of a semantic calculus that presupposes other, preliminary semiotic operations' (Eco 1984, 87). On the status of synecdoche as one of the 'master tropes', see also above, pp. 25–6.

[226] This is equally true of commentaries and of large-scale studies of stylistics and tropology, such as Pecz 1886 and Breitenbach 1934.

The root of the confusion surrounding synecdoche lies, once more, in Aristotle's broad and ambiguous usage of μεταφορά ('metaphor') in his *Poetics*.[227] After defining 'metaphor' (or rather tropicality) in substitutionalist terms as 'the transference of a term from one thing to another',[228] Aristotle suggests four ways in which such 'transference' can occur: from genus to species, from species to genus, from species to species, and by analogy. Both the theoretical exposition as well as the examples he gives make clear that only the fourth category constitutes metaphor proper, whereas the examples given for the other three range from dead metaphor (νηῦς δέ μοι ἥ δ' ἕστηκεν, 'here stands my ship') to metonymic hyperbole (ἦ δὴ μυρί' Ὀδυσσεὺς ἐσθλὰ ἔοργεν, 'indeed, ten thousand noble things did Odysseus')[229] and multiple metonymy (τεμὼν ταναήκεϊ χαλκῷ, 'cutting off with the tireless bronze'). His fourfold classification, however, is influential for the later development of a more diversified view of the tropical space. As with μετωνυμία, the term συνεκδοχή itself does not appear in Aristotle's theorizing but features as an established technical term in the later Greek rhetoricians,[230] the Stoic grammarians,[231] and in the late Hellenistic *Rhetorica ad Herennium*.[232] All of these treat synecdoche as a trope in its own right, but the definitions they give overlap with Aristotle's types of μεταφορά: synecdoche is primarily understood as a 'substitution' of a part for the whole or of the whole for a part, thus corresponding, more or less, to Aristotle's categories of species for genus and genus for species.[233] At the same time, the examples cited by these writers to illustrate synecdoche are barely distinguishable from those used to illustrate metonymy. Eco notes that this imprecision continues on the level of theoretical analysis:

> As a matter of fact, traditional rhetoric has never satisfactorily explained why a substitution genus/species... and a substitution *pars/totum*... are both synecdoches, whereas all other kinds of substitution (object/purpose, container/content, cause/effect, material/object, and so on) are called metonymies.[234]

[227] See Arist. *Poet.* 1457b7; on this point, see also above, pp. 37–8.

[228] Arist. *Poet.* 1457b7; trans. Halliwell.

[229] Cf. Silk 2003, 116–18.

[230] See, for instance, Trypho, *Trop.* 739.27–740.11, Anon. *De Trop.* 718.25–719.25, Greg. Cor. *De Trop.* 769.11–770.31.

[231] For a collection of relevant instances, see Barwick 1957, 90–1.

[232] See Auct. ad Her. 4.44–5.

[233] The correspondence is not absolute: strictly speaking, the part–whole relationship is frequently understood as referring to material reality (material parts of a whole object), whereas the genus–species relationship is understood as referring to intellectual reality (a specific class of things as part of a larger, more general class of things). Whether this differentiation is helpful for the study of poetic language is questionable; see below, pp. 163–5.

[234] Eco 1984, 116; italics in the original.

Quintilian is the first to address the relationship between metaphor, metonymy, and synecdoche explicitly. Initially he distinguishes synecdoche from metaphor and then, as he moves on to discuss metonymy, states that 'there is no great gap between synecdoche and metonymy'.[235] Accordingly, from Quintilian onwards, one strand of criticism has insisted that synecdoche should be understood as a variant and subcategory of metonymy. According to Barwick, Stoic grammarians considered metonymy, synecdoche, and antonomasia as a group of related tropes, collectively characterized by the operative principle of *vicinitas* ('proximity'), in which we can see another precursor of the more recent term 'contiguity'.[236] This view re-emerges in the rhetorical tradition, for instance in Dumarsais's view (1729) that '[s]ynecdoche, then, is a species of metonymy by which . . . I take the more for the less, or the less for the more'.[237] Likewise, in Jakobson's bipolar conceptualization of the tropical space, synecdoche is subsumed under metonymy,[238] a view endorsed by critics who accept Jakobson's basic assumption.[239] Others, however, have questioned this affiliation. Genette, for instance, views it as a consequence of an inadequate understanding of metonymic contiguity as spatial proximity or contact.[240] Yet, in his critique, in which he calls for a sharper differentiation of the various relationships that exist between constituent elements and a greater whole, he remains entirely concerned with conceptual content:

This reduction [*sc.* subsuming synecdoche under metonymy] no doubt has its origin in an almost inevitable confusion between the relation of the part to the whole and the relation of the same part to the *other parts* that make up the whole: a relation, it might be said, of the part to the *remainder* . . . one might read *ad libitum*, in the figure by attribute ('crown' for 'monarch', for example), a metonymy or a synecdoche, depending on whether one regards the crown as simply linked to the monarch, or as forming part of him, by virtue of the implicit axiom: no monarch without a crown. One then sees that every metonymy can be

[235] Quint. *Inst.* 8.6.23: *Nec ab hoc genere* [*sc.* synecdoche] *procul discedit metonymia.*

[236] Barwick 1957, 90; see also above, p. 47.

[237] 'La Synecdoque est donc une espèce de métonymie, par laquelle on done une signification particulière à un mot, qui, dans le sens propre, a une signification plus générale; ou au contraire, on done une signification générale à un mot, qui, dans le sens propre n'a qu'une signification particulière. En un mot, dans la métonymie je prens un sens pour un autre, au lieu que dans la sinecdoque [sic], je prens le *plus* pour le *moins*, ou le *moins* pour le *plus*.' Dumarsais 1729, 115; italics in the original.

[238] This is made most explicit when Jakobson notes that 'Uspenskij had a penchant for metonymy, especially for synecdoche' (Jakobson 1956, 257).

[239] See, for instance, Silk 1974, 6 and 2003, 124 as well as Landfester 1997, 92–3.

[240] 'To reduce every metonymy (*a fortiori* every synecdoche) to a pure spatial relation is obviously to restrict the play of these figures to their physical or sensory aspect alone . . .' Genette 1970a, 109–10.

converted into a synecdoche by appeal to the higher totality, and every synecdoche into a metonymy by recourse to the relations between constituent parts. The fact that each figure-event can be analysed in two ways at will certainly does not imply that these two ways are in fact one... but one can see very well how in fact this kind of double membership might cause confusion.[241]

Genette is sceptical of any attempt to reduce the various modalities of metaphorical and metonymic relations to just two principles, analogy and contiguity,[242] and he sees in synecdoche a prime example of the supposed shortcomings of this bipolar view:

The schema of intersection has never really, in any tropology, classical or modern, defined synecdoche: it concerns in fact an inclusion, or belonging... and [is] of a logical rather than of a spatial type: the inclusion of 'sail' in 'ship' might be regarded as spatial, but in no sense is that of 'iron' in 'sword', or 'man' in 'mortal'. Were it so, rhetoricians would not define the figure 'to drink a glass', as they constantly do, as a *metonymy of content*, but as a synecdoche, considering that the wine is 'included' in the glass—a blunder they have never committed.[243]

Genette's argumentation here is not original but belongs to a long-standing tradition that seeks to establish an underlying (and differential) logic of synecdoche and metonymy.[244] While metonymy persistently eludes such attempts,[245] synecdoche, understood as a 'substitution' based on a part–whole relationship, appears to promise some such logical basis. Pecz, for example, presents an equation that reflects Genette's concerns: 'Synecdoche = a pro $a + b$, or $a + b$ pro a... Metonymy = a pro b or b pro a.'[246]

[241] Genette 1970a, 108–9; italics in the original.
[242] See Genette 1970a, 115.
[243] Genette 1970a, 115–16; italics in the original.
[244] Compare, for instance, Genette's discussion here with Pecz's attempt to tackle the problem: 'Already the ancients had an adequate grasp of the nature of synecdoche and metonymy when they proposed that in the former a part stands for the whole or the whole for a part, and in the latter the cause for the result or the result for the cause... we have attempted to differentiate in a proper way between what is seemingly very similar but ultimately different. Thus we have taken, for instance, the expressions "fir for ship", "fir for fleet" as metonyms, but we considered it advisable to view the expression "beam for ship" as a synecdoche.' ('Das Wesen der Synecdoche und der Metonymie fassten schon die Alten richtig auf, als sie behaupteten, dass im einen der Theil für das Ganze oder das Ganze für den Theil, im anderen die Ursache für das Verursachte oder das Verursachte für die Ursache stehe... Ferner trachteten wir das scheinbar einander sehr Aehnliche aber doch von einander Verschiedene gebührend zu unterscheiden. Wir haben z. B. die Ausdrücke: "die Fichte für das Schiff", "die Fichte für die Flotte" als Metonymien genommen, aber den Ausdruck "der Balken für das Schiff" hielten wir schon für angerathen als Synecdoche zu betrachten.' Pecz 1886, 3 and 10). It is at once obvious that Pecz's definition of metonymy as a 'substitution' based on a cause–result relationship is unsustainable since even his own example for metonymy ('fir for fleet') falls outside this definition.
[245] See above, pp. 154–6.
[246] 'Die Synecdoche = a pro $a + b$, oder $a + b$ pro a... Die Metonymie = a pro b oder b pro a.' Pecz 1886, 4.

The first thing to note here is that both Pecz's and Genette's discussions privilege conceptual content, and the problems they attempt to confront arise primarily from having chosen an approach which offers few dividends for a systematic, structural understanding of poetic language. As Eco has rightly pointed out,

> when it is specified that the synecdoche carries out a substitution within the *conceptual content* of a term, while metonymy acts outside of that content, it is hard to see why the part for the whole is a synecdoche and the material for the object a metonymy—as though it were 'conceptually' essential for an object to have constituent parts and not to be made of some material.[247]

Moreover, given the impossibility of establishing one single 'logic' of contiguity, it is also apparent that any attempt to distinguish metonymy from synecdoche by constructing an opposition between 'logical' synecdoche and extra-logical metonymy is deeply problematic, since metonymy in its traditional sense already encompasses various logical relationships (container 'for' contained, product 'for' producer, etc.).[248] The argument that synecdoche is characterized by a particular logical relationship between its elements may therefore (at most) distinguish synecdoche as a particular type of metonymy, but it does not warrant the conclusion that synecdoche is different in kind from metonymy *on a structural level.* As we have shown, what distinguishes *metaphor* from metonymy is that the metaphorical compound is characterized by both an underlying logic of analogy/similarity and a resulting collocation of otherwise incompatible terminologies, whereas metonymy is characterized by a shift within a given terminology, that is, within a semantic field. Pecz's and Genette's focus on the 'conceptual content' ignores the terminological dimension, and thus sidelines what should be at the centre of any discussion that seeks to illuminate poetic language.

Before proposing a better way of theorizing synecdoche, which, as I will argue, should indeed be seen as a variant of metonymy, it is worth taking account of the counterargument that synecdoche should be seen as connected with metaphor. The most important proponents of this view are the Groupe μ.[249] These critics use the principle of 'decomposition' in their analyses to conclude that metaphor is a combination of two synecdoches. Culler illustrates this notion with the following example:

> Metaphor is a combination of two synecdoches: it moves from a whole to one of its parts to another whole which contains that part, or from a member to a

[247] Eco 1984, 90. [248] See above, pp. 48–9.
[249] See Groupe μ 1982, 91–119; as a precursor of this view, see also Cohen 1966, 105–35.

general class and then back again to another member of that class. Starting... from 'oak' we have:

member	→	*class*	→	*member*
oak		tall things		any tall person or object
		strong things		any strong person or object
whole	→	*part*	→	*whole*
Oak		branches		anything with branches (banks?)
				anything with roots

The move from member to class to member is the most common procedure for interpreting metaphors.[250]

The problem with this approach is the opposite of the one that compromises Genette and Pecz. While *their* focus on 'logical' relationships leads them to ignore the central fact of tropical terminology, the Groupe μ critics take terminological considerations into a dimension where it is misleading to do so. What their theory does is effectively translate the logical principle of analogy/similarity at the heart of metaphor into—itself—a terminological format: the *tertium comparationis*, which links tenor and vehicle in metaphor, is analysed as if it were—itself—actual terminology. Yet, as Ricoeur points out,

> It goes without saying that the reader of a metaphor is not conscious of the two operations. He is conscious only of the transfer of meaning from the first term to the second... This is why the reader does not sense the impoverishment involved in passing through 'the narrow path of the semic intersection,' but on the contrary feels a sense of enlargement, an opening up, an amplification.[251]

The problem is evident. If tropical language consists *structurally and aesthetically* in perceptible deviation from ordinary usage and is therefore—itself—essentially a terminological phenomenon, how can any theorizing based on something the reader can *not* perceive lead to a better understanding of the poetic mechanisms and effects of such phenomena? Moreover, the concept of two synecdoches intersecting in one point is itself misleading. One need only call to mind one of Brooke-Rose's examples to see this. By way of illustrating the verbal nature of metaphor, she argues that 'the fire of love' is based on the notion that 'if love burns, it is a fire'.[252] Are 'love' and 'fire' members of the class 'things that burn'? Does 'love' ever literally 'burn'? And what about other classes of things which both terms could be said to be members of, such as 'things that warm', 'things that consume', 'things that destroy', 'things that easily get out of control', 'forces

[250] Culler 1975, 180–1. [251] Ricoeur 1975, 165.
[252] Brooke-Rose 1958, 155; see also above, pp. 86–7.

of nature'? It is misleading to assume merely one common denominator for a metaphor's tenor and vehicle; the logical relation of analogy and similarity provides an inclusive principle that more adequately acknowledges the possibility of both single and multiple points of contact.[253]

What is remarkable about the double-synecdoche model for metaphor is that it relies on the traditional 'conceptual content' theory of semantic fields, albeit in the terminology of more recent linguistics. In order for this model to work, one must identify a field to which both tenor and vehicle belong ('things that...'), which is then said to constitute the point of contact at which the two synecdoches intersect. But any such attempt to use the traditional semantic-field theory to explain metaphor is flawed. As we have seen, not only does the 'decomposition' fail to reduce the metaphorical statement to a literal statement, but the restriction to just one semantic field also makes it impossible to accommodate any metaphors that are based on more than one point of similarity or analogy. This is important for my overall argument because the Groupe μ's position also entails the modern monistic view of the tropical space. The notion of synecdochical decomposition and reduction leads the Groupe μ to postulate an 'intermediary term' at the heart of both metaphor and metonymy. According to this view, both tenor and vehicle share a seme in metaphor (the element that indicates that both are 'things that...'), whereas, in metonymy, tenor and vehicle are included in an ensemble of semes that belong together:

> And this is the place to remember the notions of denotation and connotation... Metaphor involves denotative semes, nuclear semes, included in the definition of terms. Metonymy, on the other hand, involves connotative semes, that is to say, semes contiguous within a larger grouping and combining to define this grouping.[254]

Synecdoche is represented here as a technical linguistic operation: the isolation of a seme.[255] In synecdoche, this isolation itself would be the

[253] Although Ricoeur himself does not pursue this line of argument, the critique offered here is consistent with his criticism that 'it is certainly possible to decompose a *given* metaphor into two synecdoches; but one cannot *produce* a metaphor with two synecdoches... One may doubt that metaphorical comparison... can be equated in this way with synecdochic reduction.' Ricoeur 1975, 166–7; italics in the original. Ricoeur himself takes the view 'that metonymy and synecdoche belong on the same side, in that they can be defined and explained as accidents of denomination.' Ricoeur 1975, 346.

[254] 'Et c'est ici le lieu de se raccorder aux notions de dénotation et de connotation... La métaphore fait intervenir des sèmes dénotatifs, sèmes nucléaires, inclus dans la définition des termes. La métonymie par contre fait intervenir de sèmes connotatifs, c'est-à-dire contigus au sein d'un ensemble plus vaste et concourant à la définition de cet ensemble.' Groupe μ 1982, 118.

[255] This includes both the *pars pro toto* and the *totum pro parte* variants of synecdoche: 'being a part of something' constitutes a seme just as much as 'being a collective of'.

poetic mechanism and effect; in metaphor, this isolation is seen as an intermediary stage between the tenor and vehicle which share the seme that the implicit synecdoches isolate; in metonymy, the tenor and the vehicle are implicit synecdoches of the intermediary term. Metonymy here is not subsumed under metaphor as one of its variants but is seen as one stage in a process: the stage that leads to metonymy, where the full process results in metaphor. In Ricoeur's words: 'The same theory that demonstrates the close relationship of synecdoche and metonymy also shows that the difference between metaphor and metonymy reduces to a difference between the partial and the total character of *the self-same* addition-suppression operation.'[256] The fact is that this whole approach to analysing poetic language is defective. In the first place, it describes analytical operations which do not pertain to the actual reading experience, and therefore have little to offer by way of explaining the aesthetics of tropes; and, secondly, it relies on an inherent ambiguity in its key concept, 'seme'. The Groupe μ themselves rightly point out that traditional approaches that share their focus on extra-linguistic realities are inadequate,[257] but shifting the focus from 'things' to 'meanings' leads to a new set of complications, and the more so given that 'seme' (the smallest meaning-carrying unit in language) is used here in a way that makes it hover ambiguously between reference to actual terms and identification of conceptual contents.

It is once again clear that a focus on conceptual contents and on logical relationships between such contents fails to provide a satisfying structural analysis, while a focus on semantic components likewise fails to do justice to the aesthetics of poetic language. In the light of the shortcomings—though also the insights—of these views, we can now reassess this phenomenon of synecdoche from the perspective of descriptive poetics.

[256] Ricoeur 1975, 165; italics added.

[257] 'Among modern semanticians, for example in Ullmann's theory referred to above, metonymy is "the transfer of a term by *contiguity of meaning*", this contiguity being "spatial, temporal or causal". In this regard, there would be no great difference between metonymy and synecdoche: in both cases "the thing receives its name from something else with which it comes into contact". We do not dispute that there is in the notion of actual contiguity the beginning of a satisfactory theory of metonymy, but one sees that the problem is poorly posed by this reference to the "thing".' ('Chez les modernes sémanticiens, par example dans la théorie d'Ullmann rappelée plus haut, la métonymie est "transfert du nom par *contiguïté des sens*", cette contiguïté étant "spatiale, temporelle ou causale". A cet égard, il n'y aurait pas grande différence entre la métonymie et la synecdoche: dans l'un et l'autre cas "la chose reçoit son nom d'une autre chose avec laquelle elle se trouve en contact". Nous ne contestons pas qu'il y ait dans la notion de contiguïté réelle, l'amorce d'une théorie satisfaisante de la métonymie, mais on voit que le problème est mal posé par cette référence à la "chose".' Groupe μ 1982, 117).

In its most basic form, synecdoche involves expressing a part through the whole or the whole through a part by using the singular where ordinary language would give the plural and *vice versa*.[258] In such instances, the reader will understand the present singular as an implied plural and will perceive a sharper focus as the effect of this deviance from ordinary usage. Consider, for example, these verses from Euripides' *Iphigenia among the Taurians* and Hölderlin's 'Der Neckar':

> οἰκτρόν τ' ἐκβαλλόντων *δάκρυον*
>
> and shedding a piteous *tear*.[259]
>
> ...aus dem Tal,
> Wie Leben aus dem Freudebecher,
> Glänzte die *bläuliche Silberwelle*
>
> ...from the valley,
> like life from the cup of joy,
> shimmered the *bluish silver-wave*[260]

While this 'zooming' or 'focusing' effect is reminiscent of amplification metonymy, the grammar-based readjustment that occurs in the reading process bears a formal resemblance to grammatical metonymy. In terms of both aesthetic effect and governing structural principle, we therefore have at a most basic level clear similarities with metonymy, but no element of analogy or introduction of extraneous terminology that would point to metaphor. At this point it is worth recalling the earlier discussion of index metonymy and amplification metonymy. Both variants of metonymy are characterized by a shift within a semantic field; the shift is present in the form of a genitive compound in amplification metonymy; the shift is implicit and points to a virtual semantic field in index metonymy. One of Pecz's formulae for synecdoche ($a + b$ pro a) matches precisely the syntactical structure that constitutes amplification metonymy: a, the whole (as the partitive genitive that expresses the metonymic tenor) and b, the part (as the metonymic vehicle that specifies the compound beyond what would be expected in ordinary language). This is, of course, not in itself an argument that synecdoche is a variant of metonymy; one might as well argue, conversely, that what has been classified above as amplification metonymy should better be understood as synecdoche. What is of central importance, rather, is whether it

[258] See, for instance, Cic. *De Or.* 3.168, Auct. ad Her. 4.45, and Quint. *Inst.* 9.3.20.

[259] E. *IT* 228. Note the combination of singular for plural with a grammatical metonym: οἰκτρόν, 'piteous', is transferred from the implied subject to the tear. The teardrop is thus doubly highlighted.

[260] Hölderlin, 'Der Neckar', 7–8.

can be demonstrated that the structural principle at work in both index metonymy and amplification metonymy, namely a lateral shift within a semantic field (implicit in the former and explicit in the syntax of the latter), likewise characterizes synecdoche.

The two commonly acknowledged variants of synecdoche, part for the whole (and *vice versa*) and genus for species (and *vice versa*), find their correspondence in the linguistic concepts of meronymy/holonymy and hyponymy/hypernymy. A meronym denotes a word or other element that together with other elements constitutes a whole. Thus, 'bark', 'leaf', and 'branch' are meronyms of the holonym 'tree'. A hyponym, on the other hand, denotes a word that belongs to a subset whose elements are collectively summarized by a hypernym. Thus, 'tree', 'flower', 'bush' are hyponyms of the hypernym 'plant'. A first observation to be made here is that these two concepts describe relationships on different levels: meronymy/holonymy describes a relationship between elements of material objects. It is the referential object 'leaf' which in extralingual reality forms a part of the whole 'tree'. Hyponymy/hypernymy, by contrast, refers to a relationship between concepts. 'Flowers' and 'trees' are jointly classified as 'plants', but in extralingual reality there is no 'plant' that consists of 'flowers' and 'trees'. In other words, the first relationship is extralingual, the second relationship is conceptual.

Genette's attempted critique of the reduction of synecdoche to metonymy relies precisely on the alleged irreducibility of meronymy to hyponymy.[261] However, both meronymy/holonymy and hyponymy/hypernymy describe a relationship between a subgroup and an overarching point of reference. This is arguably the reason why synecdoche was thought of as a distinct phenomenon in poetic language in the first place, and why examples traditionally given to illustrate synecdoche indiscriminately exploit associations along the lines of both meronymy/holonymy and hyponymy/hypernymy. If one moves away from a logic-based and/or conceptual content-based analysis and adopts a terminological perspective, this becomes all the more obvious: the terms on either end of this relationship can be connected by supplying either an 'and more specifically' or an 'and more generally'. Any deviation from ordinary language in which a hyponym or a meronym is used to imply its hypernym or holonym (and *vice versa*) can easily be transformed into a non-deviant statement if the sequence is thus expanded. Here we should bear in mind Silk's 'operational' suggestion that any deviation from ordinary usage which can be expanded into a literal statement without

[261] See above, pp. 156–7.

using similarity or analogy markers (such as 'like') should be seen as metonymy.[262] The principle surely provides powerful evidence for a structural connection of synecdoche with metonymy. This finds further confirmation if we consider how the shift, which we might explicate with an 'and more specifically/generally', is realized in deviant, tropical language. We have already noted that the meronym/holonym relationship can take the form of a partitive genitive compound.[263] In addition to this *grammatical* option for the particularizing shift from holonym to meronym, the generalizing and the particularizing shift of both variants of synecdoche can be realized *lexically*—when a reading of an implied term or terms is prompted by deviant usage of a term which is too general or too specific to be compatible with the given context. And this, on a structural level, is no different from the workings of index metonymy.

In the new framework proposed, it thus becomes clear that synecdoche shares both the aesthetic effects and the structural mechanisms of metonymy, since it, too, is based on a lateral shift within a semantic field. The revised theory of semantic fields as advanced here, namely as clusters of terms pragmatically constituted through regular co-occurrence in ordinary usage, can also explain synecdoche; the fact that both variants of synecdoche can be readily expanded into non-deviant statements supports this point. Once we get beyond a preoccupation with logical, content-based 'relationships', we can see that synecdoche has to be understood as a specific variant of metonymy, just as personification has to be understood as a specific variant of metaphor.

While metaphor as such is characterized by a logical relation of analogy/similarity and the introduction of extraneous terminology, further distinctions may indeed be made that take account of either the way this logical relation is realized (as Brooke-Rose does) or the particular extraneous terminologies that are introduced (as Pecz and Breitenbach do). Metonymy, characterized by a lateral shift within a semantic field, may, of course, also be subcategorized by taking account of the various 'relationships' between the metonymic vehicle and the metonymic tenor. These 'relationships' are ultimately always abstractions of the most likely expansion of the metonym in question: 'x who/which produces/is produced by y', 'x which contains/is contained by', 'x which is made of y', and so on. Synecdoche, which can be expanded to 'x which is a part of y', 'x which includes y', 'x among which there are y' (and so on), is now shown to be just another set of such 'relationship statements'. Synecdoche is therefore to be seen as a content-specific variant of metonymy

[262] See above, p. 48. [263] See above, pp. 162–3.

but not as a structurally different trope in its own right. As with personification, it may be significant for a particular text that *this* specific variant occurs or is predominant, and for that reason synecdoche (like personification) may have a legitimate place in the critical vocabulary, but the level on which this specificity occurs is not one that warrants the assumption of a difference in kind.

My analyses of these various metonymic presences, their respective complications and complexities, demonstrate and confirm that the theory of metonymy formulated in Chapter 2 and developed over the course the earlier parts of this chapter provides a reliable basis for the analysis of more complex scenarios. The discussion of more complex examples has furthermore provided important additional vindication for Jakobson's claim that metonymy and metaphor should be seen as two basic principles under which other phenomena of tropical language can be subsumed. With the new theoretical framework for understanding metonymy thus established, the next chapter will consider some of its central implications in literary practice while also continuing to refine the new theory of metonymy proposed here. The principles extrapolated, mechanisms analysed, and categories distinguished will now be mobilized and put to use in three different areas of scholarly enquiry—translation criticism, stylistic criticism, and (post-)structuralist criticism.

4 Beyond theory

Metonymy in critical practice

Metonymy, as the opening discussion of this book has made clear, occupies a peculiar position in scholarly discourse: it is, on the one hand, the 'forgotten trope', insofar as the appreciation of its literary aesthetics and the understanding of its core operative principle and different concrete realizations as a stylistic device in poetic language are concerned; yet it is at the same time considered to be a 'master trope' of special importance to our understanding of language and literature at large, including not least as a tool for (post-)structuralist analyses of both verbal and non-verbal discourses. In this chapter, I will therefore examine the impact of the new theory of metonymy advanced in previous chapters on critical practice. In three cases studies, I will explore how the new insights into the workings of metonymy gained here allow us to read and think differently in our engagements with literary texts and how they open up new approaches, perspectives, and avenues of investigation in literary studies and beyond.

Metonymy and translation criticism

The act of translation is a further activity, alongside abstract theorizing, in which a sustained engagement with tropical language becomes unavoidable. As Stanford notes,

> A fine metaphor is one of the hardest things in the world to rationalize. The translator of a play of Aeschylus or an ode of Pindar soon finds that of all stylistic devices metaphors are by far the most fugacious of interpretation in a foreign idiom.[1]

One hastens to add: what is true for metaphor is also true for metonymy (once again deprivileged and elided here vis-à-vis metaphor),[2] but

[1] Stanford 1936, 1.

[2] As noted earlier, Stanford's study of Greek metaphor, from which this quotation is taken, is marked by a pervasive neo-Romantic bias that privileges metaphor over and above all other forms of poetic language; see above, p. 28, n. 12 and p. 35, n. 36.

Stanford's phrasing of '*interpretation* in a foreign idiom' highlights the important point that, since literary translations are inescapably forced to respond to issues of style and defamiliarized language, they become, in a way, the practical (and implicit) counterpart of abstract (and explicit) theorizing in this arena. Ortega y Gasset lucidly summarizes what is at issue here:

> To write well is to make continual incursions into grammar, into established usage, and into accepted linguistic norms. It is an act of permanent rebellion against the social environs, a subversion. To write well is to employ a certain radical courage. Fine, but the translator is usually a shy character... He finds himself facing an enormous controlling apparatus, composed of grammar and common usage. What will he do with the rebellious text? Isn't it too much to ask that he also be rebellious, particularly since the text is someone else's? He will be ruled by cowardice, so instead of resisting grammatical restraints he will do just the opposite: he will place the translated author into the prison of normal expression; that is, he will betray him. *Traduttore, traditore.*[3]

Curiously enough, in contrast to the voluminous literature on metaphor in various fields and disciplines, the translating of metaphors has been largely neglected by translation theorists.[4] Debate has been confined to brief theoretical sketches, rarely supported by (let alone based on) any substantial evaluation of empirical material, and the outcome limited to arguments about various critics' differing concepts and categorizations of metaphor rather than the actual specifics of metaphor in translation.[5] The usefulness of these contributions for practical literary criticism is reduced further by the fact that they follow, by and large, cognitive and conceptual approaches, and consequently pay little or no attention to questions of literary aesthetics.[6] And with metonymy, it is fair to say, critical-theoretical discussion has hardly begun at all.

[3] Ortega y Gasset 1937, 50.

[4] Key contributions to translation theory as compiled in Venuti's *Translation Studies Reader* (Venuti 2000, and indeed Venuti's own influential book *The Translator's Invisibility* (Venuti 1995), contain no discussion of this issue at all. It is symptomatic of the state of research in this field that even a work aimed at comprehensiveness such as the *International Encyclopedia of Translation Studies* (Kittel et al. 2007) contains a meta-critical article 'Metaphor and image in the discourse *on* translation' (Hermans 2007; italics added) but no essay on what happens to actual metaphors, or indeed to any trope, *in* translation; only puns and humour find any discussion (see Delabastita 2007 and Selle 2007, respectively).

[5] However, Dagut 1976 instigated a debate on the translatability of metaphor among linguisticians, which led to a series of responses, notably Newmark 1980, Van den Broeck 1981, Mason 1982, Snell-Hornby 1983, and Dagut 1987. A summary of this debate is given by Fung 1994.

[6] This is particularly true of more recent contributions such as Fung 1994 and Alexieva/Petrequin 2000.

The aim of the first section of this chapter is to make the new theory of metonymy fruitful for translation criticism and, in turn, to further refine this theory by studying metonymy in translation. By comparing metonyms from the ancient Greek text corpus with selected German translations, I shall look at what happens to metonymy under the impact of changed linguistic, syntactic, and cultural contexts. I will also consider whether metonyms are affected by the different translation strategies of each writer and, by way of examining these translations as literary texts in their own right, test the new theory against a wider range of examples to demonstrate its value as a tool of practical criticism. As we shall see, otherwise unrecognized translation strategies and patterns become visible and a whole new dimension of assessing and comparing literary translations emerges once we mobilize the theoretical framework for metonymy established here on the basis of descriptive poetics for the purposes of translation criticism—with implications that challenge some conventional dichotomies that still hold considerable sway in translation studies.

The texts chosen for examination are translations of Aeschylus' *Agamemnon* into German and English, dating from the late eighteenth to the late nineteenth century (by Jenisch, Humboldt, Droysen, Wilamowitz-Möllendorff, and Browning). Aeschylus' *Agamemnon*, which has already featured with some prominence in the development of the new theory of metonymy in Chapter 3, lends itself as an ideal source text for the purpose of studying metonymy in translation due to the extraordinary density and richness of tropical language that shapes its poetic texture and which, as Stanford rightly notes in the passage cited above, poses a particular challenge to translators. The period from which the translations are taken is likewise especially suitable for a comparative investigation such as the one undertaken here because it witnesses an intense debate on different ideals and models of translation, which one would expect to have a direct impact on how tropical passages in a source text are tackled in the translation process. The analysis of metonyms in translation itself will take the form of two 'cuts', allowing us to study metonymy in translation from two different angles. I shall compare and contrast the various translations in order to trace how different translation strategies affect the way metonyms in the Greek text are represented in translation practice. The discussion will be (loosely) structured according to the various categories established in Chapter 3, which will thus be re-examined from a new perspective. This will enable us to assess how different conformations of metonymy (as well as different translation strategies) influence the representation of metonymic passages in translation.

Before engaging with the translations themselves, however, some preliminary discussion and contextualization is necessary. At various points in this book, I have emphasized the ahistorical nature of tropes as possibilities inherent in language—namely as possibilities for deviance from a language's standard usage). This is, however, not to say that historical circumstances do not affect the *treatment* of metonyms in poetic practice, that is, in the way individual writers think of them, use them, respond to them, and value (or disvalue) them. The poetic choices of a Neoclassical, a Romantic and a Modernist writer or translator are bound to vary significantly in this respect. Nor is it to say that different possibilities and specificities of individual languages do not have an impact on which types of metonymy may or may not appear in any given language and its literature, or may appear with greater or lesser frequency or intensity of effect. A highly inflected language such as classical Greek and a moderately inflected language such as German, one might expect, is likely to come with possibilities not (or less) open to a weakly inflected language like English. Similarly, a language's ability to form compound words, a hallmark of both classical Greek and German but much less developed in English, might well affect the respective language's capability to manifest some forms of metonymy or have an impact on the relative intensity of their poetic effect. This means that the assessment of metonymy and metonyms in translation offered in this chapter must take into account both (*a*) how the theoretical understanding of metonymy *in general* developed in Chapter 3 relates to the question of the differences between source and target languages with respect to their grammatical and syntactical capabilities (thus filtering the aspect of linguistic as well as cultural specificities into the subsequent analyses); and (*b*) how the specific cultural-historical circumstances of this period at large and of the individual translators relate to their perception of, relation to, and treatment of metonyms in the source text and in their own translation work (thus filtering the cultural-historical dimension of literary style into the subsequent analyses). In order to achieve this, the evaluation and discussion of the chosen set of translations will be prefaced, first, by some initial reflections on the 'translatability' of metonyms, and second, by some historical contextualization of the changing ideas about language around 1800 and the development of different theoretical views on translation, represented not least by the translators of the texts studied, which are fundamentally shaped by these changes. This approach will make it possible to analyse and compare the various translations in greater depth, sensitive to their linguistic and cultural-historical specificities, to relate the individual findings to broader theoretical concerns and paradigms of translation studies—such as the differentiation between 'domesticating' and 'foreignizing' translations—which originated in this period (largely on the basis of translations like the ones examined here) and still shape critical discourse on translations today.

'TRANSLATABILITY'

First, then, let us reflect on what sort of expectations we can formulate regarding the 'translatability' of metonyms in the light of my theoretical framework as established in Chapter 3. One influential notion of translatability suggested by Benjamin has as its focus works of literature as a whole.[7] Here, we shall understand translatability in a more narrow and concrete sense as the possibility of reproducing a specific linguistic feature, a trope, in another language so that it is (*a*) still felt to be the same trope and (*b*) carries approximately the same semantic value.[8] What parameters can we expect for the translatability of metonyms?

In his classic discussion of 'translatability' from a linguistic perspective,[9] Catford notes that,

> Translation fails—or untranslatability occurs—when it is impossible to build functionally relevant features of the situation into the contextual meaning of the TL [target language] text. Broadly speaking, the cases where this happens fall into two categories. Those where the difficulty is *linguistic*, and those where it is *cultural*.[10]

In the case of cultural untranslatability, translation is impossible because the target culture has no equivalent for what is denoted by a term in the source text; the term's rendering in the target text therefore requires explanatory paraphrase. In the case of linguistic untranslatability, on the other hand,

> the functionally relevant features include some which are in fact formal features of the *language* of the SL [source language] text. If the TL [target language] has no

[7] 'Translation is a mode. To comprehend it as mode one must go back to the original, for that contains the law governing the translation: its translatability. The question of whether a work is translatable has a dual meaning. Either: Will an adequate translator ever be found among the totality of its readers? Or, more pertinently: Does its nature lend itself to translation and, therefore, in view of the significance of the mode, call for it? In principle, the first question can be decided only contingently; the second, however, apodictically... Translatability is an essential quality of certain works, which is not to say that it is essential that they be translated; it means rather that a specific significance inherent in the original manifests itself in its translatability.' Benjamin 1923, 16.

[8] Where this is the case to the highest possible degree, I will speak of 'verbatim translation' of metonyms; on this point, see below, p. 192.

[9] Catford 1965, 93–103. [10] Catford 1965, 94; italics in the original.

formally corresponding feature, the text, or the item, is (relatively) untranslatable. Linguistic untranslatability occurs typically in cases where an *ambiguity* peculiar to the SL text is a functionally relevant feature—e.g. in SL puns.[11]

As a further exemplary occasion of linguistic untranslatability, Catford goes on to mention polysemy and oligosemy, that is, cases in which one language is either more, or less, specific than the other. By way of illustration, he mentions the Russian verb *prišla*, which specifically denotes to arrive *by foot*, and cannot be expressed by any one 'equivalent' English verb.

Although Catford's linguistic theory of translation is, by and large, focused on ordinary language usage, his observations offer a helpful starting point, not least because a certain degree of 'ambiguity' is undoubtedly a 'functionally relevant feature' in tropical usage and one of the main causes of difficulty in translating poetic texts mentioned by Stanford. Yet are we to conclude from this that, where tropes turn out to be untranslatable, we are necessarily dealing with cases of linguistic rather than cultural untranslatability? The differences between metaphor and metonymy that have repeatedly surfaced and found explanation in my theoretical discussions suggest otherwise.

We have seen that metonymy is structurally more dependent on ordinary language usage than metaphor: while the effects of metaphor stem from the terminological interaction between tenor and vehicle terms, their encounter is facilitated by the principle of analogy and similarity; in other words, by an extra-linguistic principle. In metonymy, on the other hand, the effects not only occur largely outside the tenor–vehicle compound (namely in interaction with the context); the relationship of tenor and vehicle here actually assumes ordinary usage. The link between the two, in other words, is based on an intralinguistic principle. While this difference does not eliminate the potential for cultural untranslatability in the case of certain metonyms, it does situate that potential at a different location. I have argued that metonymy is to be understood as a shift within a semantic field and have suggested that this explains why it is possible to expand a metonymic expression into a literal statement without the need to add any logical markers. It follows that whenever this expanded literal version of a metonym can be translated from the source language into the target language without any intercultural complications, so can the metonym. If the expanded literal sentence is coherent and acceptable as an expression in ordinary usage in both languages (that is, that the corresponding terms are collocatable in both languages), it must be that the

[11] Catford 1965, 94; italics in the original.

lexical contiguity, which constitutes the link between metonymic tenor and metonymic vehicle, is equally available to both languages. In metaphor, on the other hand, even if an extended literal statement explicating the relationship of similarity and/or analogy can be translated into the target language without any cultural untranslatability of the terms involved, the analogy or similarity itself must also be subject to potential cultural differences. After all, what is perceived of as comparable or analogous in one culture need not necessarily be seen as such in another.[12] Metaphors, therefore, are that much more likely to be subject to culturally determined untranslatability.

However, while collocatability in ordinary usage is a *sine qua non* for potential metonymic usage, it is not the sole criterion that determines the viability of metonymic expressions. Rather, the frequency of such collocations determines the strength of the link between metonymic vehicle and tenor which the metonym exploits. The more frequently collocations occur in ordinary usage, the stronger the link, but also, as a consequence, the weaker the primary poetic effect of the metonymic shift in tropical usage. With regards to translation, this means that while a metonym may be translatable, the abrasiveness of the metonymic shift (and the strength of the poetic effect) may be felt more or less strongly in the target language depending on whether the terms in question co-occur with greater or lesser frequency and regularity in that language.

A further consideration: the most prominent effects of metaphor arise from terminological interaction within the tenor–vehicle compound between otherwise unrelated terminologies. In this sense, metaphors are more self-contained; if the isolated metaphorical compound can be translated into the target language, then the metaphor will be recognizable as such in that language, regardless of the context.[13] The poetic effects of metonymy, on the other hand, depend to a greater extent on secondary terminological interactions with the context. The metonymic

[12] This is, of course, not only a matter of denotative value but also, and especially, of connotations and their hierarchy. For instance, when Homer calls Hera βοώπις ('cow-eyed') it is the reference to the particularly long eyelashes and shininess of cow eyes that makes this epithet a flattering compliment to the queen of Mount Olympus. The corresponding expression used in contemporary English, on the other hand, is likely to be understood as unflattering, because 'cows' (when associated with women) connote dislikeability, or passive stupidity, or both. The different culturally determined connotations here impact on the translatability of this metaphor.

[13] Although a loss (or an increase) in further poetic effect may arise if additional interactions with the context outside the metaphorical compound are lost (or gained) in translation.

tenor and vehicle stand in a pre-established relationship stemming from ordinary usage and therefore do not form a compound with 'built-in' terminological interaction: they must be terminologically coherent.[14] Given this high degree of context-dependency for the overall effect of metonyms, it follows that in addition to the primary effect of the metonymic shift itself, secondary effects resulting from interaction(s) of the metonymic vehicle with the context may be a further source of increased or decreased effectiveness of the metonym in translation.

Cultural untranslatability, then, is a special risk for index metonyms and *mutatis mutandis* metonyms by association. The remaining categories of metonymy distinguished in Chapter 3, on the other hand, come with an additional potential for linguistic untranslatability. Re-examining Catford's work on translatability, Wong has pointed out that,

> Working within the framework of Indo-European languages... Catford has focused only on the lexical level, leaving the macro, syntactic level untouched, perhaps because syntax does not pose too much of a problem in translation between Indo-European languages.[15]

To illustrate his point, Wong refers to relative pronouns which are available as a syntactical feature in all Indo-European languages but have no equivalent in Chinese. Wong suggests that Chinese syntax 'is normally short and linear, with an extremely small capacity to carry subordinate clauses, parenthetical constructions, etc. so that it can never aspire after the syntactic complexity, malleability, or tortuosity of its counterpart in an Indo-European language'.[16] This lack of equivalent syntactical structures leads to one-way linguistic untranslatability: while sentences in Indo-European languages can be too complex to be rendered into Chinese, 'the sense units in a Chinese text can be readily transported in the opposite direction with little disturbance to the original configuration'.[17] As we have seen, syntax plays a structurally significant role in both amplification metonymy and in forms of grammatical metonymy. In both cases, specific linguistic features are prerequisites: the genitive case in amplification metonymy and the affiliation of an adjective to its governing noun through agreement of case, number, and gender in grammatical metonymy. I shall accordingly factor into my examination the question whether linguistic untranslatability occurs in cases where the target language does not offer these features, or only offers them to a limited extent, while also remaining

[14] See above, pp. 64, 74, and 139. [15] Wong 2006, 124.
[16] Wong 2006, 128. [17] Wong 2006, 130.

open to the possibility that a target language might offer alternative features that allow a metonymic effect through other syntactic means.

While these preliminaries bear on the translatability of metonyms in general, they in no way predetermine how translators can or will actually respond to metonyms encountered in the source text. To get a better sense of the cultural-historical and indeed epistemological factors that are bound to shape the response of the translators under discussion here, it is necessary to familiarize ourselves with the age in which they write, as well as with the views and ideals about language, poetry, and translation which they individually hold.

LANGUAGE IN THE 'AGE OF TRANSLATION': CHANGING PERCEPTIONS AND NEW PARADIGMS

A particularly broad range of responses to the challenges of literary translation is observable in Germany during the late eighteenth and early nineteenth centuries.[18] Contemporaries were acutely aware of developments in both the theory and practice of translation. Madame de Staël noted that '[t]he art of translation has been pushed further in Germany than in any other European dialect'[19] and August Wilhelm Schlegel concurred (not without a touch of irony): 'The Germans are indeed universal translators.'[20] The idiosyncratic co-existence and interpenetration of classicism and romanticism in Germany meant that the development of literary translation into German included both classical texts and texts in vernacular European languages of various epochs. However, the rise of German philhellenism, with its notion of a special affinity between Germany and ancient Greece in terms of language and culture, ensured a special place for translations of Greek texts. After only very limited engagement with Greek literature in the original during the Renaissance,[21] the radically new mode of translation represented by

[18] Good introductions to these developments in Germany are offered by Fuhrmann 1987, Louth 1998, 5–53, Bernofsky 2005a, and Kofler 2007. The most comprehensive study to date is Kitzbichler/Lubitz/Mindt 2009, 12–113. A summary of the wider European dimension of the emerging theoretical approaches to translation in this period can be found in Frank 2007.

[19] 'L'art de traduire est poussé plus loin en allemand que dans aucun dialecte européen', Staël 1813, vol. ii, 103.

[20] 'Die Deutschen sind ja Allerweltsübersetzer', Schlegel 1798, 58.

[21] 'Reuchlin is said to have been one of the five men in Germany at the beginning of the sixteenth century who had a thorough command of Greek... The knowledge of Greek did not become general in Germany until the middle of the sixteenth century. The first

Voss's Homer, along with Schleiermacher's and Goethe's contrasting theorizings, are widely seen as a turning point in the history of translation.[22] Then again, it is a prime characteristic of the period of Weimar classicism in general that,

> Nearly all the notable writers and critics in this period—Goethe, Herder, Humboldt, Hölderlin—translated the ancients, [while] even Schiller in his Hellenic period translated Euripides with the aid of Latin and French editions.... The task of the translator was to lead the reader to an authentic appreciation of the original, even if this meant exploding the usual syntax and rhythm of German. The novelty of this approach can be seen in comparison with Wieland, who strove by all faithfulness to the original to produce a work of elegance and clarity; the 'improvement' of difficult or unclear passages was a pardonable sin, if not an outright virtue. The younger generation, on the other hand, sought to retain absolute fidelity to the original, so that the translation, in the words of Humboldt, 'den Geist des Lesers gleichsam zum Geist des Schriftstellers stimmt' ['would, as it were, tune the spirit of the reader to the author's'] ...[23]

A shift of attention away from the reader and his aesthetic expectations to the author and the stylistic peculiarities of the original text are at the heart of a fundamental change in the practice and theory of translation. Several reasons have been suggested for this change. In literary-theoretical terms, a preoccupation with authors is one of the most evident features of Romantic thinking (German and other). In terms of cultural-political context, the 'specifically German mode was in large part arrived at via opposition to what they saw as the domination and assimilation foisted on foreign texts by translators in France'.[24] This opposition is pointedly illustrated in Herder's celebrated remark that,

> The French, too proud of their national taste, assimilate everything to it rather than bringing themselves to appreciate the taste of another era. Homer has to come to France a captive, dressed in their fashion so as not to offend their eyes. Stripped of his venerable beard and his old, simple dress, he is made to adopt French manners, and where his rustic nobility still shines through, he is mocked for being a barbarian.—We poor Germans, on the other hand, still virtually

translations from the Greek were Reuchlin's versions of Demosthenes' *First Olynthian Oration* and the twelfth of Lucian's *Dialogues of the Dead*. For nearly a century following Reuchlin, practically all "translations" of Greek authors were from Latin... Sophocles, Aeschylus, Euripides and the Greek poets were translated into German only long after 1550.' Thompson 1943, 348.

[22] See, for instance, Louth 1998, 27f. and Bernofsky 2005b, 4; see also below, pp. 180–2.
[23] Grair 2005, 81. [24] Louth 1998, 7. See also Kofler 2007.

without an audience, and without a fatherland, still free from the tyranny of a national taste, want to see him the way he is.[25]

The rise of German national sentiment also stands behind the frequent deployment of the *topos* which presents translation of classical literature as a means of refining and improving one's native language. While in antiquity translation had often been a personal undertaking in which individuals sought to extend their own stylistic repertoire and powers of expression,[26] it now became central to nation-building.[27] Humboldt's preface to his translation of Aeschylus' *Agamemnon* (1816) is a prime witness here:

It is impossible to count the merits Klopstock has earned himself in serving the German nation through his first successful treatment of ancient metres, and even more so Voss, about whom one can say that he has indeed introduced classical antiquity into the German language. A more powerful and beneficent influence on *Nationalbildung* [both 'nation-building' and 'national formation/erudition'] in an already highly cultivated era is hardly conceivable, and this merit is his alone.[28]

If the purpose of translation is to add to the language and spirit of a nation that which it does not possess or at least only possesses in a different way, then the first necessity is fidelity... It follows from this view, of course, that the translation will carry a certain colouring of foreignness... As long as not foreignness but the foreign is felt, the translation has fulfilled its highest purpose... If, out of some queasy timidity, one goes further still and seeks even to avoid the foreign, in the sense in which one is used to hear it said that the translator ought to write just as the original author would have written in the language of

[25] 'Die Franzosen, zu stolz auf ihren Nationalgeschmack, nähern demselben alles, statt sich dem Geschmack einer andern Zeit zu bequemen. Homer muß als Besiegter nach Frankreich kommen, sich nach ihrer Mode kleiden, um ihr Auge nicht zu ärgern: sich seinen ehrwürdigen Bart, und alte einfältige Tracht abnehmen lassen: Französische Sitten soll er an sich nehmen, und wo seine bäurische Hoheit noch hervorblickt, da verlacht man ihn, als einen Barbaren.—Wir armen Deutschen hingegen, noch ohne Publikum beinahe, und ohne Vaterland, noch ohne Tyrannen eines Nationalgeschmacks, wollen ihn sehen, wie er ist.' Herder 1805, 63f.

[26] See e.g. (from ancient Rome) Cic. *De Or.* 1.155, Quint. *Inst.* 10.5.2–3, or Plin. *Ep.* 7.9.2.

[27] As, of course, it had also been in earlier centuries for other vernacular languages: cf. e.g. Du Bellay's *Deffence et illustration de la langue françoise* (1549). And the literature of ancient Rome itself depends in the first instance on translation (and other 'imitation') of Greek texts.

[28] 'Es ist nicht zu sagen, wieviel Verdienst um die Deutsche Nation durch die erste gelungne Behandlung der antiken Silbenmasse Klopstock, wie noch weit mehr Voss gehabt, von dem man behaupten kann, dass er das klassische Alterthum in die Deutsche Sprache eingeführt hat. Eine mächtigere und wohlthätigere Einwirkung auf die Nationalbildung ist in einer schon hoch cultivirten Zeit kaum denkbar, und sie gehört ihm allein an.' Humboldt 1816, xviii.

the translator…then one destroys all translation, and all of its benefit for language and nation alike.[29]

On a more fundamental level, the massive surge of interest in translation itself can also be understood as a consequence of a radical shift in semiotics that occurs around 1800. The Enlightenment notion of linguistic signs had been based on the principle of representation: signs, if used properly, were credited with the ability to clearly represent whatever they signify.[30] On this view, signifiers are virtually transparent; the creation of meaning in literature, therefore, is exclusively a matter of content, not of form. Gottsched's *Ausführliche Redekunst* ('Comprehensive Art of Rhetoric') of 1736, for instance, is entirely based on this assumption. He holds that '[w]ords themselves are arbitrary signs of our concepts'[31] and shows no signs of any doubt regarding the general reliability of language in terms of referentiality and communication. When Gottsched displays any concern about issues of obscurity and incomprehensibility in language, he thinks only of problems of unconventionality.[32] Thus, when discussing 'the dark, unclear or incomprehensible

[29] 'Soll aber das Uebersetzen der Sprache und dem Geist der Nation dasjenige aneignen, was sie nicht, oder was sie doch anders besitzt, so ist die erste Forderung einfache Treue…Mit dieser Ansicht ist freilich nothwendig verbunden, dass die Uebersetzung eine gewisse Farbe der Fremdheit an sich trägt…Solange nicht die Fremdheit, sondern das Fremde gefühlt wird, hat die Uebersetzung ihre höchsten Zwecke erreicht…Wenn man in ekler Scheu vor dem Ungewöhnlichen noch weiter geht, und auch das Fremde selbst vermeiden will, so wie man wohl sonst sagen hörte, dass der Uebersetzer schreiben müsse, wie der Originalverfasser in der Spracher des Uebersetzers geschrieben haben würde…so zerstört man alles Uebersetzen, und allen Nutzen desselben für Sprache und Nation.' Humboldt 1816, xix–xx.

[30] For a general discussion, see Foucault 1966, 58–71 and 81–120. Based on the principles outlined there, Wellbery 1984 offers a cogent reading of Lessing's *Laocoon* as a paradigmatic text for the Enlightenment semiotics of representation.

[31] 'Die Wörter an sich selbst sind willkürliche Zeichen unserer Begriffe.' Gottsched 1736, 299.

[32] 'Insofar as comprehensible words are concerned, it is the particular duty of the orator to use them: because he cannot succeed in his intentions at all when he is not understood. Those words are comprehensible which are in general usage among the people where one gives a speech, and which the orator takes in their ordinary meaning. Incomprehensible items tend to be 1) local (provincial) words…2) very old words…3) foreign words…4) neologisms…5) artificial words…' ('Was die verständlichen Wörter betrifft, so hat ein Redner dieselben sonderlich zu befleißigen: weil er seine Absichten gar nicht erreichen kann, wofern er nicht verstanden wird. Es sind aber alle Wörter verständlich, die bey dem Volke, wo man redet, durchgehend üblich sind, und die der Redner in der gewöhnlichen Bedeutung nimmt. Hergegen unverständlich pflegen oft zu sein 1) Provinzialwörter…2) Die gar zu alten Wörter…3) Fremde Wörter…4) Die neugemachten Wörter…5) Die Kunstwörter…'). Gottsched 1736, 300–1. The Aristotelian source for this list is apparent (cf. Arist. *Poet.* 22).

way of writing' ('die dunkle, undeutliche, oder unverständliche Schreibart'), he argues that such writing originates either from a corresponding dark or unintelligible quality of the thought to be expressed or from the choice of unconventional words or from an infelicitous and obfuscating combination of words.[33] In other words: it results from misuses of language, but not from any general problem inherent in language as such.

This view inevitably has consequences for Gottsched's understanding of tropical language. He defines tropes as 'nothing but words taken in meanings other than those which they ordinarily have'[34] with the consequence that

> such expressions... [are] richer in senses and meanings than ordinary words: and whoever wishes to understand them needs to be able to intellectualize more than someone who only understands literal ways of speaking. Thus tropes have been introduced to oratory as a means to make the style more beautiful.[35]

In Gottsched's substitutionalist view, the 'proper' signifier is replaced by another, less precise sign which requires from the reader or listener a greater intellectual effort ('mehr nachsinnen') in order to reach the signified. There is a clear distinction between aesthetic effect and conceptual content which makes it possible and legitimate to translate foreign texts *ad sensum* and to add a roughly 'equivalent' level of stylistic 'decoration' according to contemporary taste without incurring any real loss.[36] The word as such has little importance; it merely provides access to the content. Translations by Wieland (whose approach to translation is based on Christian Wolff's rationalistic theory of signs),[37] like the much earlier translations by Opitz, assume this argument.[38] Only when the assumed transparency of the sign and its ability to represent reliably become questionable—only when signs themselves are seen to be opaque and historically contingent carriers of aesthetic and semantic value[39]—can

[33] Gottsched 1736, 361–7.

[34] 'nichts anderes, als Wörter, die man in anderen Bedeutungen nimmt, als die sie gemeiniglich haben...'. Gottsched 1736, 307.

[35] 'solche Ausdrückungen... allerdings reicher an Sinn und Bedeutungen als die gemeinen Worte [sind]: und wer sie verstehen will, der muß mehr nachsinnen können, als wer nur eigentliche Redensarten vernehmen kann. Dadurch wurden die Tropen, als ein Mittel, die Schreibart schöner zu machen, in die Redekunst eingeführt'. Gottsched 1736, 309.

[36] 'Gottsched emphasises the rendering of the sense rather than form. In this he is a faithful adherent to Leibniz' theory of language: words are signs, or even counters. They are freely convertible by means of what almost amounts to a mathematical operation. Equivalents can be found, imports are unnecessary.' Lefevre 1977, 13.

[37] See Fuhrmann 1987, 3–6.

[38] See Louth 1998, 10–11.

[39] Or, as Foucault has put it: 'From the nineteenth century, language began to fold in upon itself, to acquire a particular density, to deploy a history, an objectivity, and laws of its own. It became an object of knowledge among others...'. Foucault 1966, 295. For a detailed

translation become problematic enough to provoke the degree of theoretical reflection and practical experimentation that we see in Germany around 1800. Romantic aesthetics are profoundly influenced by a new notion of the sign as a 'hieroglyph' which ultimately eludes the full grasp of the writer and, consequently, also the translator.

It follows that Humboldt's notion of the general untranslatability of poetry, as expressed in the preface to his *Agamemnon* translation,[40] and Friedrich Schlegel's doubts about the reliability of linguistic communication in general, as expressed in his essay 'On Incomprehensibility' ('Über die Unverständlichkeit') of 1800,[41] can be seen as two expressions of a single underlying epistemological-semiotic problematic. The form of the sign becomes meaningful in its own right; the act of translation thus acquires a Sisyphean quality and becomes an ongoing work-in-progress engagement with a foreign text that can never hope to reach a final stage of full completion.[42] And the ubiquitous understanding of the poet as an 'original genius', whose creativity takes priority over any contemporary conventions, now pushes translators towards an ever-increasing closeness to the modes of expression used in the original.

In this context, Voss's translation of Homer's *Odyssey* (1781) marks the pioneering step that took translation onto new ground:

> Convinced of the inner relatedness of both languages, Voss dared to attempt a translation which set out not only to be faithful with regard to individual words and verses but also to maintain the word order and rhythm of the Greek original... despite much criticism, not least from Weimar, concerning the

study of the impact of these epistemological-semiotic changes on rhetoric and poetics in Germany, see Matzner 2013.

[40] 'Such a poem [as Aeschylus' *Agamemnon*] is untranslatable by its own particular nature, as well as in a very different sense insofar as this can be said of all works of great originality in general' ('Ein solches Gedicht ist, seiner eigenthümlichen Natur nach, und in einem noch viel anderen Sinne, als es sich überhaupt von allen Werken von grosser Originalität sagen lässt, unübersetzbar'). Humboldt 1816, xv.

[41] 'Of all things that have to do with communicating ideas, what could be more fascinating than the question of whether such communication is actually possible?' ('Was kann wohl von allem, was sich auf die Mitteilung der Ideen bezieht, anziehender sein, als die Frage, ob sie überhaupt möglich sei'). Schlegel 1800, 363.

[42] Humboldt is once again exemplary for this new view: 'For translations are rather works which probe, determine, and influence the state of a language at a given point in time and which need to be repeated anew time and again, as lasting works' ('Denn Uebersetzungen sind doch mehr Arbeiten, welche den Zustand der Sprache in einem gegebenen Zeitpunkt, wie an einem bleibenden Massstab, prüfen, bestimmen, und auf ihn einwirken sollen, und die immer von neuem wiederholt werden müssen, als dauernde Werke'). Humboldt 1816, xxiv.

unreadability of his translation, his Homer and with it his new mode of translation set a new standard.[43]

The novelty of Voss's translation lies in its thoroughly foreignizing approach, and the distinction between foreignizing and domesticating translation does indeed date back to the period under discussion here. In 1813, three years before Humboldt's reflections on 'foreignness' and 'the foreign' in translation, both Goethe and Schleiermacher use their experience of reading and translating Greek literature, and the stimulus of Voss's revolutionary experiment,[44] to formulate the two basic approaches to translation which are still fundamental to translation theory today:

> There are two principles of translation: the first requires that an author from a foreign nation be brought across to us in such a way that we can consider him one of us; the second conversely requires of us that we ourselves move closer to the foreign author and reconcile ourselves to his conditions, his idiom, and his peculiarities.[45]

> The translator either leaves the author in peace as far as possible and moves the reader towards him or else leaves the reader in peace as far as possible and moves the author towards him.[46]

The formulation of these two options,[47] seen today as extreme points on a scale rather than mutually exclusive positions, presupposes the shift in translation practice from the traditional, domesticating translation model advocated by the likes of Gottsched to the new foreignizing

[43] 'Überzeugt von der geistigen Verwandtschaft beider Sprachen, wagt Voss hingegen eine Übersetzung, die nicht nur wort- und versgetreu sein, sondern auch Wortstellung und Versrhythmus des griechischen Originals bewahren soll ... trotz vieler Kritik gerade auch aus Weimar an der mangelhaften Lesbarkeit der Übersetzung setzt sich sein Homer und mit ihm seine neue Art des Übersetzens durch.' Kofler 2007, 1753.

[44] 'Voss did effect a kind of revolution in taste ...'. Louth 1998, 28.

[45] 'Es gibt zwei Übersetzungsmaximen: die eine verlangt, daß der Autor einer fremden Nation zu uns herüber gebracht werde, dergestalt, daß wir ihn als den Unsrigen ansehen können; die andere hingegen macht an uns die Forderung, daß wir uns zu dem Fremden hinüber begeben und uns in seine Zustände, seine Sprachweise, seine Eigenheiten finden sollen.' Goethe 1813, 705.

[46] 'Entweder der Übersetzer läßt den Schriftsteller möglichst in Ruhe, und bewegt den Leser ihm entgegen oder er läßt den Leser möglichst in Ruhe und bewegt ihm den Schriftsteller entgegen.' Schleiermacher 1838, 218. The paper was delivered as a lecture to the Prussian Royal Academy of Sciences on 24 June 1813.

[47] There are, of course, precursors to these two famous formulations. Lefevre points out that 'in reality Bodmer deserves most of the praise which is usually lavished on Goethe and Schleiermacher as theorists of translation'. Lefevre 1977, 19; see also Louth 1998, 15–17. While Johann Jakob Bodmer (1689–1783) certainly implies the two positions in his 1746 work 'Der Mahler der Sitten' ('The Painter of Manners'), the greater precision and impact of Goethe's and Schleiermacher's theorizing surely justifies their prominent position in the history of translation theory.

promoted by Voss, Humboldt, and others. And soon, as Louth observes, the foreignizing imperative itself yields alternative positions:

> If metre was perhaps Voss's overriding concern, he was in practice always making carefully judged compromises... no one consideration was allowed to crowd the others. Still, it is easy to see how Voss gave rise to translations where one principle did prevail to the detriment of other aspects: word-order in Hölderlin's Pindar, or metre in Humboldt's *Agamemnon*.[48]

Different translators' responses to metonyms can be expected to reflect this revolutionary turn, along with their own particular preoccupations, in different ways. Bernofsky rightly points out as a caveat that,

> Inevitably, perhaps, the developments in translation practice around 1800, considerable as they were, could not entirely keep pace with the ambitious theoretical goals being set, even when translator and theorist were one and the same person.[49]

Nonetheless, programmatic statements by the translators themselves help us to assess how far each translator's response to metonyms in an original text is in line with explicit theoretical positions and objectives.

POETIC LANGUAGE IN LITERARY TRANSLATION: IDEALS AND APPROACHES

The translations of Aeschylus' *Agamemnon* chosen for examination are by Daniel Jenisch (published 1786), Wilhelm von Humboldt (1816), Johann Gustav Droysen (1832), Ulrich von Wilamowitz-Möllendorff (1900), and (by way of contrast and comparison) Robert Browning (1877). They are all prefaced by a statement from the translator in which he outlines his views on the text and the appropriate method of translating it. The selection includes texts from before and around 1800 as well as later texts that revert to a sober and philological method which, in semiotic and aesthetic terms, is much more akin to the pre-1800 mode of translation. Their markedly different strategies will make it possible to assess whether and how particular preoccupations or aesthetic-stylistic preferences on the part of the translators affect the way the source text's metonyms are represented in the target language. In the light of the earlier reflections on 'translatability', special attention

[48] Louth 1998, 29. [49] Bernofsky 2005a, 2.

will be paid to whether and how metonyms are affected by the linguistic possibilities and limitations of the target language, culture, and literary tradition, as well as to the role metonyms play in these translations in general. First, however, let us review the translation ideals, stated aims, and methodological deliberations of each translator, and consider what implications they may have for their respective engagements with metonyms in the Greek source text. In elaborating their individual approaches, I will also draw out how each translator's programme aligns with the principles of either foreignization or domestication, an opposition, which, as seen, first emerged in the period under discussion but still informs much contemporary translation criticism. Following on from these initial (and conventional) localizations, the subsequent analysis of examples will then proceed to productively challenge this blunt dichotomy: revealing its inadequacies from the perspective of tropology and stylistics, the discussion will demonstrate how the translators' patterns of engagement with and responses to tropical language in the source texts do not neatly align with the parameters of these two categories while also highlighting the divergences between what the translators purport to do and what they actually do.

An epigraph, from Salmasius' *De Hellenistica Commentarius*, on the frontispiece of Jenisch's translation underlines this translator's awareness of the high level of defamiliarized language usage in this play: 'Only Aeschylus' *Agamemnon* contains more obscurity than all the books of the Old Testament with their Hebraisms, Chaldeisms, Samaritanisms, etc.'[50] Jenisch claims to be the first to offer a translation of the entire play into German, only to stress the impossibility of such an undertaking:

> I dare to present to the public the translation of a piece by the tragic muse of antiquity which, as far as I know, has never appeared in German dress before, except for some translated choral passages published in the *Museum*... But the translation of an Aeschylean tragedy will perhaps be a daring undertaking even after this [*sc.* the latest Pindar edition by Schütz], since among others Herder, Germany's Longinus, in his *Fragments* places Aeschylus in the ranks of untranslatable poets.[51]

[50] *Unus Aeschyli Agamemnon plus habet obscuritatis quam omnes Veteris Testamenti libri cum suis Hebraismis, Chaldaïsmis, Samaritanïsmis etc. etc.* (Jenisch 1786, frontispiece). In the preface, Jenisch looks back to this same quotation: 'Salmasius said... that it is darker than the entire Old Testament with all its dialects' ('Salmasius... sagt, daß es dunkler sei, als das gesamte alte Testament mit allen seinen Dialekten'). Jenisch 1786, vii.

[51] 'Ich wage es, dem Publikum die Uebersetzung eines Stückes der tragischen Muse des Alterthums vorzulegen, welches, so viel ich wüßte, außer einigen im Museum verteutschten Chören noch niemals in einem teutschen Gewande aufgetreten ist... Aber die Uebersetzung eines Aeschylischen Trauerspiels dürfte vielleicht auch nach dem [*sc.* der neuesten Pindarausgabe besorgt durch Schütz] noch ein Wagestück seyn, da nebst andern Herder,

While the notion of the untranslatability of poetic language would seem to situate Jenisch on the side of the new, foreignizing approach to translation, the metaphorical notion of undressing and reclothing the source text echoes the earlier, domesticating approach.[52] This ambiguity continues as Jenisch proceeds to give an outline of his attitude to translation:

> ... translating is, of course, easy, if it means nothing more than exchanging words and making a foreign original somehow readable to the public in one's own mother tongue: but if it means carrying every individual idiosyncrasy of an author's words and thoughts, his genius and that of his language, into our language and into our souls, so that the author of the original might accept the translation as a second copy of his work and the public the translation as a home-grown original: in that case, translating becomes somewhat more complicated... The more original the genius of a writer, the more idiosyncratic his manner of expression, the more his language differs from ours and the spirit of his age from ours, the more difficulties will be encountered in translation... For a translator of works of genius it is therefore paramount that, in addition to linguistic proficiency, he is able to empathize with the inner situation ['idealische Situation'] of the author and that he translates in the same spirit in which the other wrote.[53]

In every line, it seems, Jenisch shifts from one approach to the other: he rejects word-for-word translation, considers it insufficient merely to communicate the meaning, and stresses the importance of conveying not only the idiosyncrasies of the author's thoughts but also the words he uses (one also notes the connection of all this with the concept of the poet

Teutschlands Longin, in seinen Fragmenten, den Aeschylus in die Reihe der unübersetzbaren Dichter zählt.' Jenisch 1786, vii. It is worth pointing out just how unusual translation of Aeschylus was until 1800: he was the last of the three tragedians to be translated into most European languages, and no complete translation of his works into German was available until 1808.

52 For the role this metaphor plays in Gottsched's concept of translation, see Louth 1998, 15.

53 '... übersezzen ist freilich leicht, wenn es nicht mehr heißt, als Worte umtauschen und ein ausländisches Original dem Publikum seiner Muttersprache irgend lesbar zu machen: aber wenn es heißt, jede Individualität der Worte und Gedanken eines Autors, seines Genies und des seiner Sprache in unsere Sprache und in unsere Seelen hinübertragen, so daß der Autor des Originals die Uebersezzung für die zweyte Abschrift seines Werkes, und das Publikum die Uebersetzung für ein einheimisches Original ansehe: dann könnte übersezzen vielleicht doch etwas schwerer seyn... Je origineller das Genie eines Schriftstellers, je eigenthümlicher die Manier seines Ausdrucks, je verschiedener seine Sprache von der unsrigen, und der Genius seiner Zeit von dem der unsrigen ist, desto mehr Schwierigkeiten wird auch die Uebersezzung haben... Bey einem Uebersezzer der Werke des Genies ist es also, außer der Sprachkenntniß, eine Hauptelforderniß, daß er sich in die ganze idealische Situation seines Verfassers hineinzuversezzen wisse, und mit eben dem Geist übersezze, mit dem jener schrieb.' Jenisch 1786, vii–viii.

as original genius). Although this points to a foreignizing approach, there is also a tendency towards *ad sensum* translation in the exhortation to write 'in the same spirit', and the expressed aim that the translation should appear to readers as if originally written in the source language clearly points to a domesticating approach. It is worth noting that later in the preface the need to do justice to the author's genius is placed in categorical opposition to attention to form: clinging to formulations in a literal-minded way is portrayed as intrinsically opposed to the elusive, sublime, spiritual quality that constitutes the genius in the first place.[54] It is this that leads Jenisch to the ideal of free translation:

> This alone I cannot leave unmentioned, that I have dealt with my Aeschylus rather freely here and there ... [s]ince a literal translation ... of Aeschylus would be the most unbearable of all unbearable things, and would degrade one of the greatest geniuses to a nonsensical, pompous creator of bombast. Aeschylus ... says everything only with half a mouth: he thinks more than he says, hints at more than he shows ...[55]

If the 'hinting rather than showing' is achieved in the original through a metonym, however, the metonymic shift will be a shift within a semantic field and, hence, a matter of terminology and its formal manipulation, for which free translation may or may not be adequate.

As noted already, metre is widely recognized as the major concern of Humboldt's translation,[56] but his innovations in translation practice and theory go far beyond this. Humboldt is one of the key thinkers associated with the new semiotic paradigm, which is also reflected in his preface to the *Agamemnon* translation:

> All forms of language are symbols, not things themselves, not conventional signs, but sounds which perpetually remain in a real and, as it were, mystical correlation with the things and concepts they represent through the spirit in which they were conceived and continue to be conceived, and which contain the content of reality,

[54] See Jenisch 1786, x–xi.

[55] 'Dies nur kann ich nicht unangemerkt lassen, daß ich mit meinem Aeschylus hier und dort noch freymüthiger umgegangen ... Daher auch eine wörtliche Uebersezzung ... vom Aeschylus, das unerträglichste aller unerträglichen Dinge seyn, und nothwendig eins der größesten Genies zu einem non-sensikalischen Bombastaufdunser herabwürdigen würde. Aeschylus ... redet alles gleichsam nur mit halbem Munde aus: er denkt mehr, als er sagt, winkt mehr, als er zeigt ... '. Jenisch 1786, xi.

[56] See above, p. 182. In the preface, Humboldt argues that German is the only language which can imitate the rhythmic nature of ancient Greek metre; see Humboldt 1816, xxiii–xxiv. This concern is shared, albeit to a lesser and less programmatic extent, by Jenisch, who renders dialogue passages into iambics while turning the play's choral passages into variants of the metres introduced into the German poetic repertoire by Klopstock in his odes. See Jenisch 1786, xxvi–xxvii.

in effect, dissolved into ideas and which can now change, determine, separate, and unite them in a way that must be thought of as infinite.[57]

Accordingly, he advocates a foreignizing approach which seeks to convey the idiosyncrasies of the original in the target language, avoiding only the most serious violations of the mother tongue:[58]

An inability to match the particular beauties of the original all too easily leads to decorating it with foreign ornaments which produce a different colour and tone altogether. I have tried to avoid un-Germanness and obscurity, although, in respect to the latter, one must not call for unjustifiable changes that will diminish the original's particular qualities. A translation cannot and need not be a commentary. It may not contain obscurities that result from vague usage or odd composition; but where the original only hints at something rather than explicitly expressing it, where it allows itself the use of metaphors whose relations are hard to grasp, where it skips pivotal ideas, there a translator would commit an injustice if he introduced on his own account a clarity that would distort the character of the text. The obscurity we find at times in the texts of the ancients, and which marks the *Agamemnon* in particular, results from the brevity and boldness with which—while discarding mediating and connecting phrases—ideas, images, emotions, memories, and premonitions are conjoined with one another just as they emerge from the mind in a state of deep emotion.[59]

[57] 'Alle Sprachformen sind Symbole, nicht die Dinge selbst, nicht verabredete Zeichen, sondern Laute, welche mit den Dingen und Begriffen, die sie darstellen, durch den Geist, in dem sie entstanden sind, und immerfort entstehen, sich in wirklichem, wenn man es so nennen will, mystischen Zusammenhange befinden, welche die Gegenstände der Wirklichkeit gleichsam aufgelöst in Ideen enthalten, und nun auf eine Weise, der keine Gränze gedacht werden kann, verändern, bestimmmen, trennen und verbinden können.' Humboldt 1816, xvii.

[58] See also Humboldt 1816, xix–xx, as cited above, see above, pp. 177–8.

[59] 'Das Unvermögen, die eigenthümlichen Schönheiten des Originals zu erreichen, führt gar zu leicht dahin, ihm fremden Schmuck zu leihen, woraus im Ganzen eine abweichende Farbe, und ein verschiedener Ton entsteht. Vor Undeutschheit und Dunkelheit habe ich mich zu hüten gesucht, allein in dieser letzteren Rücksicht muss man keine ungerechte, und höhere Vorzüge verhindernde Forderungen machen. Eine Uebersetzung kann und soll kein Commentar seyn. Sie darf keine Dunkelheit enthalten, die aus schwankendem Wortgebrauch, schielender Fügung entsteht; aber wo das Original nur andeutet, statt klar auszusprechen, wo es sich Metaphern erlaubt, deren Beziehung schwer zu fassen ist, wo es Mittelideen auslässt, da würde der Uebersetzer Unrecht thun, aus sich selbst willkührlich eine den Charakter des Textes verstellende Klarheit hineinzubringen. Die Dunkelheit, die man in den Schriften der Alten manchmal findet, und die gerade der Agamemnon vorzüglich an sich trägt, entsteht aus der Kürze, und der Kühnheit, mit der, mit Verschmähung vermittelnder Bindesätze, Gedanken, Bilder, Gefühle, Erinnerungen und Ahndungen, wie sie aus dem tief bewegten Gemüthe entstehen, an einander gereiht werden.' Humboldt 1816, xx–xxi. In the same spirit Humboldt declares later on: 'A part of such attention must also be devoted to the translation, not demanding that what in the source language is sublime, gigantic, and extraordinary should in translation be easy and immediately accessible' ('Einen Theil dieser Aufmerksamkeit muss man auch der Uebersetzung schenken, nicht verlangen, dass das, was in der Ursprache erhaben, riesenhaft und ungewöhnlich ist, in der Uebertragung leicht und augenblicklich fasslich seyn solle'). Humboldt 1816, xxi.

Once again, an awareness of 'obscurities' resulting from tropical language is apparent (metaphor is singled out, but 'hinting rather than explicitly expressing' certainly covers metonymy as well), and the stated aim is to preserve such 'obscurities' in the translation.

Droysen and Wilamowitz take a very different stance. Both produce their translations at a time when the spirit of excited experimentation with translation has already worn itself out.[60] The pendulum now swings back to a preference for domesticating, albeit in different degrees and with a residual sensitivity to stylistic features.

For Droysen, the primary objective of translations is to 'domesticate the foreign',[61] but not to the extent that all foreignness disappears:

> Insofar as the translation itself is concerned, I have, of course, followed the natural rule which follows from its rationale. It would be just as erroneous to blur all that is foreign as to force one's own language under the yoke of a foreign idiom; only the greatest fidelity can steer a course between the twin hazards of caricature and blandness.[62]

Although he emphasizes the need to convey not only the source text's content but also the aesthetic impression created by its formal features,[63]

[60] 'Translations of ancient poets have an awkward status in our literature; the public has grown tired and suspicious because of the many failed attempts; for good reasons one refers to the more congenial and incomparably richer poetry of modern peoples; famous names from antiquity slowly lose the aura of traditional partiality; and the essence of classicism, rhetorical perfection, which no longer surpasses that of modern writing, usually perishes in translations, whose tastelessness has become proverbial' ('Uebersetzungen antiker Dichter haben in unserer Literatur einen schwierigen Stand; durch viele mißglückte Versuche ist das Publikum ermüdet und mißtrauisch gemacht; mit Recht wird auf die verwandtere und ungleich reichere Poesie der modernen Völker verwiesen; berühmte Namen des Alterthums verlieren allmählig den Nimbus herkömmlicher Vorurtheile; und das Wesen der Klassicität, die rhetorische Vollendung, die sie schon nicht mehr vor dem neueren Schriftthum voraus haben, geht gewöhnlich in den Uebersetzungen zu Grunde, deren Geschmacklosigkeit zum Sprüchwort [sic] geworden ist'). Droysen 1832, i.

[61] 'If the purpose of translations is to domesticate the foreign, then it is not necessary, I believe, to display at the same time the extensive apparatus of transmission and all the untidy traces of this journey and its learned wrappings' ('Wenn Uebersetzungen Fremdes heimisch zu machen bestimmt sind, so, glaube ich, braucht nicht der weitlaeufige Apparat des Transportes und alle die unreinlichen Spuren des durchgemachten Weges und der gelehrten Emballage mit ausgestellt zu werden'). Droysen 1832, i.

[62] 'Die Uebersetzung selbst anlangend bin ich der natürlichen Regel, die aus ihrem Zwecke folgt, gefolgt. Es wäre gleich fehlerhaft, alles Fremdartige zu verwischen, wie der eigenen Sprache das Joch eines fremden Idioms aufzubürden; zwischen beiden Klippen der Karikatur und der Farblosigkeit kann die größte Treue allein hindurchleiten.' Droysen 1832, vii.

[63] 'This fidelity initially requires an understanding of the original that is as comprehensive as possible; if it were sufficient to convey the contents, a translator with dictionary and grammar book would be sufficient; the more essential and idiosyncratic the form of the original is, the more important is it to pick up and raise to awareness the immediate impression. The ancient poets present manifold difficulties in this respect... The translator

Droysen rejects foreignizing approaches that seek to remodel foreign expressions, words, and syntax in the target language.[64] Thus, despite arguing for a *via media* and despite insisting on replicating the original metre,[65] ultimately he favours a domesticating approach:

> The translator has no higher guiding principle than to represent the artistic beauty of the original in his language to the degree that it can count for a free product of that language, that it could be the form which the poet himself would have used in this language.[66]

Droysen privileges the impression created in and by the source language over the actual formal features which create it. It is the aesthetic impression which needs to be represented through the given means of the target language, and in this recreation the formal structures which create them in the source language are not considered as binding. In other words,

must seek to convey the content of the original faithfully, yet the *impression* of the form which is given to the content more faithfully; in all that remains he operates like a scholar, in this one respect like an artist' ('Diese Treue fordert zunächst möglichst vollkommenes Verständniß des Originals; genügte es, den Inhalt wiederzugeben, so möchte der Uebersetzer mit Lexikon und Grammatik ausreichen; je wesentlicher und eigenthümlicher die Form des Originals ist, desto wichtiger ist es, das Unmittelbare ihres Eindrucks herauszufühlen und zum Bewußtsein zu bringen. Die alten Dichter bieten in dieser Hinsicht mannigfache Schwierigkeit... Der Uebersetzer muß treu den Inhalt des Originals, treuer den *Eindruck* der Form, die sich der Inhalt gegeben, wiederzugeben suchen; in allem Uebrigen ist er auf gelehrte, in diesem Einen auf künstlerische Weise thätig'). Droysen 1832, viii; italics in the original.

[64] 'And yet in translations of ancient authors one has grown used to taking clumsiness for fidelity, crass crudity for the antique... Can the most repulsive German be a true translation of pure, rhetorically perfect Greek? The first demand is to translate from the beautiful into the beautiful; every cacophony, every maimed word, every contorted sentence is a worse infidelity than a word more or a word less; it is not far from the pedantry of slavishly literal translation to the absurd manner of those Persian translators who, when they could not proceed any further, honestly left the Indian word of the Upanishads in the text' ('Und doch hat man sich gewöhnt, in Uebersetzungen alter Autoren Unbehülflichkeit für Treue, krasse Rohheit für antik zu nehmen... Kann das abscheulichste Deutsch treue Uebersetzung eines reinen, rhetorisch vollendeten Griechisch sein? Die erste Anforderung ist, daß aus dem Schönen in das Schöne übertragen werde; jeder Mißlaut, jede Wortverstümmelung, jede Satzverrenkung ist eine ärgere Untreue, als ein Wort zuviel oder zu wenig; von der Pedanterei sklavischer Wörtlichkeit ist es nicht weit bis zur absurden Manier jener Persischen Uebersetzer, die, wenn es nicht weiter ging, ehrlich das Indische Wort ihres Upanischad selbst in den Text setzen'). Droysen 1832, ix.

[65] 'It goes without saying that the metre of the original had to be kept everywhere' ('Es versteht sich von selbst, daß überall die Versformen des Originals beizubehalten waren'). Droysen 1832, xi. This declaration is followed by an extensive discussion of the difficulties of metrical transposition into German, see Droysen 1832, xi–xv.

[66] 'Der Uebersetzer hat keine höhere Richtschnur, als die künstlerische Schönheit des Originals in seiner Sprache bis zu dem Grade wiederzugeben, daß sie für ein freieres Erzeugniß derselben gelten, daß sie die Form sein könnte, deren der Dichter selbst sich in dieser Sprache bedient haben würde.' Droysen 1832, ix.

Droysen's approach effectively aims at dynamic, functional equivalence as opposed to formal equivalence.[67] It remains to be seen if and how metonymy is affected by this choice, given that its specific aesthetic impression—the metonymic shift—seems to be intrinsically linked to its specific formal realizations.

Wilamowitz positions himself yet more clearly at the domesticating end of the translation spectrum. For the radical foreignizing pioneered by Humboldt almost a century earlier, the philologist only has poisoned praise:

> I adore Wilhelm von Humboldt to the utmost degree, I admire his desire to translate the *Agamemnon* and the spirit in which he has attempted it; but I no longer attempt to do it in exactly the same spirit, for now we also know the errors of classicism, and I consider his translation a complete failure.[68]

For Wilamowitz, revealingly, the provisional nature of all translation is not so much a matter of the intrinsic untranslatability of signs but of 'scientific' progress which renders earlier translations progressively obsolete.[69] Once again, this is related to an underlying change in the way language in general is understood. Apel and Kopetzki rightly point out that 'as if Herder, Goethe, Schlegel, and Humboldt had never existed, in the context of translation Wilamowitz returns to a conception of language which seems to have belonged to a pre-philological era.'[70] While Jenisch's pioneering German translation of the *Agamemnon* stands between traditional, classicizing domestication, on the one hand, and Voss's and Humboldt's new, radical foreignizing, on the other, Wilamowitz's (and Droysen's) position is more akin to that of Gottsched and Wieland than to their chronologically closer predecessors. The difference between Wilamowitz and that first wave of German

[67] These terms for the two concepts were coined by Nida; see Nida 1964.

[68] 'Ich verehre Wilhelm von Humboldt auf das höchste, ich bewundere, dass er den Agamemnon hat übersetzen wollen und in welchem Sinne er es versucht hat; aber ich versuche es nicht mehr ganz in demselben Sinne, denn wir kennen jetzt auch die Irrtümer des Klassicismus, und ich halte seine Übersetzung für ganz verfehlt.' Wilamowitz-Möllendorff 1900, 3f. Remarkably enough, in the following lines Wilamowitz cites Humboldt's translation of *Agam.* 239–47 as an illustration of precisely what he takes issue with—a passage of the play that contains one of the most striking index metonyms in Greek tragedy. Humboldt's translation of the passage, Wilamowitz's critique, and his own translation are discussed in more detail further below, see pp. 213–17.

[69] See Wilamowitz-Möllendorff 1900, 5.

[70] 'Als hätte es Herder, Goethe, Schlegel und Humboldt nie gegeben, kehrt Wilamowitz-Moellendorff im Kontext der Übersetzung zu einer Sprachauffassung zurück, die vorphilologischen Zeiten anzugehören schien . . . '. Apel/Kopetzki 2003, 93–4.

classicism, however, lies in the direction their 'domestication' takes. For the earlier classicists, the appropriate way to address the 'obscurities' of the source text was embellishment according to the contemporary taste of neoclassicism; for the philologist, such obscurities call for explanation:

> My translation aims to be as comprehensible as the original was to the Athenians, perhaps even more readily comprehensible; that is, it already wants to supply part of the interpretation.[71]

This aim of a self-explanatory translation, clearer than the original, opens up intriguing possibilities regarding the treatment of metonyms: will they be simply translated into literal expressions whenever their ambiguity is considered too 'obscure', or are there other modes of 'interpretation' ('Erklärung') that reflect at least something of the original poetic idiom even when presenting a more lucid and comprehensible sequence?

Browning's English translation, finally, though chronologically closer to Wilamowitz's than to the others, can also be counted among the foreignizing versions. Browning is prepared to use unfamiliar language in order to achieve closeness to the foreign original, but proposes to limit it to archaisms, in particular, without doing violence to the target language:

> If, because of the immense fame of the following Tragedy, I wished to acquaint myself with it, and could only do so by the help of a translator, I should require him to be literal at every cost save that of absolute violence to our language. The use of certain allowable constructions which, happening to be out of daily favour, are all the more appropriate to archaic workmanship, is no violence: but I would be tolerant for once,—in the case of so immensely famous an original,—of even a clumsy attempt to furnish me with the very turn of each phrase in as Greek a fashion as English will bear...[72]

In this set of translations, then, Humboldt represents the foreignizing approach, while Droysen and Wilamowitz set out to offer more

[71] 'Meine Übersetzung will mindestens so verständlich sein wie den Athenern das Original war, womöglich noch leichter verständlich; sie will also einen Teil der Erklärung bereits liefern.' Wilamowitz-Möllendorff 1900, 3.

[72] Browning 1877, v–vi. In addition to this (positive) programme, the (negative) rejection of a merely content-centred domestication is made explicit later on in the preface: 'Further,—if I obtained a mere strict bald version of thing by thing, or at least word pregnant with thing, I should hardly look for an impossible transmission of the reputed magniloquence and sonority of the Greek, and this with much the less regret, inasmuch as there is abundant musicality elsewhere, but nowhere else in his poem the ideas of the poet. And lastly, when presented with these ideas, I should expect the result to prove very hard reading indeed if it were meant to resemble Aeschylus, ξυμβαλεῖν οὐ ῥᾴδιος, "not easy to understand", in the opinion of his stoutest advocate among the ancients.' Browning 1877, vi. A domesticating element that should be noted, however, is the use of rhyming to express the elevated tone of the choral passages.

domesticating renderings of the Greek text. Jenisch's translation takes an intermediate position between the two. Browning, another foreignizer but the only non-German translator discussed here, will provide valuable evidence for how far specific features of the German language may be playing a role in responses to metonymy in the German versions.

METONYMY ACROSS LANGUAGES: TRANSLATING METONYMS IN AESCHYLUS' *AGAMEMNON*

'Dead' Metonyms and Metonymic Literary Clichés

Let us begin the assessment here, as in Chapter 3, with passages that contain metonyms which have become clichéd through frequent usage in Greek poetic idiom and have thus effectively gained denotative value. What happens to such metonymic clichés and 'dead' metonyms in translation? Consider the following passage in which Clytemnestra addresses Agamemnon with the following words:

> ... νῦν δέ μοι, φίλον *κάρα*,
> ἔκβαιν᾽ ...
>
> Now then, please, dear *head*,
> step out ...[73]

a) Jenisch
... mein geliebtes *Haupt* ...
... my beloved *head* ...

b) Humboldt
... geliebtes *Haupt* ...
... my beloved *head* ...

c) Droysen
... mein theures *Haupt* ...
... my precious *head* ...

d) Wilamowitz
... Trauter Freund ...
... my dear friend ...

e) Browning
... dear *headship* ...

[73] A. *Agam.* 905–6; trans. Sommerstein.

As Fraenkel *ad loc.* points out, 'This form of affectionate address, the prototype of which is as early as Homer, occurs in Aeschylus only here, whereas in Sophocles and Euripides it is to be found a number of times.' Jenisch's, Humboldt's, and Droysen's translations show that the metonymic expression can be translated verbatim into German where the clichéd literary tradition continues in the target language. Here, and in what follows, I refer to verbatim translations when the highest degree of translatability is demonstrated, whereby the term in the target language corresponds to the term in the source language in its range of both denotative and tropical significations, so that the semantic range of the two terms in ordinary usage *and* in tropical usage is roughly equivalent.[74] Wilamowitz's translation gives a literal version instead of the metonymic cliché, whereas Browning's translation gives a more striking (if bizarre) live metonym: Agamemnon is not addressed as a person, or as a body part implying one, but as an abstraction.

We find a similar outcome with the following sequence in which the chorus express their sense of foreboding and anxiety about the events about to unfold:

> προφθάσασα *καρδία*
> *γλῶσσαν* ἂν τάδ' ἐξέχει.
>
> my *heart* would be too quick for my *tongue*
> and would be pouring all this out[75]

a) Jenisch
längst schon hat die *Zung'* herausgeströmet,
was die Seele erfüllt

the *tongue* has already poured out
that which fills the soul

b) Humboldt
goss das *Herz*, voreilend, sich
über meine *Lippen* aus

the *heart* precipitately poured itself out
over my *lips*

[74] This (approximate) semantic equivalence does not, however, imply equivalence in terms of poetic effect. A literary cliché in one culture and one poetic idiom may be less clichéd or even striking in another, and vice versa.

[75] A. *Agam.* 1028–9; trans. Sommerstein.

c) Droysen
Eilen würde da mein *Herz*
Auszuströmen diesen Wunsch

Then my *heart* would rush to
Pour out this wish

d) Wilamowitz
Der *Zunge* käm' zuvor das *Herz*

The *tongue* would come second after the *heart*

e) Browning
My *heart*, outstripping what *tongue* utters,
Would have all out

In four of the translations, the metonymic cliché 'heart' (implying the emotional inner life of the subject) has been carried over into the target language with the same terminology and the same clichéd status in poetic idiom. 'Tongue' also proves to be translatable in principle. Humboldt's translation converts it to 'lips', thus replacing one stock metonym with another, but both equally imply 'speech'. Only Jenisch's translation gives a literalized translation, which renders the content of the otherwise implied speech explicit ('that which fills my soul').[76]

I take all expressions of this type to be metonymic clichés (and not literal or indeed metaphorical expressions) since they are based on a link of lexical contiguity between an organ and an abstract capacity of human subjects, with no analogy or similarity involved (which would be indicative of metaphor). It is hard to ascertain (retrospectively) which logic, if any, may have originally motivated the forging of individual connections, and so in response to Genette's question, 'what kind of "contiguity" could be maintained by the heart and courage, the brain and intelligence, the bowels and mercy?',[77] the pragmatic answer is: *lexical* contiguity. Extralinguistically, these links may be supported by physiological sensations that coincide with certain emotions ('trust your gut feeling'), by knowledge of the functions of human anatomy ('use your brain'), or by pure convention ('follow your heart'); intralinguistically, it

[76] It is worth highlighting that the different contextual associations generated by different body parts are likely to have an impact on the different treatment they receive by translators. Thus, 'heart' associations in Greek, German, and English are largely emotional and, while some may have an angry or erotic edge, they do not tend to indicate connected associations that 'tongues' can bring with them in Greek (and in the target languages), including *inter alia* sexual practices on the one hand and anxieties about verbal practices on the other.

[77] Genette 1970a, 109.

is clear that we are dealing here with contiguous relationships based on culturally and terminologically pre-established links that do not include any analogical conception. Regardless of how exactly the extralinguistic relationship between organ and non-corporeal capacity may have been conceptualized,[78] the link between them is linguistically established through regular collocation of organ terminology with human terminology in the context of abstract human faculties—and the exploitation of links established through collocation in ordinary usage is, as shown above, the core principle of metonymy.[79] All such terms, which recur frequently in both ancient and modern poetry, constitute instances of elevated poetic language; that is to say, they belong to the conventional but still stylized idiom of poetry, rather than to ordinary referential language.[80] As such, they add significantly to the poetic texture of the

[78] The debate on how we are to understand the 'speaking organs' that appear in Homer and other early Greek poets continues, albeit with less intensity, to this day. In his influential work *The Discovery of the Mind* (1946), Snell took Homer's words at face value. As part of his larger narrative of 'man's gradual understanding of himself' (Snell 1946, iii), Snell argues that 'Homeric man' had not yet developed a concept of the self as one single, unified, self-conscious entity. As Pelliccia summarizes, Snell accordingly interprets organ-speech passages in Homer as revealing a 'conflict between separate and autonomous entities instead: the person is in conflict with an actual thing or organ that he believes to be inside of him and which, like a separate person, can argue with him' (Pelliccia 1995, 19). It is beyond the remit of this study to discuss the precise nature of the ancient Greeks' mental concepts themselves and whether or how they embody a psychological conceptualization of man that is different from ours (for a good introduction to recent scholarship on 'the Greek view of man', which raises many important points of methodological criticism, see Thumiger 2007, 3–26). My concern is entirely with the literary-linguistic, or terminological, side of the argument—and in this respect we are dealing here clearly with literary clichés employed in elevated poetic diction. Having acquired denotative value over time through frequent employment, their possible origin in a one-time tropical usage is a matter for diachronic reconstruction rather than synchronic semantics and aesthetics. That said, it is apparent that these expressions are not—and seem never to have been—based on any kind of logic of analogy or similarity, and so they should not be considered 'metaphorical' in any respect.

[79] Although rarely considered, my suggestion that such expressions are (historically) metonymic is not entirely without precedent: 'But why then say you, have the Philosophers defined anger a boyling of the bloud about the hart? if it be according to that definition, then the more cholericke a man is, so much the more angry he is: because the choler is first apt to boyle, as it were brimstone to the match, in respect of the other humours. That definition of anger, is to be taken not by proper speech, but by a *metonymicall* phrase, wherebye the cause is attributed to the effect. For first the heart moveth, kindled by anger, then the bloud riseth, which being cholericke encreaseth the heate, but addeth nothing to the passion.' Bright 1586, 87–8; italics added.

[80] And for precisely this reason it is methodologically highly problematic to use literary texts as evidence for large-scale cultural studies without paying close attention to the tropological dimension of the texts in question. Trying to reconstruct denotations and conceptualizations from evidence gathered in poetic texts, in the way that Snell and his followers have attempted, runs the risk of mistaking poetic modes of expression and narrativizations for straightforward representations of realities, psychological or otherwise.

texts in which they occur and, depending on the wider context and the vehicle terminology of neighbouring metaphors, they can indeed be integrated in tropical clusters within which, as a whole, they effectively intensify a sequence.[81]

The Greek term κέαρ ('heart') also exemplifies this type of traditional literary cliché; compare the following two sets, the first from the watchman's opening monologue as he awaits, on Clytemnestra's orders, the fire signal coming from Troy, the second from Clytemnestra herself after the signal has at last arrived:

(1) γυναικὸς *ἀνδρόβουλον* ἐλπίζον *κέαρ*
a woman's hopeful *heart, which plans like a man*[82]

a) Jenisch
Wie sollt'
hier dieses Weibes freches *Männerherz* hinschmelzen
How should
here this woman's daring man-*heart* melt away

b) Humboldt
Denn so heischet es des Weibes mannhaft kühnes, tückisch hoffend *Herz*
For thus desires the woman's manly-bold, cunningly-hoping *heart*

c) Droysen
also, denk' ich, hat es mir
geboten meiner Herrin männlich ratend *Herz*
This way, I think,
has my lady's manly-counselling *heart* instructed her

d) Wilamowitz
Die Königin, an Kühnheit und Verstand ein Mann
The queen, a man in terms of boldness and intelligence

To illustrate the point: it is as if some future lexicographer of modern English attempted to establish the literal meaning of the expression 'prime minister' from instances where it is used jointly with live or dead metaphorical expressions such as 'keeping course', 'making bills watertight', 'steering the country through difficulties', and 'preparing the economy for stormy waters', and concluded on the basis of that 'evidence' that this office of state is somehow 'conceptualized' as having intrinsic nautical qualities. I plan to explore and illustrate the methodological relevance of *tropology* for research in the history of ideas in more detail in a separate publication, drawing in particular on the debate on 'speaking organs' as a prime example; for a detailed study that elucidates the *narrative function* of 'organs of will' in Homer and Pindar, see Pelliccia 1995.

[81] On the phenomenon of 'tropical clusters', see above, pp. 123–34.

[82] A. *Agam.* 11; trans. Sommerstein.

e) Browning
so prevails audacious
the man's-way-planning hoping *heart* of woman

(2) ἦ κάρτα πρὸς γυναικὸς αἴρεσθαι *κέαρ*
How very like a woman, to let her *heart* take flight[83]

a) Jenisch
Wie schwillt das *Herz* des Weibes doch so leicht der Freude
How easily woman's *heart* swells to joy

b) Humboldt
Recht Weiberart ist's, eitlen Wahns das *Herz* zu blähen
It is indeed women's way to inflate the *heart* in vain delusion

c) Droysen
Doch Weiberart ist's, außer sich gar bald zu sein
But it is women's way to be completely out of one's mind

d) Wilamowitz
Wie leicht ist doch ein Weiber*herz* entzündet
How easily a woman's *heart* is set on fire

e) Browning
Truly, the woman's way,—high to lift *heart* up

In both sequences, the majority of translations replicate the Greek metonymic cliché verbatim. The only variations are, in the first passage, Jenisch's addition of a stock metaphor ('melt away') and Wilamowitz's literalizing translation; and in the second, Wilamowitz's addition of a stock metaphor ('easily set on fire') and Droysen's literalizing translation.

With the Greek term γλῶσσα ('tongue'), the situation is slightly different. As before, a verbatim translation is possible (as other instances in the play confirm).[84] However, the semantic range of the term as a

[83] A. *Agam.* 592; trans. Sommerstein.

[84] Compare, for instance, the translation of θαυμάζομέν σου *γλῶσσαν, ὡς θρασύστομος* ('We are amazed at your language [lit.: your *tongue*]—the arrogance of it—[lit.: how *bold-mouthed*]'; A. *Agam.* 1399; trans. Sommerstein) in which all translators but Jenisch preserve the metonymic cliché in one form or another (note how Droysen first literalizes the original metonym and then reintroduces it in the form of a compound adjective): Jenisch—'Wie staun ich über deine Frechheit!' ('How I marvel at your boldness!'), Humboldt—'Wir staunen *deiner Zunge* frecher Lästerung' ('We marvel at *your tongue's* impertinent blasphemy'), Droysen—'Wir staunen deiner Rede, wie Du *zungenfrech* noch solche Worte prahlest über dich und ihn!' ('We marvel at your speech, how *bold-tongued* you boast such words about yourself and him!'), Wilamowitz—'Ob deiner *Zunge* Kühnheit staun' ich' ('I marvel at the boldness of your tongue'), Browning—'We wonder at thy *tongue*: since

metonym has become so familiar that the translators are prepared to eliminate any sense of metonymy and its directional, open-ended suggestions. Compare the following two sets, the first from the herald's reply to the chorus's enquiry on Menelaus' *nostos*, the second from the chorus's response to the herald's report:

(1) εὔφημον ἦμαρ οὐ πρέπει κακαγγέλῳ
γλώσσῃ μιαίνειν

It is not proper to defile a day of good omen
by uttering of bad news
[lit.: with a *tongue* that brings ill tidings][85]

a) Jenisch
Den Tag des Heiles ziemt's
it Unglücksbotschaften nicht zu entweihn

It is not proper to desecrate the day of salvation
with news of ill-fortune

b) Humboldt
Den Tag des Heils mit Trauerkunde schnöd' entweihn
gebühret nicht

To vilely desecrate the day of salvation with news of mourning
is not proper

c) Droysen
Mit böser Botschaft sollte man den frohen Tag
Niemals entweihen

One should never desecrate the happy day
With bad news

d) Wilamowitz
Den Tag der Freude sollte Trauerbotschaft nicht entweihn

News of mourning should not desecrate the day of joy

e) Browning
It suits not to defile a day auspicious
With ill-announcing speech

bold-mouthed truly is she who in such speech boasts o'er her husband.' Full translatability is also displayed in the translation of ἀλλὰ τούσδ' ἐμοὶ *ματαίαν γλῶσσαν* ὧδ' ἀπανθίσαι ('But to think that these men should shoot off their worthless *tongues*'; A. *Agam.* 1662; trans. Sommerstein): Jenisch—'[m]it so loser *Zunge*' ('with such loose *tongue*'), Humboldt—'der eitlen *Zunge*' ('of vain *tongue*'), Droysen and Wilamowitz—'mit frecher *Zunge*' ('with *insolent tongue*'), Browning—'the idle *tongue*'.

[85] A. *Agam.* 636–7; trans. Sommerstein.

(2) μή τις ὅντιν' οὐχ ὁρῶμεν προνοίαισι
τοῦ πεπρωμένου
γλῶσσαν ἐν τύχᾳ νέμων;

perhaps a being we cannot see,
using language [lit.: *tongue*] with accuracy
through his foreknowledge of what was fated[86]

a) Jenisch
der Unsichtbaren einer
lenkte, kundig des Schicksals
die profetische *Zunge* ihm

one of the invisibles,
knowing the ways of fate, directed
the prophetic *tongue* for him

b) Humboldt
lenket', unerschauet, nicht, ahndungsvoll
dess, was vorbestimmt war, einer recht *der Zunge* Wort?

does not someone, unseen, full of foreboding
of what was predetermined, rightly guide the *tongue's* word?

c) Droysen
Wenn nicht der, den keener schaut, der voraus all Verhängniß überdenkt,
Auch *das Wort* im Zufall lenkt

Even if the one whom nobody sees, who ponders all fate in advance,
Does not also guide *the word* by chance.

d) Wilamowitz
Fand ihn eines Dämons *Zunge*, zukunftahnend, schicksaldeutend?

Did a demon's *tongue* find him, with premonitions of the future, interpreting fate?

e) Browning
Was he someone whom we see not, by forecastings of the future
Guiding *tongue* in happy mood?

In the first example, all the translations have eliminated the vestige of a metonymic trope and thus any vestigial ambiguity. Most of the German translations conflate the adjective κακαγγέλῳ ('bringing ill tidings') and the noun γλώσση ('tongue', 'speech') into one compound noun, which indicates that it is the microcontextual specification accomplished by the adjective which prompts the disambiguation. In the second example, the microcontext is less specific and leaves more room for the ambiguity resulting from the extended semantic range of the Greek term. In the

[86] A. *Agam.* 684–6; trans. Sommerstein.

event, only Droysen's translation disambiguates the metonym, though without rendering the term entirely literal (note the singular 'word' implying a plural). Humboldt's translation gives the same disambiguated version ('Wort', 'word'), but at the same time includes a literal translation of the metonymic term ('der Zunge', 'the tongue'), albeit in a subordinate position where it carries little semantic weight. All the other translations give a verbatim representation of the stock metonym.

Translatable metonymic clichés in which the terminology of body parts is used to imply either the whole person or aspects of personhood are common enough.[87] Conversely, there are some cases where cultural specificities impede verbatim translation. Consider two cases involving the Greek term φρήν ('midriff', 'diaphragm'), the first from the chorus's response to Clytemnestra's words as Agamemnon walks over the purple fabric towards the palace door, the second from the chorus's dialogue with her after she has killed Agamemnon:

(1) οὐδ' ἀποπτύσαι δίκαν
δυσκρίτων ὀνειράτων
θάρσος εὐπειθὲς
ἵζει *φρενὸς* φίλον <u>θρόνον</u>;

Why can I not spurn it,
like a dream hard to interpret,
and let optimism persuade me and set itself
in command of my mind within?
[lit.: and let persuasive confidence
sit on the dear <u>throne</u> of my *diaphragm*][88]

a) Jenisch
Warum fliegt mir der schwarze Schreckgedanke
durch die Seele profetisch hin, und weissagt
ungelohnt, ungeheissen, dunkle Zukunft?
Warum tilg' ich ihn, gleich dem unausdeutbarn Traume, nicht aus der bangen *Brust*?

Why does the frightful black thought fly
prophetically through my soul, and prophesy
unpaid, uncalled for, a dark future?
Why do I not purge it, like an uninterpretable dream, from the anxious *breast*?

[87] Such aspects being, for instance, powers of reasoning, speech, feelings of sympathy and anger, and so on.
[88] A. *Agam.* 980–3; trans. Sommerstein.

b) Humboldt
Warum kehret, räthselhaftem Traum
gleich, es fern verbannend, nie
wieder sicherer Muth mir
zum Sitz der lieben Brust?

Why does firm courage
nevermore return
to the seat of the dear breast,
banning it far away
like a mysterious dream?

c) Droysen
Warum nicht, vergessend sein,
sein wie eines dunklen Traums,
weilt auf meines Gemüths liebem Thron getroster Muth?

Why does confident courage
not rest on the dear throne of my mind,
forgetting it, like a dark dream?

d) Wilamowitz
Und die das *Herze*
nicht wie ein wirres Traumgesicht
verscheucht und frei und ruhig schlagen mag.

And which the *heart*
does not expel like a confused dream vision
and [*sc.* so that it] may beat free and peaceful.

e) Browning
Fronting my *heart*, the portent-watcher—flits she?
Wherefore should prophet-play
The uncalled lay,
Nor—having spat forth fear, like bad dreams—sits she
On the mind's throne beloved—well-suasive Boldness?

(2) φονολιβεῖ τύχᾳ *φρὴν* ἐπιμαίνεται

your mind [lit.: your *diaphragm*] is driven mad by your experience of flowing blood[89]

a) Jenisch
als hättest du aus dem Blutbecher gesoffen,
so rasest du

you are raging
as though you had been drinking from the cup of blood

[89] A. *Agam.* 1427; trans. Sommerstein.

b) Humboldt
   da dir die *Brust*, an Mord frech sich ergötzend, rast

   since your *breast* is raging, impertinently delighting in murder

c) Droysen
   so frech von dem vergoss'nen Blut
   ras't dir der Geist noch nach

   your mind is still raging on,
   impertinent because of the shed blood

d) Wilamowitz
   Wie sich dein rasend *Herz*
   letzt an der blut'gen That

   How your raging *heart*
   feasts on the bloody deed

e) Browning
   thy mind, with its slaughter-outpouring part,
   is frantic

The difficulty in translating the term φρήν lies in the fact that a metonymic connection between the diaphragm and an abstract human faculty (encompassing both emotional, intellectual, and voluntative responses) has no direct parallel in German or English culture or in the poetic idiom of the two literary traditions. For cultural reasons, therefore, this metonymic cliché is untranslatable so far as verbatim translation is concerned. Accordingly, the translations show a variety of responses, ranging from paraphrase that drops the metonymic element in Jenisch's translation of the second passage, to literalization ('mind') and replacement with the nearest available metonymic cliché of the target language ('breast', 'heart'). In the first passage, Wilamowitz goes further by simply conflating the untranslatable φρενός with the translatable καρδίας ('heart') (a term that occurs in the preceding verses). One other noteworthy feature is the explication of the associative link on which such (clichéd) metonyms were originally based, as in Humboldt's translation of the first example: the breast is explicitly and, as it were, 'literally' said to be the seat of courage. The same is true, although less explicitly, with Jenisch's translation. In the Greek original, things are not so clear, because here the metaphorical φίλον θρόνον ('dear throne') ascribes a notion of rulership to the mental faculty at issue rather than explicating the metonymic link itself. Interestingly, this notion is dropped in most of the translations.

Many similar examples could be cited. The term σπλάγχνον, for instance, is another metonymic cliché which has come to denote not only (unspecific) internal organs but also the seat of the emotions.[90] Where it occurs in the play, the translations display a wide range of approximately equivalent metonymic clichés from the target language: 'breast', 'bosom', 'heart'.[91] Needless to say, organ terminology is not the only field in which such metonymic clichés can be found. A quite different example is 'roof' for 'house'. Here, too, translingual and transcultural equivalents are available—and yet the fact that literalization does occur in some of the translations (notably Droysen's and Wilamowitz's) shows that the term is, nevertheless, still recognized as metonymic.[92]

The issues that arise with metonymic clichés recur with mythological metonyms. The names of gods are often used as stock examples of metonymy in rhetorical handbooks ('god-for-sphere-of-operation'-type metonym) but they have been excluded from the main body of my discussion because of the difficulty of assessing whether or not, in any particular case, Greek religion treats divinities as subsuming their sphere of operation and, therefore, the impossibility of determining the exact semantic range of what is denoted (or else metonymically implied) by the name of a god. With the eighteenth- and nineteenth-century translations, the case is different: here, a literal identity or approximate synonymity of sphere and godhead is no longer a *donnée* in ordinary usage, and so the tropical status of gods' names can be reliably assessed.[93]

[90] The term denotes a physical organ at e.g. Hdt. 2.40, Arist. *PA* 667b3, and *Il.* 1.464; instances where it occurs as a metonymic cliché for the seat of the feelings or the feelings themselves include A. *Ch.* 413, S. *Aj.* 955, and E. *Med.* 220.

[91] *σπλάγχνα* δ' οὔτοι ματᾴζει ('And my *inwards*... do not speak in vain', A. *Agam.* 995; trans. Sommerstein) is translated as 'Keine Ahndung klopfte je vergebens die *Brust*' ('No premonition ever knocked at the *breast* in vain') by Jenisch, 'Nicht schwatzt eitel *der Busen*' ('The *bosom* does not speak in vain') by Humboldt, 'so täuscht sich nicht mein *Herz*' ('thus my *heart* is not mistaken') by Droysen, 'Nicht trügt das Zeichen... das treue Herz' ('The sign does not mislead the faithful *heart*') by Wilamowitz, and as 'The *heart* that's rolled in whirls... justly presageful of a fate' by Browning.

[92] κἄπειτ' Ἀτρειδῶν ἐς τόδε σκήπτει *στέγος* ('And then it fell upon this house [lit.: *roof*] of the Atreidae', A. *Agam.* 310; trans. Sommerstein) is translated as 'der Atriden *Dach*' ('the Atreidai's *roof*') by Jenisch and Humboldt, as 'Schloß der Atriden' ('the Atreidai's castle') and 'unser königliches Schloss' ('our royal castle') by Droysen and Wilamowitz, and as '*roof* of the Atreidai' by Browning. Similarly, ἆ ποῖ ποτ' ἤγαγές με; πρὸς ποίαν *στέγην*; | πρὸς τὴν Ἀτρειδῶν... ('Where on earth, what kind of house [lit.: *roof*] have you brought me to? | To the house of the Atreidae...', A. *Agam.* 1087–8; trans. Sommerstein) is translated as 'der Atriden Haus' ('the Atreidai's house') by Jenisch, 'Zum *Dach* von Atreus' ('to Atreus' roof') by Humboldt, 'Zum Hause der Atriden' ('to the Atreidai's house') by Droysen and Wilamowitz, and as 'To the Atreidai's *roof*' by Browning. Note that it is the domesticators Droysen and Wilamowitz who opt for a literalized version of the metonymic cliché while the others carry the cliché over into the target language.

[93] Needless to say, where the names of Greek gods *are* used 'metonymically', we usually have cases of metonymic cliché, since such usages are a firmly established part of the poetic idiom of classical writing and are not striking or abrasive enough to be counted as tropical in the strict sense.

Moreover, these translations illustrate the range of terms metonymically evoked by divine names. Consider the following example from the chorus's reflections on Paris' abduction of Helen:

> ὀμμάτων δ' ἐν ἀχηνίαις
> ἔρρει *πᾶσ' Ἀφροδίτα.*
>
> because they [*sc.* statues] lack eyes
> all their loveliness goes for nothing
> [lit.: in the blanks of their eyes
> *all Aphrodite* perishes][94]

a) Jenisch
Denn diese Augen ach!
sie schmachten nicht! Ganz ist sie, ganz hin—
hin—*Afrodite* mit jedem Liebreiz.

For these eyes, alas!
They do not yearn! She is utterly, utterly gone—
gone—*Aphrodite* with all loveliness.

b) Humboldt
weil in Blickes Entbehrung kalt
jede Liebe dahin welkt.

for cold, lacking a gaze,
all love dies.

c) Droysen
Ihres Auges verlorne Lust aller Liebe Verlust ihm

The lost pleasure of her eye [equalled] loss of all love for him

d) Wilamowitz
Nicht tröstete der Gatte
sein darbendes Auge
am Bild der Geliebten; er fühlte sich
von Aphrodite verlassen.

The spouse did not console
his starving eye
with the image of the beloved; he felt himself to be
deserted by Aphrodite.

e) Browning
in place of eyes
those blanks—all *Aphrodité* dies.

[94] A. *Agam.* 418–19; trans. Sommerstein.

In the Greek original, the adjective πᾶσ' ('all') prompts a reading that takes Ἀφροδίτα to signify 'loveliness', 'erotic appeal', 'beauty', and so on. Of all the translations, Browning's is the only one that would strictly speaking be a 'god-for-remit'-type metonym: his translation only makes sense if we take the goddess's name as an index metonym and infer any or all of these terms.[95] The versions offered by Humboldt, Droysen, and Wilamowitz, on the other hand, disambiguate and literalize the term, the former two by specifying 'love', the latter by rephrasing the sequence in a way that turns the goddess into a personally acting 'absent presence'. Jenisch's translation, finally, seeks a middle way by keeping the goddess's name in the text but supplementing it with an explicit term that spells out what is at issue ('loveliness'). The ambiguity inherent in the Greek original (active goddess linked unspecifically to the presence of an abstract quality) is thus expressed in literal terms[96]—a strategy we have already encountered in Humboldt's translation of another passage:[97] the term, which serves as metonymic vehicle in the source text, is carried over into the target language in literal translation but is supplemented with a term that would be the (implicit) metonymic tenor in the source text. As this translation strategy can be observed frequently, I suggest we refer to it from here on as 'literalizing supplementation'.

A range of responses similar to the one triggered by the mythological metonym above can be found in the following passage from the chorus's opening reflections on the Greek expedition to Troy:

[95] The name of the goddess taken together with the verb in this passage represents a case of conditional metonymy/metaphor as discussed above, see pp. 135–40: as soon as metonymic tenor (abstract quality) is inferred from metonymic vehicle (person), the verb must be understood metaphorically; however, the combination of the metonymic vehicle (person) and the verb ('to die') as such is perfectly literal—albeit not undramatic, since it expresses nothing less than the death of a goddess.

[96] But Jenisch's 'inspired' approach to translation, which calls for the translator to write 'in the same spirit' as the author, also leads him to deploy heightened poetic language in what follows, adding tropical elements that are not present in the source text. He translates μάταν γάρ, εὖτ' ἄν ἐσθλά τις δοκοῦνθ' ὁρᾷ,| παραλλάξασα διὰ | χερῶν βέβακεν ὄψιν ('for it is empty when one sees what seems a blessing and then the vision slips aside through one's arms and is gone', A. *Agam.* 423–5; trans. Sommerstein) as 'Denn zwiefach jammert, wem vor dem *Auge* die *Wohllust* tanzte, und lange ihm den *trunkenen* Blick geweid't' ('for twice he moans whose *eye lust* has danced in front of and has long nourished his *drunken* gaze'). Jenisch thus adds a number metonym ('eye' for 'eyes'), an index metonym ('lust' implying 'a person that arouses lust'), and a metaphorical cliché combined with grammatical amplification metonymy ('drunk' implies 'pleasure', 'saturation', 'exhilaration', and is transferred from the subject implicit in 'his' to '[his] gaze').

[97] See above, pp. 198–9.

μέγαν ἐκ θυμοῦ κλάζοντες *Ἄρη*

uttering from their hearts a great cry for war[98]
[lit.: crying from their heart (thumos) for great war (*Ares*) /
crying in anger (thumos) loudly for war (*Ares*) /
expressing in cries from their heart (thumos) their great warlike spirit (*Ares*)]

a) Jenisch
gewaltgen Krieg
und blutge Rache athmend

breathing great war
and bloody revenge

b) Humboldt
aus der Brust die Begier laut schnaubend des Kampfes

breathing out from the breast the desire for fighting

c) Droysen
Voll Zornmuth schrie'n sie gewaltigen Kampf

Full of angry valour they cried [for] great fighting

d) Wilamowitz
Grimmig scholl aus ihrer Brust der Schlachtruf

Grimly the battle cry arose from their breast

e) Browning
clamouring
'Ares' from out the indignant breast

All the German translators literalize the sequence, replacing the god's name with various terms from the field of battle terminology. In addition to the variety of terms chosen (ranging from 'war' and 'fighting' to 'revenge'), several of the translations also conflate the metonymic tenor, as inferred from the metonymic vehicle, with other elements from the source text. Wilamowitz's translation conflates κλάζοντες Ἄρη ('crying Ares') into the compound noun 'battle cry'. Jenisch's and Humboldt's versions, on the other hand, seek to integrate it with the literally untranslatable ἐκ θυμοῦ. This Greek phrase denotes a human faculty that encompasses will and passion and has no direct equivalent in German culture or language. Jenisch's translation, by contrast, duplicates Ἄρη into both 'great war' and 'bloody revenge'. That second phrase conflates θυμοῦ and Ἄρη, conveying both passionate response (θυμοῦ) and the war terminology implied by the metonymic vehicle (Ἄρη). Humboldt's translation of the sequence recalls the earlier discussion of

[98] A. *Agam.* 48; trans. Sommerstein.

the untranslatable 'dead' metonym φρήν.[99] His version splits ἐκ θυμοῦ into two terms, yielding both 'breast' (the assumed 'seat') and 'desire' (the emotion). Browning's translation, finally, preserves the god's name and might therefore seem to be the most 'faithful' translation. However, it diverges significantly from the source text so far as tropicality is concerned: the god's name is used literally—as the very word the combatants utter. This constitutes a literalization of the Greek original, in which the accusative case of Ἄρη precludes such an interpretation.[100] Despite carrying the same term over into English, therefore, Browning's translation is as much a disambiguating literalization as any of the German versions.

One final example of a mythological metonym produces quite different outcomes:

> *Ἥφαιστος* Ἴδης λαμπρὸν ἐκπέμπων σέλας
> *Hephaestus*, sending a bright blaze on its way from Mount Ida[101]

a) Jenisch
Vulkan, der bis von Ida's Gipfel her
Glanzstrahlend Fackel stets an Fackel zündt

Vulcan, who lights all the way from Ida's peak
one radiant torch with another torch

b) Humboldt
Hephästos, fern vom Ida sendend Feuerglanz

Hephaestus, sending fire-gleam from far-away Ida

c) Droysen
Hephaistos, der vom Ida hellen Strahl gesandt

Hephaestus, who sent a bright ray from Ida

d) Wilamowitz
Hephaistos, der vom Ida helles Licht gesandt

Hephaestus, who sent bright light from Ida

e) Browning
Hephaistos—sending a bright blaze from Idé

To begin with the Greek original: the sequence is the beginning of Clytemnestra's reply to the question, which messenger could have possibly brought the news of the fall of Troy with such speed. The literal answer to the question is the chain of watch posts equipped with beacons to report the Greek victory. Clytemnestra's reply is rhetorically elegant

[99] See above, pp. 199–201, and below, pp. 259–60.
[100] This would require the genitive case; on this construction, see above, p. 99.
[101] A. *Agam.* 281; trans. Sommerstein.

and effective: the question, as phrased, asks for a person to be named in the answer. Naming Hephaestus not only meets this requirement of personhood but also invokes a divinity as guarantor for the validity of her claim. Once again it is impossible for us to be sure about the Greek term's tropical status but it is interesting that all the translations reproduce the god's name; not one translation literalizes to 'fire' or 'fire signals'. The context of the passage makes it abundantly clear that what is at issue is not a divine intervention but Clytemnestra's very human machination, so the shift from fire signals to god of fire is (at least from the perspective of the translators) metonymic. However, the translations display a sensitivity for the rhetoric at work in this passage by reproducing the god's name.[102]

Synecdoche (Number Metonymy)

Before moving on to the more striking metonyms discussed in Chapter 3, let us consider a few more low-level metonyms. The discussion of synecdoche pointed to the implication of singular for plural, and vice versa, as the most basic form of this type of metonymic defamiliarization. In itself, this might seem to be a negligible, almost imperceptible deviation. Yet, when it comes to the overall poetic texture of a translation, the role of such 'minor' devices should not be underestimated. As with the examples just discussed, there are many instances where metonymic shifts in number have become clichéd and where translingual and transcultural continuation of such traditions of poetic idiom exists. To give just one example (from Cassandra's exchange with the chorus):

> ἐπεύχομαι δὲ καιρίας πληγῆς τυχεῖν,
> ὡς ἀσφάδαστος, αἱμάτων εὐθνησίμων
> ἀπορρυέντων, *ὄμμα* συμβάλω τόδε.
>
> And I pray that I may receive a single mortal stroke,
> and close these eyes [lit.: *eye*] without a struggle,
> my blood flowing out in an easy death.[103]

is translated verbatim in all the versions:[104]

[102] Jenisch's substitution of the Greek Hephaestus with the Latin Vulcan may seem striking to us but is a feature frequently found in both literary translations and classicizing poetry of this period, which often uses names from Greek and Roman mythology interchangeably and alongside each other without discernable semantic differentiation.

[103] A. *Agam.* 1292–4; trans. Sommerstein.

[104] Note that this entire sequence also illustrates the structural similarity of metonymy proper and metonymic association (see above, pp. 140–7): the instance under discussion here involves the collocation of an explicit statement on death with the mention of closing

a) Jenisch
und sich schnell *dies Auge* schließ'.

and that *this eye* may close quickly

b) Humboldt
schliessen *dieses Aug'* ich kann

and may close *this eye*

c) Droysen
sich ruhig ohne Todeskampf mein *Auge* schließt

my *eye* may close quietly without agony

d) Wilamowitz
rasch das Auge bricht, das Leben ohne Krampf und Zucken scheiden kann

the *eye* breaks quickly, life departs without agony and convulsion

e) Browning
without a struggle,—blood the calm death bringing in easy outflow,—
I *this eye* may close up

Compare, however, what happens with the following two sequences, beginning with this first one from the watchman's opening soliloquy:

ἐν ὀψικοίτοις δ' ὄμμασιν βλάβας ἔχω

And I have damaged those eyes by lying late awake
[lit.: and I have damage in my eyes *which go to bed late*][105]

a) Jenisch
Mein *Auge, das*
oft bis um Mitternacht, gewacht, ward trüb
vor Gram

My *eye, which*
often stayed awake until midnight, became overcast
with sadness

b) Humboldt
Mein *spät entschlummernd Auge* kranket schmerzerfüllt

My *eye, falling asleep late*, is sick and full of pain

one's eye/s. Regular collocations of this kind establish a link that can be exploited in metonymy by association: when closing one's eye/s is mentioned alone in a similar context but without an explicit death statement, the preceding collocations have invested the term with a semantic surplus that becomes active and implies, by metonymic association, such a death statement when only the closing of one's eye/s is mentioned.

105 A. *Agam.* 889; trans. Sommerstein.

c) Droysen
   Mein *spätentschlummernd Auge* krankt und schmerzt mich sehr

   My *eye, falling asleep late*, is sick and pains me very much

d) Wilamowitz
   und blöde ward des *überwachten Auges* Blick.

   and the vision of my *eye, which has been awake for too long*, has gone blind.

e) Browning
   And in my *late-to-bed* eyes damage have I

   Bewailing what concerned thee

Here, the Greek original has an ordinary-language plural, ὄμμασιν ('eyes'), whereas all the translations except Browning's choose a rendering which implies the plural but gives the singular. Why? ὀψικοίτοις ('going to bed late') is a grammatical amplification metonym, transferred from the implied subject (who literally goes to bed late) to the subject's eyes.[106] By adding a metonymic cliché to the grammatical amplification metonym, the translations achieve a further elaboration of the overall poetic effect. It is worth pointing out that this includes the translations by Droysen and Wilamowitz. We noted earlier that their translations disambiguate even metonymic clichés,[107] as indeed their 'domesticating' agendas would lead us to expect, but here even they make the sequence (slightly) more defamiliarized than it is in the source text. And this is not an isolated case; consider the second example (from the same scene):

> ...φόβος γὰρ ἀνθ' ὕπνου παραστατεῖ
> τὸ μὴ βεβαίως βλέφαρα συμβαλεῖν ὕπνῳ
>
> for it is Fear instead of Sleep that stands beside me,
> preventing me from closing my eyes firmly in sleep
> [lit.: from putting firmly together my eyelids in sleep][108]

a) Jenisch
   an seiner Stelle steht
   zur Seite mir *mit dem Erynnenstab*
   die *wache* Furcht, und wehrt ihm, dieses *Aug*
   fest zuzusiegeln)

   in its [Sleep's] place stands
   by my side with *the Erinyes' staff*
   wide-awake Fear, and keeps him,
   from firmly sealing *this eye*

[106] Cf. above, p. 109. [107] See above, pp. 191–202.
[108] A. *Agam.* 14–15; trans. Sommerstein.

b) Humboldt
   Dass nie ich, schlummernd, schliesse fest *das Augenlied* [sic]

   So that never, slumbering, do I close my *eyelid* tight

c) Droysen
   Zufallen könnte gar im Schlaf *mein Augenlied* [sic]

   My eyelid might even close in sleep

d) Wilamowitz
   dass nicht zu fest der Schlummer meine Lider schliesst

   so that slumber does not firmly close my [eye]lids

e) Browning
   So as that fast I fix in sleep no eyelids [sic]

The Greek original contains no metonym as such. If anything, one might suggest that the (not especially striking) collocation βλέφαρα συμβαλεῖν ὕπνῳ is one of the many Greek usages that create a link between (the Greek for) 'sleep' and (for) 'closing one's eyes' which can then be potentially drawn on in metonymic association: 'closing one's eyelids' implies 'sleep' by mere association without any literal sleep terminology being present. The only tropical element in this sequence is the phrase φόβος παραστατεῖ. Here 'fear' is personified by virtue of the fact that the verb παραστατεῖ ('stands beside') associates this abstract emotion with the terminology of human agency.[109] Compare the translations. Both Humboldt's and Droysen's give singular instead of plural ('eyelid' instead of 'eyelids'), thereby making the expression more pointed and 'poetic' than in the source text. Jenisch's translation increases the number of tropical elements in the sequence even further: personified 'fear' is supplemented by a grammatical amplification metonym in the form of an epithet, 'die wache Furcht' ('wide-awake fear'), with the adjective transferred from the implied subject; the plural of βλέφαρα ('eyelids') is represented by the singular 'Aug' ('eye') which, however, implies a plural; the verb-based personification of 'fear' is continued by the insertion of a further live metaphor, 'fest zuzusiegeln' ('to seal firmly'); and the 'Erynnenstab' ('Erinyes' staff') in the hand of personified 'Fear' not only adds to the personification but also suggests, by metonymic association, what the watchman is so afraid of (revenge of bloodshed among kin). The density of defamiliarizing elements here significantly exceeds that in the source text. Wilamowitz's translation, on the other hand, does not much increase the quantity of poetic defamiliarization; for instance,

[109] By implication, the same is true for 'sleep'. On personification as a variant of metaphor, see above, pp. 147–54.

it keeps the plural βλέφαρα ('eyelids'). Yet even this translation intensifies the personification of 'sleep', in parallel to that of 'fear' in the preceding verse, by making 'sleep' the acting subject of a clause. Only Browning's translation is verbatim in every respect, except that the poeticizing effect of his 'so as that' as a way of reproducing the Greek's negative articular infinitive arguably exceeds the degree of poeticity in the original.

Such intensification of poetic language beyond the level of the source text is not confined to exceptional moments. It pervades these translations, regardless of whether they follow a 'foreignizing' or 'domesticating' manifesto. Two more examples make the point, beginning with this first one from the herald's exchange with the chorus:

ὥστ᾽ ἐνδακρύειν γ᾽ ὄμμασιν χαρᾶς ὕπο.
So much so that my eyes now fill with tears of joy.[110]

a) Jenisch
Ach
oft standen, oft, der Sehnsucht Thränen mir
auf dieser *Wange*.

Alas
often, often were there tears of longing
on *this cheek*.

b) Humboldt
Dass jetzt der Freude *Thräne* meinem *Aug'* entquillt

That now joy's *tear* pours from my *eye*

c) Droysen
So daß die Freude Thränen meinem *Aug'* entlockt!

So that joy elicits tears from my *eye*.

d) Wilamowitz
Drum macht das Wiedersehen mir das *Auge* feucht.

Thus the reunion makes my *eye* wet.

e) Browning
So that I weep, at least, with joy, my eyes full.

In the Greek original, the sequence is perfectly literal, and yet all the translators except Browning introduce metonymic singular for plural, as if by way of (lightly) elevating the diction. Compare and contrast the range of responses in the second example, taken from the chorus's opening recollection of the tragic events at Aulis:

110 A. *Agam.* 541; trans. Sommerstein.

...*δάκρυ* μὴ κατασχεῖν.
ἄναξ δ' ὁ πρέσβυς τότ' εἶπε φωνῶν

...could not hold back their tears [lit.: the *tear*]—
And the senior king spoke, and said this[111]

a) Jenisch
Konnten sich der Thränen nicht erwehren.
Laut rief der zween Könige größter aus

Could not fend off the tears.
The greater of the two kings cried out

b) Humboldt
...nicht haltend des Grams
Thräne zurück.
Da hub das *Wort* an der ältre König

...not holding back the *tear*
of grief.
Then the older king began uttering the *word*

c) Droysen
...und selbst Thränen sie nicht hemmten.
Da also sprach *dieses Wort* der Aeltere

...and even they did not hinder [their] tears.
Then the older one said *this word.*

d) Wilamowitz
aus *unwilligem Auge*
brachen die Thränen.
Da war es, wo der ält're der Atreidenfürsten sprach

out of an *unwilling eye*
broke forth the tears.
It was then that the older of the Atreidai lords said

e) Browning
So that the Atreidai striking staves on earth
Could not withhold *the tear.*
Then did the king, the elder, speak this clear.

The Greek original here displays a very low level of defamiliarized language, with only the singular for plural of δάκρυ ('tear') deviating from ordinary usage. Once again, Browning's translation is the only one to represent the source text verbatim. The others all adjust the tropical

[111] A. *Agam.* 204–5; trans. Sommerstein.

status of elements in the sequence. Despite his openness to 'free' and 'foreignizing' translation, Jenisch normalizes the deviation, with the plural 'Thränen' ('tears'). Droysen also literalizes the tropical element of the sequence in the source text but introduces, as if in its stead, another metonymic cliché: 'sprach dieses *Wort*' ('said this *word*'). One might assume that this rendering is prompted by the formulaic and tautological εἶπε φωνῶν ('saying he said'), but it is not without significance that it thereby preserves the degree of defamiliarization of the source text, albeit without a verbatim translation. Humboldt's translation likewise introduces the same metonymic cliché, but also preserves the number-based metonym of the source. The most remarkable innovation, however, is in Wilamowitz's translation, which literalizes the modest number metonym with the plural, 'tears', but simultaneously introduces not only another number metonym but also combines it with a grammatical amplification metonym: 'aus *unwilligem Auge*' ('out of an *unwilling eye*'). A transferred adjective is used here to express the negated verb κατασχεῖν ('to hold back'). Counterintuitively, Jenisch's 'free' translation emerges in this instance as 'familiarizing', in the sense that it literalizes tropical elements, whereas Wilamowitz's 'domesticating' translation is the most 'defamiliarizing' in the sense that it introduces new elements of poetic language. This unexpected finding is noteworthy, as is the phenomenon observed here in Wilamowitz, which I propose to call 'transferred tropical replacement': a metonymic element in the source text is literalized, but another trope (metonymic or metaphorical) is introduced which, in effect, preserves the degree of poetic elevation or heightening.[112]

Index Metonymy

With these preliminary observations in mind, we can now revisit the more striking examples discussed in Chapter 3 and assess how each category of metonymy fares in translation. I shall also continue to probe the extent to which 'domesticating' and 'foreignizing' strategies correspond, in practice, with 'familiarizing' and 'defamiliarizing' translation, respectively.

As we have seen, Wilamowitz strongly criticizes Humboldt's translation, and it is a passage containing one of the play's most striking index metonyms that he cites in order to illustrate what he considers to be Humboldt's failure to provide an adequate rendering.[113] The passage he refers to is the sacrifice of Iphigenia at Aulis, recalled by the chorus

[112] On the difference between the two, see above, p. 21.
[113] See Wilamowitz-Möllendorff 1900, 4.

at the beginning of the play (a scene already briefly discussed in the introduction):

> *κρόκου βαφὰς* δ' ἐς πέδον χέουσα
> ἔβαλλ' ἕκαστον θυτήρων ἀπ' *ὄμματος* βέλει
> φιλοίκτῳ, πρέπουσα τὼς
> ἐν γραφαῖς, προσεννέπειν
> θέλουσ', ἐπεὶ πολλάκις
> πατρὸς κατ' ἀνδρῶνας εὐτραπέζους
> ἐμέλψεν, ἁγνᾷ δ' ἀταύρωτος αὐδᾷ πατρὸς
> φίλου τριτόσπονδον εὔποτμον
> παιῶνα φίλως ἐτίμα

> As she poured *saffron dye* towards the ground
> She cast on each of her sacrificers a glance darted from her *eye*,
> A glance to stir pity, standing out as if
> In a picture wanting to address them
> By name—because often
> At the rich banquets in her father's dining chambers
> She had sung, a pure virgin with pure voice,
> Duly and lovingly performing her father's
> Paean for good fortune to accompany the third libation.[114]

Humboldt's translation of the passage, cited by Wilamowitz, reads as follows:

> *Des Safrans Tünchung* zum Boden giessend,
> und sanft des Mitleids Geschosse
> vom Blick der Opfrer jedem sendend, erschien sie bildähnlich dort,
> verlangend noch, wie sonst nach Anrede,
> weil sie oft im Männergemach des Vaters versammelt einst weilten.
> Fromm ehrte dann ihres Vaters hochbeglücktes Los
> aus kindlicher Brust Stimme sie nicht ergrimmet.

> Pouring down to the ground the *saffron dye*,
> and softly sending from her gaze missiles of pity
> to each of the sacrificers, [thus] she appeared there, like an image,
> still longing to be spoken to as usual,
> since they were often gathered together in the men's chamber of her father.
> Piously, from childish breast her voice, not angered,
> then honoured her father's happy lot.

[114] A. *Agam.* 239–47; trans. Sommerstein. For a discussion of the crucial role of this index metonym within a system of kindred imagery in the *Oresteia*, in which images of 'flowing' and 'dripping' proleptically prepare the flow of Agamemnon's blood when he is killed in the bath, see Lebeck 1971, 80–6.

Wilamowitz comments:

> When I read this, I know, first, that it is not German, and it is not verse either; secondly, I cannot understand it without the Greek, and thirdly, when I put the Greek next to it, I see that Humboldt has not understood it.[115]

Let us compare Humboldt's translation with Wilamowitz's own version of the passage:

> Vom *Busen* riss rohe *Faust* das Safrankleid.
> Auf jeden ihrer Schlächter schoss sie Gnade flehend Blick um Blick,
> schön wie ein Bild, wie ein Bild der Sprache bar,
> und hatte doch so oft in ihres Vaters
> gastfreien Hallen singen dürfen. An frohen Festen pries beim Tischgebet
> der Jungfrau reiner Mund
> des Vaters Glück
> mit kindlich liebevollem Psalm
>
> The *raw fist* tore the saffron robe from the *bosom*.
> She shot at each one of her slaughterers glance after glance, begging for mercy,
> beautiful like an image, like an image without voice,
> and yet she had so often
> been allowed to sing at her father's hospitable halls. At happy feasts,
> saying grace at the table, the virgin's pure mouth praised
> her father's happiness
> with childish, loving psalm.

The translations do indeed have a very different tone to them and the felt degree of poetic defamiliarization in Wilamowitz's version is clearly less than Humboldt's. But is this a matter of tropical language usage?

When Wilamowitz remarks that Humboldt's translation is 'not German', he is primarily pointing to Humboldt's syntax, which follows the Greek closely. The key features here are word order (in particular, nouns in the genitive preceding their governing noun in prominent positions) and the extensive use of participles. While literal reproduction of these features is grammatically possible in German without making the text incomprehensible, it deviates from ordinary usage, thus creating a broadly 'poetic' impression. This is where Wilamowitz's translation

[115] 'Wenn ich das lese, so weiss ich erstens, das ist kein Deutsch, und es sind auch keine Verse; zweitens kann ich es ohne das Griechische nicht verstehen, und drittens sehe ich, wenn ich das Griechische hinzunehme, dass Humboldt dieses nicht verstanden hat.' Wilamowitz-Möllendorff 1900, 4.

most obviously differs from Humboldt's: *his* syntax runs smoothly; most participles have been converted into predicates; there are only two preceding genitives and they are in inconspicuous positions. Yet there are also important stylistic issues on the tropical level, and here Humboldt's translation reproduces its source verbatim: all the tropical elements in the first two verses of the sequence are present here with the same status and effect. Wilamowitz's translation, on the other hand, literalizes the striking index metonym and conditional metaphor compound κρόκου βαφὰς…χέουσα ('pouring down saffron dye'). However, his rendering replaces this tropical cluster with another metonymic sequence: the singular 'fist' implies a plural ('Faust' is a number metonym), but the collocation with 'raw' also suggests a possible reading as an index metonym in which it would imply ('raw') 'physical violence'. While the tropical status of 'raw' is thus conditional on the interpretation of 'fist', the term is in itself a metaphorical cliché ('raw' does not suggest 'uncooked' but 'unrefined', 'untamed', 'unmitigated'). If 'fist' is taken as (merely) singular-for-plural, the adjective is read as transferred away from the implied subjects—it is the slaughterers, not their fists, that are brutally 'raw' in the violence they are about to do to Iphigenia. Only with 'fist' taken as an index metonym is its metonymic tenor ('physical violence') directly qualified by the adjective. Similarly, 'bosom' could be read literally, but the context implies not that Iphigenia is partially exposed but that she is forcefully disrobed, making 'bosom' a metonym by association. This, then, is another case of 'transferred tropical replacement', with 'fist' constituting here the introduction of a striking 'live' metonym. In this instance, Wilamowitz's translation does not lead to a simple 'literalization' of tropical elements but to the fashioning of a new metonymic sequence. Towards the end of the sequence, conversely, we get 'domestication' in the ordinary sense. The terms 'Tischgebet' ('grace') and 'Psalm' ('psalm'), with their obvious Christian connotations, make the text culturally familiar.

As far as the metonymic elements in the passage are concerned, one can perhaps acknowledge some reduction of poetic intensity in Wilamowitz's translation and argue that the instances of metonymic defamiliarization here are relatively less striking than those in Humboldt or in the Greek original. Metonymy by association is by definition felt as less intense than metonymy proper, and the deviation from ordinary usage involved in the 'fist' index metonym is arguably less marked than the one in the 'saffron dye' index metonym. Moreover, there is a conditional metonymic element in the Wilamowitz but a conditional metaphorical element in the Humboldt, and as we have seen, metaphorical elements tend to exceed the metonymic in poetic effect.[116] However, it is difficult to pass an absolute judgement here. For one thing, the focus of the image is significantly changed: in Aeschylus and Humboldt the focus is on the yellow of the robe which dramatically glides to the ground, in Wilamowitz it is on the hand that reaches out to violate Iphigenia (note how the singulars intensify this sharp focus). The impression, though, that Wilamowitz 'tones down' the poetic effects in this passage is reinforced in the second verse. Like Humboldt, he carries the metaphor in that verse over into the target language (ἔβαλλ'...ἀπ' ὄμματος βέλει φιλοίκτῳ—'she cast...a glance darted from her eye, a glance to stir pity'). Yet, here, too, we notice a contrast of intensity: Humboldt's translation, like the Greek original, contains both a noun and a verb in vehicle terminology ('Geschosse...sendend', 'sending...missiles'); Wilamowitz, less forcefully, only has a verb in vehicle terminology ('schoss', 'shot'). This impression is confirmed by the fact that the number metonym here ('eye' for 'eyes') is maintained in the Humboldt but literalized in the Wilamowitz ('Blick um Blick', 'glance after glance'). The typical effect of tropical clusters, in which elements combine to create an intensified impression overall,[117] is lost in Wilamowitz's rendering.

The other translations, too, show an inclination to reduce the poetic intensity of this passage. None of them reproduces the striking index metonym, the 'saffron *dye*':

a) Jenisch
der safranfarbne Mantel
auf die Erde entflos—und sie dastand
gleich dem *Meißelgebild*—ein Marmorleben!
Da da blickte sie Zärtlichkeit
in der Opferer Herz

the saffron-coloured robe
poured down onto the ground—and she stood there
like a *chisel-work*—a marble-life!
Then, there she looked tenderness
into the heart of the sacrificers

b) Droysen
Ihr Safrankleid ließ sie niederfließen,
Und sah mit wehmüth'gem Blick bang zu jedem bittend ihrer Opfrer

And she let her saffron robe flow down,
And, begging, looked anxiously with wistful gaze at each of her sacrificers

[116] See above, pp. 139–40.

[117] On tropical clusters, see above, pp. 123–34.

c) Browning
   And as to the ground her saffron-vest she shed,
   She smote the sacrificers all and each
   With arrow sweet and piteous,
   From the *eye* only sped,—
   Significant of will to use *a word*
   Just as in pictures

Droysen's translation literalizes the sequence most markedly: it retains only one metaphor and drops all other tropical elements.[118] Browning drops the striking index metonym but keeps the tropical compound ('arrow' metaphor and number metonym) and adds a further number metonym ('Significant of will to use *a word*'). The effect created by these singulars is a more poignant contrast between the visual and the verbal: 'eye' and 'pictures' enclose Iphigenia's suppressed 'word', which is now stuck between the two visual terms. Jenisch translates the beginning of the passage like Droysen, but then produces a remarkably heightened sequence that has no parallel in the source text (yet another case of 'transferred tropical replacement'). Jenisch elaborates the source text's notion that the muted and restrained Iphigenia resembles a speechless picture (πρέπουσα τὼς ἐν γραφαῖς, 'as if in a picture') by comparing her to a marble statue. The outer form of the simile is kept ('gleich', 'like') but the substitution of 'statue' for 'image' is unexpected. Iphigenia's 'statuesque' appearance is now elaborated by two compound nouns, 'Meißelgebild' ('chisel-work') and 'Marmorleben' ('marble-life'). This 'chisel-work' is metonymic and, if analysed into separate words ('work of a chisel'), can be seen to resemble the Pindaric index metonym μελισσᾶν... τρητὸν πόνον ('perforated labour of bees', for 'honeycomb') discussed earlier.[119] The 'labour (of bees)' and the 'work (of a chisel)' both metonymically translate outcome into activity. Jenisch's other compound noun, 'Marmorleben' ('marble-life'), is elliptical; it would seem to conflate 'marble' and 'still life' in such a way as to emphasize the contrast of cold and fixed marble and Iphigenia's (sadly restrained) vivacity.[120]

[118] This instance also vividly illustrates how the tropical status of a conditional metaphor (χέουσα, 'pouring') changes to full, live metaphor as soon as the metonym is disambiguated: the metonymic tenor ('saffron-coloured robe'), upon which the metaphorical reading is conditional, is here literally present, the tropical status of the metaphor therefore unequivocally given. Cf. pp. 135–40 above.

[119] See above, pp. 61–2.

[120] The German language's capacity to create compound nouns is one of its most prominent distinctive features, but the compressions it produces do not affect my argument: cf. below, pp. 225–6.

Another striking element in this sequence is the 'arrow' metaphor, which in the source text expresses Iphigenia's attempt to move her sacrificers with the look of her eyes. In Jenisch's translation the metaphor is represented by the sequence 'da blickte sie Zärtlichkeit in der Opferer Herz' ('she looked tenderness into the heart of the sacrificers'). As with the compound nouns, we have a compression here: Iphigenia looks *at* her sacrificers, she looks *for* sympathetic tenderness in their hearts, she tries to stir symphathy *in* their hearts—all these notions are implicit. But what exactly is the tropical element that creates this range of implications? And are we to classify it as metonymic? Leaving the metonymic cliché 'heart' aside, we are dealing only with tenor terminology: Iphigenia literally 'looks' at her 'sacrificers' in her longing for 'tenderness'. The defamiliarization, then, does not lie in the terms used but in the way they are syntactically coordinated. The noun 'Zärtlichkeit' ('tenderness'), which functions as accusative object, requires the predicate 'blickte' ('looked') to be a transitive verb. One might be tempted to consider this as a case of verb-based index metonymy, arguing that from the present term ('look') a further term is inferred ('create/stir [a feeling]'). On closer examination, though, this thought is misleading.[121] In index metonymy, the metonymic tenor is inferred from the metonymic vehicle, with which it stands in a relationship of lexical contiguity, because the (micro-)context makes a literal reading of the vehicle impossible. While the vehicle creates poetic effects through interaction with the context, the semantic coherence of the sequence depends on the inferred tenor. The metonymic shift between vehicle and tenor and the enhanced possibilities for interaction of present and supplemented terms with the context jointly create the various poetic effects of index metonymy. The comprehensibility of the sequence, however, rests on the inferred tenor: it is the inferred term that makes the sequence semantically coherent. This is clearly not the case here. Iphigenia literally 'looks' at the sacrificers, indeed, her 'looking' is the central issue of the passage. While the grammar is deviant, the terminology is not. Given that there is no introduction of extraneous terminology nor any underlying notion of analogy or similarity, we can rule out metaphor. Moreover, we have already come across comparable metonymic phenomena, albeit involving nouns and adjectives: the reaffiliation of adjectives (as in grammatical metonymy) and the change of a noun's number (as in basic synecdoche: singular-for-plural and vice versa) also result from the manipulation of grammatical categories. Here indeed, then, we are dealing with a

[121] Cf. the earlier argument about the structural impediment that prevents verbs from being used as index metonyms: see above, pp. 91–2.

metonymic phenomenon centred on a verb. But, just as in grammatical metonymy, the tropical status of the verb here does not stem from the verb's usage but ultimately arises from the demands of the noun with which it is syntactically coordinated. I propose, therefore, that 'she looked tenderness into the heart of the sacrificers' is best understood as a variant of grammatical index metonymy. In this sequence, the accusative object combined with the preposition 'into' demand of the predicate a grammatical function that is not compatible with the verb's ordinary usage (transitive instead of intransitive). Consequently, these elements prompt the inference of *additional*, implicit notions ('create', 'plant', 'arouse', 'insert') which are superimposed on the present, literal predicate. As with adjective-based grammatical metonymy, the tropical term maintains its denotative meaning according to ordinary usage, but the demands of the context give rise to further terms which need to be supplemented. Thus understood, one can appreciate how Jenisch's translation, too, reproduces the source text's 'arrow' metaphor—in the form of a much more subtle metonym.

As the last instance shows, even a striking index metonym may not be reproduced in translation. In order to assess what happens to this type of metonymy in translation more generally, let us examine some other examples, beginning with one from the chorus's opening recollections of the Greek army's departure to Troy:

> χρόνῳ μὲν ἀγρεῖ Πριάμου πόλιν ἅδε *κέλευθος*
> In time this expedition [lit.: *path, journey*] will capture the city of Priam[122]

a) Jenisch
Nur noch ein kleines—und Priams Stadt gehört
den Streitern dieses Heers

Just a little longer—and Priam's city belongs
to the warriors of this army

b) Humboldt
Im Lauf der Zeit einst
stürmt Priamos Veste der *Pfad* hier

In the passage of time
This *path* here will one day storm Priam's stronghold

c) Droysen
Wohl wird dereinst Priamos Feste die Beute der Heerfahrt

Surely at some point Priam's stronghold will be the booty of the expedition

[122] A. *Agam.* 126; trans. Sommerstein. On the Greek original, see above, p. 84.

d) Wilamowitz
...der Tag wird kommen, wo unsere Heerfahrt
Priamos' Veste bewältigt

The day will come, when our expedition
overcomes Priam's stronghold

e) Browning
In time, *this outset* takes the town of Priamos

Only the Browning and Humboldt verbatim translations carry the metonym over into the target language. The degree of defamiliarization is arguably highest in Humboldt's version, since the Greek term κέλευθος denotes both 'path' and 'journey', and therefore has dynamic overtones, which are closer to the tenor (the attacking army); the German 'Pfad' ('path') does not have these overtones, but they are present in Browning's 'outset'. One imagines that this might well be one of the passages Wilamowitz had in mind when writing that Humboldt's translation made no sense without the Greek original. Humboldt's index metonym is certainly abrasive, but, arguably, is neither incomprehensible nor the product of 'misunderstanding' the source text. The other German translations, however, literalize the index metonym, displaying a range of metonymic tenors (from the individual soldiers of the army to the expedition as such) and thereby illustrating the directional semantics of index metonymy. Here, then, a metonymically used Greek term is either literalized or actually made more pronounced because the broader semantic range of the Greek term cannot be replicated in the target language.

In the following example, taken from Clytemnestra's exchange with the chorus following the murder of Agamemnon, the opposite is the case. A bit of Greek idiom, best seen as deviant but approaching literary cliché status, is recognized and variously reworked by the translators:

ἔθυσεν αὑτοῦ παῖδα, φιλτάτην ἐμοὶ
ὠδῖν', ἐπῳδὸν Θρῃκίων ἀημάτων

He sacrificed his own child, the most beloved
of my pangs, as a spell to soothe the Thracian winds[123]

[123] A. *Agam.* 1417–18; trans. Sommerstein (adapted). Interestingly, in this instance it is Sommerstein who emerges as a literalizing translator: he translates φιλτάτην ἐμοὶ ὠδῖν' as 'the darling offspring of my pangs', thus preserving the index metonym ὠδῖν' ('pangs'), but supplementing it with an inferred metonymic tenor, 'offspring'—just like Jenisch in his translation. On the range of meanings of ὠδίς and the difficulties in establishing this word's ordinary usage, see the following note.

a) Jenisch

... sie,—sein *Blut*,
die Tochter meiner Schmerzen, schlachtete—
ihr Blut, wie einen höllschen Zaubertrank
den Winden strömen ließ.

He sacrificed her, his *blood*,
the daughter of my pains,
letting her blood run to the winds,
like an infernal magic potion

b) Humboldt

Hinwürgte seine Tochter, mir die theuerste
der *Weh'n*, zur Sühne wilder Stürme Thrakiens.

He strangled his daughter, to me the most precious
of *labour pangs*, to reconcile the wild storms of Thrace.

c) Droysen

Sein eigen Kind doch, meines Schooßes liebste Frucht,
Ließ schlachten, thracische Winde zu beschwigtigen.

He let his very own child, the dearest fruit of my womb,
Be slaughtered so as to pacify Thracian winds.

d) Wilamowitz

Die eigne Tochter, meines Schosses liebste Frucht,
den Nordlandstürmen zur Beschwicht'gung schlachtete.

He slaughtered his own daughter, the dearest fruit of my womb,
To the pacification of the winds of the northern lands.

e) Browning

Sacrificed his child,—dearest fruit of travail
To me,—as song-spell against Threkian blowings

The Greek ὠδίς is largely a verse word so it is difficult to establish an 'ordinary' usage for it. Its usage in extant literature predominantly denotes pain, specifically the throes of childbirth, but there are also instances in poetic texts—beyond the one under discussion here—where the word refers to the (born) child itself.[124] In all the translations,

[124] For the former, see e.g. *Il.* 11.271, Pi. *P.* 9.85, *O.* 6.43, *N.* 1.36, S. *OC* 533, E. *Phoen.* 355, and, most important, Pl. *Tht.* 149d and Arist. *HA* 560b22; for the latter, see in addition to the instance under discussion e.g. Pi. *O.* 6.31, E. *IT* 1102, and *Ion* 45, 1487. The instances in Plato's *Theaetetus* and Aristotle's *History of Animals* are the only extant prose usages of the word in classical Greek literature (apart from 'metaphorical' uses: see LSJ s.v. II). The word is used of 'pangs of labour' in Plato (καὶ μὴν καὶ διδοῦσαί γε αἱ μαῖαι φαρμάκια καὶ

however, the term triggers tropically highly charged renditions. Jenisch offers us a 'literalizing supplementation': we get both the potential metonymic vehicle ('meine Schmerzen', 'my pains') and the metonymic tenor ('Tochter', 'daughter'). In addition, he introduces a metonymic cliché by referring to Agamemnon's daughter as 'sein Blut' ('his blood'). Mentioning 'blood' twice within three lines (where the Greek has none), once in (clichéd) tropical usage and once in ordinary usage, Jenisch invests the passage with an ominous quality: by sacrificing his daughter, Agamemnon not only (literally) sheds 'her blood' but also (metonymically) 'his blood'. This metonym illustrates *in nuce* how Agamemnon's own fatal bloodshed takes effect, through his own doing. In shedding his daughter's blood, he sheds his own: what the metonym suggests here will all too soon become literal reality as the play moves towards its climax, the stabbing of Agamemnon. Although unmotivated by the phrasing of the Greek lines under translation here, this effect of suggestive, imagery-based associations within the play's overall action in Jenisch's translation is remarkably similar to what Aeschylus achieves in the original via the imagery of flowing and dripping liquids, which likewise connect Agamemnon's crime and punishment.[125]

Humboldt's translation, by contrast, singles out one core component from the semantic range encompassed by the Greek term ὠδίς and thereby creates a striking index metonym, moderated only by the fact that the metonymic tenor ('Tochter', 'daughter') is co-present already. The metonym serves as a subordinated epithet that sheds new light on what is at issue rather than introducing, by implication, what is at issue. Against the backdrop of this example, it is possible to formulate an important principle for metonymy in translation: index metonymy can arise in the target language when polysemy in the source language makes for linguistic untranslatability.[126] If there is no one word in the target language which encompasses the semantic range of the term in the source language, any attempt at literal translation is bound to be selective. From the perspective of the target language, the semantic range covered by the term in the source language becomes a semantic field,

ἐπᾴδουσαι δύνανται ἐγείρειν τε τὰς ὠδῖνας καὶ μαλθακωτέρας ἂν βούλωνται ποιεῖν—'And furthermore, the midwives, by means of drugs and incantations, are able to arouse the pangs of labour and, if they wish, to make them milder'; trans. Fowler) and 'birth-giving' in Aristotle (δύνανται δ' αἱ περιστεραὶ καὶ ἤδη τοῦ ᾠοῦ ἐν ὠδῖνι ὄντος κατέχειν—'Pigeons are able to hold the egg back even when they are just on the point of laying it'; trans. Peck). In the light of this (admittedly) limited evidence, one should consider the Aeschylean usage as deviant from 'ordinary' usage, but, given the spread of comparable instances of poetic usage, as approximating the status of a literary cliché.

[125] See above, p. 214, n. 114.

[126] On this type of untranslatability according to Catford, see above, pp. 171–2.

and the translator is forced to choose one term from this field. In Humboldt's case, the term chosen is incompatible with the microcontext, which prompts a reading of the term as a striking index metonym in the target language.[127] Intriguingly, Droysen and Wilamowitz take an entirely different approach. Both give a clichéd metaphorical version of this sequence ('dearest fruit of my womb'), as does Browning (albeit in a slightly less clichéd variation). In the case of Droysen and Wilamowitz, this suits an understanding of translation as concerned less with formal equivalence than with dynamic, functional equivalence. Given the clichéd nature of the Greek term, its representation in the target language in the form of a metaphorical cliché is, in effect, closer to the source text than Humboldt's much more startling and heightened version.

The impact of polysemy/oligosemy on translatability also arises in the following example, discussed earlier as a case of conditional metonymy. Having received the news of the Greek victory over Troy, Clytemnestra imagines the fate that has now fallen upon its inhabitants:

> ...οὐκέτ' *ἐξ ἐλευθέρου*
> *δέρης* ἀποιμώζουσι φιλτάτων μόρον
>
> ...and *from throats* [or: *necks*] *that are no longer free*
> They cry out their laments for the death of their dearest.[128]

a) Jenisch

> ...Sie weinen, ach nicht mehr mit freier *Brust*!
> der Lieben Tod.
>
> ...they cry, alas, no longer with a free *breast*!
> over the death of their loved ones.

b) Humboldt

> ...weinen, schluchzend laut,
> aus nicht, wie sonst, mehr *freier Brust*, der Liebsten Tod
>
> ...they cry, sobbing loudly,
> not as before from a *free breast*, over their loved ones' death

[127] This analysis supports (in reverse, as it were) the understanding of metonymy as a shift in a semantic field. A further contributing factor in this particular case lies in the fact that the status of terms as literary clichés differs from one language, literary tradition, and period to another, and any difference in the spread of comparable poetic usages of a term in source and target language directly impacts on the perceived intensity of such usages in each language.

[128] A. *Agam.* 328–9; trans. Sommerstein.

c) Droysen
...sie beklagen nimmer mehr
Mit *freier Kehle* dieß Geschick der Theuersten

...they no longer mourn
with a *free throat* this fate of their dearest

d) Wilamowitz
...und alle jammern um des Teuersten Verlust,
und jeder *Mund*, der jammert, ist ein *Sklavenmund*.

...and all are mourning the loss of their dearest,
and every *mouth* that mourns is a *slave-mouth*.

e) Browning
from a *throat that's free no longer*,
shriekingly wail the death-doom of their dearest

As already noted, the Greek term δέρης is both 'neck' and 'throat', and the sequence consequently allows both for a literal reading that imagines the Trojan captives literally yoked together by their necks when enslaved and for a grammatical-metonymic reading in which the Trojans, and not just the 'throats' that emit their laments, are no longer free.[129] Again we observe how, for lack of a term with a comparable semantic range in the target language, the translators are forced to reduce the ambiguity of a sequence. The disambiguation observable here, however, is not straightforward literalization but rather an adjustment from conditional tropicality to tropicality proper or to tropical cliché. Thus, Droysen and Browning opt for a translation that gives a grammatical amplification metonym: the adjective 'no longer free' is transferred from the implied subjects to their throats, thereby adding emphasis to their cries, which now appear to lament the death of their loved ones and their own loss of freedom simultaneously. Jenisch and Humboldt, on the other hand, opt for 'transferred tropical replacement': the conditional metonym of the source text is replaced with a metonymic cliché which emphasizes not a concrete, physical loss of freedom to move (as the neck terminology does) but the broken spirit of the captives. Wilamowitz, finally, gives us an example of 'literalizing supplementation': his translation includes both the (potentially) metonymic vehicle term followed by an explication in the shape of tenor terminology: 'Mund' ('mouth'), as the subject governing 'der jammert' ('that mourns'), is an index metonym which implies the

[129] See above, pp. 138–9.

person through a part of the mourner's body, but the compound 'Sklavenmund' ('slave-mouth') then makes explicit what is at issue.

It is interesting to reflect further on Wilamowitz's compound noun. As a compound, it is a compressed version of a noun with genitive attribute: 'the mouth of a slave'. If we replaced the compound noun with this extended version, we would have a case of amplification metonymy, because the tenor would be present in the genitive case ('[of a] slave'); after all, what is at issue in this latter part of the sequence is that all mourners are now slaves. Yet the density of a compound seems to impinge with a greater poetic effect, because the 'Mund' ('mouth') of 'Sklavenmund' ('slave-mouth') belongs to 'body part' terminology, and as such prolongs the incompatibility of the terminology with the verb. The presence of 'slave' as a separate noun in the genitive would (however minutely) have weakened the abrasiveness. This instance, then, allows us to make two observations: first, that compound nouns can be compressed versions of amplification metonyms, since they, too, can include a metonymic tenor embedded in a context in which the emphasis is shifted from one term to another within one semantic field; and second, that the compression into a compound noun itself can add to the impression of defamiliarization, partly because of the novelty of the compound (if it is a neologism), partly because of the immediacy of the specifying shift and the additional possibility of remaining more closely within the confines of context-incompatible vehicle terminology.

Contrast what happens with translations of elevated poetic idiom in the following sequence:

οὐδ' ἐπόντισε σκάφος
nor does he submerge undersea the *hull*[130]

a) Jenisch
das Schiff selbst kämpft oft aus den Fluthen empor.
the ship itself fights its way out of the floods.

b) Humboldt
noch [sinkt] das Schiff zum Meeresgrund
nor does the ship sink to the floor of the sea

c) Droysen
Noch verschlingt die See den *Kiel*
Nor does the sea swallow the *keel*

[130] A. *Agam.* 1013.

d) Wilamowitz
so mag die Ladung überfrachtet nicht versinken
so that the cargo, overloaded, might not sink

e) Browning
Nor has fear overwhelmed the *hull.*

The term σκάφος denotes the hull but is frequently used in poetry (and beyond) to mean the entire ship.[131] Hence, we are dealing with a metonymic cliché in the source text which, in this sequence, is best classified as a (clichéd) metonym by association: a literal reading is technically possible but a metonymic inference is prompted by the context. Contrary to what one might expect, Jenisch and Humboldt literalize the term whereas Droysen's 'domesticating' translation as well as Browning's 'foreignizing' version give a verbatim rendering from which the reader infers that it is the entire ship and not just the hull that does not sink.[132] Wilamowitz conflates the metonymic term of the source text with a literal term from the preceding verse and thus evades any tropical ambiguity.

Interestingly, the same term, σκάφος, appears in another passage of the same play, but in non-tropical collocation:

ἡμᾶς γε μὲν δὴ ναῦν τ᾽ ἀκήρατον σκάφος
ἤτοι τις ἐξέκλεψεν ἢ ᾽ξῃτήσατο
θεός τις

We ourselves, on the other hand, and our ship, its hull unscathed,
were either smuggled out or begged off
by some god[133]

As one would expect, all the translations give a literal rendering of the passage—except Humboldt's, which, without anything in the source text to prompt it, introduces an amplification metonym:

Uns aber sammt *des Schiffes unversehrtem Bau*
entführte damals, oder rettet' unvermerkt
ein Gott

[131] For the more specific denotation of 'hull', see e.g. Th. 1.50, A. *Pers.* 419, and Hdt. 7.182 (the latter already bordering on metonymy by association, implying the entire ship); examples of the word referring to a ship as a whole include A. *Supp.* 440, Ar. *Ach.* 541, and D. 9.69.

[132] This is, in fact, a borderline case between index metonymy and metonymy by association: in both cases 'hull' can be taken literally without violating rules of collocation, yet the sequence effectively requires that 'ship' is inferred as the metonymic tenor—not as an additional association but as what is at issue here.

[133] A. *Agam.* 661–2; trans. Sommerstein.

But then a god
abducted us, or saved us imperceptibly
together with *the ship's undamaged construction*

Compare the responses to the index metonym in the following example, once more taken from the chorus's recollection of events preceding the play:

τραπέζας
ἀτίμωσιν ὑστέρῳ χρόνῳ

exacting delayed requital for the dishonouring
of the *host's table*[134]

a) Jenisch
Straften bald die Entweihung ihres *Mahles*,
deines heiligen Gastrechts

Soon punished the desecration of their *meal*,
of your holy laws of hospitality

b) Humboldt
...rächte schwer
noch nachher das Gastgebot

...still later took harsh revenge
for [the breach of] the laws of hospitality

c) Droysen
...für des *Gasttisches* arge Schändung einst,...

...for the former desecration of the guest-*table*...

d) Wilamowitz
Sühne für des *Herdes* Schändung, Sühne für den Bruch des Gastrechts

atonement for the desecration of the *hearth*, atonement for the breach of the laws of hospitality

e) Browning
In after-time, for the *tables'* abuse

At issue in this passage is Paris' breach of the laws of hospitality by abducting Menelaus' wife Helen while a guest in his house. The Greek term τράπεζα denotes 'table', especially 'dining table', and while there are further instances in which the term is used to connote hospitable

[134] A. *Agam.* 702–3; trans. Sommerstein.

generosity,[135] it cannot literally denote the *laws* of hospitality as such. Humboldt's 'foreignizing' translation literalizes the index metonym whereas Browning's 'foreignizing', as well as Droysen's 'domesticating', preserves the metonym verbatim. Jenisch once again opts for 'literalizing supplementation', offering both the metonymic vehicle and the metonymic tenor, albeit with a slight modification: his version has 'meal' instead of 'table' as an index metonym to imply 'laws of hospitality'. The same can be observed in the Wilamowitz: his version doubles the sequence and gives a literalized version preceded by a metonymic version in which, however, the index metonym has been replaced by a metonymic cliché ('hearth' implying 'household'). The insertion of a metonymic cliché reflects but 'tones down' the intensified idiom of the source text by gesturing towards poetic elevation. We observe, once again, that there is no inevitable correspondence between 'domesticating' and literalizing translations, or 'foreignizing' and verbatim translations. This becomes yet more obvious in the following case, another index metonym, from the herald's speech upon his return to his homeland:

> ἥρως τε τοὺς πέμψαντας, εὐμενεῖς πάλιν
> στρατὸν δέχεσθαι τὸν λελειμμένον *δορός*
>
> and the heroes who sent us forth, praying that they may
> receive back with favour the army, or what the war [lit.: *the spear*]
> has spared of it[136]

[135] Such instances are to be found e.g. at *Od.* 14.158, Xen. *Anab.* 7.2.33, and Hdt. 5.20. An example of the kind of collocation that terminologically links 'table' and 'hospitality' in Aeschylus' *Agamemnon* itself is ᾔσχυνε *ξενίαν* | *τράπεζαν* κλοπαῖσι γυναικός ('and shamed *the table of hospitality* by stealing away a wife', A. *Agam.* 401–2; trans. Sommerstein). Here the adjective expresses explicitly what the noun implies: ξενία—hospitality and the code of conduct attached to it. The translations of this sequence show a similar spread to the one above: Wilamowitz literalizes the sequence ('entweihte den Frieden des Gastrechts, entführte die Herrin des Hauses', 'desecrated the peace of the laws of hospitality, abducted the lady of the house'); Droysen's and Browning's versions are verbatim ('frech den *gastlichen Tisch* entweiht, der die Gattin entführt hat', 'impertinently he desecrated the *hospitable table*, he who abducted the wife' and (Browning) 'shamed the *guestboard* by robbery of the spouse'); Humboldt combines literalizing explication with retention of the metonymically used term, i.e. 'literalizing supplementation' ('kühn einst schmähte des Gastgebots Tisch durch Weibes Entführung', 'daringly once spurned the *table* of the law of hospitality by kidnapping the wife'); and Jenisch's translation opts for 'transferred tropical replacement', as it literalizes the metonymic term of the source text but introduces metonymic association later in the text ('Er kam—ein Fremdling—in der Atriden Haus, und scheute nicht der Gastfreundschaft heilges Recht; er schändete des Freundes *Bette*: raubte sein Weib ihm vom warmen *Busen*', 'He came—a stranger—into the Atreidai's house, and he was not respectful of the sacred laws of hospitality; he desecrated the friend's *bed*: stole his wife from his warm *bosom*').

[136] A. *Agam.* 517; trans. Sommerstein.

a) Jenisch

Ihr, die ihr Helden sandtet, führet auch
den Rest der *Schlacht*, das Heer, ins Land zurück

You, who sent out heroes, also lead
the rest of the *battle*, the army, back into the land

b) Humboldt

jetzt aufzunehmen dieses *speerverschonte* Heer

now to receive this army, spared by *the spear*

c) Droysen

das Heer empfangen, das *der Lanzen Wuth* verschont

to receive the army, which *the wrath of spears* has spared

d) Wilamowitz

nehmt uns gnädig auf,
so viel dem *Schwert* entronnen heut ihr wiederseht.

graciously receive us,
as many of us as you see again today, having escaped *the sword*

e) Browning

friendly, once more
the army to receive, the *war-spear's leavings*!

For once, all translations contain a metonymic element to represent the index metonym of the source text, albeit in a variety of conformations and with different effects. Jenisch alone comes close to literalizing the sequence. There is only a slight metonymic feel to 'der Rest der Schlacht' ('the rest of the battle'), with 'battle' implying 'the army fighting in the battle'. However, the fact that 'army' is mentioned in a clarifying parenthesis immediately afterwards greatly reduces any feeling of defamiliarization. Furthermore, 'the rest of the battle' comes with an inherent ambiguity: it feels tropical if 'rest' is understood in a partitive sense ('a part of the battle is left' implying 'a part of the [army fighting in the] battle is left'), but it seems literal if understood in a more temporal sense ('that what remains after the battle'). The elliptical expression, at all events, falls short of constituting an index metonym proper. Humboldt, by contrast, coins a compound adjective, 'speerverschont' ('spared-by-the-spear'), to represent the source text's index metonym. There is a slight change in the semantics of this sequence, since the Greek original emphasizes that only a part of the army returns, whereas Humboldt's version merely indicates that the present army has survived the battle. On the level of poetic defamiliarization, however, Humboldt's neologism is a compressed version of 'spared by the spear' (implying the onslaught of the enemy army, regardless of any specific weapon), which closely resembles the metonymic sequence in the source text, with the newly created compound intensifying the effect. Wilamowitz moves in the opposite direction by replacing 'spear' with 'sword', which is a widely used metonymic cliché in the German literary tradition and therefore comes with a reduced poetic impact. Contrary to what one might expect from his 'domesticating' agenda, Droysen heightens the poetic impact of the sequence. In describing the army as one 'which the wrath of spears has spared', his translation introduces a stark clash of incompatible terms, directly juxtaposing weapon terminology with emotion terminology in a way that evokes the aggressive onslaught of the enemy more forcefully than the other translations and, indeed, than the original. Finally, Browning's translation also features a newly created compound noun but the effect is different. Browning comes closest to a verbatim translation, but in his apposition ('the army... the war-spear's leavings') he adds the specifying prefix 'war-' to 'spear' and thereby introduces a potential metonymic tenor into the sequence; the effect is reduced correspondingly.

Metonymic Association

In the examples discussed so far, we have seen metonymic elements produce responses ranging from verbatim translation to literalizing disambiguation and transposition into other forms of defamiliarized language; and this range has been prompted not only by striking, abrasive metonyms, but also by 'dead' metonyms, literary clichés, and at times even literal terms whose semantic range has no parallel in the target language. With metonymic association, where the surplus in meaning does not stem from any deviant usage, the range of outcomes is—surprisingly?—similar. Consider, to begin with, an example from Clytemnestra's exchange with the chorus following the murder of Agamemnon already discussed earlier:

> οὔ μοι φόβου μέλαθρον ἔλπις ἐμπατεῖ,
> *ἕως ἂν αἴθῃ πῦρ ἐφ᾽ ἑστίας ἐμῆς*
> *Αἴγισθος*, ὡς τὸ πρόσθεν εὖ φρονῶν ἐμοι
>
> no fearful apprehension stalks my house,
> *so long as the fire upon my hearth is kindled by*
> *Aegisthus* and he remains loyal to me as hitherto[137]

[137] A. *Agam.* 1434–6; trans. Sommerstein.

a) Jenisch
so lang
Aegisthus Feu'r auf meinem Heerde brennt,
wohlwollend, wie er's war

For as long as
Aegisthus' fire burns on my hearth,
Benevolent, as he used to be

b) Humboldt
So lange meines Heerdes Flamme zündet an
Aigisthos

As long as Aegisthus kindles the flame at my hearth

c) Droysen
so lang auf meinem Heerd das Feuer noch
Aigisthos anschürt, wie bisher mir treugesinnt

as long as Aegisthus kindles the flame at my heath,
As loyally minded as ever

d) Wilamowitz
so lange wohlgesinnet, wie er bisher war,
Aigisthos über meines Herdes Flamme wacht.

as long as, loyally minded as he has been so far,
Aegisthus stands guard over my hearth's flames

e) Browning
So long as on my hearth there burns a fire,
Aigisthos as before well-caring for me

As I have argued, what is at issue here is not whether Aegisthus literally lights a fire (at the 'hearth'), but rather that he is and remains present in Clytemnestra's house and, moreover, that he does so as (stand-in) head of the household.[138] The metonymic cliché 'hearth' (implying 'household') is part of the traditional poetic idiom of Greek, German, and English, and has the same evocative power in each of these languages: hence the similarity of metonymic association in each translation. The evocation of such associations is then reinforced by the explicit comment on Aegisthus' continued loyalty. The metonymic association in the source is thus a feature common to all the translations of this passage.[139]

[138] See above, p. 142.

[139] The only significant variant belongs to Browning, whose version—inadvertently?—creates a conditional metaphor: 'Aigisthos' either introduces the English equivalent of a genitive absolute construction (i.e. 'with Aigisthos... well-caring') or else is in apposition to 'fire'.

However, such equivalence is not invariable, as this example from Cassandra's words of warning to the chorus shows:

ἐν μέρει δ' ἀπέπτυσαν
εὐνὰς ἀδελφοῦ τῷ πατοῦντι δυσμενεῖς

and one after another they [the Erinyes] show their abhorrence of [also: spit out at]
the brother's *bed* that worked harm to him who defiled it.[140]

a) Jenisch
Auch ihnen ist das *Bruderbett* verhaßt,
in das ein Bruder stieg

And they hate the brother's bed [lit.: the *brother-bed*]
to which a brother went

b) Humboldt
fluchen abscheuvoll zugleich
des Bruders *Ehbett*...

at the same time they curse full of abhorrence
the brother's *marriage bed*

c) Droysen
verfluchen dann
Des Bruders *Ehbett*

then they curse
the brother's *marriage bed*

d) Wilamowitz
sein Fluch vergisst
auch dessen nicht, der seines Bruders Ehe brach

neither does his curse forget
the one who broke his brother's marriage

e) Browning
in turn spit forth at
the brother's *bed*, to him who spurned it hostile.

Clytemnestra is elaborating on the long-running curse of familial violence and revenge that plagues her house, and here she refers to Thyestes' corruption of Aerope, the wife of his brother Atreus. As discussed earlier, the term εὐνή is used widely throughout Greek texts to refer to acts of lovemaking and constitutes a literary cliché.[141] These overtones are

[140] A. *Agam.* 1192–3; trans. Sommerstein.

[141] See above, p. 56, n. 7.

undoubtedly present here: what the Erinyes spurn is not the item of furniture but the forbidden acts that occurred in it. The Greek sequence gains a certain elegance from the way that the ambiguity of εὐνή as 'bed' on the one hand, and 'lovemaking' on the other, is matched by the semantic range of ἀπέπτυσαν as 'spit (on)' and 'spurn'. The personified goddesses of revenge and fury spit on the beds and spurn the illicit lovemaking—both concrete and abstract are harmoniously co-present.[142] This elegance disappears in translation, both because the polysemy of ἀπέπτυσαν cannot be reproduced in either of the target languages and because 'Bett' and 'bed' do not have quite the same status as metonymic clichés for 'acts of lovemaking' in the poetic idiom of the target languages. In Jenisch's translation, the reader is nevertheless likely to assume that the reason for the Erinyes' hatred of the bed cannot simply be that a brother lay in it. However, the immediacy of the metonymic association is not as straightforward here as in the Humboldt or the Droysen. Where Jenisch offers a disconcerting neologism, in the shape of the compound noun 'Bruderbett' ('brother-bed'), these give 'Ehebett' ('marriage bed'). This unremarkable ordinary-language compound noun points more directly to what is at issue in this sequence: matrimony, and its violation. Once again, tenor terminology that explicates what is at issue is introduced through a compound noun, albeit somewhat more concealed in this instance. Wilamowitz, finally, makes this entirely explicit. He literalizes the sequence and completely removes the source text's 'bed' terminology, and with it any possibility or need for metonymic associations. The fact that literalization occurs here is remarkable, given that there is no actual deviance from ordinary language in the source text. The effect of metonymic association elicited by the source text is clearly strong enough to prompt a mode of translation appropriate for the treatment of tropes in the strict sense and, by extension, of literary clichés.

The following example, a passage from Clytemnestra's address to Cassandra, illustrates this yet more forcibly:

> καὶ παῖδα γάρ τοί φασιν Ἀλκμήνης ποτὲ
> πραθέντα *τλῆναι δουλίας μάζης τυχεῖν*
>
> they say, you know, that even the son of Alcmene was once
> sold and *brought himself to touch the coarse food of the slave.*[143]

[142] This is comparable to the effect achieved in a similar configuration (involving an index metonym) in one of Pindar's *Odes*, discussed earlier, in which Aphrodite 'sheds loving reverence' on the lover's 'bed'; see above, pp. 60–1.

[143] A. *Agam.* 1041–2; trans. Sommerstein.

a) Jenisch
Zwar bist Alkmenens Tochter du: (so sagen sie)
doch jetzt—hieher verkauft: und mit Gewalt dem Joche unterworfen

Although you are Alcmene's daughter (or so they say)
you are now sold to this place: and with force subjected to the yoke

b) Humboldt
Alkmenens Sprössling, sagt man, auch erduldete
verkauft, und schmeckte wider Willen einst das Joch

Alkmene's son too, they say, suffered,
when sold, and once against his will tasted the yoke

c) Droysen
Denn auch Alkmene's Sohn, so sagt man, trug es einst
verkauft zu leben und gezwungen Knecht zu sein

For Alcmene's son too, so they say, once endured
living as a sold man and being forced to be a servant

d) Wilamowitz
Selbst Herakles, erzählt man, hat von Sklaven*brot*,
als er verkauft war, sich zu nähren nicht verschmäht

Even Heracles, so they say, did not refuse to nourish himself
with slaves' *bread* when he was sold

e) Browning
And truly they do say Alkmene's child once
bore being sold, slaves' *barley bread* his living.

In the Greek original, the sequence τλῆναι δουλίας μάζης τυχεῖν ('brought himself to touch the coarse food of the slave') prompts metonymic association. It is clear from the context that what is at issue here is not that Heracles was prepared to master an unwelcome diet but that he accepted the lot of slavery when it fell upon him. The association is prompted and framed by the terms πραθέντα ('sold') and δουλίας ('belonging to a slave'), describing in explicit terms Heracles' being a slave, which is consequently taken to be the implicit, general point of the sequence all together. Stanford comments on this idiom:

Another such [cliché] is 'to eat the bread of slavery' for simply 'to be a slave.' It occurs in Archilochus 79,6, Hipponax 39,6, and Aeschylus *A.* 1041 (as well as in Sophocles *Ajax* 499, Euripides *Alcestis* 2). Another is 'to trample oaths under foot' in place of 'to break an oath' (*Iliad*, IV, 157, Archilochus, 79, 13, Theognis 847, Aeschylus *E.* 110). These, and others like them, may sound fresh and vivid to our ears. But so it is with *clichés* in general—some hundred years from now such phrases as 'the long arm of the law' or 'in the nick of time' may charm posterity, though they are nerveless to us.[144]

All the more interesting is what actually happens to the 'fresh and vivid'-sounding cliché in the translations. Only Wilamowitz's 'domesticating' translation and Browning's 'foreignizing' translation give verbatim renderings of the passage. Both preserve the contextual elements that inspire metonymic association in the source text. Jenisch and Humboldt, on the other hand, alter the sequence along the lines of 'transferred tropical replacement': metonymic association is replaced with metaphorical cliché.[145] The 'yoke' as a metaphor for 'slavery' is a well-established literary cliché in German poetic idiom and both translators offer it here as a functional equivalent to the metonymic cliché of the source. Humboldt's translation has a slightly stronger tropical feel to it because it combines two metaphorical clichés whose terminologies are unaligned: 'taste' implying 'experience' and the 'yoke' implying 'slavery'. Coming from the Greek original, it is easy to see how the first metaphorical cliché ('taste') might be inspired by the food terminology of δουλίας μάζης ('slave's bread'); the resulting juxtaposition of the two clichés, however, creates a certain abrasiveness that is not present in the source. Droysen, finally, gives a literalized translation of the sequence, making explicit what a reader will read in (by association) to the other translations and to the original: Heracles 'endured living as a sold man and being forced to be a servant'.

As the different translations of this sequence show, metonymic association in the source text elicits the same range of responses as index metonymy: verbatim translation, transferred tropical replacement, and literalization. Here is confirmation that this seemingly insignificant form of metonymy does impact on readers (represented here by our translators). And the correspondence of responses to those elicited by index metonymy also tends to validate the categorization of this phenomenon as a variant of metonymy, albeit one that is not tropical in the strict sense.

Grammatical Metonymy

A picture of metonymy in translation is emerging. Metonymic passages are widely translatable, but there are limited instances of cultural

[144] Stanford 1942, 47; italics in the original.

[145] Jenisch, by way of an incidental variant, appears also to have misunderstood the Greek παῖδα, 'son', to mean 'daughter' (along with the syntax of the sentence as a whole).

untranslatability (with culturally specific 'dead' metonyms and metonymic clichés) and linguistic untranslatability (with polysemy/oligosemy). One type of metonymy, however, would seem to be particularly at risk in translation: grammatical metonymy. After all, as Apollonius Dyscolus (in effect) recognized, the transfer of an adjective from its governing noun to another noun depends to a degree on the possibilities of interchange between inflectional endings.[146] The question therefore arises: what happens to grammatical metonyms when they are translated from a highly inflected language like ancient Greek into a moderately inflected language like German or a weakly inflected language like English?

We begin with three straightforward cases of grammatical metonymy. Consider first this example from Agamemnon's return speech:

> τούτων θεοῖσι χρὴ *πολύμνηστον* χάριν
> τίνειν
>
> For this we must be deeply mindful of the gods' favour and pay them
> Thanks [lit.: pay them *much-remembering* thanks][147]

a) Jenisch
Deswegen ziemt's den Göttern Preisgesäng'
hinaufzutönen

Therefore it is proper to let the gods' praises
resound up high

b) Humboldt
Dafür gebührt's, den Göttern Dank, lautschallenden,
zu weihen

Therefore it is becoming to dedicate to the gods
loud-resounding praise

c) Droysen
Dafür gebührt den Göttern *vielgedenker* Dank
Therefore the gods deserve *much-remembering* thanks

[146] On grammatical metonymy and ἐναλλαγὴ πτώσεως ('enallage of the case'), see above, p. 100. Pertinently enough, Puttenham argued that speakers of English, 'having no such variety of accidents [i.e. inflections], have little or no use of this figure' (Puttenham 1589, 171). This view is still held by some contemporary rhetoricians, such as Fowler, who likewise posits that '[s]ome figures of classical rhetoric, indeed, could not be used at all in non-inflected languages—like *enallage*, variation of endings' (Fowler 1990, 105; italics in the original).

[147] A. *Agam.* 821; trans. Sommerstein.

d) Wilamowitz
   Des Dankes für der Götter Beistand dürfen wir niemals vergessen

   We must never forget to thank the gods for their aid

e) Browning
   Of these things, to the gods grace *many-mindful* 'tis right I render...

In the source text's grammatical amplification metonym, the adjective is transferred from implicit subject to accusative object, for it is not the expression of gratitude itself that is 'mindful' and 'much-remembering' but the subject that expresses this gratitude. Jenisch's and Humboldt's 'foreignizing' translations entirely drop the adjective and literalize the sequence.[148] Wilamowitz's 'domesticating' translation, too, literalizes the term but does so by turning the adjectival trope into a literal verb—a move that effectively reunites the transferred adjective with the implied subject, albeit with a slight adjustment of the message: the source text's emphasis is on the gods' aid in the past which is not to be forgotten, whereas in the Wilamowitz it is the duty to give thanks that is not to be forgotten. Both the 'domesticating' by Droysen and the 'foreignizing' by Browning produce verbatim translations, though Browning changes the word order and thereby increases the feeling of defamiliarization further.

Compare this outcome with that in the following instance from the chorus's shocked response to the murder of Agamemnon:

βιάζεται δ᾽ *ὁμοσπόροις*
ἐπιρροαῖσιν αἱμάτων
μέλας Ἄρης

black Ares forces his way,
with... streams of kindred blood
[lit.: with *kindred* streams of blood][149]

a) Jenisch
   Ströme des Blutes, euch fürcht ich, von eurem Rauschen versinket einst dieses Haus: denn es träuft nicht mehr in Tropfen das Blut

   Streams of blood, I fear you, in your gushing this house will sink one day: for the blood no longer drizzles in drops

[148] In both cases, one suspects a misunderstanding of the Greek term πολύμνηστον as an adjectival compound based on πολύ ('many') and ὕμνος ('song').

[149] A. *Agam.* 1509–11; trans. Sommerstein.

b) Humboldt
   Gewaltsam fortgetrieben stets
   von Strömen gleich entstammten Bluts

   Always driven away violently
   By streams of kindred blood

c) Droysen
   In Strömen gleich entsprungnen Bluts
   Drängt fort und fort der öde Kampf

   In streams of kindred blood
   the bleak fighting pushes further and further

d) Wilamowitz
   In Strömen des Verwandtenblutes stürmt einher
   der schwarze Mord

   In streams of kindred blood storms in
   black murder

e) Browning
   He is forced on and on
   By the kin-born flowing of blood,
   Black Ares

In the Greek, the adjective ὁμοσπόροις ('kindred') has been transferred from αἱμάτων ('blood') to ἐπιρροαῖσιν ('streams'), by grammatical amplification metonymy. All the German translators literalize this instance, Humboldt, Droysen, and Wilamowitz by reaffiliating the adjective, Jenisch by turning it into a noun ('dieses Haus', 'this house', implying 'the kin of this family') and by paraphrasing the sequence freely. 'Foreignizing' and 'domesticating' translators alike are happy to eliminate the metonym. Browning's English, by contrast, approximates a verbatim translation: the semantic affinity of 'kin-born' and 'blood' is felt, but the adjective goes with 'flowing' unmistakably. Browning's rendering of ὁμοσπόροις as 'kin-born' rather than as 'kindred', however, makes the term all but compatible with its governing noun, expressing the causal background of the bloodshed: the 'flowing of blood' is 'born' of [strife and violence among] 'kin'. The example is complicated further, but trivially, by the fact that 'born' here is a metaphorical cliché. While there is an element of discourse compression here, the juxtaposition of adjective and noun perhaps falls short of the abrasiveness and incompatibility needed to constitute grammatical amplification metonymy as in the source text.

In the next example from Agamemnon's dialogue with Clytemnestra, already discussed,[150] several of the translators do carry the grammatical metonym into the target language:

> ... μηδὲ βαρβάρου φωτὸς δίκην
> *χαμαιπετὲς* βόαμα προσχάνηις ἐμοί
>
> do not fall to the ground before me and utter open-mouthed cries
> in the manner of a barbarian
> [lit.: do not, in the manner of a barbarian, open your mouth to me with
> A cry *that falls to the ground*][151]

a) Jenisch
...grüß mich auch nicht,
auf Barbaren Art, zur Erde hingestreckt

...nor greet me,
in barbarian manner, stretched out on the ground

b) Humboldt
...noch mir senden, gleich ausländischem
Weichlinge, *staubgesunknen* Ehrfurchtsruf empor

...nor send up to me, like a foreign
weakling, cries of reverence *that have sunk into the dust*
[lit.: *sunk-into-dust* reverence-cries]

c) Droysen
Auch wolle sonst nicht mit mir zärteln, nach der Art
der Weiber, noch am Boden liegend tief herauf
so wie's Barbaren thun, mir knechten *deinen Gruß*

And do not attempt to indulge me otherwise, in the manner
of women, nor subjugate *your greetings* to me, like barbarians do,
lying low on the ground

d) Wilamowitz
Ich bin kein Barbar,
vor dem ein *plumpes Schmeicheln* in den Staub sich wirft.

I am not a barbarian
in front of whom a *clumsy flattering* throws itself into the dust

e) Browning
...nor—as in mode of barbarous man is—
To me gape forth a *groundward-falling* clamour!

[150] See above, p. 105.

[151] A. *Agam.* 919–20; trans. Sommerstein.

Jenisch literalizes the sequence through paraphrase. Humboldt and Browning give verbatim translations, incidentally indicating that striking grammatical amplification metonymy is possible in both languages, regardless of the degree to which they are inflected. More remarkable is what happens in the two programmatically 'domesticating' translations. Wilamowitz replaces the grammatical amplification metonym of the source text with a striking index metonym: 'clumsy flattering' implies the person who does the flattering. The direct juxtaposition of abstract elements and the physical description of the act itself is 'poetic' in spirit. Droysen likewise transforms the grammatical metonym into a tropical cluster consisting of conditional metaphor and conditional metonym. The sequence is perfectly literal until the clause finishes with the words 'mir knechten deinen Gruß' ('subjugate your greetings to me'). The expression is startling and violates collocation rules in ordinary usage. Two different readings are possible. The 'greeting' could be taken as tenor terminology, expressing what is at issue here; in that case the verb 'knechten' ('subjugate', 'treat like a slave') must be understand tropically. It would then imply by analogy that the proper form of greeting among freeborn persons is violated in the same way that their dignity would be violated if they were treated as slaves. On this reading, the verb is a metaphor. Alternatively, the verb can be taken as tenor terminology, with 'you' literally treated as a slave. In this case, the accusative object will be understood as an index metonym. What is subjugated and treated like a slave is not 'deinen Gruß' ('your greetings') but the metonymic tenor implied by the possessive pronoun: do not subjugate *yourself* to me. Both readings are possible and are co-present in a remarkable instance of 'transferred tropical replacement'.

To conclude this survey of grammatical metonymy, let us examine two more examples, both powerful and both discussed earlier. The second will serve as a bridge to the assessment of tropical clusters in translation, but first consider these verses from the watchman's opening monologue:

> εὖτ' ἂν δὲ *νυκτίπλαγκτον* ἔνδροσόν τ' ἔχω
> εὐνὴν ὀνείροις οὐκ ἐπισκοπουμένην
>
> But while I keep this night-walker's bed, wet with dew,
> [lit.: But while I keep this bed *that causes wandering at night* wet
> with dew,]
> this bed of mine not watched over by dreams[152]

[152] A. *Agam.* 12–13; trans. Sommerstein.

a) Jenisch
Seit ich dieses Lager mir
hier bette, das der Thau so oft durchnezzet, das
der Schlummer flieht

Since I am preparing for myself this bed here,
which the dew drenches,
which sleep flees away from

b) Humboldt
Wann hier mich *nachtdurchirrend* Lager, thaubenetzt,
von Traumgesichten freundlich nie besuchet, hält

When a bed, *wandering through the night*, drenched with dew,
never visited by friendly dream visions, keeps me

c) Droysen
Und halt' ich so nachtgestörte Ruh
vom Thau durchnäßt, nie mehr von Träumen aufgesucht

And thus I have a night-disturbed rest,
drenched with dew, nevermore visited by dreams.

d) Wilamowitz
Da muss ich liegen, nachtumwittert, thaubenetzt,
und meinem Lager nahet nimmer sich ein Traum

There I have to lie, night-weathered, dew-drenched,
and never does a dream approach my bed

e) Browning
But when I, driven from night-rest, dew-drenched, hold to
this couch of mine—not looked upon by visions

Jenisch's translation is the only one that literalizes the sequence by dropping the metonymic adjective altogether. Browning keeps the term as 'driven from night-rest', but reaffiliates it with the subject of the sentence, thereby undoing the grammatical metonymy (and tacitly affirming my earlier analysis).[153] The other translators offer different compound adjectives that variously remodel the Greek νυκτίπλαγκτον ('causing to wander by night, rousing from the bed'), in itself an adjectival neologism coined by Aeschylus.[154] Like Browning, Wilamowitz affiliates the adjective, along with the accompanying adjective ἔνδροσον ('wet with dew'), with the subject rather than the accusative object as in the source text. His translation is arresting only in the sense that 'nachtumwittert' ('night-weathered') is a neologism which conflates 'exposure to bad weather' and 'at night time' into one expression. In the Droysen,

[153] See above, pp. 113–14. [154] See above, pp. 113–14, n. 133.

εὐνήν ('bed') has been converted into 'Ruh' ('rest'), as if the Greek term had been an index metonym to be literalized in translation. Like Wilamowitz, Droysen also introduces a newly coined compound adjective—'nachtgestörte' ('night-disturbed')—which likewise conflates 'disturbed from one's rest' and 'at night time'. In both cases, the adjective attracts the reader's attention as a newly coined compound but the collocation is not so abrasive that we can speak of any metonymy. Only Humboldt offers anything approaching a verbatim translation, with the neologistic compound adjective 'nachtdurchirrend' ('wandering through the night') transferred from the subject (who literally wanders during his night watch), to the bed.[155] As this example shows, the capacity of the German to recreate Greek compound words does not in itself ensure that grammatical metonyms are preserved. On the contrary, while the novelty of the compound adjective is reproduced (variously) in all but one of the German translations, the grammatical metonym is only reproduced in one of them.

Tropical Clusters

Our next instance takes us back to the riddle of the sphinx and a notable tropical cluster:

> *τό θ' ὑπέργηρων* φυλλάδος ἤδη
> κατακαρφομένης *τρίποδας* μὲν ὁδοὺς
> στείχει
>
> While *extreme old age*, its leaves already
> withering, walks its way
> On three feet [lit.: walks *three-legged* paths][156]

a) Jenisch

> stüzzen *Kinderkraft hingeschwundener Körper*
> auf den Stäben des Greisen-Alters, nähren
> Mark, dem Säuglinge gleich im milchnen Busen—jede Blüthe der Jugendkraft
> hin—
> hin mit Zweig und mit Blatt!—der dürre Stamm nur
> trocknet saftlos dem nahen Sturz entgegen.
> Da—da schleichen wir nun auf dreyen Füßen . . . einher.
>
> They support *the child-strength of bodies that have wasted away*
> with the canes of old-age, nourishing

[155] This is the case irrespective of the fact that Humboldt's translation swaps subject and accusative object in the sentence compared to the source text.

[156] A. *Agam.* 79–81; trans. Sommerstein. For a discussion of the various elements of this tropical cluster, see above, pp. 125–7.

marrow, like the infant at the milky bosom—every blossom of youth-strength
gone—
away with twig and with leaf!—only the arid trunk
dries, juiceless, towards its near collapse.
There—there we slink now on three feet

b) Humboldt
Was dem Alter erliegt, wenn herbstlich das Laub
hinwelket, das schleicht *dreifüssigen* Pfad

That which succumbs to old age, when the foliage withers away
autumnally, that slinks down the *three-footed* path

c) Droysen
Wer dem Alter erliegt, wem herbstlich die Stirn sich entlaubet,
er wankt dreifüssigen Gang

He who succumbs to old age, whose forehead autumnally sheds leaves,
staggers in a three-footed walk

d) Wilamowitz
Und *das letzte Menschenalter* wieder,
wann das Laub am Lebensbaum vertrocknet,
wankt dahin, dreifüssig

and *the last age of man*, again,
when the foliage of the tree of life dries up,
staggers along, three-legged, weak and childish,

e) Browning
...but in *oldest age's* case,
Foliage a-fading, why, he wends his way
On three feet

The translations of this cluster vividly confirm that metaphors are more likely to be preserved and carried over into the target language than metonyms. Of all these five translations only one, Humboldt's, gives a verbatim rendering that reproduces all the tropical elements of the source text: index metonym (the abstract 'that which succumbs to old age' implying concrete 'old persons'), metaphor (the defoliating tree implying human ageing), and metaphor conjoined with grammatical metonym ('three-legged': both the metaphorical walking with a cane as a third 'leg' and the metonymic transference from walking persons to path walked on). In all the other translations, the metaphorical adjective is reaffiliated to the subject as its governing noun, and no grammatical metonymy results. Droysen's translation is the most literalizing, as it removes all metonymic elements. Jenisch's highly poetic paraphrase, by contrast, involves a change from one variant of metonymy to another: the index metonym ('extreme old age' implying 'old persons') is replaced by an amplification metonym ('the child-strength of bodies that have wasted away'). The limited, child-like strength left to the elderly is the metonymic vehicle in a compound within which the noun (and adjective) in genitive case spell out the metonymic tenor, on which the remainder of the sequence depends. In Jenisch's version, the 'withering tree' metaphor is greatly elaborated and the 'three leg' metaphor maintained (although the metaphor's tenor, 'canes of old age', is also literally present). But in all the translations, and in clear contrast to the changes or literalizations to which the metonymic elements of the source text are subjected, the 'three leg' metaphor and the 'withering tree' metaphor are reproduced.

Amplification Metonymy

To conclude this analysis, let us consider one final example of amplification metonymy. Unlike those instances where translators introduce amplification metonyms themselves, the following passage contains an amplification metonym in the source text. As she is led towards the altar to be sacrificed, Iphigenia is being gagged by Agamemnon's henchmen:

> *βίᾳ χαλινῶν τ' ἀναύδῳ μένει*
>
> by force, by *the silencing power of a bridle*
> [lit.: by force, and by *the speechless power of bridles*][157]

a) Jenisch
Auch die Diener des Opfers heißt er grausam
ihr die Lippen von Rosen dicht zu fesseln
mit *verstummender Kraft*!

And cruelly he orders the servants of the sacrifice
to bind her lips of roses firmly
with *muting force*.

b) Humboldt
mit Zaum, und *sprachlosen Zwangs harter Kraft*

with bridle, and *speechless coercion's hard force*

c) Droysen
Sie schwieg dem Machtwort in *lautlosem* Zwang

She said nothing to the decree in *soundless* coercion

d) Wilamowitz
Die Fessel hielt. Stumm und starr lag sie da.

The fetter held. Mute and stiff she lay there.

[157] A. *Agam*. 238; trans. Sommerstein.

e) Browning
...and the fair mouth's guard
and frontage hold,—press hard
from utterance a curse against the house
by dint of bit—violence bridling speech.

In the Greek, there is a metonymic shift, with an over-specifying metonymic vehicle ('power') acting as the noun governing the metonymic tenor in the genitive ('bridle').[158] In addition, the adjective ἄναυδος is used here as a grammatical amplification metonym: it is the gagged Iphigenia who is without speech, not the force that is gagging her.[159] Interestingly, none of the translators gives a verbatim rendering of this verse. Wilamowitz literalizes the sequence altogether, the others change it significantly; Droysen eliminates the concrete instrument used to gag Iphigenia ('bridle') but maintains the grammatical amplification metonym. While it might be imaginable that 'soundless' should qualify the 'coercion' exercised on Iphigenia, what is at issue here is clearly not that the sacrificers act in silence but that Iphigenia is being silenced. The adjective is transferred away from the noun it would literally qualify, namely Iphigenia, who is 'soundless' as she hears her father's decree in subjection to her sacrificers. Humboldt rearranges the word order, which allows 'bridle' to be kept in the text (in ordinary, literal usage) but undoes the collocation that constitutes the source text's metonym. Instead, his translation offers a less intense amplification metonym, 'coercion's hard

[158] On the amplification metonymy in the Greek, see above, p. 85.

[159] LSJ s.v. gives 'silencing' as a denotative meaning of the term but can only cite this one instance here in support of the claim. The overwhelming majority of other verse occurrences show it denoting the absence of speech and/or of the ability to speak, i.e. 'speechless', 'without speech', 'unable to articulate'; see *Od.* 5.456, 10.378, Hes. *Th.* 797, A. *Sept.* 82, *Pers.* 577, S. *OC* 1274, 1404, *El.* 1284, and E. *Med.* 1183. But more reliable evidence for ordinary usage in any case comes from the Hippocratic corpus, where the adjective clearly denotes the effect of speechlessness, as at Hp. *Epid.* 5.50: πάλιν ἐπετείνετο τῷ πυρετῷ, καὶ κατεφέρετο, καὶ ἄναυδος ἦν—'Again she was prostrated by the fever; she was depressed, speechless'; trans. Jones. Cf. also the term's usage at Hp. *Coac.* 291, *Mul.* 2.110, *Epid.* 3.79. This conclusion finds further support in the usage of the adverbial form, ἀναύδως, at Hp. *Prorrh.* 1.90, where it denotes 'without speech' (αἱ ἐν πυρετοῖσι πρὸς ὑποχόνδριον ὀδύναι ἀναύδως, ἱδρῶτι λυόμεναι, κακοήθεες—'in a person who loses his speech, pains to the hypochondrium that occur during fevers and are resolved with a sweat are malignant'; trans. Potter), and of the nominal form, ἀναυδία, which denotes 'speechlessness' at Hp. *Coac.* 353 (ἐν τοῖσι σπασμοῖσιν ἀναυδίη ἐπὶ πολὺ, κακόν—'In convulsions, a longer loss of speech is bad'; trans. Potter). Against the background of this prose usage and the term's predominant usage in verse texts, the usage of the term here is unmistakably deviant, tropical usage. This would also apply to the usage at S. *Aj.* 947, ὤμοι, ἀναλγήτων | δισσῶν ἐθρόησας ἄναυδ' | ἔργ' Ἀτρειδᾶν τῷδ' ἄχει ('Ah me, you named unspeakable [lit.: *speechless*] actions of the ruthless twin sons of Atreus when you voiced this grief'; trans. Lloyd-Jones), even if we see this as influenced by the related term ἀναύδητος ('not to be spoken', 'unutterable', 'horrible').

force': less intense, because both terms involved are abstract and the shift in semantic field is therefore less strong than in the Greek (concrete to abstract). In Humboldt, the affiliation of 'speechless' is ambiguous, as between reference to Iphigenia (the result of her gagging) or to the sacrificers (while gagging her). In either case, the abrasive collocation of human terminology ('speechless') with abstract ('coercion') shows that the adjective has been transferred from its proper governing noun. Jenisch, finally, undoes the source text's amplification metonym by turning its metonymic tenor (χαλινῶν, 'of the bridle') into the predicate in the target language ('zu fesseln', 'to bind'). This has consequences for the grammatical amplification metonym, which is represented as 'mit verstummender Kraft' ('with muting force'). The term that corresponds to the transferred adjective in the Greek here is the participle of a transitive verb. As such, it is affiliated to the following noun and at the same time qualifies Iphigenia without any deviant usage. At most, the noun 'Kraft', or indeed the combination of participle and noun, might be read as a metonym by association which evokes the bridle as the object through which this muting power is exercised without literally mentioning it. Then, as if to compensate for loss of defamiliarization and without any prompting from the source text, Jenisch introduces a metaphorical cliché ('lips of roses'): 'transferred tropical replacement', once again.

Found in Translation: Supplementary Metonyms and Poetic Texturing

Before we leave the *Agamemnon* and its translations, let us return once more to the way metonyms are sometimes introduced during the translation process. As we have seen, this phenomenon is attested in both 'domesticating' and 'foreignizing' translations. The following passage from the chorus's opening remarks on the Trojan expedition illustrates the pattern:

> στόλον Ἀργείων χιλιοναύτην,
> τῆσδ' ἀπὸ χώρας
> ἦραν, στρατιῶτιν ἀρωγὰν
>
> launched the thousand-ship expedition of the Argives
> from this land
> as military backers for their suit[160]

[160] A. *Agam.* 45–7; trans. Sommerstein.

a) Jenisch
   und tausend Schiffe
   ins Schlachtgefild' hinreihten

   and lined up a thousand ships
   into the battle zone

b) Humboldt
   zu der Hülfe des Kriegs von dem heimischen Land
   fern lösten den Zug
   einst tausend Argeiischer *Segel*

   once, as an aid to war, they released and sent
   far from the homeland the expedition
   of a thousand Argive *sails*

c) Droysen
   der Argiver tausendschiffigen Zug
   Von jenem Gestad
   Fortführten, Genossen des Krieges.

   comrades of war led
   the Argives' thousand-shipped expedition
   away from these shores

d) Wilamowitz
   der Hellenenflotte tausend *Segel*
   aus den Häfen unsres Landes führten,
   auszufechten ihren Rachekrieg

   [they] led the Hellenic fleet's thousand *sails*
   out of our country's ports
   to battle out their war of revenge

e) Browning
   Did from this land the aid, the armament dispatch,
   the thousand-sailored force of Argives

In the Greek, the Argives' fleet is qualified by the compound adjective χιλιοναύτην ('[consisting] of a thousand ships'). Both Droysen's 'domesticating' and Browning's 'foreignizing' translation use similar compound adjectives to represent this epithet, whereas Jenisch drops στόλον ('expedition', 'fleet') and splits the compound adjective into adjective and noun in literal usage. Humboldt's 'foreignizing' and Wilamowitz's 'domesticating', on the other hand, give metonymic renderings of this passage: Humboldt's translation adds an index metonym, 'a thousand Argive sails' (implying the 'thousand ships of the Argives' fleet'); Wilamowitz's adds an amplification metonym, 'the Hellenic fleet's thousand sails' (focusing on the 'sails', when what is at issue is the 'fleet' itself). Both yield limited deviations from ordinary usage, because the context leaves little room for ambiguity, yet the feeling of a new trope clearly appeals to both translators as adequate reflection of the overall stylistic quality of the Greek.

Generally speaking, it is Humboldt who uses metonymic elements to enrich poetic texture most strikingly. More than any other translator he adds metonyms to intensify the idiom. Three examples may suffice by way of illustration. Example one—the chorus warns:

> βαρεῖα δ' ἀστῶν φάτις ξὺν κότῳ
> The talk of citizens, mixed with anger, is a dangerous thing[161]
>
> Humboldt:
> *Des Bürgerzorns Schmähungswort* lastet schwer
>
> The reviling *word* of citizens' anger weighs heavily
> [lit.: citizen-anger's *condemnation-word* weighs heavily]

Here, Humboldt juxtaposes two neologistic compound nouns (neither paralleled in the source text), which also introduce a number metonym, with 'word' invoking expressions of discontent denoted in the Greek by φάτις ('talk', 'speech').[162] Example two—the chorus remarks to Cassandra:

> ταχεῖα δ' ἄτα πέλει.
> Disaster comes swiftly[163]
>
> Humboldt:
> Denn rasch hin eilt *Ate's Fuss*.
>
> For *Ate's foot* travels quickly.

Humboldt's translation to a certain extent preserves the ambiguity of the Greek term ἄτα, which can be taken to denote literally both 'disaster' or 'ill fate' and Ate, the personified goddess of ruin. Regardless of whether we take Humboldt's 'Ate' as the goddess or the 'disaster', his translation introduces an amplification metonym, 'Ate's foot', thereby emphasizing the swiftness of the movement, where what is at issue is the sudden arrival of the goddess and/or the ills she brings. This added element, which has no pretext in the Greek, is testimony to Humboldt's familiarity with Greek poetic idiom. His translation echoes innumerable tragic foot metonyms, from the chorus's plea to Apollo in *Antigone*, μολεῖν καθαρσίῳ *ποδὶ* Παρνασίαν ὑπὲρ κλειτὺν ('[Apollo,] come with cleansing movement [lit.: with purifying *foot*] over the slope of Parnassus!'),[164] to

[161] A. *Agam.* 456; trans. Sommerstein.

[162] In this instance Browning also takes the singular of φάτις as pretext for a new metonym: 'And grave with anger goes *the city's word*, | And pays a debt by public curse incurred'.

[163] A. *Agam.* 1124; trans. Sommerstein.

[164] S. *Ant.* 1144–5; trans. Lloyd-Jones.

Orestes' invocation of Athena as a helper in *Eumenides*, τίθησιν ὀρθὸν ἢ κατηρεφῆ *πόδα* | φίλοις ἀρήγουσ' ('planting a straight or a covered leg [lit.: *foot*]').[165] And example three—the last words of the chorus prior to the return of Agamemnon:

> γνώσῃ δὲ χρόνῳ διαπευθόμενος
> τόν τε δικαίως καὶ τὸν ἀκαίρως
> πόλιν οἰκουροῦντα πολιτῶν.
>
> In time you will know by inquiry
> which of the citizens has acted honestly
> when staying at home in the city, and which inappropriately[166]
>
> Humboldt:
> In der Folge der Zeit kennst prüfend du leicht
> wer billig und recht, wer sonder Gebühr
> dir der Bürger *die Mauern* verwaltet.
>
> As time goes by, you recognize easily by investigation
> which of the citizens is supervising *the walls* for you
> duly and justly, which improperly

This is another case which illustrates how Wilamowitz may have reached his conclusion that one needed the Greek text to make sense of Humboldt's translation. With or without the source text, 'die Mauern' ('the walls') will be taken as an index metonym, implying civic institutions rather than actual structures; but without the Greek text the overtones are likely to be more military, the inferred term more likely to be 'the city's defence' or indeed even 'the city's fortifications' rather than 'the city' itself, as the Greek has it. This instance may involve only a slight divergence from the source, but from an aesthetic point of view the cumulative effect of such defamiliarizing divergences is not without impact. We should certainly acknowledge that Humboldt's experimentation with Greek metres, his neologistic compounds, and his willingness to stretch German syntax are central to the overall 'foreignizing' and 'defamiliarized' impression of his translation. Nevertheless, his consistent deployment of metonymic devices throughout the translation surely adds to this impression and its role should not be underestimated.

[165] A. *Eum.* 294–5; trans. Sommerstein. The exact interpretation of these verses is a matter of dispute (see e.g. Sommerstein *ad loc.*). As elsewhere, I would argue that uncertainty is built into the metonymic nature of the expression. It is not open to scholarly erudition to provide a definitive and unambiguous 'explanation'.

[166] A. *Agam.* 807–9; trans. Sommerstein.

METONYMY IN TRANSLATION: FINDINGS AND CONCLUSIONS

What happens to metonymy in translation? My analysis of contrasting translations of Aeschylus' *Agamemnon* has produced a series of important findings:

1) It is in principle possible to give verbatim translations of all the variants of metonymy distinguished in Chapter 3, with the exception of certain cases of cultural untranslatability (where the lexical link, on which a metonym is based, is not available in the target language) or linguistic untranslatability (where the semantic range of a term is different in source and target language). Both cases of untranslatability, and their outcomes in practice, validate *per contrarium* my fundamental definition of metonymy as a shift in a semantic field established through regular collocation in ordinary usage.
2) While verbatim translation is often, still, a possible option, metonyms in practice elicit a wide range of responses. Literalization is common, either in part or whole (to the entire elimination of defamiliarized language). There are two translation strategies through which partial literalization can take place. In one, the source text's metonymic vehicle is carried over into the target language but is explicitly supplemented with a term that would otherwise constitute the implicit metonymic tenor in the source; I propose to refer to this as *literalizing supplementation.* In the other, the source text's metonym is literalized but a degree of defamiliarization is maintained through the insertion of new tropical elements (metonymic or other), which create a comparable effect of intensified language without reproducing the original metonymic phenomenon. I suggest we refer to this as *transferred tropical replacement.*
3) In this sample, translations serving an explicit 'domesticating' programme display a greater overall tendency towards literalization, but there is no consistent or predictable equivalence between 'domestication' and 'literalization' on the one hand, or 'foreignization' and verbatim translation on the other. On the contrary, some of the most striking metonymic defamiliarizations are observable in translations that purport to be 'domesticating'—either by way of preserving metonyms of the Greek source text or by introducing new metonyms into the translated text.[167]

[167] There seems to be some correlation between domesticating and literalizing versus foreignizing and verbatim translations in the most extreme cases, i.e. those of Wilamowitz (who very often opts for literalizing tropes) and Browning (the most consistent verbatim

4) Linguistic specificities and differences between source and target language, such as the degree to which a language is inflected or its propensity to create compound words, do not necessarily have a significant impact on the translatability of metonyms nor do they affect in any consistent manner different translators' approaches to metonyms. As far as compound nouns in particular are concerned, the samples show them used as index metonyms, as compressed amplification metonyms, or merely as compressed discourse without any tropical element.
5) The existence of diachronic or translingual traditions of poetic idiom means that metonymic clichés can sometimes be represented verbatim or with equivalents from the target language and culture. In this sample, however, the fact that some translations offer literalized versions of clichés suggests that in such cases there remains a residual defamiliarization that continues to be poetically effective. The same is true of metonymic association whose outcomes vary from translatability with comparable effect to literalization. Although neither metonymic cliché nor metonymic association can be said to involve tropicality in the narrow sense, the effects they elicit in translation vindicate the decision to count them among metonymic phenomena.

Studying metonymy in translation has presented us, moreover, with a panorama of concrete readings of individual metonyms—as made manifest in the different translation choices made by each translator upon encountering them—which unfolded for every example discussed (some of) the range of semantic possibilities (perceived to be) inherent in the metonyms of the Greek source text. Surveying the different translatorial responses confirmed several of the key assumptions underpinning my earlier theorizing. The plurality of translation solutions in and of itself

translator); yet this impression is immediately complicated by that fact that Wilamowitz's translation is also characterized by a strong tendency to simultaneously flatten out the Greek tropes *and* introduce new 'abrasions' to compensate ('transferred tropical replacement'), while Browning's poeticizing preserves the original most closely on a word-by-word level but does so at the expense of idiomatic English, which gives his translation consistently an even greater degree of intense defamiliarization than is felt in the Greek original. This is particularly intriguing in the light of Wilamowitz's positivistic indifference to referential indeterminacy inherent in language, which might lead us to expect the exact opposite of what these findings show, yet his translation—somewhat ironically—indicates exactly this indeterminacy to a far greater extent than Browning's. Both observations, that much is clear, only become possible through the nuanced perspective of descriptive poetics, as developed and mobilized here, and they are indicative of what can be gained by incorporating tropological-stylistic perspectives more rigorously into translation criticism.

vividly demonstrated the directional aesthetics of metonymy, that is, the way metonyms point to clusters or chains of lexically associated terms, as the metonymic vehicle present in the text opens up a semantic field that includes a range of possible metonymic tenors, only narrowed down (or not) by the (more or less) determinative context. The core argument advanced in this book, namely that metonymy is to be understood as a shift within a semantic field, found further support in the translation of non-tropical passages, in which the issue of untranslatable polysemy arose: where no one word in the target language encompasses the semantic range of a term in the source language, any attempt at literal translation is forced to be selective. From the perspective of the target language, the semantic range covered by the term in the source language becomes a semantic field, and the translator is forced to choose one term from this field—which illustrates and supports, in reverse (as it were), the understanding of metonymy as a shift in a semantic field. The evaluation of the different translations also highlighted the impact that metonyms, even clichéd or dead metonyms, have on readers (here represented by the translators): though they may seem rather unremarkable (when analysed as low-level stylization devices in their own right), it became apparent that translators do respond to them as poetically active elements and seek to somehow convey their effect and presence in their translations. The analysis of translations of Aeschylus' *Agamemnon* as literary texts in their own right has furthermore demonstrated the value of the categories developed in Chapter 3 for practical literary criticism. These categories have proved to be reliable tools for the analysis and assessment of metonymic phenomena; they have made it possible to distinguish metonyms from other tropes and to compare the intensity of their respective poetic effects. They have enabled us to conduct an analysis that (*inter alia*) has shown how some of the most striking index metonyms of a source text may be eliminated in translation, while compensatory metonymic (or other) elements may be introduced. This finding in particular underscores the important role metonymy plays in enriching the poetic texture of texts—without necessarily attracting much attention.

It goes without saying that (had it been a practical possibility) it would have been desirable to examine further German translations of other Greek texts from this period to confirm or further qualify my results, for instance through a comparative evaluation of Sophocles' *Oedipus Tyrannus* and its translations by Friedrich Hölderlin (1804), Karl Wilhelm Ferdinand Solger (1824), and Christian Graf zu Stolberg (1827). Different poets' styles are, after all, markedly shaped by their different ways of using tropical language—subsuming both the *types* of metonymic expressions they tend to use (e.g. recurring or dominant conformations of metonymy, typical levels of intensity of poetic effect, etc.) and the *role* metonyms play within their overall strategies of stylization (e.g. gently elevating poetic language across a text, dramatic heightening at key moments, etc.)—which means that the very starting position and overall framework against which translators model their respective approach to individual metonyms in any particular text differ significantly from one poet to the next. Translating metonyms in Pindar is, therefore, bound to be a very different process than translating those in Sophocles, since the former's use of tropical language is so unusually elaborate and bold, while the latter's is much more measured and restrained (which would suggest, among other things, a larger number of instances of untranslatability in Pindar than in Sophocles). These differences of style in the source text then compound with differences of translatorial style. For the record: preliminary research suggests that a contrastive analysis of the translation of Pindar's *Odes* by Friedrich Gedike (1777) and Hölderlin (1800) would have allowed us to shed more light on metonymy's dependency on a stable syntactic environment, which is generally provided by Gedike but often on the verge of collapse (or beyond it) in the Hölderlin. One has the impression, also, that a comparison of translations of Sophocles' *Antigone* by Martin Opitz (1636), Hölderlin (1804), Solger (1824), and August Boeckh (1843) would serve to illuminate the impact of classicizing, Romantic, and positivistic-philological aesthetics and stylistics on metonymy in translation. For lack of space, however, it seemed best to limit this study to the examination of translations of a single text. While, therefore, it is necessary to end my discussion of metonymy in translation here, I hope that the theoretical framework established and the insights gained in this first exploration of a largely uncharted field will encourage further research in this area.

Metonymy and stylistic criticism

Metonymy—this much should be by now abundantly clear—is not a marginal phenomenon in literary texts. Whether adding to the poetic texture by elevating poetic idiom or creating intense effects of heightening in significant passages, metonyms play an important role in the formal-aesthetic conformation of literary works. The analysis of metonymy in translation in the first section of this chapter has demonstrated that the categories distinguished in Chapter 3 are valuable tools for critical practice, but it is, of course, not just translation criticism that the theoretical framework offered here promises to illuminate. Without a finely tuned critical apparatus it is virtually impossible to appreciate how individual texts create their overall aesthetic impression. A case in point is the large body of texts that can be characterized as 'hellenizing' in terms of their content and style. The imitation, emulation, and evocation of the poetic idiom of classical Greek literature plays an important role in a huge number of texts from different periods and different literatures; yet while it is usually relatively easy to determine which elements in the *content* of a text forge a connection with ancient Greece, ascertaining what exactly marks such texts as 'hellenizing' in terms of their *style*, that is, elucidating how they create a recognizably 'hellenizing' mode of poetic expression, appears to be a less straightforward affair—and is indeed much less frequently attempted.

In this section, I will mobilize the theoretical framework developed in the previous chapter to do just this. The two texts chosen for this purpose are Schiller's play *Die Braut von Messina* ('The Bride of Messina') of 1803 and Housman's 'Fragment of a Greek Tragedy' of 1883. While this may, admittedly, at first seem to be a rather unlikely pairing, it is precisely the imitation of the poetic idiom of Greek tragedy that lies at the core of both texts: in Schiller's attempt to reconnect modern theatre with its ancient roots, in Housman's aim of parodying over-literal translations (such as Browning's), if not Greek tragic idiom itself. The pairing of a text with a serious and tragic outlook with another of a playful and humorous character is particularly attractive as it makes it possible to show how literary devices, such as metonymy, can be used to strikingly different ends while aiming at evoking and (re-)creating a broadly similar overall style. In both cases, criticism has explored the classical hypotexts quoted, imitated, or alluded to, but little has been said about the actual stylistic features of the texts themselves. Arguably, the fact that source criticism has all too often eclipsed textual analysis stems not least from the lack of the necessary tools to conduct such analysis.

In the case of Schiller's play, much has been written (not least by the author himself) about the use of the chorus, the conflation of classical pagan and fatalistic world views with Christian and Islamic elements, and the classical tragedies which are alluded to or have inspired individual passages, characters, or plot lines of the play.[168] The play's most

[168] As in both earlier scholarship, for instance, Gerhard 1919 and Clark 1937, and more recent contributions like Schadewaldt 1969, Janz 1984, Frick 1998, Guthke 1998, Ritzer 1998, Silk 1998, and Ewans 2005, 208–9. Gerhard's study contains a section entitled 'Griechische Elemente in Schillers Dramen, Kapitel 1: Form, a) Sprachliches' ('Greek Elements in Schiller's Plays, Chapter 1: Form, a) Idiom'). However, Gerhard only dedicates 15 out of 135 pages to this topic (see Gerhard 1919, 40–54) and, more important, confines herself to reflections on the general nature of tropical language rather than close, textual

immediate 'hellenizing' feature, however, is without doubt its poetic idiom. This is duly acknowledged by Hibberd (in the only significant study of the play's imagery), who argues that '*Die Braut von Messina* may be best understood and appreciated through its formal elements . . . the motivation here is achieved through stylistic and rhetorical means.'[169] His discussion begins with some interesting observations:

> The stylization of the play is not least apparent in its language. The pathos of the dramatic situations is expressed in imagery that is rarely startlingly original but is none the less dramatically effective. The play contains few neologisms, but a higher proportion of adjectives than any other of Schiller's dramas . . . Among the many traditional rhetorical devices, the *explanatio* and the Homeric simile figure frequently.[170]

However, instead of shedding more light on which rhetorical devices are used where and how, Hibberd recalibrates his perspective and concentrates on 'the preponderance of recurring images',[171] namely fire and water imagery. While such studies can indeed add to our understanding of particular texts,[172] they are different in kind from stylistic analysis proper, since the focus here is on the conceptual content of imagery rather than on the mechanisms through which images are deployed and the way they affect poetic texture and aesthetic effect.

Housman's parody, on the other hand, has attracted practically no critical attention in its own right, despite the fact that the text has become a common point of reference for classicists, especially in unfavourable reviews of translations,[173] but also as a teaching tool to give Greek-less students a taste of Greek tragic diction. The latter prompted Marcellino to compile a commentary on the parody for those who 'have read all of the *Oresteia* in translation, [yet] do not realize how clever it is, although

analysis. To give just two examples: 'Schon an sich wird die Metapher einer toten Sprache leicht umgedeutet . . . Man läuft Gefahr, Wendungen als Metaphern anzusprechen, die von dem Griechen nicht mehr als solche gefühlt wurden, oder umgekehrt' ('Metaphors in a dead language are easily misinterpreted . . . One runs the risk of taking expressions as metaphorical which are no longer felt by the Greeks as such, or vice versa'; Gerhard 1919, 41) or 'der moderne Leser wird hier versucht sein, als Personifizierung oder Allegorie zu empfinden, was für den Griechen infolge seiner Religion durchaus konkret war . . . Anwendungen griechischer Mythologie werden stets leicht in Allegorien oder Personifizierungen umschlagen' ('the modern reader will be tempted to take as personification or allegory what for the Greeks was quite concrete, in line with their religion . . . Uses of Greek mythology will always easily turn into allegory or personification'; Gerhard 1919, 42). While these are valid and relevant considerations, which have also informed my own theorizing, they nevertheless fall short of a concrete examination of the specifics of the text.

169 Hibberd 1967, 306. 170 Hibberd 1967, 307. 171 Hibberd 1967, 307.

172 A prime example in the criticism of Greek tragedy is Lebeck 1971.

173 See, for instance, Bers 2000.

they do find it hilarious'.[174] Again, much effort is invested in tracking down hypotexts for individual passages, providing historical background information, and (in this case) adducing classical witnesses for the stylistic peculiarities of the authors parodied. Yet, here too, very little is said about the stylistic devices of the text itself, which, after all, create the 'hilarity' in the first place.

Both texts serve to demonstrate how the theoretical framework established earlier in this book enables us to reach a better understanding of aesthetic effects—in this case the effect of a 'hellenizing' style. Right from the start, metonymy plays an important role. Compare the two opening sequences, beginning with Schiller's play:

> Der Noth gehorchend, nicht dem eignen Trieb,
> Tret' ich, ihr greisen *Häupter* dieser Stadt,
> Heraus zu euch aus den *verschwiegenen*
> *Gemächern* meines Frauensaals, das Antlitz
> Vor euren Männerblicken zu entschleiern.
>
> Not following my own urge but obeying necessity
> I step out of the *discreet rooms* of my lady-chambers
> to you, *elderly heads* of this city,
> to unveil my countenance
> in front of your manly gaze.[175]

The index metonym 'elderly heads' for 'elders' is a literary cliché and, as such, elevates the diction from the outset.[176] The grammatical amplification metonym 'discreet rooms of my lady-chambers' (for 'rooms in which discreet ladies live') further intensifies the idiom and thus sets the tone for the dramatic poetry that is to follow.

The famous opening lines of the chorus in Housman's parody at once introduce a superficially comparable usage:

> O suitably-attired-in-leather-boots
> *Head of a traveller*, wherefore seeking whom
> Whence by what way how purposed art thou come
> To this well-nightingaled vicinity?

[174] Marcellino 1953, 171. [175] Schiller, *Die Braut von Messina*, ll. 1–5.

[176] The expression is not a 'dead' metonym or indeed a 'dead' metaphor, as 'head' is in English (e.g. in 'head of school'); the equivalent denotative term in German is 'Oberhaupt' rather than just 'Haupt', which belongs to poetic idiom rather than ordinary language. Rather, when used as a form of direct address, this is a metonymic cliché equivalent to the pervasive φίλον κάρα ('dear head'), *vel sim.*, of Greek tragedy (see e.g. S. *OC* 1631 or A. *Agam.* 905). The metonymic impression is retrospectively enforced through the focus on facial features in 'countenance' ('Antlitz') and 'manly gaze' ('Männerblicken') in ll. 4–5.

The pseudo-compound adjective 'suitably-attired-in-leather-boots' imitates a specific type of adjective that features prominently in the idiom of Greek epic and (subsequently) tragic poetry, namely adjectives that assert the aptness or well-builtness of their governing noun. At the same time, it is evocative of Aeschylus' special predilection for heavy compound adjectives. Likewise, the amplification metonym 'head of a traveller' reproduces a widespread metonymic cliché of Greek tragic idiom.[177] Both expressions, needless to say, are comical in their own right by virtue of their sheer un-Englishness. The comic effect, however, is significantly enhanced by the abrasive juxtaposition of the metonymic vehicle and its qualifying adjective in tenor terminology: a *head* (MV) is said to be suitably attired in leather *boots*. It is precisely the metonymic shift within the amplification metonym, foregrounding the 'head' of the 'traveller', that creates the absurd juxtaposition.

LAUGHING WITH METONYMY: HOUSMAN'S HUMOROUS 'HELLENIZING'

This first impression of the two texts is borne out by a close reading of the respective 'hellenizings' that follow. Housman's parody contains comical metaphors, such as the chorus's question whether Alcmaeon arrived 'Sailing on horseback, or with feet for oars',[178] its mock-gnomic assertion that 'Life, I say, is not a stranger to uncertainty',[179] as well as a metaphor taken over almost unchanged from Aeschylus (and, in its unchanged state, presented as in itself ridiculous): 'Mud's sister, not himself, adorns my shoes'.[180] Two further metaphors occur in the lines,

> Nay even the palace appears
> To my yoke of circular eyes
> (The right, nor omit I the left)
> Like a slaughterhouse, so to speak,
> Garnished with woolly *deaths*
> And many shipwrecks of cows.

[177] See n. 176; compare also the famous opening verse of Sophocles' *Antigone*: ὦ κοινὸν αὐτάδελφον Ἰσμήνης κάρα ('O kindred sisterly head of Ismene').

[178] Housman, 'Fragment of a Greek Tragedy', l. 10; 'feet for oars' is arguably a simile rather than a metaphor, as Marcellino implies (see Marcellino 1953, 73), owing to the presence of 'for', which makes the analogy explicit.

[179] Housman, 'Fragment of a Greek Tragedy', ll. 39–40.

[180] Housman, 'Fragment of a Greek Tragedy', l. 13; cf. A. *Agam.* 494–5: μαρτυρεῖ δέ μοι κάσις | πηλοῦ ξύνουρος διψία κόνις τάδε, ('and the thirsty dust, the sister and neighbour of mud, testifies to me'; trans. Sommerstein).

The last two lines, however, derive their humorous force not least from the combination of an index metonym and a metaphor. Both tropes are equally far-fetched and mutually dependent on each other when it comes to making sense of the sequence. The index metonym implies the concrete 'dead bodies' through the abstract 'deaths' and uses the adjective 'woolly' to qualify the dead bodies, indirectly, as 'sheep carcasses'.[181] This instance illustrates how metonyms, too, can be quite startling, provided that the metonymic shift leads to a significant, abrasive terminological clash between metonymic vehicle ('deaths') and the tenor terminology of the surrounding context ('woolly'). In metaphor, as 'shipwrecks of cows' shows, this terminological clash is built into the trope itself.

A further metaphor occurs in a passage that is otherwise dominated by metonyms:

> Nor did the *Delphine tripod* bark it out,
> Nor yet *Dodona*.
> Its native ingenuity sufficed
> My self-taught *diaphragm*.[182]

The 'Delphine tripod' and 'Dodona' denote seats of oracles but not the actual oracles at these seats; they are index metonyms, albeit somewhat clichéd. The expression '[to] bark it out' is arguably so close to conventional colloquial English that is constitutes a borderline case between metaphorical cliché and 'dead' metaphor. However, the juxtaposition with the metonymic vehicle, an object instead of a living being, reinvigorates the felt degree of defamiliarization: a tripod is said to be barking. Once again, humour arises from a terminological clash, here between metonymic cliché and metaphorical cliché. The comic effect of the last two lines, on the other hand, is based on the collapse of a Greek metonym in translation:[183] the effect works, because the cultural-lexical link of contiguity that exists in Greek poetic idiom between 'diaphragm' and 'intelligence' has no equivalent in English. In effect, the sentence does nothing other than state the cultural assumption (and recreate the lexical connection) that lies behind the term's usage in Greek, namely that the seat of ingenuity is the diaphragm. The humour arises from the terminological clash that occurs between 'ingenuity' and 'diaphragm'—by virtue of the unfamiliarity of this collocation in English (but also,

[181] Cf. the similar construction in the opening stanza of Keats's poem 'The Eve of St Agnes': 'And silent was the flock in *woolly* fold' (l. 4).

[182] Housman, 'Fragment of a Greek Tragedy', ll. 43–6.

[183] On the metonymic nature of the Greek terms φρήν and πραπίς (both 'diaphragm', 'midriff') in Greek poetic idiom, see above, pp. 192–202 and 259–60.

prospectively, from the reader's knowledge of Greek poetic idiom and the issues of untranslatability arising from it).[184] Likewise, Housman transplants other classical metonymic clichés, as in the chorus's question, 'Beneath a shining or a rainy *Zeus*?',[185] as well as grammatical metonymy and metonymy by association.

Consider now this passage from Housman's mock-stichomythia:

> ALCMAEON: A *shepherd's questioned mouth* informed me that—
> CHORUS: What? for I know not yet what you will say—
> ALCMAEON: Nor will you ever, if you interrupt.
> CHORUS: Proceed, and I will hold my *speechless* tongue.
> ALCMAEON: This house was Eriphyle's, no one else's.
> CHORUS: Nor did he shame *his throat* with shameful lies.
> ALCMAEON: May I then enter, passing through the door?
> CHORUS: Go chase into the house a lucky *foot.*[186]

The first line contains a prime example of a forceful amplification metonym. The metonymic shift from the 'shepherd' to his 'mouth' may be unremarkable in itself; after all, the shepherd as the metonymic tenor is co-present in the genitive case. Yet as the participle 'questioned', which semantically belongs to the implied subject (the 'shepherd'), is affiliated with the grammatical subject (the metonymic vehicle 'mouth'), this collocation breaches ordinary collocation rules. The amplification metonym is thus combined with a grammatical amplification metonym ('questioned' transferred from 'shepherd' to 'mouth'), which creates the comic image of a conversational exchange between a speaker and just a mouth. The next defamiliarized sequence in this passage, 'I hold my speechless tongue', is taken by Marcellino as an instance of prolepsis, in which the adjective is applied to a noun in anticipation of the results of the action denoted by the verb.[187] Surely, though, what we have here is grammatical amplification metonymy with the adjective 'speechless' transferred from the subject 'I' (which can literally be said to be speechless) to 'tongue'. The expression '[n]or did he shame his throat' is likewise metonymic; in ordinary usage the verb 'to shame' only takes persons as direct objects, and it is ultimately the speaker (rather than 'his

[184] The same is true of 'midriff' ('This truth I have written deep | In my reflective *midriff* | On tablets not of wax', ll. 35–7) and 'liver' ('Never may Cypris for her seat select | My dappled *liver*!', ll. 61–2). This latter example also includes the mythological metonym 'Cypris' for 'erotic attraction'.

[185] Housman, 'Fragment of a Greek Tragedy', l. 12. Note, however, that this metonymic cliché is arguably more evocative of Latin than Greek poetic idiom; see Marcellino 1953, 174.

[186] Housman, 'Fragment of a Greek Tragedy', ll. 17–24.

[187] See Marcellino 1953, 174.

throat') which was not shamed with lies. Thus understood, 'his throat' constitutes a case of amplification metonymy, since the metonymic tenor is present in the genitive ('his'). In the final line, the chorus encourages Alcmaeon to 'chase a lucky foot', a comic image which has him running after his own feet (which also constitutes number metonymy, since clearly both his feet are at issue). The adjective 'lucky' adds to the impression of deviation: either it can be taken as a grammatical amplification metonym (transferred from Alcmaeon, the implicit addressee of the imperative, whom the chorus wishes to be 'lucky') or else it prompts an index-metonymical reading of 'foot' as 'run' (the sequence being understood as 'have a successful run into the house'). Throughout the mock-stichomythia, not only is the humour heavily dependent on individual metonyms; there is also a cumulative effect of almost grotesque physicality from the constant focus on organs: mouth, tongue, throat, foot—all in the space of eight lines, and all arising from the metonymic usage of the terms involved.[188]

FROM TROPES TO FIGURES: STYLISTIC PACING IN SCHILLER'S *BRIDE OF MESSINA*

Tropological analysis of Schiller's play likewise illuminates its inner workings. Overall, *Die Braut* seems to be particularly rich in two poetic devices, metonymy and *figura etymologica*. From a classical perspective, the latter might be thought to evoke the style of Homer or Plato rather than Greek tragedy.[189] However, the distribution of the two devices is interesting. As the play moves on from the first tableau-like scenes and the dramatic action gathers pace and finally reaches its climax, the language becomes increasingly more direct, and tropical language usage is reduced—and it is here that we find the most dense deployment of *figurae etymologicae*. Instances of *figura etymologica* also occur earlier on in the play, as at ll. 809–10: 'Als eine Fürstin fürstlich will ich sie | Einführen in die Hofburg meiner Väter' ('I shall give her as noblewoman

[188] In this respect, Housman's parody of Greek tragic idiom approximates a characteristic metonymic strategy of Attic comedy that reduces—to comic effect—abstract concepts, especially domestic ones, to bits and pieces.

[189] In more general terms, Gerhard notes: 'Auch gehen die Spracheigenheiten Schillers oft wohl eher auf Homer als auf die Tragödie zurück' ('The idiosyncrasies of Schiller's idiom can be traced back to Homer rather than to tragedy.' Gerhard 1919, 41). For a general discussion of *figura etymologica* in Greek and Latin literature, with copious examples from Plato, see McCartney 1927. Detailed discussions of *figurae etymologicae* in Homer are provided by Reece 1997 and Clary 2009.

a noble entrance into my forefathers' castle'). The vast majority, however, can be found in the second half of the play, and with increasing frequency—witness the crescendo as the play moves towards its finale: 'Entsetzt vernehm' ich das Entsetzliche' ('Shocked I hear the shocking news'; l. 1588); 'Der liebend nur um deine Liebe warb' ('who but lovingly wooed for your love'; l. 1817); 'Der sich gesät die tödtliche Saat' ('who has sown himself a deathly sowing'; l. 2004); 'Bis er die tödtliche That nun gethan' ('until he finally did the deadly deed'; l. 2016); 'Die Traumkunst träumt, und alle Zeichen trügen' ('the art of interpreting dreams is dreaming, and all signs are deceiving'; l. 2393); 'Du leugnest der Sonne leuchtendes Licht' ('You deny the sun's shining shine'; l. 2395); 'Lebe, wer's kann, ein Leben der Zerknirschung' ('Live, who can, a life of contrition'; l. 2721); 'Aufblicken muß ich freudig zu den Frohen' ('I must happily look upward to the happy ones'; l. 2725); 'Er lebt in deinem Schmerz ein selig Leben, | Ich werde ewig todt sein bei den Todten' ('He lives a blissful life in your pain, I will forever be dead among the dead'; ll. 2815–16). It is as though this figure is deployed to maintain 'Greek' colouring when, for dramatic reasons, stylized, tropical speech becomes inappropriate.[190] The strategy did not convince all critics: it is arguably this shift that lies behind the rather vague comment by Schiller's contemporary Solger that in this play 'the diction is Schillerian, but unfortunately it becomes increasingly flowery and grandiloquent, and therefore less antique'.[191] In the rest of the play, metonymy is more prominent and more frequently used. The text is positively saturated with all types of metonymy, including index metonyms, such as

Denn auch *das Wort* ist, das heilende, gut.
Aber treff' ich dich draußen im Freien,
Da mag der blutige Kampf sich erneuen,
Da erprobe *das Eisen* den Muth.

For also *the word*, the healing one, is good.
But if I meet you outside in the open,
there the bloody fight might start again,
there *iron* may test courage.[192]

[190] This is one of the many instances in which it becomes apparent just how important and helpful it is to maintain the distinction between figures and tropes argued for above (see pp. 30–6), since the significance, aesthetic consequences, and dramaturgical motivation of this entire 'change of gear' in Schiller's handling of the play's poetic idiom only become fully visible in the light of this difference.

[191] 'Die Diction ist schillerisch, aber leider wird sie immer blumiger und schwülstiger, und also immer weniger antik.' Solger 1826, 110.

[192] Ll. 166–71; the last three lines are immediately repeated at ll. 172–4.

Und jeder *Fußtritt* wandelt auf *Zerstörung*

And every *footstep* wanders on *destruction*[193]

... Eine Schwester
Dacht' ich euch zuzuführen; doch ich selbst
Soll jetzt sie eurem *Heldenarm* verdanken

I thought I would bring you a sister;
yet now I shall owe her to your *heroic arm*[194]

amplification metonyms, such as

Denn mit der nächsten *Morgensonne Strahl*
Ist sie die Meine...

For with the *ray of the next morning sun*
she will be mine...[195]

Diese Zypresse laßt uns zerschlagen
Mit der mörderischen *Schneide der Axt*

Let us smash this cypress
with the murderous *blade of the axe*[196]

and metonyms by association, such as

Dein ist die *Krone*,
Dein ist der Sieg!

Yours is the *crown*,
yours is the victory![197]

Ihrer stillen Zuflucht sie entreißend,
Zurück an meine *mütterliche Brust*
Sie führt und in die *brüderlichen Arme*

snatching her from her quiet refuge,
leading her back to my *maternal breast*
and into *brotherly arms*[198]

In neuen Kampf willst du zurück mich stürzen?
Das *Licht der Sonne* mir noch theurer machen
Auf meinem Wege zu der ew'gen Nacht?

[193] L. 403.
[194] Ll. 1618–20; similarly l. 1806. Further examples for index metonymy include 'Weh, weh mir! O, entsetzensvolles *Licht*! ('Woe, woe me! Alas, dreadful *light*!', l. 2246), 'Wie mir das *Herz* gebietet, will ich reden' ('As my *heart* commands me, so I shall speak', l. 2381), 'Du, Bruder, rette dein geliebtes *Haupt*' ('You, brother, save your beloved *head*', l. 2806; similarly l. 2674).
[195] Ll. 657–8. [196] Ll. 1975–6.
[197] Ll. 1176–7. Similarly: 'Und das *goldene Scepter* in stetiger Reihe | Wandert vom Ahnherrn zum Enkel hinab' ('And the *golden sceptre* wanders | in a steady line from forefather to grandson', ll. 1187–8).
[198] Ll. 1389–90.

You wish to throw me into a new fight?
Making the *light of the sun* dearer to me
while I am on my way to eternal night?[199]

Needless to say, the play also contains metaphors, but these are rarely striking or new. Consider, for instance, 'Ausgeleert hab' ich | Der Worte Köcher und erschöpft der Bitten Kraft' ('I have emptied the quiver of words and exhausted the power of petitions', ll. 439–40)—an interesting metaphor, but modelled on Pi. *O.* 2.83–5: πολλά μοι ὑπ' ἀγκῶνος ὠκέα βέλη | ἔνδον ἐντι φαρέτρας φωνᾶντα συνετοῖσιν ('I have many swift arrows under my arm in their quiver | that speak to those who understand'; trans. Race). In fact, the more potent tropical elements of the play are often tropical clusters involving both metaphor and metonymy or metonyms of different types. Examples range from combinations of fairly clichéd expressions to more complex images. Thus we find index metonym followed by metaphor in

Manch *Segel* rettet sich in diese Buchten
Vor des Orkanes Wuth—Wo ist das Schiff?

Many *a sail* found refuge in these bays
from a hurricane's wrath—where is the ship?[200]

and

So unterwerf' ich mich, wie kann ich's ändern?
Der unregiersam stärkern Götter*hand*,
Die meines Hauses Schicksal dunkel spinnt

How could I change it? So I submit myself,
to the unswayable, stronger *hand* of the gods,
which weaves my house's fate in darkness;[201]

metaphor followed by amplification metonym in

Und jetzt liegst du, dem Staube vermählt,
Von *des Brudermords Händen* entseelt

And now you lie, married to the dust,
killed by *the hands of fratricide*;[202]

amplification metonym combined with metaphor in

Und unter *eines Joches Eisenschwere*
Bog er vereinend ihren starren Sinn

[199] Ll. 2782–3; this example combines metonymy by association with a metaphorical cliché.
[200] Ll. 1593–4. [201] Ll. 1557–9. [202] Ll. 1967–8.

He united their stubborn wills,
bending it under *a yoke's brazen weight*;[203]

and amplification metonym combined with grammatical amplification and followed by an index metonym in

In *eines Gartens abgeschiedner Stille*,
Der von der *Neugier* nicht betreten wird

In the *secluded silence of a garden*,
which *curiosity* never enters.[204]

What is especially interesting, however, is that Schiller, much like Humboldt in his translation of Aeschylus' *Agamemnon*, predominantly uses low-level metonyms and metonymic clichés to create the desired 'hellenizing' impression, repeatedly employing expressions that simultaneously elevate the play's tone and connect the play with the traditional poetic idiom of Greek tragedy.[205]

Is such usage as analysed above at all representative of the literary style of Weimar classicism, or indeed even of European classicism as a whole?[206] Only a fuller investigation could answer such a question—but surely it is essential to conduct such analyses on a larger scale before one can countenance sweeping statements about the characteristic style of literary movements. A prime example of top-down criticism that forgoes such analysis is Jakobson's claim that 'it is generally realized that Romanticism is closely linked with metaphor, whereas the equally intimate ties of Realism and metonymy remained unnoticed'.[207] The posited affinity between particular movements and individual tropes may, or may not, be true—but the only way to prove or disprove any such claim would be to evaluate metonymic occurrences in a representative set of realist texts and to contrast the results with a comparable Romantic set. As the discussion in this section has shown, the theory and

[203] Ll. 37–8. [204] Ll. 794–5.

[205] In addition to the relevant examples cited above, Schiller uses number metonymy, for instance, 'Aber das Schönste | Erlebt *mein Auge*' ('But *my eye* experiences the most beautiful thing', ll. 1207–8; see also 535 and 2112) or 'Und des Meers rings umgebende *Welle*, | Sie verräth uns *dem* kühnen *Corsaren*' ('And *the wave* of the sea surrounding us makes us known to *the* daring *corsair*', ll. 217–18) as well as mythological metonyms such as 'Nicht, wo die *goldene Ceres* lacht | Und *der friedliche Pan*, der Flurenbehüter, | Wo das Eisen wächst in der Berge Schacht, | Da entspringen der Erde Gebieter' ('Not where *golden Ceres* laughs and *peaceful Pan*, protector of meadows, but where iron grows in the depths of mountains, that is where the lords of the earth come from', ll. 223–7).

[206] The case for such studies as essential to a comprehensive understanding of *literary* history (rather than mere cultural history) was convincingly made (over sixty years ago) by Wellek/Warren 1949, 174–85.

[207] Jakobson 1956, 259.

the categories of metonymy worked out and proposed in this book can serve to facilitate precisely such evaluations.

Metonymy and (post-)structuralist criticism

An important further aim of the theoretical investigation of metonymy undertaken in this book has been to clarify the understanding of the order of the tropical space, that is, to gain a better understanding of relationships between the different tropes. This, in turn, is a fundamental prerequisite for a long overdue critical reassessment of (post-)structuralist reappropriations of tropology—from the perspective of tropology. The proposed understanding of metonymy as based on lexical contiguity has vindicated Jakobson's proposition of a bipolar model of the tropical space by substantiating his claim with reference to concrete, literary material. As I have sought to demonstrate, metaphor's underlying principle of similarity or analogy is intrinsically verb-centred, since it is actions or states which are being compared, whereas metonymy's underlying principle of lexical contiguity is intrinsically noun-based, since (for linguistic reasons) nouns create stronger links with other nouns through ordinary collocation and thereby determine all metonymy's variants. Metaphor and metonymy are thus indeed shown to be two distinct and independent forms of tropical language; furthermore, they are the two essential forms of tropical language under which other, supposedly separate, tropes should be subsumed.

While my findings thus corroborate Jakobson's understanding of the bipolar order of the tropical space, they also cast a new light on structuralist reappropriations of tropology in the wake of his influential discussions. Although the transfer of metonymy from poetics to semiotics took place *prior* to any comprehensive theoretical understanding of metonymy as a literary phenomenon, these ('metaphorical') applications of the term 'metonymy' can now be scrutinized from a better informed perspective.[208] Two studies, by de Man and Lodge, which were instrumental in popularizing Jakobson's structuralist tropology within the field of literature, may serve as illustrations.[209]

[208] Earlier critiques of Jakobson-inspired studies lack this basis and are often witnesses to the twentieth-century 'theory wars' in literary studies rather than detailed discussions of underlying presuppositions and lines of argument; see, for instance, Vickers 1988, 464–7, and Fowler 1990, 110–11.

[209] De Man 1979 and Lodge 1977.

In *Allegories of Reading* de Man presents his reflections as a 'theory of reading', based on consideration of Rilke, Proust, Nietzsche, and Rousseau; and '[w]hat emerges is a process of reading in which rhetoric is a disruptive intertwining of trope and persuasion or . . . of cognitive and performative language'.[210] Many of de Man's central lines of argument here are intimately connected with the premises of 'deconstruction',[211] and this cannot be the place to engage with such large reconsiderations of language, rhetoric, and poetics. An issue worth raising, however, is de Man's use of the terms 'metaphor' and 'metonymy'. After all, even if both are given a much wider signification than ours and are used within a radically different theoretical framework, we are sure to find statements on their relatedness, which can be compared and contrasted with the results of the present inquiry into their relationship.

No matter how far-reaching his general redefinition of tropology in literary analysis, de Man's fundamental understanding of tropes is based on the traditional (and outdated) notion of 'substitution'.[212] This leads to difficulties within his arguments which are exacerbated further by his persistent blurriness regarding the relationship of the 'substitute' and 'substituted' in metonymy. His remarks on synecdoche exemplify the problem. De Man appeals to synecdoche in two of his readings, and in both cases he associates it with metaphor. The first mention of synecdoche occurs in a discussion of the rhetorical question, with reference to a passage from Yeats's poem 'Among School Children':

> O chestnut-tree, great-rooted blossomer,
> Are you the leaf, the blossom or the bole?
> O body swayed to music, O brightening glance,
> How can we know the dancer from the dance?[213]

De Man comments: 'one finds powerful and consecrated images of contiguity from part to the whole that makes synecdoche into the most seductive of metaphors: the organic beauty of the tree, stated in the parallel syntax of a similar rhetorical question, or the convergence, in the dance, of erotic desire with musical form'.[214] While de Man's main interest in the poem is the way it lends itself to a metapoetic, semiotic

[210] Both quotations from de Man 1979, ix.

[211] As explicitly acknowledged in the preface; see de Man 1979, x.

[212] Many remarks throughout the book make this obvious. Thus e.g.: 'All rhetorical structures, whether we call them metaphor, metonymy, chiasmus, metalepsis, hypallagus, or whatever, are based on substitutive reversals' (de Man 1979, 113) and 'Neither are we helpless when confronted with figures of speech: as long as we can distinguish between literal and figural meaning, we can translate the figure back to its proper referent' (de Man 1979, 201).

[213] As cited by de Man 1979, 11.

[214] De Man 1979, 11.

reading, his prima facie assessment of the technicalities of the passage (after all, the basis of his subsequent reflections)[215] is deeply problematic. Certainly, the two pairs of lines constitute rhetorical questions, but how far is his appeal to contiguity, synecdoche, and metaphor legitimate? There is a 'contiguous' relationship between (on the one hand) the tree and its parts as well as (on the other) between body, music, dancer, and dance—regardless of whether we understand this contiguity in conceptual or lexical terms. There is, however, no overt deviance from ordinary usage in these lines. The rhetorical question as such articulates a statement that conflicts with referential language in its most narrow definition as representational language that reproduces empirical reality in the code of linguistic signs. Nevertheless, the use of the individual terms does not conflict with ordinary usage: each term denotes what it denotes in common parlance.

What these lines do, from a terminological perspective, is in fact *proto*-tropological: they unfold two semantic fields, enumerating terms which are linked by lexical contiguity and therefore have the potential to be used in metonymic expressions. It is only the parallelism of the rhetorical questions which prompts the thought that the individual terms might refer to the same signified. One might argue that the parallelism of the two paired lines, each comprising an apostrophe marked by 'O' followed by a rhetorical question, suggests an implicit analogy between the two rhetorical questions. On this basis, the four lines are (we must conclude) metaphorical by association as they conjure up, in this combination, the image of the chestnut tree swaying its leaves and blossoms in the wind *like* a dancer's body swaying to music. It is, in other words, not the '*contiguity* of images' that 'makes synecdoche into the most seductive form of metaphor'—the 'images' merely co-occur jointly here. It is the parallel syntactic structure of the lines which confers an impression of metaphor onto this sequence, and the 'seductiveness' results precisely from the absence of any felt abrasiveness (which would prompt a restructuring of the sequence or the inference of a term in order to make sense of the sequence). A metaphorical reading is merely suggested and arises as an additional layer, a further possible reading. And what de Man's discussion of this passage shows, incidentally, is that appeal to synecdoche hardly illuminates the passage or his own argument. After all, is the 'dancer' really a 'part' of the 'dance'? And if so, is he a 'part' in the same way as the 'leaf' is a 'part' of the 'tree'?

[215] See de Man 1979, 11–13.

Such confusions multiply as the discussion progresses. De Man cites a passage from Proust's *À la recherche du temps perdu*, acknowledges the occurrence of concrete metaphors in the passage, then focuses on its 'metafigural' aspect and claims that a

> preference is expressed by means of a distinction that corresponds to the difference between metaphor and metonymy, necessity and chance being a legitimate way to distinguish between analogy and contiguity. The inference of identity and totality that is constitutive of metaphor is lacking in the purely relational metonymic contact: an element of truth is involved in taking Achilles for a lion but none in taking Mr Ford for a motor car.[216]

The association of metaphor/analogy with 'necessity' and of metonymy/contiguity with 'chance' is fraught with difficulties. From the perspective developed in the earlier chapters of this book, we can agree that there is a logical element to metaphor which can be (more or less) compelling, whereas metonymy is rooted in pragmatic collocations of ordinary language, but the radical opposition of 'necessity' and 'chance' adds nothing but obfuscation.[217]

A more serious inconsistency here arises from the fact that if 'identity' and 'totality' are inferred because an actual inference is required to make sense of a sequence, then this is equally true for both metaphor and metonymy (or, to be precise, for certain variant forms of both tropes).[218] The association of 'truth' with the logic of analogy is also problematic, considering that metaphors not only 'reveal' 'truths' by exploiting analogies but also suggest and create analogies. But unsustainable as de Man's claims may be, they are certainly consistent with the pervasive neo-Romantic privileging of analogy over lexicon. From there, it is only a small step to denying metonymy its status as a trope altogether: 'the superiority of the "symbolic" metaphor over the "literal", prosaic, metonymy is reasserted in terms of chance and necessity'.[219] Rather: the explanation of metonymy as rooted in semantic fields, established

[216] De Man 1979, 14.

[217] *Inter alia*, the semantic fields of any language at any given time are a necessary given for the individual speaker—regardless of how arbitrary the circumstances of their historical emergence may be.

[218] De Man himself would seem to admit this much when he writes a few pages later: 'The crossing of sensory attributes in synaesthesia is only a special case of a more general pattern of substitution [sic] that *all tropes have in common*. It is the result of an exchange of properties *made possible by a proximity or an analogy so close and intimate* that it allows the one to substitute for the other without revealing the difference necessarily induced by the substitution. The relational link between the two entities involved in the exchange then becomes so strong *that it can be called necessary*' (de Man 1979, 62; italics added).

[219] De Man 1979, 70.

through collocation in ordinary usage, explains why metonymy is associated (by de Man and many others) with 'prose' and at the same time clearly recognized as a trope—a problematic conjunction that haunts many structuralist studies.

In de Man's case, one outcome is the misleading association of synecdoche with metaphor, which he elaborates in some detail. Citing another passage from Proust that includes the metaphorical expressions 'the flies executing their little concert, the chamber music of summer',[220] de Man argues:

> The relational link between the two entities involved in the exchange then becomes so strong that it can be called necessary: there could be no summer without flies, no flies without summer. The 'necessary link' that unites flies and summer is natural, genetic, unbreakable; although the flies are only one minute part of the total event designated by 'summer', they nevertheless partake of its most specific and total essence. The synecdoche that substitutes part for whole and whole for part is in fact a metaphor, powerful enough to transform a temporal contiguity into an infinite duration... Compared to this compelling coherence, the contingency of metonymy based on only the casual encounter of two entities that could very well exist in each other's absence would be entirely devoid of poetic power... [Metonymy] may be able to stimulate memory in a mechanical way, but fails to lead to the totalizing stability of metaphorical processes. If metonymy is distinguished from metaphor in terms of necessity and contingency (an interpretation of the term that is not illegitimate), then metonymy is per definition unable to create genuine links...[221]

One might perhaps be willing to accept (however grudgingly) de Man's 'scandalously loose and slippery'[222] notions of metaphor, metonymy, and synecdoche as specific to his reading of this passage in Proust and grant that, terminological infelicities aside, his remarks have their own merit as aids to interpreting the texts under discussion. But his further comments in a footnote to this passage make clear that he considers that these thoughts have a more general bearing:

> Classical rhetoric generally classifies synecdoche as metonymy, which leads to difficulties characteristic of all attempts at establishing a taxonomy of tropes; tropes are transformational systems rather than grids. The relationship between part and whole can be understood metaphorically, as is the case, for example, in the organic metaphors dear to Goethe. Synecdoche is one of the borderline figures that create an ambivalent zone between metaphor and metonymy and that, by its spatial nature, creates the illusion of a synthesis by totalization.[223]

[220] As cited by de Man 1979, 13. [221] De Man 1979, 62–3.
[222] Barnouw 1982, 460. [223] De Man 1979, 62–3.

What we have here is ultimately a projection of de Man's individual associative readings back onto the primary, rhetorical arena. His remarks on a text's 'metafigural' dimension lead him to redefine 'figures' (*sc.* tropes). Of course, structuralism is based precisely on the premise that comparable structures occur on the various levels of verbal expression as well as in non-linguistic discourse. However, the comparability of structures can only ever be validly assumed if it is supported by analyses on each level (or in each discourse) in its own right. Where reflections on one such order are pitched against others without empirical validation, the fundamental comparability of structures is no longer an intrinsic given but an externally imposed perspective. In this particular case, my structural analysis of synecdoche and metonymy as they occur in poem after poem, passage after passage, points in the exact opposite direction to de Man's.

Although Lodge's contribution to Jakobson-inspired literary scholarship is far less controversial than de Man's, one nevertheless soon encounters similar paradoxes. Lodge explains that his objective is to reconsider 'some fundamental questions of literary theory and critical practice' and to develop 'a comprehensive typology of literary discourse ... capable of describing and discriminating between all types of text without prejudice' by exploring 'a theory of language upon which such a typology may be based—Roman Jakobson's distinction between metaphor and metonymy'.[224] Writing in the 1970s, Lodge can be credited with (and it is one of his main concerns) mediating new critical approaches developed in Russian, Czech, and French literary theory to an initially less than receptive audience in the world of Anglo-Saxon scholarship. The more specific problem he addresses is the question of how to come to terms with 'realism', and in particular with the 'realistic novel', within the framework of essentially formalist criticism.

The most fundamental tenet of formalism (certainly in its Russian heartland) is its characterization of literature as art based on defamiliarized language. Realism, however, defies this definition: it defines itself precisely through its closeness to ordinary, familiar language and aims at concealing its artificiality. If realist literature neither requires suspension of disbelief (criterion of fictionality) nor contains literary devices (criterion of stylization), how can it be understood as 'literature' from a formalist perspective?[225] Lodge points out that texts centred on realist aesthetics nevertheless remain representations of reality and that '[f]or obvious reasons, a verbal text can never be mistaken for the reality it refers to, as

[224] Lodge 1977, ix. [225] See Lodge 1977, 1–71.

an object of visual or plastic art may be mistaken. Writing cannot imitate reality directly (as a film, for instance, can)'.[226] Because the realist text is representational, it is bound to be partial, foregrounding certain aspects over others (through new perspectives, alternative viewpoints, leitmotifs, and so on).[227] This is the point at which Lodge invokes Jakobson, who had postulated (without much explanation) intrinsic connections between metaphor, symbolism, and poetry, as between metonymy, realism, and prose.[228] Based on Jakobson's association of metaphor with the 'selection' axis of language and metonymy with the 'combination' axis of language, Lodge views metonymy as the result of an omission of elements from an extended version of a kernel sentence.[229] Realist literature is deemed to be 'metonymic' because individual elements are chosen over others, which are omitted, and because the text as a whole represents 'a slice of life as it is' but remains recognizable as a 'slice' of a larger totality which it thus invokes.[230] Lodge contrasts this with another 'type' of literature, which operates in the 'metaphorical' mode and is understood as referring to the totality of reality not by representing it selectively but by implying that its discourse relates to it by way of analogy.[231] Moreover, in addition to the way a text relates to referential reality, the way its internal progress is structured is also understood in terms of 'metaphor' and 'metonymy'. Lodge now appeals directly to Jakobson's notion that prose is 'forwarded essentially by contiguity'[232] and claims that linearity of progress is characteristic of prose (and 'metonymic', since it establishes a 'contiguous' line of one thing after the other), whereas poetry establishes relations of similarity between elements through its formal rules (metre, rhyme, stanza, and so on) and is therefore 'metaphorical'.[233]

[226] Lodge 1977, 25. [227] See Lodge 1977, 25 and 40–1.

[228] See Jakobson 1956, 254–5 and 259. For a critique of Jakobson's associative argumentation here, see Silk 2003.

[229] See Lodge 1977, 76.

[230] '[M]etonymy and synecdoche... are transformations of literal kernel sentences produced by a process of combination and nonlogical deletion. This would seem to correspond to what we commonly refer to as a novelist's "selection" of details in narrative description.' Lodge 1977, 93.

[231] A related notion can also be found in de Man, albeit in the context of his 'metafigural' deconstructionism: 'The sheer *metonymic enumeration* of things that Rousseau describes in the Discourse ("if one oak was called A, and another was called B...") is an entirely negative moment that does not describe language as it is or used to be at its inception, but that dialectically infers literal denomination as the negation of language. Denomination could never exist by itself although it is a constitutive part of all linguistic events. All language is language about denomination, that is, a conceptual, figural, *metaphorical metalanguage*.' De Man 1979, 152–3; italics added.

[232] Jakobson 1956, 258.

[233] Lodge 1977, 88. For a critical discussion of the Jakobsonian basis of this proposition, see Silk 2003.

Lodge's answer to the problem realism poses for formalist criticism entails serious complications. First, his notion of 'metonymic' and 'metaphoric' modes of writing suggests that both are options available on the same level. Yet, on reflection, it is clear that the selectiveness ascribed to metonymy is an unavoidable consequence of the representational nature of *all* verbal expression, whereas the presence of an element of analogy is specific only to *certain* verbal expressions. In other words, in one case we are dealing with the fact that something *is* represented (and is therefore inevitably selective: 'metonymic'), in the other with *how* something is represented (by analogy: 'metaphorical'). Lodge himself shows some awareness of these complications when he writes:

> if we interpret the formula . . . to mean simply that contiguity, or context, controls the field of selection, then we have nothing more than a simple description of the way ordinary referential discourse works. This is in fact what we might expect, since literature written in the metonymic mode tends to disguise itself as nonliterature.[234]

Once more we note the recurring tendency to deny metonymy its status as a trope. Lodge tries to get round this awkwardness by arguing that 'metonymic' texts are characterized by a 'systematic internal foregrounding'[235] and that

> [w]riting that emphasizes the differences between things in the world . . . will tend to operate mainly along the axis of combination or contiguity . . . This way of representing reality can be rhetorically heightened by metonymic devices which delete or rearrange contiguous items, and this is the method of realism . . .[236]

Yet this does not resolve the problem but only reformulates it: 'metaphoric texts' are still seen as different *in kind* from ordinary, non-literary texts, 'metonymic texts' as different *in degree*. It is (to say the least) hard to reconcile this essentially a priori notion of the relationship between 'metaphor' and 'metonymy' with the results yielded by my analyses.

In any case, it remains doubtful what, if anything, is gained by appealing to 'metaphor' and 'metonymy' in this way and whether in particular it adds to the precision of our critical apparatus. When Romeo and Juliet argue about whether they heard a lark or a nightingale,[237] they have not suddenly discovered an ornithological interest: what is at issue is whether it is still evening or already morning, and although their conversation makes perfect sense on a literal level, the birds evoke these times of day through metonymic association. This is different in

[234] Lodge 1977, 93. [235] Lodge 1977, 96. [236] Lodge 1977, 132.
[237] Shakespeare, *Romeo and Juliet*, Act 3, Scene 5.

kind from the chorus's assertion in Aeschylus' *Agamemnon* that Helen had 'bequeathed to her people the clang of shields and spears'.[238] The difference lies in the fact that in the Shakespeare the sequence makes sense when taken literally but does not pertain to what really is at issue, whereas in the Aeschylus everything, if taken literally, is both comprehensible and pertinent to what is at issue. Lodge and many other scholars regularly refer to instances of both kinds as 'synecdochic details',[239] but, again, one might ask: given the constraints of selectivity that apply to all representation in verbal expression, can any element of a text ever *not* be a detail? And can any detail ever *not* be 'synecdochic'? It is questionable whether our ability to describe and analyse literary texts gains from this radically extended use of rhetorical terms. Yet even if one is prepared to go along with this mode of commentary, it must be granted that the terminology used blurs the lines between stylistic analysis on the level of poetic idiom and criticism on the level of compositional structure. The outcome is such paradoxical statements as:

> the opening of *A passage to India* is not 'poetic' prose. It is metonymic writing, not metaphoric, even though it contains a few metaphors and no metonymies; it is metonymic in structure, connecting topics on the basis of contiguity not similarity.[240]

Passages like this one demonstrate that Lodge's comments on the text's structure are entirely dissociated from tropological-stylistic analysis, thereby disproving Mosher's view that 'New Criticism, though somewhat maligned of late, is protean and survives apparently either by changing its name—literary stylistics, explication du texte, Structuralism—or by changing its language.'[241] Quite the contrary: Lodge's paradoxical claims suggest that structural analysis and stylistic criticism are actually incommensurable and somewhat incompatible, or at least only tortuously relatable. If this is indeed the case, then it raises the question whether it is really helpful to use the *same* critical term to describe *unrelated* phenomena on *different* levels of analysis. Regardless of the merit or validity of structuralist analyses in their own right (questionable though some may be), and irrespective even of one's definition and understanding of metonymy as a poetic trope, it seems evident that clarity of argument suffers from this way of using critical terminology.

[238] λιποῦσα δ' ἀστοῖσιν ἀσπίστοράς | τε καὶ κλόνους λογχίμους (A. *Agam.* 403–4).
[239] Inspired by Jakobson's comment that the realist author is 'fond of synecdochic detail' (Jakobson 1956, 255).
[240] Lodge 1977, 98–9.
[241] Mosher 1976, 75.

The ensuing obscurity and lack of precision diagnosed here also affect other parts of Lodge's discussion, for instance his reading of Joyce's *A Portrait of the Artist as a Young Man*. Lodge argues that

> in accord with the development of Stephen's romantic, egocentric and literary sensibility, the prose becomes more 'poetic': metaphor is overt, and the progress of the syntagm is deliberately impeded by repetition of key words and elaborate rhythmical patterning...for example...'Her bosom was as a bird's soft and slight, slight and soft as the breast of some darkplumaged dove. But her long hair was girlish: and girlish, and touched with the wonder of mortal beauty, her face.'[242]

One notes immediately that the cited passage does not display a single metaphor—but two similes (as well as chiasmic sentence structure). Of course, if 'metaphor' is equated with all structures based on analogy, the distinction between simile (which explicitly states an analogy) and metaphor (which implies it) becomes irrelevant. However, this distinction is fundamental to metaphor, and if it becomes irrelevant for the purpose of structural analysis, then why not appeal directly to analogy in the first place? At the same time one wonders whether it could not be argued that the repetition of key words in the Joyce emphasizes precisely the continuity of the movement in the passage from one element to the next—which would in that sense make it 'metonymic' rather than 'metaphorical'.

To avoid any misunderstanding: my critique is not meant to suggest that every appeal to metonymy or metaphor beyond stylistic analysis is illegitimate. Lodge himself, as a novelist, offers a more compelling application of the terms. When English literature lecturer Robyn tries to explain to engineer Vic the intricacies of structuralist semiotics in Lodge's comic novel *Nice Work*, she refers to two different types of cigarette advertisements.[243] The brand 'Silk Cut', she explains, operates on the basis of metaphor:

> [S]ilk has nothing to do with tobacco. It's a metaphor, a metaphor that means something like, 'smooth as silk'. Somebody in an advertising agency dreamt up the name 'Silk Cut' to suggest a cigarette that wouldn't give you a sore throat or a hacking cough or lung cancer.[244]

[242] Lodge 1977, 132.

[243] The scene (Lodge 1988, 154–7) is probably the only theoretical discussion of metonymy within a novel and is presumably inspired by Barthes's discussion of an advertisement for 'Panzani' pasta which 'metonymically' connects the product with 'Italianicity': see Barthes 1964.

[244] Lodge 1988, 155.

The advertisements for 'Marlboro' cigarettes, depicting a cowboy smoking in the great outdoors, on the other hand, are described as metonymic:

> The Marlboro ad . . . establishes a metonymic connection—completely spurious of course, but realistically plausible—between smoking that particular brand and the healthy, heroic, outdoor life of the cowboy. Buy the cigarette and you buy the lifestyle, or the fantasy of living it.[245]

It is important to point out that what is described in the metonymy example is the advertising *strategy* rather than the advertisement itself: the image of a smoking cowboy can hardly be deemed 'tropical' (and thus defamiliarizing) in any meaningful way. What happens is that the advertisement *creates* a link of contiguity which is then 'metonymically' exploited. By repeatedly collocating the image of the cowboy with a particular brand of cigarettes on suitable visual sites, the cigarette acquires the potential to evoke the cowboy and his lifestyle 'metonymically'. This example of metonymy as an advertising strategy is particularly interesting because it shows that the principle of collocation in ordinary usage (or ordinary experience) is transferable to other media. One of the familiar charges levelled against structuralism is that its suggestion that 'everything is text' makes it blind to the specific idiosyncrasies of different media.[246] My efforts to determine concretely what 'contiguity' means in a literary context have led us from the theory of semantic fields to the principle of collocation in ordinary usage. It would, no doubt, be worthwhile to attempt to determine the media-specific expression of 'contiguity' in other arts, such as photography, film, and drama. If all art forms can indeed be understood as semiotic systems, it should be possible to find equivalents to ordinary language collocation and to probe whether there, too, deviance from the ordinary collocation can take the form of an explicit or implicit metonymic shift based on such ordinary collocations.

Instead of concerning themselves with the specificities of particular media, however, let alone with comparative scrutiny of more than one, the majority of Jakobson-inspired scholars have adopted his top-down approach. Following Jakobson's association of 'metaphorical' with

[245] Lodge 1988, 157.

[246] It is telling that the most sophisticated debate on this issue has taken place (a generation ago) in the context of film theorists' responses to structuralist notions of 'metaphor' and 'metonymy'. The main point of contention here follows from this medium's seeming ability to reproduce reality without mediation and the complications that arise from this for the notion of a 'language of film', language being obviously and undeniably a mediated form of representation in its own right. A summary of the debate is provided by Nichols 1976a, key contributions are Abramson 1976, Eco 1970, Metz 1964, 1972, and 1973, Nichols 1976b, Pasolini 1965, and Wollen 1969.

'similarity', 'selection', 'paradigm', and 'metonymy' with 'contiguity', 'combination', 'syntagm',[247] structuralist studies tend simply to appeal to these notions as guarantors of a structural comparability of phenomena in different media and discourses. In consequence, they often arrive at hugely disparate conclusions. Take, for instance, two contrasting studies of metonymic and metaphorical structures in drama, by Dévényi and Osterwalder, both of whom accurately reproduce Jakobson's lines of argument and terms of reference.[248] On this basis, Dévényi calls plays 'metonymic' if they can be seen as a dramaturgical expression of an experience through a foregrounded fragment, whereas plays are deemed to be 'metaphorical' if they aim at dramaturgical presentation of an experience in its entirety.[249] Osterwalder, on the other hand, suggests that '[e]very type of parallelism in the structure of a play is metaphoric', whereas, 'In a purely metonymic play the complete absence of structure, of an inner organizing design behind the outward action, would be the most striking characteristic.'[250] Neither of them asks what 'contiguity', as the structural principle of metonymy, might mean in the context of dramaturgy.

Dévényi's study also illustrates once more the undesirable terminological blurriness we have observed in Lodge when she writes that

> [m]etaphor... is dear to Homer... He employs metaphor as the principle of narrative representation (Achilles' revenge precipitates further violence just as it does in the cultural framework of Homer's time) even if his descriptive terms are often metonymic (e.g., Nausikaa of the white arms or Hektor of the shining helmet).[251]

Not only are Dévényi's particular applications of 'metaphor' and 'metonymy' wholly unconvincing; the deployment of parallel critical terms (metaphor and metonymy) on different and unrelated levels (referential reality and poetic idiom) is surely unhelpful; and the resulting opacity is aggravated further by the fact that Jakobson himself had associated the entire epic genre as such with metonymy.[252] Worse still: Dévényi asserts that 'whether dramatic or not, I consider metonymic structures just as poetic as metaphoric structure. As an artistic strategy, metonymy can be as powerful as metaphor can be'[253]—in diametrical opposition to the demonstrable and explicable difference in degree between the poetic potency of metaphor and metonymy as literary tropes.[254]

[247] See Jakobson 1956, 243 and 254.
[248] See Dévényi 1996, 15–18 and Osterwalder 1978, 4–21.
[249] See Dévényi 1996, 15. [250] Osterwalder 1978, 56.
[251] Dévényi 1996, 19. [252] Jakobson 1956, 255. [253] Dévényi 1996, 18.
[254] Compare further both the position developed here and Dévényi's position with the view put forward by Hayward within the context of film studies: 'Metaphors... are very

A more detailed discussion would be needed to do justice to either of these studies, but also to demonstrate their inadequacy in terms of the theory of metonymy put forward here. Yet what emerges, even after such a brief comparison, is the astonishing diversity of definitions of 'metonymy', implicit or explicit, in studies that invoke 'metonymy' as a structural principle. To put it bluntly: while it is just possible to formulate a general principle behind the traditional stock examples given for metonymy in ancient rhetorical treatises, it is often virtually impossible to deduce any one structural principle from a set of structuralist studies that appeal to it;[255] and, to make it worse, most do not even feel the need to make their own definition of metonymy explicit—owing to the term's widespread use in contemporary critical literature.

It is true that metaphor has an important heuristic function in the creation of knowledge, and (to restate the point) my critique here is far from implying that 'metonymy' cannot or should not be used 'metaphorically' as an analytical tool to describe underlying structures. The potential benefit of such technical metaphors, however, lies in the fact that they enable us to address what is new, unfamiliar ,and opaque through a framework of familiar, well-defined, and well-understood terms and concepts.[256] As soon as one employs a technical metaphor that draws on an ill-defined term, any hermeneutic benefit vanishes. It would seem that the fate of metonymy in many of its structuralist reappropriations has been shaped not only by Jakobson's free associations in his seminal essay, but also by his teacher Peškovsky's dictum, cited approvingly by Jakobson: 'Let's not quibble about terminology...

visible, they draw attention to themselves. Metonyms are not. And this is why the two terms can be seen as two sides of the same coin. Metaphors render the unknown visible... Metonyms represent what is absent' (Hayward 2006, 251–2). The first proposition here directly contradicts Dévényi's position, the second is so narrow that it only captures a fraction of the actual function and potential of either metaphor or metonymy in poetic language, and misrepresents the relationship between the two tropes.

[255] One extreme example within one single work: in his attempt to develop a 'tropology of discourse', White associates tropes with general modes of experience as well as specific modes of emplotment, argument, and ideological implication and cites representative historians and philosophers for each tropological type of discourse. In his scheme, metaphorical discourse, represented by Michelet and Nietzsche, is said to be representational, Romantic, 'formist', and anarchistic; metonymic discourse, represented by Tocqueville and Marx, is reductionist, tragic, mechanist, and radical; synecdoche, represented by Ranke and Hegel, is integrative, comic, organicist, and conservative (see White 1973, 1–42). One is hard-pressed to formulate the shared structural principle that lies behind the members of each list, let alone to connect them in a meaningful way to my (or even any) understanding of metaphor and metonymy as literary tropes, either individually or in their relationship to each other.

[256] See, for instance, Blumenberg 1960, Jones 1982, Stambovsky 1988, and Haverkamp-Mende 2009.

You may even call it "Ivan Ivanovich" so long as we all know what you mean.'[257] While some structuralist studies may well make illuminating observations about their respective objects by elaborating patterns then referred to as 'metonymic', significant problems at once arise for interdisciplinary dialogue and criticism. Already this brief discussion of just a few representative cases illustrates how easily a sensible-sounding appeal to metonymy achieves nothing but confusion in the event. The central purpose and objective of the 'semiotic turn' (with its focus on structures that transcend any one medium, culture, language, or form of expression) is seriously undermined by this lack of consistency and clarity regarding one of its fundamental points of reference: metonymy.

[257] Jakobson 1953, 557.

5 Conclusion

The chief deficiency of earlier attempts to theorize metonymy has been their recurrent failure to formulate a single, unifying principle behind metonymy. As the Groupe μ correctly notes, 'ancient rhetoric was unable to formulate a satisfactory definition of metonymy, the majority of treatises contenting themselves with enumerating different types'.[1] Landfester explains that the underlying problem is structural: 'metonymy is the trope with the most variants; these often come with their own names, which prevent the recognition of the inner relatedness of these variants'.[2] I have approached this issue by revisiting the concept of 'contiguity', which, under various names and forms, has long been suggested as a potential principle of metonymy but has rarely found explicit discussion and concrete definition.[3] In order to do justice to metonymy as a phenomenon of poetic language, I have redefined contiguity as lexical contiguity and drawn on semantic-field theory to define metonymy as, precisely, a shift within a semantic field. This definition has two special advantages: first, it allows us to explain metonymy in both its unity and its diversity; secondly, it allows us to establish the relationship of metonymy to metaphor and to explain the respective differences in their poetic effect. I have defined semantic fields (pragmatically) as consisting of the terms that are collocatable with a given term in ordinary usage. The assessment of different forms of metonymy has indicated that the characteristic metonymic shift within a semantic field can be realized in two ways: either explicitly, by the reorganization, within a syntactic unit, of terms that are otherwise collocatable in ordinary usage (amplification metonymy, grammatical amplification metonymy); or implicitly, by the effective requirement to infer a term from the semantic field (index metonymy, grammatical index metonymy, metonymy by association). The principle of lexical contiguity thus enables us simultaneously (*a*) to demonstrate the intrinsic connectedness of a number of tropes (metonymy, enallage, synecdoche) through their

[1] '[L]a rhétorique ancienne a été incapable de formuler une définition satisfaisante de la métonymie, la plupart des traités se contentant d'en énumérer les espèces.' Groupe μ 1982, 117.

[2] 'Die Metonymie ist der Tropus mit den meisten Formen; diese haben häufig eigene Namen, die verhindern, die innere Zusammengehörigkeit dieser Formen zu erkennen.' Landfester 1997, 92.

[3] Cf. pertinently Allan 2008, 12.

shared structural principle, and (*b*) to trace their differences in structure and effect to alternative grammatical realizations of the metonymic shift and to explicit or implicit action. Moreover, on this basis, we can also explain and assess the aesthetic impact of the various forms of metonymy, both relative to each other and to metaphor.

If, with Shklovsky, we take defamiliarization to be the hallmark of poeticity (or, more cautiously, of poetic language), then it follows that the more an expression deviates from ordinary usage, the greater its prospective poetic effect (in formal-aesthetic terms). Metonymy's basis in pre-existing links established *through* ordinary usage necessarily limits its potential to deviate *from* ordinary usage. My analyses suggest that where metonymy creates significant effects, these are rarely caused by the primary effect of the metonymic shift itself, but instead stem from the interaction of the metonym with its context. It is on this interface that terminological interaction occurs. In metaphor, on the other hand, the underlying principle of analogy and similarity calls forth extraneous terminology and a terminological clash *within* the trope itself, prior and in addition to further terminological interaction with the context. It is for these structural reasons that metaphor's potential to create startling terminological juxtapositions is higher than metonymy's.[4] The fact that metonymy has received so little scholarly attention and is so frequently dismissed as a 'lesser form of metaphor' is surely a consequence of its basis in lexis rather than logic—which fails to excite critics trained in Aristotelian rationalism or in (neo-)Romantic aesthetics.[5]

The study of metonymy in translation confirmed this emerging picture: metonymy can produce striking effects, but its overwhelming usage is of a refined or restricted kind. The pattern is one of relatively few intense outcomes, and relatively many less intense ones. Given the difference in the degree of poetic intensity between metonyms and metaphors due to their differences in terminological interaction (which

[4] See also above, pp. 52–3 and 139–40.

[5] Despite their fundamental differences, both these major traditions of Western criticism share an admiration for the analogy principle at the heart of metaphor. While Aristotle made this explicit in a famous passage in his *Poetics* (Arist. *Poet.* 1459a5–8), more recent scholars have argued (along Jakobsonian lines) that '[a]nalogical thinking was dear to Hölderlin... and to the Romantic writers generally; it was their characteristic mode of thought' (Louth 1998, 3); see also Abrams 1953, 47–69. In any case, the argument advanced here is surely more to the point than the alleged lack of a specific critical language necessary to discuss metonymy (so Jakobson 1956, 258) or the self-contradictory assertion that easily decipherable 'metonyms' frequently occur in ordinary language (see Martin 1993, 783); the notion that 'metonymies are common in ordinary usage' (ibid.) is in itself nonsensical: whatever is common in ordinary usage is by definition not tropical and therefore *a fortiori* not pertinent to an understanding of the trope metonymy.

are themselves a result of a fundamental difference in their respective governing core principles), it is now apparent why metonymy should have featured in literary scholarship for so long as 'the forgotten trope'. This is surely the true explanation for the lack of attention given to metonymy—this, and not (for instance) Jakobson's homoeopathic suggestion that the 'meta-language' of criticism is inherently metaphorical, so that critics are only equipped to interpret metaphors but have no adequate means to come to terms with metonyms.[6]

Explaining how metonymy came to be 'the forgotten trope' is important. More important still, however, are the consequences for critical practice and future research that can be drawn from its tropological rediscovery offered here. My study of metonymy was in part motivated by the wish to offer a reappraisal of descriptive poetics as an insightful perspective and productive methodology for literary studies. The results yielded by this approach, namely the theoretical framework and the categories of metonymy established on this basis, vindicate my advocacy for this methodology since both proved to be of great value for small-scale stylistic criticism as well as large-scale structuralist analyses. As the discussion of a wide range of sample passages throughout this book has richly illustrated, a finely tuned critical apparatus is a key prerequisite for a nuanced appreciation and critical discussion of the formal-aesthetic dynamics and stylistic idiosyncrasies of literary texts. Due to metonymy's (often) less eye-catching poetic effects, its (equally often) crucial contributions to the creation and sustainment of complex imagery are all too frequently overlooked in the close reading of individual texts. A lack of awareness and sensitivity for metonymic elements means losing sight of an entire layer of textual dynamics. The consequences of such oversights, though in any case regrettable, compound further when it comes to making broader literary-aesthetic claims, for instance about the characteristic use of poetic language in certain authors, periods, or genres, either in their own right or in comparison with one another. As the discussion of personification and synecdoche has shown, the perception of similarities and differences between authors in their use of poetic language is likely to be significantly skewed and obfuscated when commentary on their use of the same *terminology* is confused with commentary on

[6] 'Similarity in meaning connects the symbols of a metalanguage with the symbols of the language referred to. Similarity connects a metaphorical term with the term for which it is substituted. Consequently, when constructing a metalanguage to interpret tropes, the researcher possesses more homogeneous means to handle metaphor, whereas metonymy, based on a different principle, easily defies interpretation. Therefore nothing comparable to the rich literature on metaphor can be cited for the theory of metonymy.' Jakobson 1956, 258.

their use of the same *poetic devices*. What holds true for the comparison of the style of different authors also applies to the evaluation of stylistic tendencies in literary movements or traditions. Does metonymy feature more prominently in Latin than in Greek literature?[7] Does metaphor dominate Romantic poetry,[8] while metonymy gains popularity in modernist and postmodern poetry?[9] Such questions are immensely interesting and hold a significant potential to develop the genuinely *literary* dimension of our accounts of literary history. Yet all claims of this sort require validation and substantiation, no matter how *prima facie* plausible they may seem, which can only be achieved through the evaluation of representative samples of literary material and not (or at least not only, and certainly not primarily) through cultural-historical explanations. Such evaluations, however, require a clear understanding of both of these tropes in their respective core principles and different conformations in the first place. Thus, whichever dimension of literary style a discussion may be focusing on, the general theory and typology of metonymy offered here makes it possible to conduct text-/author-/genre-/period-specific tropological analyses and evaluations with much greater insight and precision.

The disadvantages and risks associated with limitations in perceptiveness and imprecisions in analysis that beset stylistic criticism powerfully reoccur in (post-)structuralist appeals to metonymy that are equally insufficiently grounded in a sound understanding of metonymy as a literary trope—again with the consequence of an impairment or downright loss of comparability. The almost total separation of (post-)structuralist applications, appropriations and (re-)conceptualizations of the term 'metonymy' from *actual* metonyms in poetic action (and their description and theorization in literary stylistics) following Jakobson's momentous extension of 'metaphor' and 'metonymy' beyond their original context in poetics and rhetoric has resulted in a progressive 'incomparability creep': as my critical re-examination of some (post-)structuralist reappropriations of 'metonymy' in the light of the insights gained over the course of this study has shown, the continued absence of a sound, reliable point of reference for such studies has led to a highly problematic vagueness and

[7] 'In some of the best ancient literature, however, metaphor and simile are not predominant. In particular, the most characteristic tropical movements in much Latin poetry and literary prose involve not metaphor but metonymy. . . '. Silk 2012, 941.

[8] As the predilection of Romantic writers for analogy, noted by Louth, might seem to suggest; see Louth 1998, 3.

[9] 'Modernists (and even more pronouncedly, contemporary Postmodernists) tend to use metonymy rather than metaphor because metonymy allows them to deconstruct experience horizontally through paratactic and horizontal juxtaposition.' Gelpi 1998, 116.

slippage in the use of a central critical concept and term that now enjoys currency in a wide range of disciplines across (and beyond) the humanities. The new theory of metonymy advanced here can help to support best practice in transdisciplinary structuralist scholarship and inter-arts criticism by (re-)establishing comparability of 'metonymic' phenomena, both verbal and non-verbal. Inter-arts criticism has particularly much to gain from the reflections on contiguity as metonymy's core principle offered here. If metonymy as a *literary* trope, realized in the medium of *language*, is to be understood as operative on the basis of *lexical* contiguity, then what are the media-specific expression of 'contiguity' that might give rise to metonymy in other arts, such as photography, film, and drama? Following on from one of the key tenets of structuralism, namely that all art forms can be understood as semiotic systems, it should be possible to find equivalents to ordinary language collocation in media other than language, and to probe whether there, too, deviance from the ordinary collocation can take the form of an explicit or implicit metonymic shift based on such ordinary collocations. Investigations along these lines would put discussions of metonymy in the various visual and performance arts on a much sounder footing and would allow for the comparative study of the various expressions metonymy takes in different media, both in general and in particular cases. Taking the reflections offered in the present study further, such investigations would open up highly promising avenues of intermedial translation studies that would be sensitive not just to the treatment of themes and representations of contents in different media, but also to strategies of converting, imitating, and responding to media-specific artistic devices and defamiliarization strategies.

My explorations in translation criticism from a tropological perspective have, likewise, only scratched the surface of this field. Much awaits further investigation. There seems, for instance, to be no comparable study of how metaphor fares in literary translations. On the basis of such a study, it would be interesting to analyse how metaphor and metonymy fare relative to each other: how does the 'survival rate' of metaphors and metonyms in individual translations and/or translators compare? Likewise, in the general context of translations and translation strategy, one might well ponder how the translating of metaphors and metonyms relates to and is interlinked with other outcomes of domestication or foreignization, such as modifications of syntax and vocabulary, explanatory paraphrase, word order, and so on.

Rethinking metonymy thus gives rise to far-reaching (re-)considerations in several fields of literary scholarship and beyond. Metonymy may not embody the logical 'genius' or the terminological 'sparkle' of metaphor, but its greater subtlety and closer connection to ordinary usage make for a strikingly frequent employment in literary texts and a stylistic impact that is far from negligible. Whether in stylistic analysis, translation criticism, or structuralist studies, we need a sound understanding of this forgotten trope before we can appeal to it—whether literally or even 'metaphorically'.

BIBLIOGRAPHY

Lexica

Authenried, G. and Kaegi, A. (1999) *Wörterbuch zu den Homerischen Gedichten*. 13th edn. (Leipzig: Teubner)

Bonitz, H. (1870) *Index Aristotelicus*. (Berlin: Reimer)

Buck, C. D. and Petersen, W. (1945) *A Reverse Index of Greek Nouns and Adjectives: Arranged by Terminations with Brief Historical Introduction*. (Chicago: University of Chicago Press)

Chantraine, P. (1968) *Dictionnaire étymologique de la langue grecque: Histoire des mots*. (Paris: Klincksieck)

Dindorf, G. et al. (1831–65) *Thesaurus Linguae Graecae*. 3rd edn. (Paris: Didot)

Ebeling, H. (1885) *Lexicon Homericum*. (Leipzig: Teubner)

Frisk, J. I. H. (1960–72) *Griechisches etymologisches Wörterbuch*. (Heidelberg: Winter)

Kretschmer, P. and Locker, E. (1963) *Rückläufiges Wörterbuch der griechischen Sprache*. (Göttingen: Vandenhoeck & Ruprecht)

Kühn, J.-H. and Fleischer, U. (1986) *Index Hippocraticus*. (Göttingen: Vandenhoeck & Ruprecht)

LSJ. Liddell, H. G. and Scott, R. (1996) *A Greek–English Lexicon*. 9th edn. (Oxford: Clarendon Press)

Slater, W. J. (1969) *Lexicon to Pindar*. (Berlin: de Gruyter)

TLG. Pantelia, M. et al. *Thesaurus Linguae Graecae: A Digital Library of Greek Literature*. <http://www.tlg.uci.edu> [last accessed: 06/11/2015]

Text editions and translations

Aeschylus. *Oresteia: Agamemnon. Libation-Bearers. Eumenides*. Ed. and trans. A. H. Sommerstein. (Cambridge, MA: Harvard University Press, 2008)

Aeschylus. *Persians. Seven Against Thebes. Suppliants. Prometheus Bound*. Ed. and trans. A. H. Sommerstein. (Cambridge, MA: Harvard University Press, 2008)

Aeschylus. *Persians and Other Plays*. Trans. C. Collard. (Oxford: Oxford University Press, 2008)

Aeschylus. *Septem quae supersunt tragoedias*. Ed. D. Page. (Oxford: Clarendon Press, 1972)

Aeschylus. *Suppliant Maidens. Persians. Prometheus. Seven Against Thebes*. Ed. and trans. H. W. Smyth. (Cambridge, MA: Harvard University Press, 1922)

Anthologia Lyrica Graeca. Ed. E. Diehl. 2 vols, vol. ii: *Poeta Melici: Chori, Peplus Aristotelicus, Scolia, Carmina Popularia, Poetae Alexandrini*. (Leipzig: Teubner, 1925)

Anthologie Grecque. Première partie: Anthologie Palatine. Ed. P. Waltz, trans. G. Soury. 13 vols, vol. vii: *Livre IX.* (Paris: Les Belles Lettres, 2002)

Aristophanes. *Fabulae.* Ed. N. G. Wilson. 2 vols., vol. i: *Acharnenses, Equites, Nubes, Vespae, Pax, Aves.* (Oxford: Clarendon Press, 2007)

Aristotle. *Historia Animalium.* Ed. and trans. A. L. Peck. (Cambridge, MA: Harvard University Press, 1970)

Aristotle. *Historia Animalium.* Ed. D. M. Balme and A. Gotthelf. 2 vols, vol. i: *Books I–X. Text.* (Cambridge: Cambridge University Press, 2003)

Browning, Robert. *The Agamemnon of Aeschylus.* (London: Smith-Elder, 1877)

Droysen, Johann Gustav. *Des Aischylos Werke.* 2 vols, vol. i. (Berlin: Finke, 1832)

Euripides. *Bacchae, Iphigenia at Aulis, Rhesus.* Ed. and trans. D. Kovacs. (Cambridge, MA: Harvard University Press, 2002)

Euripides. *Fabulae.* Ed. J. Diggle. 3 vols, vol. ii: *Supplices, Electra, Hercules, Troades, Iphigenia in Tauris, Ion.* (Oxford: Clarendon Press, 1982)

Euripides. *Fabulae.* Ed. J. Diggle. 3 vols., vol. iii: *Helena, Phoenissae, Orestes, Bacchae, Iphigenia Aulidensis, Rhesus.* (Oxford: Clarendon Press, 1994)

Euripides. *Trojan Women, Iphigenia among the Taurians, Ion.* Ed. and trans. D. Kovacs. (Cambridge, MA: Harvard University Press, 1999)

Goethe, Johann Wolfgang von. *Sämtliche Werke.* Ed. K. Eibl. 40 vols, vol. i: *Gedichte. 1756–1799.* (Frankfurt am Main: Deutscher Klassiker Verlag, 1987)

Goethe, Johann Wolfgang von. *Sämtliche Werke.* Ed. D. Borchmeyer. 40 vols, vol. v: *Iphigenie auf Tauris. Egmont. Torquato Tasso. Dramen 1776–1790.* (Frankfurt am Main: Deutscher Klassiker Verlag, 1988)

The Greek Anthology. Ed. and trans. W. R. Paton. 5 vols, vol. iii. (London: Heinemann, 1915)

Hesiod. *Theogonia, Opera et dies, Scutum.* Ed. F. Solmsen. 2nd edn. (Oxford: Clarendon Press, 1983)

Hesiod. *Theogony and Works and Days.* Trans. C. M. Schlegel and H. Weinfield. (Ann Arbor, MI: Michigan University Press, 2006)

Hippocrates. *Ancient Medicine, Airs-Waters-Places, Epidemics I and III, The Oath, Precepts.* Ed. and trans. W. H. S. Jones. (Cambridge, MA: Harvard University Press, 1923)

Hippocrates. *Des lieux dans l'homme, Du système des glandes, Des fistules, Des hémorroïdes, De la vision, Des chais, De la dentition.* Ed. and trans. R. Joly. (Paris: Les Belles Lettres, 1978)

Hippocrates. *Des vents. De L'art.* Ed. and trans. J. Jouanna. (Paris: Les Belles Lettres, 1988)

Hippocrates. *La maladie sacrée.* Ed. and trans. J. Jouanna. (Paris: Les Belles Lettres, 2003)

Hippocrates. *Places in Man, Glands, Fleshes, Prorrhetic, Physician, Use of Liquids, Ulcers, Haemorrhoids, Fistulas.* Ed. and trans. P. Potter. (Cambridge, MA: Harvard University Press, 1995)

Hölderlin, Friedrich. *Sämtliche Werke. Frankfurter Ausgabe*. Ed. D. E. Sattler. 20 vols, vol. xv: *Pindar*. (Frankfurt am Main: Stroemfeld/Roter Stern, 1987)

Hölderlin, Friedrich. *Sämtliche Werke. Frankfurter Ausgabe*. Ed. D. E. Sattler. 20 vols, vol. xvi: *Sophokles*. (Frankfurt am Main: Stroemfeld/Roter Stern, 1988)

Hölderlin, Friedrich. *Sämtliche Werke und Briefe*. Ed. J. Schmidt. 3 vols, vol. i: *Friedrich Hölderlin, Gedichte*. (Frankfurt am Main: Deutscher Klassiker Verlag, 1992)

Hölderlin, Friedrich. *Hölderlin's Sophocles. Oedipus & Antigone*. Trans. D. Constantine. (Tarset: Bloodaxe, 2001)

Homer. *Iliad*. Ed. and trans. A. T. Murray and W. F. Wyatt. 2nd edn. (Cambridge, MA: Harvard University Press, 1999)

Homer. *Odyssey*. Ed. and trans. A. T. Murray and G. E. Dimock. 2nd edn. (Cambridge, MA: Harvard University Press, 1995)

Homer. *Opera*. Ed. D. B. Monro and T. W. Allen. 3rd edn. (Oxford: Clarendon Press, 1920)

The Homeric Hymns. Trans. S. C. Shelmerdine. (Newburyport, MA: Focus, 1995)

Homeric Hymns, Homeric Apocrypha, Lives of Homer. Ed. and trans. M. L. West. (Cambridge, MA: Harvard University Press, 2003)

Housman, Alfred Edward. 'Fragment of a Greek Tragedy', *The Bromsgrovian* 2.5 (1883), 107–9

Humboldt, Wilhelm von. *Aeschylos Agamemnon: Metrisch übersetzt*. (Leipzig: Fleischer, 1816)

Jenisch, Daniel. *Agamemnon: Ein Trauerspiel des Aeschylus. Aus dem Griechischen rythmisch übersetzt und mit erläuternden Anmerkungen begleitet*. (Berlin: de Lagarde & Friedrich, 1786)

Manetho. *Apotelesmaticorum qui feruntur libri iv*. Ed. A. Koechly. (Leipzig: Teubner, 1858)

Orpheus. *Hymni*. Ed. W. Quandt. (Zurich: Weidmann, 1941)

Pindar. *Carmina cum fragmentis*. Ed. C. M. Bowra. 2nd edn. (Oxford: Clarendon Press, 1947)

Pindar. *Carmina cum fragmentis*. Ed. A. Turyn. (Oxford: Blackwell, 1952)

Pindar. *Carmina cum fragmentis. Pars I: Epinicia*. Ed. B. Snell and H. Maehler. (Teubner: Leipzig, 1987)

Pindar. *Carmina cum fragmentis. Pars II: Fragmenta, Indices*. Ed. B. Snell and H. Maehler. (Teubner: Leipzig, 1989)

Pindar. *Nemean Odes. Isthmian Odes. Fragments*. Ed. and trans. W. H. Race. (Cambridge, MA: Harvard University Press, 1997)

Pindar. *Olympian Odes, Pythian Odes*. Ed. and trans. W. H. Race. (Cambridge, MA: Harvard University Press, 1997)

Pindar. *Pythiques*. Ed. and trans. A. Puech. (Paris: Les Belles Lettres, 1951)

Plato. *Euthyphro, Apologia, Crito, Phaedo, Cratylus, Theaetetus, Sophista, Politicus*. Ed. E. A. Duke et al. (Oxford: Clarendon Press, 1995)

Plato. *Theaetetus. Sophist.* Ed. and trans. H. N. Fowler. (Cambridge, MA: Harvard University Press, 1921)

Poetae Melici Graeci (= PMG). Ed. D. L. Page. (Oxford: Clarendon Press, 1962)

Schiller, Friedrich. *Werke und Briefe.* Ed. M. Luserke. 12 vols, vol. v: *Dramen IV: Maria Stuart, Die Jungfrau von Orleans, Die Braut von Messina, Wilhelm Tell, Die Huldigung der Künste.* (Frankfurt am Main: Deutscher Klassiker Verlag, 1996)

Schiller, Friedrich. *Werke und Briefe.* Ed. F. Stock. 12 vols, vol. iv: *Dramen III: Wallenstein.* (Frankfurt am Main: Deutscher Klassiker Verlag, 2000)

Sidney, Sir Philip. *The Poems of Sir Philip Sidney.* Ed. W. A. Ringer Jr. (Oxford: Clarendon Press, 1962)

Sophocles. *Ajax. Electra. Oedipus Tyrannus.* Ed. and trans. H. Lloyd-Jones. (Cambridge, MA: Harvard University Press, 1994)

Sophocles. *Antigone. The Women of Trachis. Philoctetes. Oedipus at Colonus.* Ed. and trans. H. Lloyd-Jones. (Cambridge, MA: Harvard University Press, 1994)

Sophocles. *Fabulae.* Ed. H. Lloyd-Jones and N. G. Wilson. (Oxford: Clarendon Press, 1990)

Sophocles. *Fragments.* Ed. and trans. H. Lloyd-Jones. (Cambridge, MA: Harvard University Press, 1996)

Thucydides. *Historiae.* Ed. H. S. Jones and J. E. Powell. (Oxford: Clarendon Press, 1942)

Wilamowitz-Möllendorff, Ulrich von. *Griechische Tragödien.* 14 vols, vol. ii: *Orestie.* (Berlin: Weidmann, 1900)

Ancient criticism and scholia

Alexander. *De Figuris*, in *Rhetores Graeci.* Ed. L. Spengel. 3 vols, vol. iii. (Leipzig: Teubner, 1856)

Anonymus. *De Figuris*, in *Rhetores Graeci.* Ed. L. Spengel. 3 vols, vol. iii. (Leipzig: Teubner, 1856)

Apollonius Dyscolus. *De Pronominibus*, in *Grammatici Graeci.* Ed. R. Schneider and G. Uhlig. 4 vols, vol. ii.1. (Leipzig: Teubner, 1878)

Aristotle. *Ars rhetorica.* Ed. W. D. Ross. (Oxford: Clarendon Press, 1959)

Aristotle. *De arte poetica liber.* Ed. I. Bywater. 2nd edn. (Oxford: Clarendon Press, 1958)

Aristotle. *The Poetics of Aristotle: Translation and Commentary.* Trans. S. Halliwell. (London: Duckworth, 1987)

Aristotle. *On Rhetoric: A Theory of Civic Discourse.* Trans. G. A. Kennedy. (Oxford: Oxford University Press, 2007)

Auctor ad Herennium. *De ratione dicendi (Rhetorica ad Herennium).* Ed. and trans. H. Caplan. (Cambridge, MA: Harvard University Press, 1954)

Cicero. *Brutus. Orator.* Ed. and trans. G. L. Hendrickson and H. M. Hubbell. (Cambridge, MA: Harvard University Press, 1952)

Cicero. *On the Ideal Orator.* Trans. J. M. May and J. Wisse. (Oxford: Oxford University Press, 2001)

Cicero. *Rhetorica. Tomus I: Libri de oratore tres.* Ed. A. S. Wilkins. (Oxford: Clarendon Press, 1951)

Cicero. *Rhetorica. Tomus II: Brutus, Orator, De optimo genere oratorum, Partitiones oratoriae, Topica.* Ed. A. S. Wilkins. (Oxford: Clarendon Press, 1950)

Hippocrates. *Testimonien zum Corpus Hippocraticum.* Ed. A. Anastassiou and D. Irmer. 2 vols, vol. i: *Nachleben der hippokratischen Schriften bis zum 3. Jahrhundert n. Chr.* (Göttingen: Vandenhoeck & Ruprecht, 2006)

Incerti auctoris. *De ratione dicendi ad C. Herennium libri quattuor.* Ed. F. Marx. (Leipzig: Teubner, 1964)

Quintilian. *Institutionis oratoriae libri duodecim.* Ed. M. Winterbottom. (Oxford: Clarendon Press, 1970)

Quintilian. *The Orator's Education.* Ed. and trans. D. A. Russell. (Cambridge, MA: Harvard University Press, 2001)

Trypho. *De Tropis*, in *Rhetores Graeci.* Ed. L. Spengel. 3 vols, vol. iii. (Leizpig: Teubner, 1856)

Zonaeus. *De Figuris*, in *Rhetores Graeci.* Ed. L. Spengel. 3 vols, vol. iii. (Leipzig: Teubner, 1856)

Commentaries

Denniston, J. D. and Page, D. (1957) *Aeschylus' Agamemnon.* (Oxford: Clarendon Press)

Dodds, E. R. (1960) *Euripides' Bacchae.* 2nd edn. (Oxford: Clarendon Press)

Douglas, A. E. (1966) *M. Tulli Ciceronis Brutus* (Oxford: Oxford University Press)

Farnell, L. R. (1932) *The Works of Pindar.* (London: Macmillan)

Fraenkel, E. (1950) *Agamemnon.* 3 vols. (Oxford: Clarendon Press)

Gentili, B. et al. (1995) *Pindaro. Le Pitiche.* (Milan: Mondadori)

Gerber, D. E. (1982) *Pindar's Olympian One: A Commentary.* (Toronto: University of Toronto Press)

Gildersleeve, B. L. (1885) *Pindar: The Olympian and Pythian Odes.* (New York, NY: American Book Company)

Griffith, M. (1999) *Sophocles. Antigone.* (Cambridge: Cambridge University Press)

Groeneboom, P. (1966) *Aeschylus' Agamemnon.* (Amsterdam: Hakkert)

Jebb, R. C. (1896) *Sophocles: The Plays and Fragments. Part VII: The Ajax.* (Cambridge: Cambridge University Press)

Jebb, R. (1900) *Sophocles: The Plays and Fragments. Part III: Antigone.* (Cambridge: Cambridge University Press)

Kamerbeek, J. C. (1978) *The Plays of Sophocles. Part III: The Antigone.* (Leiden: Brill)

Mankin, D. (2011) *Cicero, De Oratore. Book III.* (Cambridge: Cambridge University Press)

Müller, G. (1969) *Sophokles, Antigone.* (Heidelberg: Winter)

Pearson, A. C. (1957) *The Ajax of Sophocles.* (Cambridge: Cambridge University Press)

Stanford, W. B. (1963) *Sophocles' Ajax.* (London: Macmillan)

Verrall, A. W. (1904) *The 'Agamemnon' of Aeschylus.* 2nd edn. (London: Macmillan)

West, M. L. (1966) *Hesiod, Theogony.* (Oxford: Clarendon Press)

West, M. L. (1978) *Hesiod, Works and Days.* (Oxford: Clarendon Press)

Secondary literature

Abrams, H. (1953) *The Mirror and the Lamp: Romantic Theory and the Critical Tradition.* (Oxford: Oxford University Press)

Abramson, R. (1976) 'Structure and Meaning in the Cinema', *Movies and Methods: An Anthology.* Ed. B. Nichols. 2 vols., vol. i. (Berkeley, CA: University of California Press), 558–68

Alexieva, B. and Petrequin, S. (2000) 'Birds: Metaphor and Metonymy in Translating Children's Books', *Across Languages and Cultures* 1.1, 29–48

Allan, K. (2008) *Metaphor and Metonymy: A Diachronic Approach.* (Chichester: Wiley-Blackwell)

Apel, F. and Kopetzki, N. (2003) *Literarische Übersetzung.* 2nd rev. edn. (Stuttgart: Metzler)

Bakhtin, M. M. and Medvedev, P. N. (1928) *The Formal Method in Literary Scholarship: A Critical Introduction to Sociological Poetics.* Trans. A. J. Wehrle. (Baltimore: Johns Hopkins University Press, 1978)

Barcelona, A. (ed.) (2000) *Metaphor and Metonymy at the Crossroads: A Cognitive Perspective* (Berlin: De Gruyter)

Barnouw, J. (1982) 'Review: De Man, *Allegories of Reading*', *Comparative Literary Studies* 19, 459–46

Barthes, R. (1964) 'Rhetoric of the Image', *Roland Barthes: Image, Music, Text.* Ed. and trans. S. Heath. (New York, NY: Hill and Wang, 1977), 32–51

Barwick, L. (1957) *Probleme der stoischen Sprachlehre und Rhetorik.* (Berlin: Akademie Verlag)

Benjamin, W. (1923) 'The Task of the Translator: An Introduction to the Translation of Baudelaire's *Tableaux Parisiens*', *The Translation Studies Reader.* Ed. L. Venuti, trans. H. Zohn. (London: Routledge, 2000), 15–25

Bernofsky, S. (2005a) 'What Did Don Quixote Have for Supper? Translation and Cultural Mediation in Eighteenth-Century Germany', *Monatshefte* 97.1, 1–17

Bernofsky, S. (2005b) *Foreign Words: Translator-Authors in the Age of Goethe.* (Detroit, MI: Wayne State University Press)

Bers, V. (1974) *Enallage and Greek Style.* (Leiden: Brill)

Bers, V. (2000) 'Review: David R. Slavitt (trans.), *Aeschylus, 1: The Oresteia.* Philadelphia: University of Pennsylvania Press, 1998', *Bryn Mawr Classical Review* 10.6, <http://bmcr.brynmawr.edu/2000/2000-10-06.html> [last accessed: 06/11/2015]

Bierwiaczonek, B. (2012) *Metonymy in Language, Thought and Brain* (Sheffield: Equinox)

Black, M. (1962) *Models and Metaphors: Studies in Language and Philosophy.* (Ithaca, NY: Cornell University Press)

Blumenberg, H. (1960) 'Paradigmen zu einer Metaphorologie', *Archiv für Begriffsgeschichte* 6, 7–142

Bohn, W. (1984) 'Roman Jakobson's Theory of Metaphor and Metonymy: An Annotated Bibliography', *Style* 18.4, 534–50

Bowra, C. M. (1964) *Pindar.* (Oxford: Clarendon Press)

Bredin, H. (1984) 'Metonymy', *Poetics* 5.1, 45–58

Breitenbach, W. (1934) *Untersuchungen zur Sprache der euripideischen Lyrik.* (Stuttgart: Kohlhammer)

Bright, T. (1586) *A Treatise of Melancholie.* (London: Thomas Vautrollier)

Brooke-Rose, C. (1958) *A Grammar of Metaphor.* (London: Secker & Warburg)

Budelmann, F. (2000) *The Language of Sophocles: Communality, Communication and Involvement.* (Cambridge: Cambridge University Press)

Burke, K. (1941) 'Four Master Tropes', *The Kenyon Review* 3.4, 421–38

Burke, K. (1945) *A Grammar of Motives.* (New York, NY: Prentice Hall)

Burton, R. W. B. (1980) *The Chorus in Sophocles' Tragedies.* (Oxford: Clarendon Press)

Catford, J. C. (1965) *A Linguistic Theory of Translation.* (London: Oxford University Press)

Clark, R. T. (1937) 'The Union of the Arts in *Die Braut von Messina*', *PMLA* 52.4, 1135–46

Clary, T. (2009) *Rhetoric and Repetition: The Figura Etymologica in Homeric Epic.* (unpublished PhD thesis, Cornell)

Cohen, J. (1966) *Structure du langage poétique.* (Paris: Flammarion)

Coleridge, S. T. (1818) 'Lectures of 1818', *Coleridge's Miscellaneous Criticism.* Ed. T. Middleton Raysor. (Cambridge, MA: Harvard University Press, 1936), 3–228

Culler, J. (1975) *Structuralist Poetics: Structuralism, Linguistics and the Study of Literature.* (London: Routledge)

Dagut, M. B. (1976) 'Can "Metaphor" Be Translated?', *Babel* 22.1, 21–33

Dagut, M. B. (1987) 'More about the Translatability of Metaphor', *Babel* 33.2, 77–83

Davidson, J. F. (1983) 'The Parodos of the Antigone: A Poetic Study', *BICS* 30, 41–51

Deguy, M. (1969) 'Pour une théorie de la figure genéralisée', *Critique* 21, 841–61

Delabastita, D. (2007) 'Literary Style in Translation: Wordplay', *Übersetzung/Translation/Traduction: Ein internationales Handbuch zur Übersetzungsforschung/An International Encyclopedia of Translation Studies/Encyclopédie internationale de la recherche sur la traduction.* Ed. H. Kittel, A. P. Frank, N. Greiner, et al. 2 vols, vol. i. (Berlin: De Gruyter), 870–4

Delacroix, H. (1927) *Psychologie de l'art: Essai sur l'activité artistique.* (Paris: Librairie Félix Alcan)

De Man, P. (1979) *Allegories of Reading: Figural Language in Rousseau, Nietzsche, Rilke, and Proust.* (New Haven, CT: Yale University Press)

Dévényi, J. (1996) *Metonymy and Drama: Essays on Language and Dramatic Strategy.* (Lewisburg, PA: Bucknell University Press)

Dirven, R. Pörings, R. (eds) (2002) *Metaphor and Metonymy in Comparison and Contrast* (Berlin: De Gruyter)

Dornseiff, F. (1921) *Pindars Stil.* (Berlin: Weidmann)

Dumarsais, C. C. (1729) *Les Tropes.* Ed. G. Genette (Paris: Slatkine, 1967)

Eco, U. (1970) 'Articulations of the Cinematic Code', *Movies and Methods: An Anthology.* Ed. B. Nichols. 2 vols, vol. i. (Berkeley, CA: University of California Press, 1976), 590–607

Eco, U. (1984) *Semiotics and the Philosophy of Language.* (Bloomington, IN: Indiana University Press)

Eichenbaum, B. (1923) *Анна Ахматова: Опыт анализа* ('Anna Akhmatova: An Attempt at Analysis'). (Petrograd: Petropečat)

Eichenbaum, B. (1926) 'The Formal Method', *Literary Theory: An Anthology.* Ed. J. Rivkin and M. Ryan. 2nd edn. (Oxford: Blackwell, 2004), 7–14

Erlich, V. (1981) *Russian Formalism: History—Doctrine.* 3rd edn. (New Haven, CT: Yale University Press)

Evans, R. O. and Martin, W. (1986) 'Metonymy', *The Princeton Handbook of Poetic Terms.* Ed. A. Preminger (Princeton: Princeton University Press), 144

Ewans, M. (2005) '*Agamemnon*'s Influence in Germany', *Agamemnon in Performance, 458 BC to AD 2004.* Ed. F. Macintosh et al. (Oxford: Oxford University Press), 107–17

Firth, J. R. (1951) 'Modes of Meaning', *J. R. Firth: Papers in Linguistics, 1934–1951.* (London: Oxford University Press, 1957), 190–215

Foucault, M. (1966) *The Order of Things: An Archaeology of the Human Sciences.* Trans. A. Sheridan. (London: Tavistock Publications, 1970)

Fowler, A. (1990) 'Apology for Rhetoric', *Rhetorica* 8.2, 103–18

Frank, A. P. (2007) 'Main Concepts of Translating: Transformations during the Enlightenment and Romantic Periods in France, Great Britain, and the German Countries', *Übersetzung/Translation/Traduction: Ein internationales Handbuch zur Übersetzungsforschung/An International Encyclopedia of Translation Studies/ Encyclopédie internationale de la recherche sur la traduction.* Ed. H. Kittel, A. P. Frank, N. Greiner, et al. 2 vols, vol. ii. (Berlin: De Gruyter), 1531–1608

Frick, W. (1998) 'Schiller und die Antike', *Schiller-Handbuch.* Ed. H. Koopmann. (Stuttgart: Kroener), 91–116

Fuhrmann, M. (1987) 'Von Wieland bis Voss: Wie verdeutscht man antike Autoren?', *Jahrbuch des Deutschen Hochstifts* 29, 1–22

Fung, M. M. (1994) *Translating Poetic Metaphor: Explorations of the Process of Translating.* (PhD thesis, Warwick). <http://go.warwick.ac.uk/wrap/2311> [last accessed: 06/11/2015]

Gelpi, A. (1998) *Living in Time: The Poetry of C. Day Lewis* (Oxford: Oxford University Press)

Genette, G. (1970a) 'Rhetoric Restrained', *Figures of Literary Discourse.* Trans. A. Sheridan. (Oxford: Blackwell, 1982), 103–26

Genette, G. (1970b) 'Métonymie chez Proust, ou la naissance du Récit', *Poétique* 2, 156–73

Gerhard, M. (1919) *Schiller und die griechische Tragödie.* (Weimar: Duncker)

Goethe, J. W. v. (1813) 'Zum brüderlichen Andenken Wielands', *Johann Wolfgang von Goethe: Sämtliche Werke.* Ed. E. Beutler. 24 vols, vol xii: *Biographische Einzelschriften.* 2nd edn. (Zurich: Artemis), 693–716

Goheen, R. F. (1951) *The Imagery of Sophocles' Antigone: A Study of Poetic Language and Structure.* (Princeton: Princeton University Press)

Goossens, L., Pawels, P., Rudzka-Ostyn, B., et al. (1995) *By Word of Mouth: Metaphor, Metonymy, and Linguistic Action from a Cognitive Perspective* (Amsterdam: Benjamins)

Gottsched, J. H. (1736) 'Ausführliche Redekunst', *Johann Christoph Gottsched: Ausgewählte Werke.* Ed. H.-G. Roloff. 12 vols, vol. vii: *Ausführliche Redekunst.* (Berlin: de Gruyter)

Grair, C. A. (2005) 'Antiquity and Weimar Classicism', *The Literature of Weimar Classicism.* Ed. S. Richter (Rochester, NY: Camden House), 63–88

Groupe μ. (1982) *Rhétorique générale.* (Paris: Seuil)

Guthke, K. S. (1998) 'Die Braut von Messina', *Schiller-Handbuch.* Ed. H. Koopmann. (Stuttgart: Kroener), 466–85

Guthrie, E. R. (1952) *The Psychology of Learning.* (New York, NY: Harper and Brothers)

Guthrie, E. R. (1959) 'Association by Contiguity', *Psychology: A Study of a Science.* Ed. S. Koch. 2 vols, vol. ii: *General Systematic Formulations, Learning, and Special Processes.* (New York, NY: McGraw-Hill), 158–95

Handl, S. and Schmid, H.-J. (eds) (2011) *Windows to the Mind: Metaphor, Metonymy and Conceptual Blending* (Berlin: De Gruyter)

Harding, D. W. (1963) *Experience into Words.* (London: Chatto & Windus)

Haverkamp, A. and Mende, D. (eds) (2009) *Metaphorologie: Zur Praxis von Theorie.* (Frankfurt am Main: Suhrkamp)

Hayward, S. (2006) *Cinema Studies: The Key Concepts.* 3rd edn. (London: Routledge)

Headlam, W. (1902) 'Metaphor, with a Note on Transference of Epithets', *Classical Review* 16, 434–42

Herder, J. G. v. (1805) 'Von der griechischen Literatur in Deutschland', *Johann Gottfried von Herder's Fragmente zur Deutschen Literatur.* Ed. C. G. Heyne. (Tübingen: Cotta), 57–147

Hermans, T. (2007) 'Metaphor and Image in the Discourse on Translation: A Historical Survey', *Übersetzung/Translation/Traduction: Ein internationales Handbuch zur Übersetzungsforschung/An International Encyclopedia of Translation Studies/Encyclopédie internationale de la recherche sur la traduction*. Ed. H. Kittel, A. P. Frank, N. Greiner, et al. 2 vols, vol. i. (Berlin: De Gruyter), 118–28

Hibberd, J. L. (1967) 'Imagery in Schiller's "Die Braut von Messina"', *German Life and Letters* 20, 306–15

Homberger, D. (2000) 'Wortfeld', *Sachwörterbuch zur Sprachwissenschaft*. (Stuttgart: Reclam), 631–2

Innes, D. C. (1995) 'Introduction' in *Demetrius: On Style*. Ed. and trans. D. C. Innes. (Cambridge, MA: Harvard University Press), 311–42

Jakobson, R. (1935) 'The Dominant', *Readings in Russian Poetics: Formalist and Structuralist Views*. Ed. and trans. L. Matejka and K. Pomorska. (Cambridge, MA: Massachusetts Institute of Technology Press, 1971), 82–7

Jakobson, R. (1953) 'Results of a Joint Conference of Anthropologists and Linguists', repr. in *Roman Jakobson: Selected Writings*. Ed. S. Ruby. 6 vols, vol. ii: *Word and Language*. (The Hague: Mouton, 1971), 554–67

Jakobson, R. (1956) 'Two Aspects of Language and Two Types of Aphasic Disturbances', repr. in *Roman Jakobson: Selected Writings*. Ed. S. Ruby. 6 vols, vol. ii: *Word and Language*. (The Hague: Mouton, 1971), 239–59

Jakobson, R. (1960) 'Closing Statement: Linguistics and Poetics', *Style in Language*. Ed. T. E. Sebeok. (Cambridge, MA: Massachusetts Institute of Technology Press), 350–77

Jakobson, R. (1968) 'Poetry of Grammar and Grammar of Poetry', *Lingua* 21, 597–609

Jakobson, R. and Tynjanov, J. (1928) 'Problems in the Study of Literature and Language', *Readings in Russian Poetics: Formalist and Structuralist Views*. Ed. and trans. L. Matejka and K. Pomorska. (Cambridge, MA: Massachusetts Institute of Technology Press, 1971), 79–81

Janz, R.-P. (1984) 'Antike und Moderne in Schillers "Braut von Messina"', *Unser Commercium: Goethes und Schillers Literaturpolitik*. Ed. W. Barner et al. (Stuttgart: Cotta), 329–49

Johansen, H. F. (1959) *General Reflection in Tragic Rhesis: A Study of Form*. (Copenhagen: Munksgaard)

Johnson, M. and Lakoff, G. (1980) *Metaphors We Live By*. (Chicago: University of Chicago Press)

Jones, R. S. (1982) *Physics as Metaphor*. (Minneapolis, MN: University of Minneapolis Press)

Kittel, H., Frank, A. P., Greiner, N., et al. (eds) (2007) *Übersetzung/Translation/Traduction: Ein internationales Handbuch zur Übersetzungsforschung/An International Encyclopedia of Translation Studies/Encyclopédie internationale de la recherche sur la traduction*. 2 vols. (Berlin: De Gruyter)

Kitzbichler, J., Lubitz, K., and Mindt, N. (2009) *Theorie der Übersetzung antiker Literatur in Deutschland seit 1800*. (Berlin: de Gruyter)

Knapp, S. (1985) *Personification and the Sublime: Milton to Coleridge.* (Cambridge, MA: Harvard University Press)

Kofler, P. (2007) 'Die Rezeption der Antike in deutschen Übersetzungen des 18. und 19. Jahrhunderts', *Übersetzung/Translation/Traduction: Ein internationales Handbuch zur Übersetzungsforschung/An International Encyclopedia of Translation Studies/Encyclopédie internationale de la recherche sur la traduction.* Ed. H. Kittel, A. P. Frank, N. Greiner, et al. 2 vols, vol. ii (Berlin: De Gruyter), 1752–7

Kosecki, K. (ed.) (2007) *Perspectives on Metonymy: Proceedings of the International Conference 'Perspectives on Metonymy', Held in Łódzí, Poland, May 6–7, 2005* (Frankfurt: Lang)

Kövecses, Z. (2002) *Metaphor: A Practical Introduction.* (Oxford: Oxford University Press)

Landfester, M. (1997) *Einführung in die Stilistik der griechischen und lateinischen Literatursprachen.* (Darmstadt: Wissenschaftliche Buchgesellschaft)

Lausberg, H. (1960) *Handbook of Literary Rhetoric: A Foundation for Literary Studies.* Ed. D. E. Orton and R. D. Anderson, trans. M. T. Bliss, A. Jansen, and D. E. Orton. (Leiden: Brill, 1998)

Lebeck, A. (1971) *The Oresteia: A Study in Language and Structure.* (Cambridge, MA: Harvard University Press)

Lefevre, A. (1977) *Translating Literature: The German Tradition, from Luther to Rosenzweig.* (Amsterdam: Van Gorcum)

Levin, S. R. (1977) *The Semantics of Metaphor.* (Baltimore: Johns Hopkins University Press)

Lodge, D. (1977) *Modes of Modern Writing: Metaphor, Metonymy, and the Typology of Modern Literature.* (London: Edward Arnold)

Lodge, D. (1988) *Nice Work.* (London: Secker and Warburg)

Louth, C. (1998) *Hölderlin and the Dynamics of Translation.* (Oxford: Legenda)

Lyons, J. (1977) *Semantics.* 2 vols, vol. i. (Cambridge: Cambridge University Press)

Marcellino, R. (1953) 'A. E. Housman's "Fragment of a Greek Tragedy"', *The Classical Journal* 48.5, 171–8, 188

Martin, W. (1993) 'Metonymy', *The New Princeton Encyclopedia of Poetry and Poetics.* Ed. A. Preminger and T. V. F. Brogan. (Princeton, NJ: Princeton University Press), 783–5

Mason, K. (1982) 'Metaphor and Translation', *Babel* 28.3, 140–9

Matzner, S. (2013) 'The Collapse of a Classical Tradition? "The End of Rhetoric" in Germany around 1800: Gottsched, Kant, Schlegel', *Publications of the English Goethe Society* 52.2, 104–23

McCartney, E. S. (1927) 'Modifiers that Reflect the Etymology of the Words Modified, with Special Reference to Lucretius', *Classical Philology* 22.2, 184–200

Meillet, P. J. A. and Vendryes, J. (1927) *Traiteí de grammaire compareíe des langues classiques.* (Paris: Champion)

Metz, C. (1964) 'Le cinéma: langue ou langage?', *Communications* 4.4, 52–90

Metz, C. (1972) 'On the Notion of Cinematographic Language', repr. in *Movies and Methods: An Anthology*. Ed. B. Nichols. 2 vols, vol. i. (Berkeley, CA: University of California Press, 1976), 582–90

Metz, C. (1973) 'Current Problems of Film Theory: Mitry's *L'Esthétique et psychologie du cinéma*, Vol. II', *Screen* 14.1–2, 40–88

Miller, D. G. (1969) *Studies in Some Forms of the Genitive Singular in Indo-European.* (unpublished PhD thesis, Harvard)

Mosher, H. F. (1976) 'The Structuralism of Genette: A Review of Gérard Genette *Figures, Figures II* and *Figures III*. Paris: Seuil, 1966, 1969, 1972', *Poetics* 5, 75–86

Nerlich, B. and Clarke, D. D. (2001) 'Serial Metonymy: A Study of Reference-Based Polysemisation', *Journal of Historical Pragmatics* 2.2, 245–72

Newmark, P. (1980) 'The Translation of Metaphor', *Babel* 26.2, 93–100

Nichols, B. (1976a) 'Structuralism-Semiology', *Movies and Methods: An Anthology*. Ed. B. Nichols. 2 vols, vol. i. (Berkeley, CA: University of California Press), 461–8

Nichols, B. (1976b) 'Styles, Grammar and Movies', *Movies and Methods: An Anthology*. Ed. B. Nichols. 2 vols, vol. i. (Berkeley, CA: University of California Press), 607–28

Nida, E. (1964) 'Principles of Correspondence', repr. in *The Translation Studies Reader*. Ed. L. Venuti. (London: Routledge, 2000), 126–40

Ortega y Gasset (1937) 'The Splendour and Misery of Translation', *The Translation Studies Reader*. Ed. L. Venuti, trans. E. G. Miller. (London: Routledge, 2000), 49–63

Osterwalder, H. (1978) *T. S. Eliot: Between Metaphor and Metonymy: A Study of his Essays and Plays in Terms of Roman Jakobson's Typology.* (Bern: Francke)

Palmer, L. R. (1962) 'The Language of Homer', *A Companion to Homer*. Ed. A. Wave and F. H. Stubbings. (London: Macmillan), 75–178

Panther, K.-U. and Radden, G. (eds) (1999) *Metonymy in Language and Thought* (Amsterdam: Benjamins)

Panther, K.-U., Thornburg, L. L., Barcelona, A. (eds) (2009) *Metaphor and Metonymy in Grammar* (Amsterdam: Benjamins)

Pasolini, P. P. (1965) 'The Cinema of Poetry', *Movies and Methods: An Anthology*. Ed. B. Nichols. 2 vols, vol. i. (Berkeley, CA: University of California Press, 1976), 542–58

Pecz, W. (1886) *Beiträge zur vergleichenden Tropik der Poesie. I. Teil: Systematische Darstellung der Tropen des Aeschylus, Sophocles und Euripides.* (Berlin: Calvary)

Peirce, C. S. (1903) 'Nomenclature and Division of Triadic Relations, as Far as They Are Determined', *The Collected Papers of C. S. Peirce*. Ed. C. Hartshorne and P. Weiss. 6 vols, vol ii: *Elements of Logic* (Cambridge, MA: Harvard University Press, 1932), 233–72

Pelliccia, H. (1995) *Mind, Body, and Speech in Homer and Pindar.* (Göttingen: Vandenhoeck & Ruprecht)

Pelz, H. (1996) *Linguistik: Eine Einführung.* (Hamburg: Hoffmann und Campe)

Porzig, W. (1934) 'Wesenhafte Bedeutungsbeziehungen', *Beiträge zur deutschen Sprache und Literatur* 58, 70–97

Prechtl, Peter (1999) 'Kontiguität', *Metzler Philosophie Lexikon*. Ed. P. Prechtl and F.-P. Burkard. (Stuttgart: Metzler), 300

Puttenham, G. (1589) *The Arte of English Poesie*. Ed. G. D. Willcock and A. Walker. (Cambridge: Cambridge University Press, 1936)

Reece, S. (1997) 'A Figura Etymologica in the Homeric Hymn to Hermes', *The Classical Journal* 93.1, 29–39

Richards, I. A. (1936) *Philosophy of Rhetoric*. (repr. New York, NY: Oxford University Press, 1965)

Ricoeur, P. (1975) *The Rule of Metaphor: Multi-Disciplinary Studies of the Creation of Meaning in Language*. Trans. R. Czerny. (London: Routledge, 1978)

Ritzer, M. (1998) 'Schillers dramatischer Stil: Tragik in Reinform: Die Braut von Messina', *Schiller-Handbuch*. Ed. H. Koopmann. (Stuttgart: Kroener), 261–5

Rosenberg, I. (1916) 'Letter to Gordon Bottomley (Postmark, July 23, 1916)', repr. in *The Collected Works of Isaac Rosenberg: Poetry, Prose, Letters and Some Drawing*. Ed. G. Bottomley and D. Harding. (London: Chatto & Windus, 1937), 371.

Russell, D. A. (1981) *Criticism in Antiquity*. (London: Duckworth)

Schadewaldt, W. (1969) 'Antikes und Modernes in Schillers "Die Braut von Messina"', *Jahrbuch der deutschen Schiller-Gesellschaft* 13, 286–307

Schenkeveld, D. M. (1964) *Studies in Demetrius on Style*. (Amsterdam: Hakkert)

Schlegel, A. W. (1798) 'Die Sprachen: Ein Gespräch über Klopstocks grammatische Gespräche', *Athenaeum: Eine Zeitschrift von August Wilhelm Schlegel und Friedrich Schlegel. Ersten Bandes Erstes Stück*. (Berlin: Vieweg), 3–69

Schlegel, F. (1800) 'Über die Unverständlichkeit', *Kritische Friedrich Schlegel-Ausgabe*. Ed. E. Behler. 23 vols, vol. ii: *Charakteristiken und Kritiken I (1796–1801)*. (Paderborn: Schöningh, 1967), 363–72

Schleiermacher, F. D. E. (1838) 'Ueber die verschiedenen Methoden des Uebersetzens', *Friedrich Schleiermacher's Sämmtliche Werke III/2*. (Berlin: Reimer), 207–45.

Selle, R. (2007) 'Literary Style in Translation: Humour and Irony', *Übersetzung/Translation/Traduction: Ein internationales Handbuch zur Übersetzungsforschung/An International Encyclopedia of Translation Studies/Encyclopédie internationale de la recherche sur la traduction*. Ed. H. Kittel, A. P. Frank, N. Greiner, et al. 2 vols, vol. i. (Berlin: De Gruyter), 875–82

Shklovsky, V. (1917) 'Art as Technique', *Literary Theory: An Anthology*. Ed. J. Rivkin and M. Ryan. 2nd edn. (Oxford: Wiley-Blackwell, 2004), 15–21

Silk, M. S. (1974) *Interaction in Poetic Imagery: With Special Reference to Early Greek Poetry*. (Cambridge: Cambridge University Press)

Silk, M. S. (1983) 'LSJ and the Problem of Poetic Archaism: From Meaning to Iconyms', *Classical Quarterly* 33, 303–30

Silk, M. S. (1995) 'Language, Poetry and Enactment', *Dialogos* 2, 109–32

Silk, M. S. (1998) '"Das Urproblem der Tragödie": Notions of the Chorus in the Nineteenth Century', *Der Chor im antiken und modernen Drama*. Ed. P. Riemer and B. Zimmermann (Stuttgart: Metzler), 195–226

Silk, M. S. (2003) 'Metaphor and Metonymy: Aristotle, Jakobson, Ricoeur, and Others', *Metaphor, Allegory, and the Classical Tradition*. Ed. G. R. Boys-Stones. (Oxford: Oxford University Press), 113–47

Silk, M. S. (2004) *Homer, The Iliad*. 2nd edn. (Cambridge: Cambridge University Press)

Silk, M. S. (2010) 'The Language of Greek Lyric Poetry', *A Companion to the Ancient Greek Language*. Ed. E. J. Bakker. (Oxford: Wiley-Blackwell), 424–40

Silk, M. S. (2012) 'Metaphor and Simile', *Oxford Classical Dictionary*. Ed. S. Hornblower and A. Spawforth. 4th edn. (Oxford: Oxford University Press), 940–1

Snell, B. (1946) *The Discovery of the Mind: The Greek Origins of European Thought*. Trans. T. G. Rosenmeyer. (Oxford: Blackwell, 1953)

Snell-Hornby, M. (1983) 'Metaphorical Thought and Translation: Taking a Stand on P. Newmark', *Linguistic Agency University of Trier*, Series A, Paper 108, 1–12

Sojcher, J. (1969) 'La métaphore généralisée', *Revue internationale de philosophie* 87, fol. 1, 58–68

Solger, K. W. F. (1826) *Nachgelassene Schriften und Briefwechsel*. Ed. L. Tieck and F. V. Raumer. (Leizpig: Brockhaus)

Staël, A. L. G. de. (1813) *De l'Allemagne*. 3 vols. (London: Murray)

Stafford, E. (2000) *Worshipping Virtues: Personification and the Divine in Ancient Greece*. (London: Duckworth)

Stambovsky, P. (1988) 'Metaphor and Historical Understanding', *History and Theory* 27.2, 125–34

Stanford, W. B. (1936) *Greek Metaphor: A Study in Theory and Practice*. (Oxford: Blackwell)

Stanford, W. B. (1942) *Aeschylus in his Style: A Study in Language and Personality*. (Dublin: University College Dublin Press)

Steen, G. (2005) 'Metonymy Goes Cognitive-Linguistic', *Style* 39.1, 1–11

Stefanowitsch, A. and Gries, S. T. (eds) (2006) *Corpus-Based Approaches to Metaphor and Metonymy* (Berlin: Mouton de Gruyter)

Steiner, P. (1984) *Russian Formalism: A Metapoetics*. (Ithaca, NY: Cornell University Press)

Steiner, P. (1995) 'Russian Formalism', *The Cambridge History of Literary Criticism*. Ed. R. Selden. 9 vols, vol. viii: *From Formalism to Poststructuralism*. (Cambridge: Cambridge University Press), 11–29

Thompson, L. S. (1943) 'German Translations of the Classics between 1450 and 1550', *The Journal of English and Germanic Philology*, 42.3, 343–63

Thumiger, C. (2007) *Hidden Paths: Self and Characterization in Greek Tragedy*. (London: Institute of Classical Studies)

Trier, J. (1931) *Der deutsche Wortschatz im Sinnbezirk des Verstandes: Von den Anfängen bis zum Beginn des 13. Jahrhunderts*. (Heidelberg: Winter)

Trier, J. (1934) 'Das sprachliche Feld: Eine Auseinandersetzung', *Neue Jahrbücher für Wissenschaft und Jugendbildung* 10, 428–49

Ullmann, S. (1964) *Language and Style.* (Oxford: Blackwell)

Van Den Broeck, R. (1981) 'The Limits of Translatability Exemplified by Metaphor Translation', *Poetics Today* 2.4, 73–87

Venuti, L. (1995) *The Translator's Invisibility: A History of Translation.* (London: Routledge)

Venuti, L. (ed.) (2000) *The Translation Studies Reader.* (London: Routledge)

Vickers, B. (1988) *In Defence of Rhetoric.* (Oxford: Clarendon Press)

Vivante, P. (1982) *The Epithets in Homer: A Study in Poetic Values.* (New Haven, CT: Yale University Press)

Wackernagel, J. (1908) 'Genetiv und Adjectiv', *Mélanges de linguistique offert à M. Ferdinand Saussure.* Ed. La société de la linguistique de Paris. (Paris: Champion), 125–52

Weisgerber, L. (1962) *Grundzüge der inhaltbezogenen Grammatik.* (Düsseldorf: Schwann)

Wellbery, D. E. (1984) *Lessing's Laocoon: Semiotics and Aesthetics in the Age of Reason.* (Cambridge: Cambridge University Press)

Wellek, R. and Warren, A. (1949) *Theory of Literature.* (London: Jonathan Cape)

White, H. (1973) *Metahistory: The Historical Imagination in Nineteenth-Century Europe.* (Baltimore, MD: Johns Hopkins University Press)

Williger, E. (1928) *Sprachliche Untersuchungen zu den Komposita der griechischen Dichter des 5. Jahrhunderts.* (Göttingen: Vandenhoeck & Ruprecht)

Wojciechowska, S. (2012) *Conceptual Metonymy and Lexicographic Representation* (Frankfurt: Lang)

Wollen, P. (1969) *Signs and Meaning in the Cinema.* (Bloomington, IN: Indiana University Press)

Wong, L. (2006) 'Syntax and Translatability', *Babel* 52.2, 124–32

GENERAL INDEX

INDEX OF PASSAGES DISCUSSED

This index includes only passages from the corpus of ancient Greek texts (defined on p. 17) that receive discussion in the development of the book's argument. Most of the passages include metonymic expressions and some contain metaphors and/or metaphors and metonyms in interaction. For discussions of passages from literary and literary-theoretical texts by other authors, classical or modern, see the general index.